Remembrance AND DENIAL

Remembrance AND DENIAL

The Case of the Armenian Genocide

Edited by

Richard G. Hovannisian

Wayne State University Press Detroit

Manufactured in the United States of America.

03 02 5 4

Library of Congress Cataloging-in-Publication Data

Remembrance and denial : the case of the Armenian genocide / edited by Richard G. Hovannisian.
p. cm.
Includes bibliographical references (p.) and index.
ISBN 0-8143-2777-X (pbk. : alk. paper)
1. Armenian massacres, 1915–1923. 2. Armenian massacres survivors—Psychology. 3. Genocide—Turkey—Historiography. I. Hovannisian, Richard G.
DS195.5R46 1999
956.6'2015—dc21 98–28282

In tribute to

SOUREN *and* VERKIN PAPAZIAN *of* PALU-HAVAV

and all other survivors

Contents

Contributors 9

Introduction: The Armenian Genocide

Remembrance and Denial

RICHARD G. HOVANNISIAN 13

1 Modern Turkish Identity and the Armenian Genocide

From Prejudice to Racist Nationalism

STEPHAN H. ASTOURIAN 23

2 The Archival Trail

Authentication of *The Treatment of Armenians in the Ottoman Empire, 1915–16*

ARA SARAFIAN 51

3 The Baghdad Railway and the Armenian Genocide, 1915–1916

A Case Study in German Resistance and Complicity

HILMAR KAISER 67

4 Finishing the Genocide

Cleansing Turkey of Armenian Survivors, 1920–1923

LEVON MARASHLIAN 113

5 *The Forty Days of Musa Dagh*

Its Impact on Jewish Youth in Palestine and Europe

YAIR AURON 147

6 **Survivor Memoirs of the Armenian Genocide as Cultural History**

LORNE SHIRINIAN 165

7 **Problematic Aspects of Reading Genocide Literature**

A Search for a Guideline or a Canon

RUBINA PEROOMIAN 175

8 **The Role of Historical Memory in Interpreting Events in the Republic of Armenia**

DONALD E. MILLER 187

9 **Denial of the Armenian Genocide in Comparison with Holocaust Denial**

RICHARD G. HOVANNISIAN 201

10 **Freedom and Responsibility of the Historian**

The "Lewis Affair"

YVES TERNON 237

11 **The Truth of the Facts**

About the New Revisionism

MARC NICHANIAN 249

12 **Professional Ethics and the Denial of the Armenian Genocide**

ROGER W. SMITH, ERIC MARKUSEN, AND ROBERT JAY LIFTON 271

Works Cited 297

Index 317

Contributors

STEPHAN H. ASTOURIAN has taught Armenian, Caucasian, and Middle Eastern history and Western Civilization at the University of California, Los Angeles, University of Michigan-Ann Arbor, and California State University, Long Beach. His doctoral dissertation is titled "Testing World-System Theory, Cilicia (1830s–1890s): Armenian-Turkish Polarization and the Ideology of Modern Ottoman Historiography," and he has published research articles on Caucasian historiography, the Karabagh conflict, and the Armenian Genocide. He serves on the editorial boards of several scholarly journals.

YAIR AURON is a specialist in Contemporary Judaism at the State Teachers College, Seminar Hakibutzim, Tel Aviv, and the College of Yezreel, where he heads the Division of Cultural Studies. He has published numerous essays on the impact of the Holocaust on Jewish identity in Israel and the Diaspora. His books in Hebrew include *Between Paris and Jerusalem: Selected Passages of Contemporary Jewish Thought in France; Jewish-Israeli Identity;* and *The Banality of Indifference: Attitude of the Jewish Community in Palestine and the Zionist Movement towards, the Genocide of the Armenians,* which will be published by the University of Toronto Press.

RICHARD G. HOVANNISIAN is holder of the Armenian Educational Foundation Chair in Armenian History at the University of California, Los Angeles. His numerous publications include *Armenia on the Road to Independence;* a four-volume comprehensive study titled *The Republic of Armenia; The Armenian Genocide in Perspective; The Armenian Genocide: History, Politics, Ethics;* and four edited volumes on Middle Eastern and Islamic studies. A Guggenheim Fellow, he has been honored by election as Academician in the National Academy of Sciences of Armenia and by the bestowal of honorary doctorate degrees from Yerevan State University and from Artsakh State University.

HILMAR KAISER is a doctoral candidate in history and civilization at the European University Institute in Florence, Italy, and a scholar-in-residence at the Armenian Research Center of the University of Michigan-Dearborn. Specializing in late Ottoman social and economic history, he has conducted extensive archival research in the Middle East, Europe, and the United States. Among his publications are *Imperialism, Racism, and Development Theories: The Construction of a Dominant Paradigm on Ottoman Armenians,* and "Germany and the Armenian Genocide: A Review Essay."

Robert Jay Lifton is Distinguished Professor of Psychiatry and Psychology at John Jay College and The Graduate Center of the City University of New York. He is the author of *The Nazi Doctors; The Future of Immortality and Other Essays for a Nuclear Age; Death in Life: Survivors of Hiroshima; Home from the War: Vietnam Veterans—Neither Victims nor Executioners; History and Human Survival,* and is the co-author of *Indefensible Weapons* and *The Genocide Mentality.*

Levon Marashlian is professor of history at Glendale Community College, where he teaches Armenian, Middle Eastern, Russian, and United States history and politics. A Fulbright scholar, he has lectured in Erevan and Stepanakert and is a frequent contributor to national and international journals and newspapers. He is the author of *Politics and Demography: Armenians, Turks and Kurds in the Ottoman Empire.*

Eric Markusen is professor of sociology and social work at Southwest State University in Minnesota. He is the co-author of *The Genocide Mentality; The Holocaust and Strategic Bombing: Genocide and Total War in the Twentieth Century;* and *Nuclear Weapons and the Threat of Nuclear War,* and has written articles on collective violence, including "Professions, Professionals, and Genocide."

Donald E. Miller is professor of religion at the University of Southern California. With his wife, Lorna Touryan Miller, he is the author of *Survivors: An Oral History of the Armenian Genocide,* and he has contributed several chapters and essays based on oral history interviews and studies. His other works include *Writing and Research in Religious Studies; The Case for Liberal Christianity;* and *Reinventing American Protestantism: Christianity in the New Millennium.*

Marc Nichanian has taught philosophy at the University of Strasbourg and Armenian language and literature in Paris and at the University of California, Los Angeles, and currently at Columbia University. He has lectured widely on the historical interpretations and literary responses to the Armenian Genocide and has offered the course "Holocaust and Catastrophe" at the Collège International de Philosophie in Paris. Among his publications are *Âges et usages de la langue arménienne;* "La dénégation au coeur du génocide"; "Sous l'empire de la catastrophe"; "L'Empire du sacrifice"; "L'Ecrit et le mutisme"; and "The Style of Violence." He has translated Armenian poetry into French and has edited the Armenian-language literary journal, *Gam.*

RUBINA PEROOMIAN has taught Armenian language and literature at the University of California, Los Angeles, Glendale Community College, and the University of La Verne. She is the author of *Literary Responses to Catastrophe: A Comparison of the Armenian and the Jewish Experience,* and, in the Armenian language, *Armenia in the Context of Relations between the Armenian Revolutionary Federation and the Bolsheviks, 1917–1921,* and *The Armenian Question,* a series of secondary school textbooks.

ARA SARAFIAN is a doctoral candidate at the University of Michigan-Ann Arbor. He specializes in the history of the late Ottoman Empire. He has published *United States Official Documents on the Armenian Genocide* (3 volumes to date), is an editor of *Armenian Forum: A Journal of Contemporary Affairs,* and serves as a director of the Gomidas Institute.

LORNE SHIRINIAN is professor of English at the Royal Military College of Canada. A poet and author, he has published two scholarly volumes of literary criticism on Armenian literature in North America. His most recent works are a collection of stories, *History of Armenia and Other Fiction;* a novel, *Ripe for Shaking;* and a collection of poetry, *Rough Landing.*

ROGER W. SMITH is professor of government at the College of William and Mary. He is the co-author of *Guilt, Man and Society,* and has written and taught extensively on the nature and history of genocide, women and genocide, the denial of genocide, the language of genocide, and the United Nations Genocide Convention. He is a founder of the Association of Genocide Scholars and a regular contributor to the *Internet on the Holocaust and Genocide.*

YVES TERNON holds a doctoral degree in medicine and another in history from the Sorbonne. He is the author of several volumes on human rights and genocide, including *Les Arméniens: Histoire d'un génocide,* and *L'État criminel: Les génocides au XX*[e] *siècle.* He has taken a prominent role in responding to the phenomenon of denial or "*négation*" in Europe.

Introduction

The Armenian Genocide

Remembrance and Denial

RICHARD G. HOVANNISIAN

The year 1995 marked several significant milestones, most notably the fiftieth anniversary of the end of World War II and the liberation of the Nazi concentration camps. These important events received worldwide attention. The same year was also the hundredth anniversary of the 1895–96 massacres of Armenians in the Ottoman Empire, which claimed some 100,000 victims and set in rapid motion the processes that would culminate in the death or exile of almost all Ottoman Armenians. And, finally, 1995 was the eightieth anniversary of the beginning of the Armenian Genocide itself.

Although the world commemorates in many ways the Holocaust and the downfall of the Nazi regime and these momentous turning points have become integral parts of world literature, national and international educational programs, and policies of many governments, there is virtual silence regarding the Armenian Genocide, and it often seems that the struggle of memory against forgetting is in retreat. The silence in the Armenian case continues to grip governments concerned with considerations of geopolitics, military alliances, and international investment and trade. These factors cause some governments and agencies to become accomplices in the rationalization, trivialization, and outright denial of the Armenian Genocide.

The Armenian Genocide of 1915 was the supremely violent historical moment that removed a people from its homeland and wiped away most of the tangible evidence of its three thousand years of material and spiritual culture. The calamity, which was unprecedented in scope and effect, may be viewed as a part of the incessant Armenian struggle for survival and the culmination of the persecution and pogroms that began in the 1890s. Or, it may be placed in the context of the great upheavals that brought about the disintegration of the multiethnic and multireligious Ottoman Empire and the emergence of a Turkish nation-state based on a monoethnic and monoreligious society. The Ottoman government, dominated by the Committee of Union and Progress (CUP) or the Young Turk party, came to regard the Armenians as alien and a major obstacle to the fulfillment of its political, ideological, and social goals. Its ferocious repudiation of plural society resulted in a single society, as the destruction of the Armenians was followed by the expulsion of the Greek population of Asia Minor and the suppression of the non-Turkish Muslim elements with the goal of bringing about their turkification and assimilation. The method adopted to transform a plural Ottoman society into a homogeneous Turkish society was genocide.

Mass killings under the cover of major conflicts did not begin with the Armenian Genocide. Throughout history, civilian populations have fallen victim to the brutality of invading armies and other forms of indiscriminate killing. In the Armenian case, however, the Turkish government openly disregarded the fundamental obligation to defend its own citizens and instead turned its might against one element of the population. In international law, there were certain rules and customs of war which were intended to protect in some measure noncombatant, civilian populations, but these regulations did not cover domestic situations or a government's mistreatment of its own subjects. Only after World War II was that aspect included in the United Nations Convention on the Prevention and Punishment of the Crime of Genocide. Nonetheless, at the time of the Armenian deportations and massacres, many governments termed the atrocities as crimes against humanity and made public their intent to hold the Turkish authorities individually and collectively accountable.

According to the United Nations Genocide Convention, genocide means to destroy with intent, in whole or in part, a national, ethnic, racial, or religious group in any one of the following ways:

(a) Killing members of the group;
(b) Causing serious bodily or mental harm to members of the group;
(c) Deliberately inflicting on the group conditions of life calculated to bring about its physical destruction in whole or in part;
(d) Imposing measures intended to prevent births within the group;
(e) Forcibly transferring children of the group to another group.

What is compelling in the Armenian case is that the victims were subjected to each and every one of the five categories. Such drastic and absolute methods not only underscore the premeditated nature of the violence but the single-minded determination of the perpetrator regime to expunge the Armenians from the new society it was determined to create.

Estimates of the Armenian dead vary from 600,000 to 2 million. A report of a United Nations human rights subcommission gives the figure of "at least one million." The important point in understanding a tragedy of such magnitude is not the precise count of the number who died—that will never be known—but the fact that more than half the Armenian population perished and the rest were forcibly driven from their ancestral homeland. What befell the Armenians was by the will of the government. Although a large segment of the general population participated in the massacres and plunder, many Muslim leaders were shocked by what was happening, and a significant number of Armenian women and children were rescued and sheltered by compassionate individual Turks, Kurds, and others.

The defeat of the Ottoman Empire and the collapse of the Young Turk dictatorship at the end of 1918 presented the Allied Powers the opportunity to fulfill their pledges regarding punishment of the perpetrators and rehabilitation of the Armenian survivors. A Turkish military court martial tried and actually sentenced to death in absentia several of the notorious organizers of the genocide. Because of subsequent developments, however, no attempt was made to carry out the sentences, and thousands of other culprits were neither tried nor even removed from office. Within a few months the judicial proceedings were suspended and many accused and imprisoned war criminals were freed and sent home.

The release of the perpetrators of genocide signaled a major shift in the political winds. The Allied Powers, having become bitter rivals over the spoils of war, failed to act in unison to implement the harsh Treaty of Sèvres or to deal with a stiff Turkish resistance movement. Unable or unwilling to commit the requisite force to quell the Turkish Nationalists led by Mustafa Kemal, who rejected any compensation to the Armenian victims or even the repatriation of surviving refugees, they ultimately came to terms with the new Turkey. The Treaty of Lausanne in 1923 contained no provision for rehabilitation, restitution, or compensation for the Armenians and marked the final Allied abandonment of the Armenian Question.

During the years that followed, the dispersed Armenian survivors concentrated their collective energies on refugee resettlement and the creation of a new diasporan infrastructure of cultural, educational, and religious institutions. Embittered by world indifference to their plight, the diaspora communities internalized their frustrations, trauma, and even creative activities. They commemorated the genocide through requiem services and programs, yet on substantive issues they could not make their voice heard in the international arena. Meanwhile, the strategy of the perpetrators and their successor government, that of the Republic of Turkey, was to avoid public discussion of the genocide, believing that in the course of time the survivors would pass from the scene, their children would become acculturated and assimilated in the diaspora, and the issue would be forgotten. And in fact by the outbreak of World War II, the Armenian Genocide had virtually become the "forgotten genocide." In some ways, it became even more remote as new millions of victims were claimed in the conflagration of warfare and the Holocaust. The Armenians continued to remember their dreadful losses, but in this they were alone.

It was not until the fiftieth anniversary of the genocide in 1965 and the growing attention paid in the media and in official circles to the Holocaust in all its ramifications that the Armenians began to find some means to externalize the question and to broaden remembrance of the genocide to include certain educational and political circles. The consolidation of Armenian legal and political action undermined the Turkish strategy of avoiding discussion of the Armenian case while enjoying the benefits of the collective confiscated Armenian goods and properties. Hence, an active campaign of denial was initiated in the 1970s and became progressively more sophisticated and professional through the 1980s. This development was attributable largely to the input and assistance of sympathetic or professionally hired Americans and Europeans who could write and translate with native-language fluency and produce materials in the accepted form and style of scholarly treatises in the West. They understood well the importance and effect of placing the Armenian issue in a relativist and rationalizing context, rather than the hitherto unconvincing approach of absolute denial. By the 1990s the denial literature had become slick and polished, inclusive of archival references, notations, and bibliographies.

The perpetrators and those who have followed them—the governments and individuals that continue to deny or rationalize the enormity of the crime—have defined the arena for the encounter between memory and forgetting. They have repeatedly placed the Armenians in a defensive position that has consumed great energy in the urgency to prove that the Catastrophe (*Aghed*) actually occurred and to win international recognition of what the entire world acknowledged and knew to be the truth during and in the immediate aftermath of the genocide. Hence, the victim side has been forced to play by the rules laid down by the side of the perpetrators rather than finding and employing its natural ways to memorialize, to comprehend, to instruct, to gain recompense, to heal, and to surmount the psychological obstacles to progressing toward a state of normalcy. The suppression of truth has lasting effects and underscores the error of those who assert that the present generation is not responsible for past crimes. Governments, institutions, scholars, and individuals who engage in denial and rationalization prevent the healing of wounds and the unfolding of the full creative energies of the victimized group.

In his studies, Erwin Staub has shown that genocide shapes not only the outlook of the immediate victims but of subsequent generations. Victim groups, rather than viewing the world as a good place with a sense of order, are filled with mistrust, fear, and a sense of danger of what may come from the world. It becomes essential, therefore, for victims to understand that the horrible events are not normal but rather are aberrations of a generally good world order. Continued denial makes this impossible and reinforces the sense of insecurity, abandonment, and betrayal. To overcome these feelings, the victims need to share their sentiments of pain and sorrow, to voice their outrage, to have the world recognize their suffering, and especially to receive expressions of regret and apology from the perpetrator side. Only then can a sense of justice and rightness be restored. Until such time, the pain and the rage fester and the healing process is blocked.

For the descendants of the perpetrators, it is of vital importance to engage in introspection, to face and learn from their history, to question how such violations could have occurred, to examine what there was and may even still be in their society that led them down the road to genocide, and to find some redemption through appropriate acts of contrition—beginning with a knowledge and acceptance of the truth. If they are unable or unwilling to deal with the truth and instead try to maintain a righteous self-image, then they may again be placed on a path toward the victimization of other groups. What has been occurring to the Kurds in the former Armenian provinces of Turkey (now referred to as Eastern Anatolia) may be taken as a case in point.

Milan Kundera has written that the struggle of man against power is the struggle of memory against forgetting. The late Terrence Des Pres has added that national catastrophes can be survived only if those to whom disaster happens can recover themselves through knowing the truth of their suffering. Powerful states, on the other hand, seek to vanquish not only the peoples they subjugate but also the cultural mechanisms that would sustain vital memory of historical crimes. He concludes: "Kundera is right; against historical crimes we fight as best we can, and a cardinal part of this engagement is 'the struggle of memory against forgetting'."

The collection of essays in this volume deals with remembrance and denial. They are the product of a symposium organized at UCLA in April

The Armenian Homelands

1995 on the occasion of the eightieth anniversary of the Armenian Genocide. The first four chapters are historical in nature. Stephan Astourian assesses the impact of the development of modern Turkish identity on the minority populations of the Ottoman Empire. Using Turkish sources and sayings, he maintains that popular anti-Armenian prejudice engendered official genocidal policies with the adoption of the exclusivist ideology of Turkism. Ara Sarafian analyzes a major contemporary source on the genocide, the British "Blue Book," *The Treatment of Armenians in the Ottoman Empire.* The volume, compiled by Arnold Toynbee, contains many official and eyewitness accounts of the Armenian calamity and has frequently been the target of deniers of the genocide. Sarafian presents the deniers' arguments and then demonstrates that the publication was in fact meticulously prepared and effectively withstands the assaults of revisionist historiography.

Hilmar Kaiser, utilizing official German archival sources, examines the positive and negative aspects of Imperial Germany's policies and actions during the Armenian Genocide, especially the internal dissension over the degree to which German officials and officers should become involved in the issue. He focuses on the Baghdad Railway, which was being built through the Ottoman Empire by German interests and which employed large numbers of Armenian laborers and technicians. The fate of these workers lay in the balance of competing German strategies. Levon Marashlian shows what happened to the Armenian survivors in Turkey after World War I and demonstrates that a major factor in the continuing denial of the Armenian Genocide stems from the uncompensated wholesale confiscation of individual and collective Armenian wealth, not only by the Young Turk wartime regime, but also by the Republic of Turkey headed by Mustafa Kemal (Atatürk). More than the use of outright massacre, however, Kemal applied intense pressure on the survivors to flee the country and abandon their goods and properties.

Four chapters concentrate on different aspects of remembrance. Yair Auron weighs the impact of Franz Werfel's celebrated novel, *The Forty Days of Musa Dagh,* on Jewish youth in Palestine and in Europe during the rise of Nazi power in Germany and during the Holocaust. He shows how the saga of resistance against overwhelming odds affected both the young people living under the British mandate in Palestine and the Jewish underground during the Holocaust. Lorne Shirinian sees the memoirs of survivors of the Armenian Genocide as an important aspect of cultural history. He maintains that written accounts have a very different dynamic and process from oral histories. Survivor memoirs are part history and part literature and are driven by a need to unburden the writer of the memory of the tragedy and to place the individual experience within a broader social and historical context.

Rubina Peroomian addresses issues relating to genocide literature. Many readers choose to avoid this genre because of its depressing nature in a world all too ridden with disaster. Peroomian uses a comparative approach in drawing on examples of both Armenian Genocide and Holocaust literature to demonstrate that the authors are desperately seeking means to cope with the tragedy. Sometimes they are condemned to silence, incapable of portraying the full force of their subject, even as they continue to pour out words. Donald Miller observes that historical memory has a strong role in interpreting current events. As a case in point, he examines the Sumgait tragedy in 1988, a violent event that presaged the flight or expulsion of nearly all Armenians from Azerbaijan as the conflict over Nagorno-Karabagh evolved during the decline and collapse of the Soviet Union. The Armenian victims made immediate comparisons with the 1915 Genocide and came to regard their Azeri neighbors as the direct heirs of the Turkish perpetrators in the Ottoman Empire decades earlier. The chapter is based on interviews and oral histories conducted with refugees in Armenia in 1993–94.

The final section of four chapters deals specifically with the issue of denial. Richard Hovannisian compares the arguments and strategies of deniers of the Armenian Genocide and of the Holocaust. Although denial in the Armenian case is far more advanced and has even entered the academic mainstream, there are marked similarities in the recent approach of substituting rationalization, relativization, and trivialization in place of absolute denial. Decimation of the victim group is shown as a part of the general wartime losses sustained by all involved peoples. Absence of intent to destroy the purported victims is paramount in the denier's brief, as are selfish economic and political motives ascribed to the survivors. On a positive note, the intensified campaign of denial has begun to draw together some scholars who have hitherto limited their concerns to one particular genocide.

In France, the Gayssot law makes it a criminal offense to deny the Holocaust. Several groups in that country have attempted to make the law applicable to the Armenian Genocide as well. The most notable case involves historian Bernard Lewis, who in an interview with *Le Monde,* reiterated certain of the denial arguments and discounted the Armenian tragedy in Turkey as having been a genocide. The "Lewis Affair" raises many questions about academic freedom and academic responsibility. Although one French court ruled that the Gayssot law is specific and cannot apply to the Armenian case, another tribunal found that Lewis had not fulfilled his duties as a thorough scholar and ordered him to pay a nominal, symbolic fine for his failure to uphold academic standards. This verdict, too, gave rise to widely differing responses and assessments regarding academic freedom and responsibility. The "Lewis Affair," as well as the broader question of remembrance and denial, is addressed by Yves Ternon and Marc Nichanian, whose contributions complement each other while maintaining distinct approaches and conclusions. Ternon contends that the issue is not a matter of academic freedom but rather of the right of a man of science to prevaricate by rejecting a historical reality no less established than Napoleon's invasion of Russia in the nineteenth century or the conflagration of two world wars in the twentieth century. Nichanian views Lewis's statements as part of a troubling new wave of negationism with well defined, albeit very subtle, parameters to distance the Armenian experience from any comparability with the Holocaust.

In the United States, denial of the Armenian Genocide is of long standing. In recent years, however, the connection between certain scholars and the Turkish government has become pronounced. There have been historians who have undertaken denial-oriented research for that government and have even drafted correspondence to be dispatched by the Turkish embassy. Roger Smith, Eric Markusen, and Robert Jay Lifton raise one such blatant example involving the American executive director of the tax-exempt Institute of Turkish Studies, established with a grant from the Turkish government. The director's internal correspondence with the Turkish ambassador regarding the Armenian Genocide was inadvertently sent to one of the authors and lays bare a deplorable side of the connection between scholarship and politics. The authors believe that serious issues of professional ethics are involved and that the transgressors should to be exposed. Their call for scholars to bear witness to historical truths draws us back to Terrence Des Pres's caveat: "Against historical crimes we fight as best we can, and a cardinal part of this engagement is the struggle of memory against forgetting."

1

Modern Turkish Identity and the Armenian Genocide

From Prejudice to Racist Nationalism

STEPHAN H. ASTOURIAN

À Michel Baumont

The Turkish nationalist ideologies that emerged in the Ottoman Empire at the turn of the twentieth century entailed two concomitant and interrelated processes: the exclusion of non-Muslims from the nation, by various degrees of violence combined with both legal and informal discrimination, and the construction of a modern Turkish identity. This exclusion was rooted in the pre-existing, widespread prejudice against those groups, of which Ottoman idioms, sayings, and proverbs best suggest the scope and virulence. A better understanding of the transition from prejudice to racist nationalist theories could shed much light on the worldview, values, and behavior of the Ottoman Turks when the empire faced European imperialism, territorial losses, financial bankruptcy, and significant socioeconomic transformations. Not only could such an understanding explain why large-scale massacres and the genocide of the Armenians characterized the end of that state (1870s–1923), it could also elucidate the reasons why these massacres were acceptable to broad segments of the Turkish and Kurdish population who often participated en masse in the violence.

Some Theoretical Considerations

The meaning of sayings and proverbs about non-Muslims and Armenians cannot be understood in isolation. They form clusters of words that are embedded in a social structure and sociopolitical worldview or, at a semantic level, in meaning systems. Thus, the representation of "the non-Muslim" or "the Armenian" in those linguistic expressions also defines the self-perception of "the Muslim Turk," along with his or her normative expectations about "the non-Muslims" or "the Armenians" and how they should behave. Not only do the discourse types to be studied reproduce *subject positions* in society, they also naturalize them. Thus, this naturalization of subject positions shapes the socialization of these subjects and defines their available social identities—in this case for non-Muslims in general, the Armenians in particular. Naturalization, then, is a weapon in the struggle to legitimize power.[1]

To be sure, the social power that sociologists and political scientists analyze is a relation between people, rather than a relation between texts or meanings. "But it is always a mediated relationship, and cannot exist without the signifying systems that constitute it. So it is also possible to say that power is also an effect of discourse, if 'discourse' has a general sense equivalent to 'semiosis' (the process of construction and circulation of signs)."[2] The Ottoman words, idioms, sayings, and proverbs about non-Muslims and Armenians constitute just such an effect of power.

In the symbolic interactionist perspective on which this essay relies, race or ethnoreligious prejudice can be better understood by studying "the process by which racial groups form images of themselves and of others."[3] That process, which is collective, defines another racial or ethnoreligious group and, by contrast, ends up characterizing one's own. As Herbert Blumer puts it, "it is the sense of social position emerging from this collective process of characterization which provides the basis of race prejudice."[4]

Four types of feeling seem always to characterize race prejudice in the dominant group. First, there is a feeling of superiority, which is demonstrated in the tendency to disparage "qualities" attributed to the subordinate group. Greediness, deceit, stupidity, and other such debasing traits usually figure among those qualities. Second, there is a feeling of distinctiveness, to the effect that the subordinate outgroup is essentially alien. Thus, its exclusion is justified. According to Blumer, these two feelings do not constitute prejudice by themselves. Third, there exists a sense of proprietary claim, a feeling of entitlement to exclusive or prior rights. These exclusive claims could pertain to some occupations, professions, or positions of power in the government, the legal system, and the army; to the ownership of various types of property including choice lands; or to the display of symbols of various kinds. Although this sense of proprietary claim is particularly strong in race prejudice, it does not explain its appearance. Indeed, such proprietary claims existed in societies displaying no prejudice, for example in various feudal or caste societies. Blumer contends that "where claims are solidified into a structure which is accepted or respected by all, there seems to be no group prejudice."[5]

The fourth feeling is a suspicion, apprehension, or fear that the subordinate outgroup is intent on threatening the superior status of the dominant group in the present or the future. This is indeed the most important feeling, for race prejudice stems precisely from the impression—whether well founded or not—on the part of the dominant group that the subordinate group is "getting out of place." Thus, "the source of race prejudice lies in a felt challenge to this sense of group position" and racism tends "to emerge and develop when racial stratification is under challenge and the position of the dominant group is being threatened."[6] The emergence of anti-Armenian prejudice in the Ottoman Empire took place precisely in such a context, from the period of reforms known as the Tanzimat (1839–76) onward.

Throughout history the power discrepancy among groups coming into contact has been the main determinant of their relations, be they racial (defined in a biological or phenotypical sense) or ethnoreligious groups. Thus, this essay uses the term "race" in the context of broadly defined "race relations," that is, situations in which groups endowed "with distinct identities and recognisable characteristics" live together in a conflicting relationship in which "ascriptive criteria are used to mark out the members of each group." According to John Rex, "true race relation situations" occur "when the practices of ascriptive allocation of roles and rights referred to are justified in terms of some kind of deterministic theory, whether that theory be of a scientific, religious, cultural, historical, ideological or sociological kind and whether it is highly systematised, or exists only on the everyday level of folk wisdom or in the foreshortened factual or theoretical models presented by the media."[7]

The Ottoman Context

The period of reform and centralization known as the Tanzimat, or "Reordering," put an end to the existing paternalistic type of intergroup relations, whereby both the inferior and superior groups internalize the subservient status of the subordinate community, and led to the emergence of racism. Indeed, the two imperial decrees central to this era, the *Hatt-i Sherif-i Gülhane* (the Noble Rescript of the Rose Chamber), promulgated in 1839, and especially the *Hatt-i Hümayun* (the Imperial Rescript) of 1856 polarized the relations between the dominant and subordinate groups by putting forward the concept of Ottomanism (*Osmanlılık*), namely, equality between Muslims and non-Muslims. This principle of equality undermined the established relations of power and paved the way for a potential end to the supremacy of the ruling element, the Muslim Ottomans in general and, by the end of the nineteenth century, the Turks in particular. Ahmed Jevdet Pasha (1822–95), the distinguished Ottoman historian and jurist, aptly captured the deep Muslim resentment against the newly proclaimed *Hatt-i Hümayun*: "Many among the people of Islam began complaining thus: 'Today we lost our sacred national rights [*hukuk-ı mukaddese-i milliyyemizi*] which were earned with our ancestors' blood. The Muslim community [*millet-i islamiyye*], while it used to be the ruling religious community [*millet-i hâkime*], has [now] been deprived of such a sacred right. For the people of Islam, this a day to weep and mourn'."[8]

During the Tanzimat era many Armenians reached high positions in the Ottoman government in such fields as foreign affairs and finances. None, however, wielded decisive power; rather, they mostly owed their positions to their technical, financial, or linguistic skills and to patron-client relationships. On the whole, they were excluded from decision-making positions in the ministries of war and foreign affairs and the grand vizierate.[9] In addition, even the wealthiest Armenians, such as the members of the *amira* class (bankers and industrialists-technocrats serving the Ottoman state), lacked real power in the Ottoman financial and economic administration. They had even less power in the Ottoman political sphere, so that the author of a seminal dissertation on the *amira*s concludes that his study "lends strong support to the theory of the supremacy of the political over the economic in pre-modern states, a theory which . . . has been extended to apply to states in transition from pre-modern to the industrialized stage."[10]

Perception of reality, however, is sometimes more important than reality itself in shaping people's actions. In the eyes of the Muslim Ottomans, it mattered little that the Tanzimat had not devolved substantial power on non-Muslims. In the long run, Muslim Ottomans felt that the Tanzimat decrees and laws would undermine their superior status as members of "the ruling religious community," thus, in effect, turning the world upside down. Ziya Pasha, one of the so-called "Young Ottoman" writers of the Tanzimat era, gave an early expression to the feeling of upheaval on the part of the Turkish Ottomans in his *Zafernâme Şerhi* (Commentary on the epic of victory). In this satirical poem criticizing the failures of the Sublime Porte (*Bab-ı Ali,* or the offices of the central government, including the grand vizierate) during the crisis with Greece over the possession of Crete (1868), he waxed ironic about Grand Vizier Ali Pasha and his policies:

If but God's plan assists in his project
The Gypsies' place will soon be in the Grand Vizier's seat
Only for the Jews he has made an exception
Since from amongst Greeks and Armenians he has [already] nominated
marshals and *balas*
To perfection has he [clearly] brought the system of equality of rights.[11]

The feeling of entitlement to exclusive rights by the Turks and their apprehension that former subordinate groups were "getting out of place" could hardly be better, and more bitterly, expressed. From those feelings stemmed Turkish racism, which also functioned to legitimize the inferior status of the non-Muslims in general and the Armenians in particular.

None perhaps was more concerned, not to say obsessed, with the perception that Armenians were overstepping the boundaries of their position in society, being ungrateful and disloyal to the empire, and constituting a danger to its territorial integrity than Sultan Abdülhamid II (1876–1909). His reign was characterized by an attempt at reverting to the traditional society which was crumbling under the impact of the Tanzimat, of the European economic penetration of the empire, and of the numerous Ottoman defeats and territorial losses since the 1770s. Indeed, in view of the widespread opposition among Turkish Ottomans to the doctrine of Ottomanism and in order to muster the support of the Muslim Ottomans in general, Abdülhamid II emphasized the utmost importance of Muslim unity and superiority within the empire and of Pan-Islamism without. As a supplement to anti-Westernism, attachment to the past was officially promoted.

The debates leading to the promulgation of the Ottoman Constitution on December 23, 1876, the apex of the Tanzimat era, give a good idea of public opinion among Ottoman Turks. These debates emphasized themes such as anti-constitutionalism and the natural inequality between Muslims and non-Muslims. They stressed that the sovereign's rights should not be curtailed by any constitutional restrictions. Many also wanted to add the attribute of sacredness to the asserted caliphal function of the sultan. The editorial introduction to an Arabic treatise on statecraft, presented at that time to Abdülhamid, captures how anti-constitutionalist *ulema* (the learned men of Islam) and the sultan himself viewed the traditional Islamic state.

> Every person knew his position and rank (*makam* and *mertebe*) and would not transgress the limits assigned to him. He would obey those above him, and would not attempt to compete in station, value, administration, or government with those above him. In this way, the affairs of the world and of human beings would reach the hierarchies of aims delimited by divine wisdom, by prophetic

Şeriat and by rational [?] traditions, and attain the peace and prosperity of the realm. . . . The man in the highest rank was the one possessing the required virtues, and as long as he ruled in justice, the graces of God continued to favour him.[12]

In view of such ideas, it comes as little surprise that Sultan Abdülhamid dissolved the newly elected Ottoman Parliament on January 31, 1878, dismissed on February 5, 1878 Grand Vizier Midhat Pasha, who had inspired the constitution, and then suspended the constitution de facto. In those actions, he enjoyed the support of "the great mass of the people—with all their beliefs and superstitions, and also their sense of honor and decency." Besides, not only was he backed by "the Ulema, the ministers, and the intellectuals," but also by the " 'men of religion'—*şerifs, seyyids, nakibs,* and *amirs*—genuine or spurious, representing either traditionalism or obscurantism."[13] Midhat Pasha, not unlike Fuad Pasha, an earlier minister of foreign affairs and grand vizier of the Tanzimat period, was accused of serving the interests of the "infidels" and of being one of them.[14] But, what did it mean, in the Ottoman Turkish mind, to be an "infidel"?

The Collective Image of Non-Muslims and Armenians

Whereas the writings of Ottoman scholars and statesmen quoted above suggest how the elite reacted to the emancipation of non-Muslims, a selection of idioms, sayings, and proverbs sketches the mentality of the Turkish Ottoman masses in relation to their inferiors.

Disloyalty characterizes the ghiaour's relations with others. "Fidelity from a ghiaour, healing from poison" (*Gâvurdan vefa, zehirden sifa*) goes a proverb, which suggests that loyalty from an unbeliever is as likely as recovery of one's health from taking poison.[15] Disloyalty is matched by ingratitude: "to a ghiaour, kindness does no good" (*Gâvura iyilik yaramaz*), for whatever you do he is ungrateful.[16] Ungratefulness is one of the essential meanings associated in Arabic with the triliteral, consonantal root *kfr,* meaning "to be an infidel," "not to believe," "to be ungrateful." Two Ottoman Turkish words, based on Arabic derivations from that root, associate the meaning of "unbelief" with "ungratefulness."[17] Shemseddin Sami's nineteenth-century Ottoman Turkish dictionary defines the first one, *kâfir,* as "one who forgets the kindness he has experienced, who does not understand [or appreciate] kindness."[18] It also defines the compound *kâfir-i nimet* as "ungratefulness."[19] The second word, *küfran,* also meant "ingratitude," whereas its compound *küfran-i nimet* referred to "ungratefulness toward a benefactor."[20] The ghiaours' ingratitude reaches an apex in the Turkish

perception that "the infidel weeps over our wretched state of affairs" (*Kâfir ăglar bizim ahval-i perişanımıza*).[21] What makes this proverb particularly strong and bitter is irony, the macrostructural rhetorical figure on which it is based. That figure is reinforced by a microstructural trope, the antiphrasis concerning "weeps over" (*ăglar*), which means the opposite of its literal meaning ("rejoices over") and reveals the irony of the whole proverb.[22]

In view of these characteristics of the ghiaours, friendship with them was excluded: "From amongst ghiaours, it is impossible [or, wrong] to make friends" (*Gâvurdan dost olmaz*).[23] Although it makes a difference whether either "impossible" or "wrong" applies in this case, the ambiguity of *olmaz,* which allows both meanings, makes the proverb polysemous, and thus better. A related proverb states that "it is impossible to make pelt from swine and friends with ghiaours" (*Domuzdan post, gâvurdan dost olmaz*). Not only is the rhymed terseness of this proverb remarkable, but so is the parallel between swine and infidels. As the Quran forbids the consumption of pork, extremely negative connotations have been associated with *domuz* in Turkish culture. In Ottoman times, *domuz* connoted "filth," "obstinacy," and "cruelty," and it appeared in highly insulting expressions.[24] It is no coincidence that most of these characteristics also constituted the salient attributes of the ghiaours. A variant of the previous proverb sheds some light on one of its meanings. It goes thus: "It is impossible to make pelt from the skin of swine and friends from old enemies" (*Domuz derisinden post olmaz, eski düşmandan dost olmaz*).[25] Obviously, "ghiaours" and "old enemies" are structurally interchangeable in these proverbs. On the whole, friendly relationships with the infidels being excluded, coexistence with them seems to be viewed only in terms of domination or hostility, a clear negation of Ottomanism.

One proverb, perhaps either foreboding or reflecting the Turkist economic nationalism of the period from 1908 to 1914 and the then Turkish boycotts of foreign and non-Muslim enterprises and shops, suggests that "he who works for the ghiaour will bear his sword as well" (*Gâvurun ekmeğini yiyen gâvurun kılıcını çalar* [*çeker, kuşanır, sallar*]).[26] Clearly, this proverb is in keeping with the theory and policies of *Millî İktisat* (National economy) which aimed at ridding the Ottoman economy of its non-Muslim bourgeoisie and replacing it with a Turkish middle-class on the eve of World War I and during it.[27] The gist of this proverb is that non-Muslim economic power should be ostracized. On the other hand, the Turkish masses and conservative elements were very reluctant to accept and adopt European inventions, especially technology, which they viewed as the creations of unbelievers. Thus, they were commonly called *gâvur icadı* ("ghiaour's invention" or

"invention imported from the West").[28] In some regions, Cilicia in particular, the Turkish and Turcoman peasantry called some of those inventions, such as tractors, the creation of the devil.

Undoubtedly, all of the proverbs about the ghiaours apply to the Armenians; however, some proverbs were more specific to them. What do they tell us about Turkish perceptions of the Armenians? "Intriguer like an Armenian" (*Ermeni gibi gammaz*), goes one proverb.[29] This perception is confirmed by another that states that "trickery [characterizes] the Armenian as procuring [or pimping] does the Greek" (*Ermeniye müzevvirlik, Ruma pezevenklik*).[30] Endowed with these negative traits, the Armenian is devoid of more desirable ones: "Spiritual knowledge in the Armenian, and [physical] might in the Jew do not exist" (*Ermenide irfan, Yahudide pehlivan olmaz*).[31] In some regions of the empire, there also existed "the Armenian illness" (*Ermeni hastalığı*) which referred to "avarice," presumably a typical attribute of the Armenian character.[32]

Resentment against the emerging Ottoman elite of Armenian origin or faith, against their "getting out of place," is best captured in two proverbs. "The Armenian grandees" (*Ermeni kibari*), goes the first one, which in fact is a derogatory reference to the "Armenian parvenus" of the Tanzimat period and their alleged ostentatious arrogance.[33] The other states: "Converted to Islam from the Armenian faith, nouveau riche" (*Ermeniden dönme, sonradan görme*). In case one might miss the meaning of the proverb, Shinasi, the great nineteenth-century Ottoman intellectual, gives its French equivalent: *Il n'y a rien qui soit plus orgueilleux qu'un riche qui a été gueux* ("Nothing is more arrogant than a rich person who used to be a beggar").[34]

The study of proverbs reveals a hierarchy in the objects of Turkish prejudice and racism, a ranking of sorts of the most despised or hated non-Turkish communities. By the end of the nineteenth-century, the Armenians were ahead of the Greeks and Jews in that ranking because they had undergone a "Renaissance" (*Zartonk*) and "emancipation" in the second half of the century. The Armenian Question had been internationalized from 1878 on, and the Turks envied the commercial successes of some urban Armenians. Thus, despite the fact that 70 percent of the Ottoman Armenians were poor peasants, derogatory stereotypes with an economic coloration were frequent. "One Greek cons two Jews, and one Armenian cons two Greeks," reported a German traveler who fully agreed with this view.[35] Another German traveler and student of things Ottoman expatiated on the nature and intensity of this prejudice: "But why, then, are the Armenians so hated? The main reason is the commercial talent of the Armenian race. The Armenians are born merchants. Their skills and craftiness in all trades are superior."[36]

Ernst Jäckh, a German Turkophile scholar who visited Cilicia in 1909, asserts that Armenians were known in the maritime and commercial cities of the Middle East for their "avaricious greed." Sayings like "Two Greeks equal an Armenian, and an Armenian equals two devils" were supposed to describe Armenians best. He went on to say that one of the causes of the Hamidian massacres, including those of 1909 in Cilicia, was precisely an attempt at weakening Armenians politically and economically.[37]

Clearly, prejudice against the Armenians had many causes other than the economic ones, but the latter were significant in important maritime and trading cities. There, as some Armenians had welcomed western culture and technology and were performing remarkably well in the economy, they were perceived as symbols of western modernity and exploiters. As a result, they were demonized.

"Exclusive" Ideologies and Turkish Identity

Not only do denigrating stereotypes legitimize domination and justify hatred, in most cases of racial and ethnic polarization they also "dehumanise the antagonist and prepare the ground for collective slaughter."[38] These stereotypes, combined with "a fantasy of power or redemption or salvation" crystallized in a "guiding ideology," result more often than not in deadly outcomes.[39] Indeed, such ideologies are often highly rationalized variants of the more popular stereotypes. They usually exclude the despised, dominated group from the nation and provide the dominant group with a megalomaniac sense of national or racial greatness as well as a delusory vision of world hegemony. Turkism and Pan-Turkism fulfilled all of these functions.

Turkism and Pan-Turkism

The emergence of Turkism, the ideological core of Turkish nationalism, led to a shift from ethnoreligious racism to a more biological version of it, for Turkism centered upon the concept of race (*cins* or *ırk*).[40] The three major thinkers who shaped Turkism and Pan-Turkism were Yusuf Akchura or Akchuraoghlu (1876–1935), Moiz Cohen, alias Munis Tekin Alp or Tekinalp (1883–1961), and Ziya Gök Alp (1876–1924).

As early as his famous article titled "Three Types of Policy" (March 1904), Akchura was in favor of constituting "a Turkish political nationality [*Türk milliyet-i siyasiyesi*] founded on race [*ırk*]."[41] He elaborated further on this idea in numerous articles published in the periodical *Türk Yurdu* (Turkish homeland) beginning in November 1911. By 1914, he defined the concept of Turkish political nationality as that of belonging to "a race, a language, a tradition," that is, Turkism.[42] On the outbreak of World War I, Akchura participated in the creation of the Pan-Turkic "Turco-Tatar Committee" (1915) and got involved in a number of Pan-Turkic activities.

Tekinalp proposed two plans for the realization of Turan, the asserted homeland of all Turkic peoples and the symbol of their future unity in a mighty state. The "minimum" plan "would consist of setting up a relatively easy-to-achieve 'small Turan,' from Istanbul to Lake Baykal . . . and from Kazan to Mongolia." This was to be but a stage, however, toward the "maximum" plan which "would involve the establishment of 'Great Turan,' from the frontiers of Japan to the Scandinavian mountains and from the Arctic Ocean to the Tibetan Plateau."[43] The logic behind these irredentist designs was a vision of the future: "Ours is the age of nationality and race. To the extent that nationality even is coming to an end, the age of race is arriving."[44] The means to achieve "Great Turan" was what Tekinalp called "New Genghizism"—a reference to Genghis Khan's methods of conquest—to be carried out by the Ottoman Turks:

> Turan will be saved!
> —But how and with what?
> —How and with what? Very simple: with iron and with fire! The iron of our swords and the fire of our thoughts will conquer and free Turan![45]

Throughout his life, Tekinalp was also consistent in preaching the Turkification of all non-Turkish minorities living in the Ottoman Empire and subsequently in Kemalist Turkey.[46]

The most influential thinker, however, was Mehmed Ziya, known under his pen name of Ziya Gök Alp, who, from 1909 to 1918, was a member of the secretive Central Committee of the Committee of Union and Progress (CUP), the party that ruled the Ottoman Empire for most of that period. As the main ideologue of that organization, he was among a handful of leaders who formulated the values and provided the vision that led the empire to enter World War I. He deemed the basis of morality to be total and unquestioning service to the nation, which he conceived as strictly limited to Turkish-speaking Muslims.[47] The territory of the Turks, however, was to be larger than the Ottoman Empire. Indeed, as he suggested in one of his poems, "Turan":

> Fatherland for the Turks is neither Turkey, nor yet Turkestan
> Fatherland is a great and eternal country: Turan.[48]

On the outbreak of World War I, he stated the aims and methods of the Ottoman Empire in no uncertain terms.

> The land of the enemy shall be devastated,
> Turkey shall be enlarged and become Turan.[49]

Despite these writings, Taha Parla, the author of a monograph on Ziya Gök Alp's thought, claims that many "have taken literally the Turkist and Turanist myths, legends, slogans, and figures of speech he used in a number of poems he published especially between 1910 and 1915." Parla believes that "the cultural myth" should not be mistaken with "Turanism, the racist and irredentist brand of Turkish nationalism," which allegedly does not appear in Gök Alp's prolific "theoretical or political articles and essays."[50]

Gök Alp's theoretical treatises on which Parla relies were written after the Ottoman defeat in World War I shattered the Turanist projects of the CUP and made them look utopian. In addition, they were written during the ascendancy of Mustafa Kemal, who had little patience with irredentist ideas that could endanger his alliance with the Bolsheviks and, therefore, his struggle for the independence of Turkey.[51] What about Gök Alp's views before and during the war?

Gök Alp was then somewhat of a visionary who announced a "New Life" (*Yeni Hayat*) for the Turkish race. In contradistinction with the purportedly decaying Europeans, the Turks would strengthen themselves by starting "a new civilization" endowed with "genuine values" and characterized by economic achievements:

> [This "New Life"] will show that the civilizations of Europe were based on rotten, sick, putrid foundations. These civilizations are condemned to decline, annihilation. The genuine civilization is the Turkish civilization which will start only with the development of the New Life. The Turkish race, unlike other races, has not been corrupted by alcohol and dissipation. The Turkish blood has been steeled, rejuvenated in glorious battles.

Convinced of the superiority of the Turks, he did not hesitate about asserting that "the supermen whom the German philosopher Nietzsche imagined are the Turks. The Turks are the 'new men' [*yeni insanlar*] of every age." Gök Alp held these ideas throughout the war. He first published these views in July 1911 and saw fit to include them six years later in the first installment of a series of essays titled "What is Turkism?"[52]

A famous Turkish journalist, who during the war was an assistant professor of sociology at Constantinople University where Ziya Gök Alp was then professing the same discipline, reports that "for him [Gök Alp], Pan-Turkism was a monomania." The World War, which he "sincerely welcomed," was "a means of realizing Pan-Turkish dreams." The Unionist leaders were "those dreamed-of men of action who could translate his theories into deeds." In view of his intellectual stature and membership in the Central Committee of the ruling party, "the military leaders let him become almost an intellectual dictator."[53] Actually, Gök Alp did not hide his irredentist Turanian opinions during World War I. In a testimonial to the publication in 1915 of Tekinalp's *Türkismus und Pantürkismus* in Weimar, he writes:

> Turan is no illusory fatherland. The Turkic tribes which live next to each other in Asia will gather under the Turkish flag and form a great empire. Turan is the fatherland of Greater Turkey [Grosstürkentum]. . . . Turan is the Ideal of a "realité sociale," born of the Turkish national consciousness. Those who consider it a Utopia are themselves living in a utopian world. . . . "L'idéal se réalise" ["The Ideal is being realized"]. This is our kısmet [destiny].[54]

As late as April 1918, Gök Alp propounded that the Turkic peoples of Russia should succeed in freeing themselves and forming independent governments. Delegates from those governments to a subsequent congress should choose a supreme leader who would receive the title of *Sahibkıran* ("Lord of the fortunate conjunction [of planets]"), which centuries earlier *ulema* had bestowed upon Timur Lenk. The *Sahibkıran*, who could also be called a *Münci* ("Savior"), would be the supreme military leader of Turan, the federation of these Turkic peoples. He would establish his general headquarters in some place of his choice in the Caucasus, Turkestan, or Kazakhstan. In many ways reminiscent of the ideal fascist leader, the *Sahibkıran* should be a charismatic and dignified hero, who would concentrate absolute civil and military powers in his hands. Turan would have an official common language, Ottoman Turkish, which would unite all its Turkic peoples.[55] It would seem that the *Sahibkıran* Gök Alp had in mind, in 1918 at least, was none other than Enver Pasha, the war minister and leader of the military wing of the Committee of Union and Progress who also happened to be a leading perpetrator of the Armenian Genocide. In a poem titled "Enver Pasha," Gök Alp celebrated the greatness of the man. Its conclusion reads:

> History teaches thus: "All great conquerors
> Are like their people inspired by God."
> Today the people is like you joyful [because of good news]
> But what is clear to you is vague to them:

The secret voice of God coming from the heavens
The glad tidings that "The Turks are at last being liberated."[56]

Ideologies, like Turkism and Pan-Turkism, have consequences and intellectuals involved in the highest political bodies, like Ziya Gök Alp, have responsibilities. Indeed, Enver Behnan Şapolyo, his biographer and disciple, reports that, as a member of the ruling central committee, Gök Alp "investigated very carefully the question of minorities, in particular the question of the Armenians in Anatolia. As a result, the Armenian deportation [*tehcir*] took place."[57] Gök Alp was thus directly guilty of the Armenian Genocide, for the word *tehcir* is but a cipher in Turkish historiography for that event.

The Theory and Policies of *Millî İktisat* (National Economy)

Whereas Turkism and Pan-Turkism excluded the Armenians from the nation, the theory and policies of *Millî İktisat* aimed at eliminating them, along with the Ottoman Greeks, from economic activities. Indeed, Gök Alp's "solidarism," opposed as it was to the liberalism of the Manchester School in the economic sphere, paralleled his collectivistic tendencies, which rejected liberalism and the free will of the individual in the political sphere. Influenced by Durkheim and the Pan-Germanist Friedrich List, Gök Alp disapproved of class struggle and propounded peaceful economic cooperation among various classes, on condition that they belong to the same homogeneous ethnic group, namely, Turkish. In this regard, he argued that the division of labor in the Ottoman Empire—Turkish soldiers and bureaucrats versus Greek and Armenian traders and artisans—had brought about a "mutual parasitism." According to him, this division of labor between Turks and non-Turks was not genuine, for the groups lacked a "common conscience." As a matter of fact, the realization of "national solidarism" (*millî tesanüd*) required the existence of a community endowed with such a "common conscience." Thus, Gök Alp concluded, the "national economy" could be materialized with its inherent organic division of labor only if the Turks undertook by themselves all kinds of economic activities.[58]

To create a strong Turkish state based on a Turkish bourgeoisie was, in a nutshell, the crux of his thought. Indeed, as the Turks had been deprived of "economic classes" (*iktisadî sınıflar*), those involved in important trading, financial, or "industrial" activities, they were unable to establish a strong state. Gök Alp, however, had a grand vision. The Turks would soon be "more modern" than the non-Muslims in all the professions they would engage in. Whereas the non-Muslims were "unwavering imitators" of Europe, the

Turks would "produce the life of a new civilization" endowed with "genuine values." The Turks "would not [merely] deign to accept the arts and crafts"; rather, they would "directly start factories" and would dominate the seas with "the very best merchant-ships."[59] In a famous nationalistic poem portraying the ideal, enlightened "fatherland," Gök Alp also suggests that "fatherland" is where "maritime arsenals, factories, steamers, trains belong to the Turk."[60] Although he argued that the Turks should control the economy of the empire in the near future, he also stressed that they were de facto the bulwarks of the Muslim world and of "Ottomanness" against "cosmopolitanism," a reference to the non-Turks and Europeans both inside and outside the empire. "The Turkish nationality [*Türklük*] is the genuine point of support of the Muslim world [*İslamiyet*] and of Ottomanness [*Osmanlılık*] against cosmopolitanism."[61]

If non-Muslim Ottomans were a hindrance to Turkish control of the economy, so was "laissez-faire" liberalism. Indeed, Gök Alp argued that the dominance of the Manchester School of political economy in the Ottoman Empire prevented the development of "economic patriotism" by promoting "cosmopolitanism." How could the spirit of "economic patriotism" be developed among the Turks so that they should spawn a national bourgeoisie, which in turn would constitute the foundation of a strong state? With somewhat circular reasoning, Gök Alp stated that "for economic conscience to become patriotic, I gather it was necessary for the state to follow the policy of the national economy!"[62] In this view, Armenians were identified with liberalism both politically, because of their reformist and decentralizing aspirations, and economically, because of their prominence in circles supporting "laissez-faire" and of their achievements in international trade. In short, they incarnated cosmopolitanism at its worst.

In the same vein, Tekinalp stressed the utmost importance for Turks to improve the economic condition of their country, to control its economy, and to develop entrepreneurial skills with the support of the state.[63] Tekinalp's portrayal of the Turks as victims of the Greeks and Armenians, mixing fantasy with Pan-Turanian dreams, economic nationalism, and a modicum of historical analysis, is particularly striking. Suggestive of a mood of revanchist bitterness, his depiction shows the links between *millî iktisat,* Turkism, and Pan-Turkism:

> On the other hand, the Christian population of Turkey has been consistently progressing, partly by means of privileges too easily granted, and partly by their own initiative, and they are ousting the real owner of the country more and more from their heritage. Two nations, pressing upon them from either

> side, have succeeded in driving the old "conquerors" more and more into the interior of the country. The Greeks from the sea and the islands have taken possession of the harbours and coast towns of Anatolia, and pressed the Turks further and further back into the salt steppes of the interior. The Armenians, who, thanks to their friendly relations with England, have become very rich, have cut off their retreat. The Turk is such a miserable wretch that he has forgotten the plains of Turania, without even having been able to assure his footing in the country he has conquered. He was so convinced of his power that he omitted to build bridges between his old and new homes, bridges between the different conquered territories.[64]

Akchura, for his part, emphasized the historical role of the bourgeoisie, which he viewed as being nationalistic by essence. Arguing that the kingdom of Poland lost its independence at the end of the eighteenth century because its middle class was made up of Jews and Germans only, he called on the Turks to develop a capitalistic bourgeoisie that would assume the role so far played by the Jews, Armenians, Greeks, and Levantines. To class struggle, he opposed, as did Gök Alp, solidarism and corporatism.[65]

The impact of those ideas is clearly attested by the Turkish boycott of Greek Ottoman shops during the negotiations between the Ottoman Empire, Greece, and the European powers over the Aegean islands (from the end of 1912 to the beginning of 1913). Without any clear political reason, that boycott was extended to the Armenians and other non-Muslim groups. A similar boycott took place during and in the wake of the Balkan Wars (1912–14).[66] These boycotts were the first applications of *millî iktisat.* As Tekinalp put it, they "caused the ruin of hundreds of small Greek and Armenian tradesmen," and he added:

> The systematic and rigorous boycott is now at an end, but the spirit it created in the people still persists. There are Turks who will not set foot in foreign shops unless they are certain that the same articles cannot be purchased under the same conditions in the shops of men of their own race, or at least of their own religion. This feeling of brotherhood has taken firm root in the hearts of the people all over the empire.[67]

Some eyewitnesses of that period aptly describe the frenzy bent on racist ostracism that took over the Turkish masses: "Newly opened restaurants, coffeehouses and barbershops everywhere bore the name of Turan, or some other racistic name."[68]

Millî iktisat resulted in Turkish control of the economy and the creation of a Turkish bourgeoisie during World War I. Insofar as the Armenians were concerned, the main mechanism for such a transformation was the state-sponsored plundering of Armenian properties, whether urban or rural, consequent upon the Armenian Genocide. As one Turkish scholar puts it cautiously, "during the war years, political factors played also a role in the fact that some business sectors came into the possession of Turkish-Muslim notables: Muslim-Turkish entrepreneurs filled the voids generated by the 'Armenian deportation'."[69] In the countryside, on the other hand, whereas big landlords and the emerging class of "middle peasants" acquired a good share of the lands vacated by the Armenian peasants, Muslim immigrants from the Balkans and the Caucasus settled on the rest.

On the Uses of Racism

Turkish racism served many purposes. Stereotyping elevated Turkish self-esteem by degrading the outgroup, that is, the ghiaours, including Armenians.[70] There was even perhaps a part of "projection" in the Turkish racism toward the ghiaours. Some derogatory proverbs that in the 1850s referred to the Turks themselves—"The Turk's wisdom comes later" or "They gave a Turk the title Bey, first he killed his father"—ended up referring to the non-Muslims on the eve of World War I.[71] By then, "Turk" was no longer a derogatory adjective and Turkishness had become the positive identity of the former Turkish-speaking Muslim Ottomans. The emergence of a proud Turkish identity was a significant achievement of the Turkists, for it paved the way to the formation of the Turkish nation-state after World War I.

The founder of ethno-psychoanalysis points out that negative formulations—in this case the stereotypical perception of the non-Muslims and the Armenians—often reflect a historical process leading to ethnic differentiation and the formation of a positive ethnic identity. Turkish nationalism constituted that positive identity. Its genesis was clearly linked with this racist process of ethnic differentiation in relation not merely to the "cosmopolitan" ghiaours but also to non-Turkish Ottomans such as the Kurds and the Arabs.[72] As a radical rejection of Ottomanism, Turkism excluded the ghiaours from the nation and denied the identity of the Kurds, thereby promoting a racially and culturally homogeneous nation: modern Turkey.

The self-identification of most Turkish-speaking Muslim Ottomans as Turks occurred in great part between 1908 and 1914. The emancipation of the non-Muslims and Armenians gained substantial momentum during these seven years as a result of the restoration in 1908, with important additions, of the Ottoman constitution of 1876. In the Ottoman Empire, much as in the United States and South Africa, a more biological form of racism emerged at a time when the dominant group (the Turks) felt that their position was most threatened.[73]

There were, however, a few major distinctions with the American and South African situations. For one thing, biological racism in the Ottoman Empire coincided with the redefinition in racial terms first and foremost of the identity of the dominant, and not the dominated, group. For another, biological racism emerged in the context of a multiethnic, multiconfessional empire crumbling at full speed. It led to the extermination or expulsion of the subordinate group from the remnants of the empire rather than to its intense exploitation. Finally, nationalism and biological racism were combined with an irredentist ideology, Pan-Turkism. In this perspective, the location of the Armenians in Eastern Anatolia was considered a barrier between Turkish Anatolia and the Turkic peoples living in the Russian Empire, from today's Azerbaijan to Central Asia. The elimination of this hindrance played no small part in the execution of the Armenian Genocide.[74]

On the whole, the main purpose of racism was to counter the transformation of the traditional order and the emergence of a society based on rational, universal norms, for such a society would have given rise to competitive race relations and consequently to irresistible non-Muslim and Armenian advances in the economic, social, and political realms. The Turks felt deprived of what they considered to be theirs naturally: their superior power in the empire.

Most Turks and Turkists explained the perceived Armenian superiority in the economy by attributing it to the vicious and cunning character of the Armenians, to their artificial "imitation" of Western culture, or to the putative support they enjoyed from the British. Thus, these Turks avoided examining the causes for Turkish economic inferiority in the nature of the Ottoman state, its class structure, its economic practices, its guilds, and by the nineteenth century the backwardness of that state in education. The direct result of Turkish economic envy and inferiority complex was indeed the widespread looting, combined with the forced expropriations and sham auctions of Armenian properties, that went on after the various massacres, including those of 1895–96 and 1909.[75] Pillage was, therefore, both an incentive and a reward for the pogroms. The theoretical formulation of this sense of economic envy and inferiority was *millî iktisat* and the practices stemming from it, including the state-sponsored, forced expropriation of Armenian properties during World War I.

Racist theories (Turkism and *millî iktisat*) constituted the apex of the hostility already manifest in stereotypical idioms, sayings, and proverbs. As intellectualized expressions of enmity, these theories formulated solutions to the ills the stereotypes had vaguely diagnosed. Turkism, Pan-Turkism, and to a lesser extent *millî iktisat,* were also forms of "national compensation" and "national idealization."[76] They made up for the feeling of frustration, jealousy, inferiority, or decline underlying the stereotypes of the dominant group. Whereas Turkism aggrandized and idealized the Turkish character and past and offered the prospect of a homogeneous new civilization, Pan-Turkism promised a glorious and powerful future. As for *millî iktisat,* it announced a world in which the Turks would be efficient entrepreneurs, and Turkey a modern industrial country. Gök Alp, eager to boost the badly damaged Turkish self-esteem in economic matters, contended even that the Turks would not be mere imitators of Europe, like the much despised but more economically and technologically advanced Armenians and Greeks, but would build a new civilization based on "genuine values." All these promises and hopes failed the test of reality to a great extent. Turkism did rid Turkey of its Armenians, but it resulted in defeat and huge territorial losses. Pan-Turkism remained a mere dream. Although *millî iktisat* brought about Turkish control of the economy and the development of a Turkish bourgeoisie, it also led to Unionist profiteering and large-scale corruption, massive inflation, failure of most of the "nationalized" enterprises formerly belonging to non-Muslims, misery for most Turkish wage-earners and small farmers, and overall economic decline.[77]

Finally, the formulation of racist theories combined with the boycotts of non-Muslim shops and the formation of exclusive organizations, such as the associations of Turkish small industries and workers, or cooperative societies of Turkish consumers, point to "the increasing aggregation of a population into exclusive groups. . . . At the subjective level, aggregation is associated with heightened salience of sectional identity, and with increasing perception in terms of antagonistic racial or ethnic interests. At the objective level, it is expressed in the growth of exclusive organisations, in the superimposition of lines of cleavage, and in the rapid escalation of local and specific disturbances to the level of general, nationwide intersectional conflict."[78] Tension ran high in the fall and winter of 1914 and local clashes multiplied in the provinces. Against this background of racism and aggregation into hostile groups, there would be no intersectional conflict, however, but a genocide.

The main consequence of Turkish Ottoman racism was the Armenian Genocide, which marked the "ejection" of the Armenians from the empire. The genocide was not irrational. First and foremost, it made possible the formation of a homogeneous Turkish nation and the realization of Pan-Turkish goals. It also was rational from the economic viewpoint dear to world-systems theory, for it constituted an opportunity for the forcible expropriation or phony sale of Armenian properties. To be sure, these expropriations were a fiasco. As one scholar puts it, the Armenian "companies were given to the new Muslim entrepreneurs, who in many cases proved incapable of making a go of them, deprived as they were of overseas contacts, markets and management skills."[79] The United States consul in Aleppo put it more tersely: "one does not become a trader by killing a trader."[80] Nonetheless, the expropriations resulting from the genocide ended up creating a small Turkish bourgeoisie from among the Turkish artisans, small traders, and provincial landlords affiliated with the ruling party. Finally, both Talât Pasha and Enver Pasha, the two most powerful leaders of the CUP, cared little about the negative economic consequences of the Armenian Genocide.[81] This fact shows the primacy of political over economic considerations in its commission, among the top decision-makers at least.

Notes

1. Norman Fairclough, *Language and Power* (1989; reprint, New York: Longman, 1991), 106.
2. Robert Hodge and Gunther Kress, *Language as Ideology,* 2d ed. (New York: Routledge, 1993), 158–59.
3. Herbert Blumer, "Race Prejudice as a Sense of Group Position," *Pacific Sociological Review* 1, no. 1 (Spring 1958): 3.
4. Ibid., 4.
5. Ibid.
6. Ibid., 5; William J. Wilson, *Power, Racism, and Privilege: Race Relations in Theoretical and Sociohistorical Perspectives* (New York: The Free Press, 1973), 42.
7. John Rex, *Race Relations in Sociological Theory,* 2d ed. (London: Routledge and Kegan Paul, 1987), 160. For a survey of the concepts of "racism," see Robert Miles, *Racism,* Key Ideas Series (London: Routledge, 1989), 41–68. Miles stresses the biological dimension of racism. According to him, "the distinguishing content of racism as an ideology is, first, its signification of some biological characteristic(s) as the criterion by which a collectivity may be identified" (Ibid., 79). For essays presenting a broad spectrum of views on race and ethnicity, see John Rex and David Mason, eds., *Theories of Race and Ethnic Relations,* 2d ed. (Cambridge: Cambridge University Press, 1990).
8. Cevdet Paşa, *Tezâkir* (Memoranda), I, ed. Cavid Baysun, 2d ed. (Ankara: Türk Tarih Kurumu, 1986), 68. In this study, most proper names, geographical names, and administrative terms are transliterated in the text itself, but left in their original Turkish alphabet in the notes and bibliography. The names of twentieth-century Turkish authors of secondary sources, articles, or monographs about Ottoman history are not transliterated. Longer quotations in Turkish, such as full sentences, are spelled in the Turkish alphabet. Ottoman expressions, names, or terms have been assimilated to modern Turkish orthography. With a few

exceptions, the orthographic reference for this chapter is *Redhouse Yeni Türkçe-İngilizce Sözlük* (New Redhouse Turkish-English dictionary), 2d ed. (İstanbul: Redhouse Press, 1974).

9. Carter V. Findley, *Bureaucratic Reform in the Ottoman Empire: The Sublime Porte, 1789–1922* (Princeton: Princeton University Press, 1980), 207–8.
10. Hagop Levon Barsoumian, "The Armenian Amira Class of Istanbul" (Ph.D. diss., Columbia University), 215, 220.
11. Ziya Paşa, *Zafernâme Şerhi* (Commentary on the epic of victory) (İstanbul: 1289/1872–73), 14, 86. The reference to the Jews means that none of them had yet been promoted to the rank of marshal or bala. Bala was the highest grade, after vizier, in the civil register of the Ottoman Empire. As for the Gypsies, they were considered as the group least able to establish a government and to preside over it. In the Balkans, Gypsies who had converted to Islam would still have to pay the poll tax imposed on non-Muslims, for they were viewed as schismatics bent on straying from the precepts of the law on ritual and moral matters. See Angus Fraser, *The Gypsies* (1992; reprint, Oxford: Blackwell, 1993), 175–76. Hilmar Kaiser drew my attention to the special position of Muslim Gypsies in relation to taxation.
12. As quoted from the introduction of the Ottoman Turkish translation of Shihâb al-Dîn Ahmad ibn Muhammad ibn Abî al-Rabî, *Kitâb sulûk al-mâlik fî tadbîr al-mamâlik* (Istanbul, 1878), in Niyazi Berkes, *The Development of Secularism in Turkey* (Montreal: McGill University Press, 1964), 238. See ibid., 232–70 for the currents of thought during the Hamidian period.
13. Berkes, *Development of Secularism in Turkey,* 258.

> The term *şerif* originally meant a descendant of the Prophet through his grandson Hasan, *seyyid* a descendant through his other grandson Hüsayn; in time these descendants came to constitute an officially recognized religious aristocracy, whose leaders were called *nakibs.* The *amirs* were chieftains or tribal princes; they no longer represented any genuine descent or relationship. Arab *shaikhs* also occupied a special place with Abdülhamid. The shaikhs or patriarchs of the orthodox religious orders came mostly from Syria, Arabia, and North Africa. Some had great reputations as astrologers, necromancers, and sorcerers. . . . The presence of these men served to symbolize the link between the Caliph and the Muslim *umma.* (Berkes, 258)

Umma refers to the community of the Muslim believers.

14. Ibid., 236. See also "Fuad Pasha's Political Testament," in J. Lewis Farley, *Egypt, Cyprus and Asiatic Turkey* (London: Trubner and Co., 1878), 244. This text has also been published in modern Turkish by Engin Deniz Akarlı, trans. and ed., *Belgelerle Tanzimat: Osmanlı Sadrıazamlarından Ali ve Fuad Paşaların Siyasî Vasiyyetnâmeleri* (The Tanzimat with documents: The political testaments of the Ottoman grand viziers Ali and Fuad Pashas) (İstanbul: Boğaziçi Üniversitesi Matbaası, 1978), 7. For decades there has been a debate about whether Fuad Pasha did write a "political testament." The best study on that question asserts that, even if Fuad Pasha did not write the testament, he may have

inspired or dictated it to one of his close collaborators. The testament may also have been written by someone who knew him well. On the whole, however, one can "accept it as a second-hand if not a first-hand expression of Fuad's views." See Roderic H. Davison, "The Question of Fuad Paşa's 'Political Testament'," *Belleten* 23 (January 1959): 119–36.

15. Metin Yurtbaşı, *A Dictionary of Turkish Proverbs* (Ankara: Turkish Daily News, 1993), s.v. "Loyalty"; E. Kemal Eyüboğlu, *On Üçüncü Yüzyıldan Günümüze Kadar Şiirde ve Halk Dilinde Atasözleri ve Deyimler* (Proverbs and idioms in poetry and popular language from the thirteenth century until now) (İstanbul: N.p., 1973), 1:101; Mustafa Nihat Özön, *Ata Sözleri* (Proverbs) (İstanbul: İnkilâp Kitabevi, 1956), 132; Feridun Fazıl Tülbentçi, *Türk Atasözleri ve Deyimler* (Turkish proverbs and sayings) (İstanbul: İnkilâp ve Aka Kitabevleri, 1963), 172.
16. Kerest Haig, *Dictionary of Turkish-English Proverbial Idioms* (Amsterdam: Philo Press, 1969), 96. This proverb was also recited to me by my aunt and my mother.
17. Hans Wehr, *A Dictionary of Modern Written Arabic,* ed. J. M. Cowan, 3d rev. ed. (Ithaca, N.Y.: Spoken Language Services, 1976), s.v. "kafara."
18. Şhemseddin Sami, *Kâmûs-i Türkî* (The Turkish dictionary) (1899; reprint, Beirut: Librairie du Liban, 1989), s.v. "kâfir."
19. Ibid. See also James W. Redhouse, *A Turkish and English Lexicon* (1890; reprint, Beirut: Librairie du Liban, 1974), s.v. "kyafir."
20. *Kâmûs-i Türkî,* s.v. "küfran." See also Redhouse, *Lexicon,* s.v. "kyufran." Redhouse defines "küfran" as "callous denial or contempt of a favor" and translates the compound *küfran-i nimet* as "ingratitude, base ingratitude." For an interesting use of that compound in Ahmed Cevdet Paşa, *Tarih-i Cevdet* (Cevdet's history) (İstanbul: 1271/1855–1856), 1:244, see J. Deny, *Grammaire de la langue turque* (*dialecte osmanli*) (1921; reprint, Wiesbaden: Dr. Martin Sandig, 1971), 671. The expression *küfran-i nimette bulunmak* also means "to be ungrateful; not to appreciate (a favour); to act callously." See A. Vahid Moran, *Türkçe-İngilizce Sözlük* (Turkish-English dictionary) (1945; reprint, İstanbul: Millî Eğitim Basımevi, 1971), s.v. "küfran (küfran-i nimet)."
21. Ahmed Vefik Paşa, *Müntahabât-ı Durûb-ı Emsal* (Anthology of proverbs) ([İstanbul]: N.p., [1871]), 225.
22. For the concepts of "microstructural," "macrostructural," "irony," "figure," "trope," and "antiphrasis," see Georges Molinié, *Dictionnaire de rhétorique* (Paris: Le livre de poche, 1992).
23. Hüseyin Kâzim Kadri, *Türk Lûgati* (Turkish dictionary) (İstanbul: Cumhuriyet Matbaası, 1945), 4: s.v. "gâvur."
24. *Kâmûs-i Türki,* s.v. "domuz"; Redhouse, *Lexicon,* s.v. "doñuz," "domuzlanmaq," and "doñuzluq."
25. See Nikolai A. Baskakov et al., *Turetsko-Russkii Slovar'* (Moscow: Russkii Iazyk, 1977), s.v. "domuz." The word "it," which means "dog" but is also commonly used as an insult with the meaning of "cur," "brute," or "swine," appears in similar proverbs.

26. Yurtbaşı, *A Dictionary of Turkish Proverbs,* s.v. "Loyalty"; Eyüboğlu, *Şiirde ve Halk Dilinde Atasözleri ve Deyimler,* 1:101; Türk Dil Kurumu, comp., *Bölge Ağızlarında Atasözleri ve Deyimler* (Proverbs and idioms in regional dialects), with introduction by Ömer Asım Aksoy (Ankara: Ankara Üniversitesi Basımevi, 1969), 122; *Redhouse Çağdaş Türkçe-İngilizce Sözlüğü* (Redhouse contemporary Turkish-English dictionary) (İstanbul: Redhouse Yayınevi, 1983), s.v. "gâvur."
27. Stephan H. Astourian, "Genocidal Process: Reflections on the Armeno-Turkish Polarization," in *The Armenian Genocide: History, Politics, Ethics,* ed. Richard G. Hovannisian (New York: St. Martin's Press, 1992), 69–71.
28. H. Fathi Gözler, *Örnekleriyle Türkçemizin Açıklamalı Büyük Deyimler Sözlüğü* [A–Z] (Great dictionary of our Turkish idioms explained with examples) (İstanbul: İnkilâp ve Aka Kitabevleri, 1975), 169; E. Kemal Eyüboğlu, *On Üçüncü Yüzyıldan Günümüze Kadar Şiirde ve Halk Dilinde Atasözleri ve Deyimler* (Proverbs and idioms in poetry and popular language from the eleventh century until now) (Istanbul: N.p., 1975), 2:186; *Redhouse Yeni Türkçe-İngilizce Sözlük* (1974), s.v. "gâvur"; and *Redhouse Çağdaş Türkçe-İngilizce Sözlüğü,* s.v. "gâvur."
29. İbrahim Şinasi, *Durûb-ı Emsâl-i Osmaniyye* (Ottoman proverbs), 3d ed. (Dersaadet [İstanbul]: Matbaa-i Ebüzziya, 1302/1886–87), 49; Ali Seydi, Ali Reşad, Mehmed Izzet, L. Feuillet, eds., *Musavver Dâiret ül-Maârif* (Illustrated encyclopedia) (Dersaadet [İstanbul]: Kanaat, 1332/1913), 1: s.v. "Ermeni"; Eyüboğlu, *Şiirde ve Halk Dilinde Atasözleri ve Deyimler,* 1:93; Tülbentçi, *Türk Atasözleri ve Deyimler,* 156; Özön, *Ata Sözleri,* 119.
30. This proverb was reported to me by my aunt.
31. Eyüboğlu, *Şiirde ve Halk Dilinde Atasözleri ve Deyimler,* 1:92; Tülbentçi, *Türk Atasözleri ve Deyimler,* 156; Özön, *Ata Sözleri,* 119. Ahmed Vefik Pasha gives a more cryptic variant: *Ermeniden irfan, Yahudiden pehlivan* ("From the Armenian refinement and from the Jew might [cannot be expected]"). See his *Müntahabât-ı Durûb-ı Emsal,* 36. Şinasi's variant is also slightly different: *Ermenide irfan Yahudide pehlivan bulunmaz* ("In the Armenian refinement and might in the Jew cannot be found"). See his *Durûb-ı Emsal-i Osmaniyye,* 49.
32. *Bölge Ağïzlarında,* 308.
33. Ahmed Vefik Paşa, *Müntahabât-ı Durûb-ı Emsal,* 36; Tülbentçi, *Türk Atasözleri ve Deyimler,* 156.
34. Şinasi, *Durûb-ı Emsâl-i Osmaniyye,* 48–49, and *Musavver Dâiret ül-Maârif,* s.v. "Ermeni." For the proverb without the French equivalent, Eyüboğlu, *Şiirde ve Halk Dilinde Atasözleri ve Deyimler,* 1:93; Tülbentçi, *Türk Atasözleri ve Deyimler,* 156; Özön, *Ata Sözleri,* 119.
35. Alfred Körte, *Anatolische Skizzen* (Berlin: Julius Springer, 1896), 62. For a broader view of the extent of such prejudice, see ibid., 53–59.
36. Heinrich Gelzer, *Geistliches und Weltliches aus dem türkisch-griechischen Orient* (Leipzig: B. G. Teubner, 1900), 246.
37. Ernst Jäckh, *Der aufsteigende Halbmond: Beiträge zur türkischen Renaissance* (Berlin: Buchverlag der "Hilfe," 1911), 99–101.

38. Leo Kuper, *The Pity of It All: Polarisation of Racial and Ethnic Relations* (Minneapolis: University of Minnesota Press, 1977), 282.
39. Israel W. Charny, *How Can We Commit the Unthinkable? Genocide, the Human Cancer* (Boulder, Colo.: Westview Press, 1982), 323–24.
40. *Cins* (Jins) was mostly used in the nineteenth century to refer to "race." See David Kushner, *The Rise of Turkish Nationalism, 1876–1908* (London: Frank Cass, 1977), 23, 26, 48, 54–55, 102 for its use by early Turkists. For the concept of *ırk,* see François Georgeon, *Aux origines du nationalisme turc: Yusuf Akçura (1876–1935)* (Paris: Editions ADPF, 1980), 26–27; Masami Arai, *Turkish Nationalism in the Young Turk Era* (Leiden: E. J. Brill, 1992), 20, 41–42, 49, 68, 75. Some of the examples given by Arai show that the concept of "race" (*ırk*) came to be confounded with that of "nation" among some Ottoman intellectuals.
41. See the French translation of "Three Types of Policy" in Georgeon, *Yusuf Akçura,* 95, 98. A recent English translation of this essay distorts the meaning of this quotation by rendering it as "a policy of Turkish nationalism based on ethnicity." See David Thomas's translation in H. B. Paksoy, *Central Asian Reader: The Rediscovery of History* (Armonk, N.Y.: M. E. Sharpe, 1994), 103. "Türk milliyet-i siyasiyesi" does not mean "a policy of Turkish nationalism," neither does *ırk* mean "ethnicity." It is indeed interesting to note that both Georgeon and Thomas are not comfortable with translating *ırk* into "race," an idea of which the connotations have been understandably disturbing since the Holocaust. Thomas chooses to translate *ırk* into "ethnicity," whereas Georgeon translates it into "race" but explains that it refers in fact to what anthropologists call an "ethnie." The fact is that the best Ottoman Turkish dictionary of the end of the nineteenth-century indicates that *ırk* means "race." See Sami, *Kâmûs-i Türkî* (1899), s.v. "ırk." On the other hand, the words closest to the meaning of "ethnic group" in the 1890s were *ümmet* (plural *ümem*) and *kavim*; see Ch. Samy-Bey Fraschery, *Dictionnaire français-turc,* 2d rev. ed. (Constantinople: Mihran, 1898), s.v. "ethnique," "ethnographe," and "ethnographie." In 1912, a Turkist ideologue, Ahmed Aghayef (Aghaoghlu), used the expressions *ilm-i ensab-i beser* ("science of the relationships [or, genealogy] of mankind") to refer to "ethnology" and *ta'rif-i ahval-i milel* ("description of the conditions of peoples") to refer to "ethnography." Thus, *beser* (mankind, man) and *milel* (plural of "millet" which means "nation," "people," or "religious community") were also used to refer to ethnic groups. "Nationalism" was then rendered by *kavmiyet.* See Ahmed Agayef, "Turk Alemi" (The Turkish world), part 4, *Türk Yurdu* 1, no. 5 (July 17, 1328 [1912]): 136. By the second half of the 1910s, *kavim* referred to the French word "ethnie." See its use by Ziya Gök Alp, " 'Turan' nedir?" (What is "Turan"?), *Yeni Mecmua* 2, no. 31 (February 8, 1918): 82. *Irk* has kept its meaning of "race," as well as of "blood," "lineage," and "vein," since the turn of the century. See Moran, *Türkçe-İngilizce Sözlük* (1945); Hony, *A Turkish-English Dictionary,* 2d ed. (Oxford: Oxford University Press, 1980); *Redhouse Yeni Türkçe-İngilizce Sözlük* (1974); and *Redhouse Çağdaş Türkçe-İngilizce Sözlüğü* (1983). As a matter of fact, *ırkçı* means "racist," *ırkî*

and *ırksal* "racial," *ırkçılık* "racism," *ırkan* "racially," and *ırktaş* "a (person) of the same race" in modern and contemporary Turkish. In addition, Persian compounds (izafets) commonly used in Ottoman Turkish such as *ırk-ı asfer* ("yellow race") or *ırk-ı ebyaz* ("white race") clearly show that *ırk* had little to do with "ethnicity." See Sami, *Kâmûs-i Türkî* and *Redhouse Yeni Türkçe-İngilizce Sözlük,* s.v. "ırk." There is a printing mistake in Sami's dictionary which gives *ırk-ı asferi* and *ırk-ı ebyazi.* Of interest are also the expressions *ırk kavgaları* ("racial conflicts") and *ırk münaferatı* ("racial hatred"). See Moran, *Türkçe-İngilizce Sözlük,* s.v. "ırk."

42. Georgeon, *Yusuf Akçura,* 26. This definition of "milliyet" appears in A. Y. [Yusuf Akçura], "1329 Senesinde Türk Dünyası" (The Turkish world in the year 1913), *Türk Yurdu* 6, no. 3 (June 3, 1330 [1914]): 2098.
43. Jacob M. Landau, *Tekinalp: Turkish Patriot, 1883–1961* (Istanbul: Nederlands Historisch-Archeologisch Instituut, 1984), 26. These ideas are developed in Tekin (Moiz Cohen), *Turan* (İstanbul: "Kader" Matbaası, 1330 [1914–15]), 113–26.
44. Tekin, *Turan,* 138. His irredentist views are also expounded in Tekin Alp, *Türkismus und Pantürkismus* (Weimar: Gustav Kiepenheuer, 1915).
45. Tekin, *Turan,* 138, 143. For a slightly different translation which omits a phrase, see Landau, *Tekinalp,* 273–74.
46. For the Ottoman period, see Landau, *Tekinalp,* 22; for the Republican era, see Tekin Alp, *Türkleşdirme* (Turkification) (İstanbul: "Resimli Ay" Matbaası, 1928), in particular his "ten commandments," which include "Turkify Your Names!" (65).
47. For his conception of morality as total service to the nation, see his poem *Vazife* (Duty), which he first published in 1915 and then republished with slight changes in his collection of poems titled *Yeni Hayat* (New life) (İstanbul: Evkaf-i İslamiyye, 1918), n.p.
48. Gök Alp first published this poem in Salonika in 1911. "Turan" was later included in the volume of poetry titled *Kızıl Elma* (The red apple) (İstanbul, 1330 [1914–15]). My translation is based on the text in Enver Behnan Şapolyo, *Ziya Gökalp: İttihat ve Terakki ve Meşrutiyet Tarihi* (Ziya Gök Alp: Union and progress and the history of the constitutional period) (İstanbul: Güven Basïmevi, 1943), 206–7.
49. This couplet, written "in the first months of the war," is from his poem "Kızıl Destan" (The red epic) as translated in Uriel Heyd, *Foundations of Turkish Nationalism: The Life and Teachings of Ziya Gökalp* (London: Luzac and Company and The Harvill Press, 1950), 128.
50. Taha Parla, *The Social and Political Thought of Ziya Gökalp 1876–1924* (Leiden: E. J. Brill, 1985), 34–35, 61, 135n. 53. This work originated in a doctoral dissertation at Columbia University in 1980.
51. On the two periods in Ziya Gök Alp's thought, before and after World War I, see Zarevand (Zaven and Nartouhie Nalbandian), *United and Independent Turania: Aims and Designs of the Turks,* trans. Vahakn N. Dadrian (Leiden: E. J. Brill, 1971), 48–49.

52. These opinions first appeared in "Yeni Hayat ve Yeni Kıymetler" (New life and new values), *Genç Kalemler* 2, no. 8 (July 26, 1327 [1911]), as reproduced in Ziya Gök Alp, *Makaleler* (Articles), ed. Süleyman Hayri Bolay (Ankara: Başbakanlık Basımevı, 1982), 2:40–46. Ziya Gök Alp included this essay in his series titled "Türkçülük Nedir?" (What is Turkism?), *Yeni Mecmua* 1, no. 25 (December 27, 1917): 482–85.
53. Ahmed Emin, *Turkey in the World War* (New Haven: Yale University Press, 1930), 195–96. On the full support that Gök Alp enjoyed on the part of Talât, Enver, and Jemal Pashas, the leading triumvirate of the Committee of Union and Progress during World War I, and his special intellectual status, see Şapolyo, *Ziya Gökalp,* 78–79.
54. See Gök Alp's testimonial in Tekinalp, *Türkismus und Pantürkismus,* 109–10.
55. Ziya Gök Alp, "Rusya'daki Türkler Ne Yapmalı?" (What ought the Turkes of Russia to do?) *Yeni Mecmua,* 2, no. 38 (June 4, 1918): 233–35. For a summary, see also Tarîk Zafer Tunaya, *Türkiye'de Siyasal Partiler,* vol. 3: *İttihat ve Terakki: Bir Çağın, Bir Kuşağın, Bir Partinin Tarihi* (Political parties in Turkey, vol. 3: Union and progress: The history of a period, a generation, a party) (İstanbul: Hürriyet Vakfı Yayınları, 1989), 320–21.
56. See "Enver Paşa" in *Yeni Hayat,* n.p. See also Tunaya, *Türkiye'de Siyasal Partiler,* III, 321.
57. Şapolyo, *Ziya Gökalp,* 108.
58. For this analysis of Gök Alp's economic thought in relation to the non-Turks, see Zafer Toprak, *Türkiye'de "Millî İktisat," 1908–1918* ("National economy" in Turkey, 1908–1918) (Ankara: Yurt Yayınları A. Ş., 1982), 32, and 30–35 for a broader summary of his economic views. On solidarism and Gök Alp, see Heyd, *Foundations of Turkish Nationalism,* 140–48. Also Parla, *The Social and Political Thought of Ziya Gökalp,* 106–16. Parla tends to underplay the importance Ziya Bey assigned to heavy industries. On specific aspects of the "national economy," see Zafer Toprak, "II. Meşrutiyet'te Solidarist Düşünce: Halkçılık," (Solidarist thought in the second constitutional period: Populism) *Toplum ve Bilim* 1 (Spring 1977): 92–123, and idem, "Türkiye'de Korporatizmin Doğuşu" (The birth of corporatism in Turkey), *Toplum ve Bilim* 12 (Winter 1980): 41–49.
59. For the quotations, see Ziya Gök Alp, "Türkçülük Nedir?" 484. On the lack of Turkish "economic classes," see Gök Alp, "Türkleşmek, İslamlaşmak, Muasırlaşmak" (Turkification, Islamization, modernization), *Türk Yurdu* 1, no. 2 (March 7, 1329 [1913]): 333.
60. See his poem "Vatan" (Fatherland), in *Yeni Hayat,* n.p.
61. Gök Alp, "Türkleşmek, İslamlaşmak, Muasırlaşmak," 1:334.
62. Ziya Gök Alp, "İktisadî Vatanperverlik" (Economic patriotism), *Yeni Mecmua* 2, no. 43 (May 9, 1918): 323.
63. Tekin Alp, *Türkismus und Pantürkismus,* 35–40. See also J. M. Landau, "Munis Tekinalp's Economic Views Regarding the Ottoman Empire and Turkey," in *Osmanistische Studien zur Wirtschafts- und Sozialgeschichte: In Memoriam Vančo Boškov,* ed. Hans Georg Majer (Wiesbaden: Otto Harraßowitz, 1986), 94–103.

64. Tekin Alp, *Türkismus und Pantürkismus,* 61–62, as translated in Landau, *Tekinalp,* 133.
65. See A. Y. [Akçura Yusuf], "1329 Senesinde Türk Dünyasi," 2102–04 and A. Y. [Akçura Yusuf], "İktisad" (Economy), *Türk Yurdu* 12, no. 12 (August 2, 1333 [1917]): 3521–23. For a French translation of the most important sections of these articles, see Georgeon, *Yusuf Akçura,* 128–30; for an interpretation, 58.
66. Zafer Toprak, "İslam ve İktisat: 1913–1914 Müslüman Boykotajı" (Islam and the economy: The Muslim boycott of 1913–1914), *Toplum ve Bilim* no. 29/30 (Spring–Summer 1985): 179–99.
67. Tekin Alp, *Türkismus und Pantürkismus,* 39, cited in Landau, *Tekinalp,* 122.
68. Zarevand, *United and Independent Turania,* 74. Confirmation can be found in Tekin Alp, *Türkismus und Pantürkismus,* 37–38.
69. Toprak, *Türkiye'de "Millî İktisat,"* 57. Parla puts also the matter in somewhat diplomatic terms. He states that the creation of a "national bourgeois class" resulted from "the collaboration of the nationalistic bureaucracy with a national commercial bourgeoisie to expropriate and replace Levantine and minority mercantile groups." See Parla, *The Social and Political Thought of Ziya Gökalp,* 110. Words and expressions like "expropriation" and "filled the voids" do not convey a clear sense of what happened, namely, state-sponsored plundering. For some examples, see Astourian, "Genocidal Process," 71–72.
70. On stereotyping, its nature, and functions, see Rupert Brown, *Group Processes: Dynamics within and between Groups* (New York: Basil Blackwell, 1988), 231–45.
71. The proverbs are in Ahmed Vefik Paşa, *Müntahabât-ı Durûb-ı Emsal,* 102. In psychiatry, projection is "an ego defense or mental mechanism operating outside of and beyond conscious awareness through which consciously disowned aspects of the self are rejected or disowned and thrown outward, to become imputed to others." See H. P. Laughlin, *The Ego and Its Defenses,* 2d ed. (New York: Jason Aronson, 1979), 221. In cases of projection, "the other person thereby becomes a mirror, in thus unwittingly reflecting back the consciously disowned emotional feelings" (ibid., 226).
72. Georges Devereux, "L'identité ethnique: Ses bases logiques et ses dysfonctions," in *Ethnopsychanalyse complémentariste* (Paris: Flammarion, 1985), 165–211.
73. For the United States and South Africa, see Wilson, *Power, Racism, and Privilege,* 104–5, 168–71.
74. Jacob M. Landau, *Pan-Turkism in Turkey: A Study of Irredentism* (Hamden, Conn.: Archon Books, 1981), 52–53.
75. Baron Wladimir Giesl, *Zwei Jahrzehnte im Nahen Orient* (Berlin: Verlag für Kulturpolitik, 1927), 119. See also Malcolm MacColl, "The Constantinople Massacre and Its Lesson," *Contemporary Review,* November 1895, 754–55. For 1909, see Astourian, "Genocidal Process," 63–66.
76.

> Compensation is an ego defense or mental mechanism, operating outside of and beyond conscious awareness, through which the individual seeks to offset, to make up for, or to "compensate" for his

> deficiencies or defects. These deficiencies may be actual, or may be so imagined to varying degrees. . . . Idealization is an ego defense or mental mechanism operating outside of and beyond conscious awareness through which a person, group, nation, family or some other object is overvalued and emotionally aggrandized. This dynamism is often marked by an attachment of attention, interest, and significance to a particular love-object which has become exalted, overestimated, and overvalued. Idealization is the process through which one sets up or creates an ideal. Persons, positions, situations, possessions, and goals can thus become regarded as ideals or as idealistic. (Laughlin, *The Ego and Its Defenses,* 18, 123)

77. For the economy, see Ahmed Emin, *Turkey in the World War,* 107–67, 290–96; Erik J. Zürcher, *Turkey: A Modern History* (New York: I. B. Tauris, 1994), 130–31; Toprak, *Türkiye'de "Millî İktisat,"* 346–51. See also Feroz Ahmad, "War and Society under the Young Turks, 1908–18," *Review: Fernand Braudel Center* 11, no. 2 (Spring 1988): 274–83. Ahmad's overview is perhaps somewhat optimistic in its assessment of the period.
78. Kuper, *The Pity of It All,* 257.
79. Zürcher, *Turkey,* 130.
80. As quoted in Johannes Lepsius, *Rapport secret sur les massacres d'Arménie* (1916; reprint, Beirut: Hamaskaine, 1968), 296.
81. Henry Morgenthau, *Ambassador Morgenthau's Story* (Garden City, N.Y.: Doubleday, Page, 1918; reprint, Plandome, N.Y.: New Age Publishers, 1975), 338, 348.

2
The Archival Trail
Authentication of *The Treatment of Armenians in the Ottoman Empire, 1915–16*

Ara Sarafian

Introduction

In February 1916, James Bryce and Arnold Toynbee began compiling evidence for a publication concerning "recent events in Armenia."[1] The reports which Bryce and Toynbee subsequently collected were used for a detailed treatise called *The Treatment of Armenians in the Ottoman Empire.*[2] Bryce and Toynbee organized these reports into a set of local narratives which demonstrated, region by region, how Ottoman Armenians were systematically uprooted and annihilated in 1915.[3] The Bryce and Toynbee volume is composed of 591 pages of documentary evidence and 144 pages of discussion and appendixes. Nearly all the evidence came from primary sources, and the main facts were established beyond question. The Ottoman government had unleashed a systematic program to annihilate Armenians in the Ottoman Empire.

The case of Trebizond, for example, was presented on the evidence of local American Consul Oscar Heizer, Italian Consul-General Giacomo Gorrini, a Montenegrin employee at the local branch of the Ottoman Bank, and a local Armenian girl.[4] The American consul's report was sent to Washington, D.C., at the time of the events, the Italian Consul's testimony was given to the *Messaggero* in Rome, the Montenegrin employee's story was printed in the Armenian newspaper *Arev* of Alexandria, and the Armenian girl's account was recorded by Mr. K. Hovadjian in Romania. These testimonies were made independently of each other, yet they corroborated a common set of events regarding the destruction of Armenians in Trebizond. Similarly, the victimization of Armenian deportees from Baiburt (near Erzerum) was narrated by three independent sources: Victoria Khatchadour Baroutdjibashian, who was in the convoy of exiles which left Baiburt on June 14, two Danish nurses, Flora A. Wedel Yarlesberg and a colleague, who observed the passage of Armenian deportees at Erzinjan, and another Danish nurse, Hansina Marcher, who observed the march of these same caravans at Harput (Kharpert).[5] Victoria Baroutdjibashian's statement was sent to Washington, D.C., by Ambassador Henry Morgenthau, the two Danish nurses communicated their report to Johannes Lepsius, and Hansina Marcher's statement was sent to Ivan Zavrieff in Switzerland.

In this critical fashion, based on the independent corroboration of eyewitness accounts, Bryce and Toynbee constructed their local narratives and formulated their overall conclusion regarding the treatment of Armenians in the Ottoman Empire. This work was the first systematic articulation of the Armenian Genocide thesis.[6] Whatever the political considerations of the British Government in printing and distributing such a book—and the Armenian Genocide did afford ample material for the British propaganda effort against the Central Powers—this publication had a serious documentary quality because of its explicit presentation of data and careful analysis.

Deviant Historiography

In recent years, a number of partisan authors have argued that the Bryce and Toynbee work was simply part of a British misinformation campaign aimed against the Ottoman Empire and its allies. These authors have insisted that the British publication had no scholarly merit either in method or in content. According to Enver Zia Karal, *The Treatment of Armenians in the Ottoman Empire* was merely "one-sided British propaganda," produced for public consumption in Great Britain, and was simply "not worth dwelling upon" any further.[7] Another author, Ismet Binark, the current general director of the State Archives in Turkey, has claimed that the "events described in the reports presented as the records of the so-called Armenian massacre . . . [were] all falsified information taken from the English's files relating to the East." *The Treatment of Armenians in the Ottoman Empire* was "ornamented with massacre stories, unrelated with the truth, biased, written with Armenian fanaticism, and misleading the world's public opinion."[8] Mim Kemal Öke has argued that this work was based "on Armenian sources and documents gathered by Armenian supporters from second and third hand sources. . . . Toynbee created hair-raising scenes of massacres without mentioning his sources, without comparing his sources, and without giving the names and surnames of his witnesses. He [Toynbee] described the alleged massacres in great detail as if he had been one of the victims."[9] Şinasi Orel has even postulated that "German, American, Austrian and Swiss missionaries and charitable organizations were present in almost every corner of Anatolia throughout this period [and] this factor alone would have been sufficient to ensure that any ill-treatment to which the Armenians were subjected would have been broadcast worldwide immediately."[10] The inference here was that there were no such reports or "broadcasts." Foreign nationals residing in the Ottoman Empire, however, provided the "core" accounts for *The Treatment of Armenians in the Ottoman Empire,* and such reports were indeed "broadcast" in the periodical press of Europe, the United States, and beyond.[11]

The most accessible record describing the origins of the materials contained in this British publication is the published work itself and its supporting publication printed separately in 1916, *Key to Names of Persons and Places Withheld from Publication in the Original Edition of "The Treatment of Armenians in the Ottoman Empire, 1915–16."*[12] These two publications gave a meticulous account for each individual record printed in the British volume and listed the identities of the primary sources and communicants who forwarded these materials. Parallel to these printed records, the Toynbee Papers, located today at the Public Record Office in London, provide further documentation regarding the compilation of this British wartime publication.[13] Specifically, the Toynbee Papers are comprised of Arnold Toynbee's original working copy of *The Treatment of Armenians in the Ottoman Empire,* his daily correspondence soliciting materials and information from his sources, as well as the pamphlets, newspapers, and journal cuttings he consulted. The Toynbee Papers provide a full record of the origins and the methodology used to compile the British publication.

As most of the materials in this work came from the United States, the archives of the U.S. State Department, and the American Board of Commissioners for Foreign Missions (ABCFM) contain many of the original and ancillary materials.[14] Consequently, one can locate a whole spectrum of archival and printed records pertaining to this publication, including the actual reports themselves, the correspondence between the different parties involved (that is, between sources and communicants), and the actual manuscript copy of the original book in question. Any balanced discussion of *The Treatment of Armenians in the Ottoman Empire* has to acknowledge and account for these printed and archival records, as each document is clearly connected to other records, and these records, as a whole, form a clear trail between the Ottoman Empire, the United States, and Great Britain in 1915–16.

In view of these printed and archival records that are readily available to scholars today, the aforementioned authors, who call *The Treatment of Armenians in the Ottoman Empire* a forgery, may also be termed as "denialists." This is because their academic strategy relies on the deliberate disregard of pertinent records on their subject matter, the wanton misrepresentation of these records when they are cited, and the use of innuendo and outright untruths to make contentions that are otherwise unsustainable by scholarship. Salahi Sonyel, for example, who has addressed *The Treatment of Armenians in the Ottoman Empire* in a number of publications, has never acknowledged the existence of Bryce and Toynbee's *Key to Names of Persons.* This supporting publication is an important accompaniment to the main volume and its existence is a matter of record.[15] Yet Sonyel has simply ignored this published key in his discussions of *The Treatment of Armenians in the Ottoman Empire.* Although Sonyel has cited the Toynbee Papers at the Public Record Office, he has never acknowledged their content.[16] The Toynbee Papers alone are enough to cast aside the questions Sonyel raises regarding the authenticity of the materials comprising *The Treatment of Armenians in the Ottoman Empire.* Similarly, although Sonyel has cited the National Archives in his bibliographies, he has never discussed the American consular despatches on the Armenian Genocide contained in these archives, even though many copies of these reports were forwarded to Bryce and Toynbee and appeared in the British publication in 1916.[17] Sonyel simply ignores these primary materials and asserts that the documents comprising the Bryce and Toynbee volume were "second or third-hand sources."[18]

The United States and Reverend James L. Barton, 1915–16

The records comprising *The Treatment of Armenians in the Ottoman Empire* can be examined at three levels. First, who communicated reports on the Armenian Genocide to the British in 1916? Second, who were the original eyewitnesses who supplied these documents? Third, how can we examine the authenticity of these documents?

Most of the reports were communicated to Bryce and Toynbee from the Ottoman Empire via the United States. The main conduit in the transmission of these reports was Rev. James L. Barton, the head of three American organizations during this period, the ABCFM, the Committee on Armenian Atrocities (October 1915), and the American Committee for Armenian and Syrian Relief (ACASR) (November 1915).[19] Barton, who was highly respected in President Woodrow Wilson's administration, had direct access to American consular reports from the interior of the Ottoman Empire and was allowed to use these materials in publicizing the plight of Ottoman Armenians.[20] The first major American publication of reports on the Armenian Genocide, a press release, issued in New York on October 4, 1915 which drew on American diplomatic, consular, and missionary reports from the Ottoman Empire, was compiled by Barton with the active involvement of the United States government.[21]

The British were aware of American records on the destruction of Ottoman Armenians, and the October press release in New York marked the opening for Toynbee's correspondence with Barton.[22] Toynbee began this correspondence which led to Barton and his aides supplying Bryce and Toynbee with additional information which was used in the compilation of *The Treatment of Armenians in the Ottoman Empire*[23] (see Appendix A).

Toynbee's modus operandi in dealing with these reports is traceable by examining his papers at the Public Record Office in London. Toynbee attempted to collect as many records on the condition and treatment of Ottoman Armenians in 1915–16 as possible. He made every effort to establish direct contact with witnesses to obtain supporting or additional documentation.[24] The least problematic of these materials, from Bryce and Toynbee's perspective, were the reports from American consulates and missionaries in the Ottoman Empire. Their authenticity as genuine reports was not in question. Nevertheless, even in these cases, when these documents had omissions of detail, Toynbee asked for further information before accepting them for consideration.[25] For example, on February 15, 1916, Toynbee wrote to Barton requesting further details regarding the reports printed in the October 4 press release by the Committee on Armenian Atrocities (New York). Toynbee wanted to authenticate the press release and ask for additional reports. He also inquired whether Barton had (or could obtain) reports on the treatment of Armenians from Mr. Ernest Yarrow of Van, Dr. James McNaughton of Bardizag, and Miss Olive Vaughan and Dr. William N. Chambers of Adana. He also requested a fuller version of the 1915 "Statement of the Medical Department at Urmia" (BFMPC). Furthermore, he requested Barton's mediation in obtaining the cooperation of the Swiss publishers of a collection of documents on the Armenian Genocide, *Quelques documents sur le sort des Arméniens en 1915*.[26] Once more, Toynbee wanted to authenticate the documents printed in the Swiss publication and to request more material.[27]

Each report sent to Toynbee was examined, as the Toynbee Papers at the Public Record Office clearly indicate. Often the American communicants who forwarded to Bryce and Toynbee various materials on the destruction of Ottoman Armenians also provided important commentaries. These Americans clearly considered it their interest to give a clear and forthright appraisal of the materials they were sending. For example, on one occasion, Rev. William Rockwell sent Toynbee a copy of an "amazing article" that appeared in the *Boston Sunday Globe* on April 23, 1916 titled "German's Kick Caused the Fall of Erzerum." Rockwell cautioned Toynbee that the report was was grossly exaggerated and of questionable value in the opinion of Reverend Robert Stapleton, an American missionary who was in Erzerum at the time of the events described in that report.[28] In the absence of further supporting materials regarding the authenticity of this report as a primary source, Toynbee did not include it in his compilation. On another occasion, Toynbee himself investigated the claim of a certain Eleanor Franklin Egan, who wrote an article titled "Behind the Smoke of Battle" in the *Saturday Evening Post* (February 15, 1916).[29] This report was also omitted from his compilation because of insufficient verification regarding the location of the author at the time of the events described.[30]

In only 22 out of 150 reports did Toynbee include materials that had to be qualified because they entailed missing information regarding sources or locations. Each of these reports was clearly identified and included in this work because of the detail it presented, and because it was verified by the other "core" materials that Toynbee regarded as authentic. Furthermore, as Toynbee pointed out, these 22 reports were not essential to the case set forth in the volume.[31] For example, the work contained several reports communicated by the Armenian Revolutionary Federation (ARF), even though these reports did not disclose the full identities of the actual witnesses. Although these ARF materials supplemented the information provided in the "core" materials, they were not essential for the Bryce-Toynbee thesis. Bryce and Toynbee pointed out the various classes of materials and the critical interrelationship between these records. This publication even provided an insert for their readers listing "forty or fifty of the most important documents."[32]

Most of the reports compiled in *The Treatment of Armenians in the Ottoman Empire* were written by nationals of neutral countries residing in the Ottoman Empire in 1915. These "core" materials, which were sent to England through trustworthy intermediaries, formed the basis of the Bryce-Toynbee thesis on the destruction of Armenians between 1915 and 1916. Toynbee also collected a smaller number of original statements directly from individuals who had been in the Ottoman Empire in 1915. *The Treatment of Armenians in the Ottoman Empire* and the Toynbee Papers thus contain a few original depositions in their own right[33] (see Appendix B).

Toynbee's success in collecting eyewitness accounts on the Armenian Genocide through dependable intermediaries can be best demonstrated by locating original copies of those reports today. For example, since most of the materials were communicated to the British via the United States, and since a significant number of these reports came from the U.S. State Department, many of the original reports can now be located in the National Archives in Washington, D.C.[34] An examination of these archives yields significant results and demonstrates the fidelity with which Rev. Barton and his associates copied and transmitted the reports to Bryce and Toynbee in 1916.

These original materials also demonstrate the careful manner used to collect and print the American documents in *The Treatment of Armenians in the Ottoman Empire.*[35] Though Barton was selective in the materials he forwarded to Toynbee from these American consular files, the reports he did send represented a fair sample. The addition of the remaining American materials today would only lend additional support to the central thesis of *The Treatment of Armenians in the Ottoman Empire*[36] (see Appendix C).

Conclusion

Unlike the compilation of some other documentary publications during World War I, Bryce and Toynbee left a clear account of the methodology of their work, both in their publication and archival records. As these records show, the volume was based largely on primary sources written by nationals of neutral countries who resided in the Ottoman Empire in 1915 during the Armenian Genocide. These persons communicated most of their reports to American consuls in the interior provinces, the U.S. Embassy in Constantinople, the U.S. State Department in Washington, D.C., as well as American missionary organizations in the Ottoman Empire and the United States. Subsequently, some of these materials were released to the American and British public.

The Treatment of Armenians in the Ottoman Empire and its supporting publication, *Key to Names of Persons and Places Withheld from Publication in the Original Edition of "The Treatment of Armenians in the Ottoman Empire, 1915–16,"* provide details on the procedure used to collect these documents, and the manner in which they were arranged to demonstrate the systematic destruction of the Armenian population. These details can be examined today in the Public Record Office, Rev. Barton's correspondence at the Houghton Library (Harvard University), and the National Archives in Washington, D.C. Many of these archival sources have been microfilmed and printed in documentary publications and are readily available at major university and research libraries.[37] These records support *The Treatment of Armenians in the Ottoman Empire* as an exemplary academic exercise which documented, verified, and accounted for its methodology—a task assumed under extraordinary circumstances in 1916.[38] This book shows that the Turkish government had embarked on a systematic policy to destroy Armenians in the Ottoman Empire.

Given the compelling documentation at hand, the denial of the Bryce and Toynbee work as "Armenian propaganda" cannot be accepted as a matter of "interpretation" or "scholarly debate." The evidence is too overwhelming to be dismissed in such a fashion. *The Treatment of Armenians in the Ottoman Empire* remains a solid milestone in the historiography of the Armenian Genocide.

Appendix A

The following table lists those individuals and organizations which provided documentation to Bryce and Toynbee. As this table shows, the single most important source was Barton's ACASR, followed by the American-Armenian journal *Gotchnag (Hayastani Kochnak),* followed by the Board of Foreign Missions of the Presbyterian Church (BFMPC). The information presented in the following table comes from *The Treatment of Armenians in the Ottoman Empire* itself.

Table 1

Sources of Reports Appearing in
The Treatment of Armenians in the Ottoman Empire, 1915–16,
by number communicated

76 reports: American Committee for Armenian and Syrian Relief (report numbers: 2, 3, 10, 11, 14, 23, 26, 44, 51, 52, 54, 59, 61, 65, 66, 69, 70–72, 77, 80, 85–87b, 88–91, 93, 96, 97, 101, 102, 104, 107–115g, 116, 117a–117d, 118, 120, 121, 124–128, 133, 136, 138a, 138b, 139a–139d, 140, 141, 143, 149, 150)

11 reports: *Gotchnag* of New York (4, 5, 17, 60, 63, 68, 84, 98–98c, 134)

10 reports: Board of Foreign Missions of the Presbyterian Church (27–32, 35, 38, 41, 42)

8 reports: Boghos Nubar Pasha in Egypt (6–9, 87c, 119, 131, 132)

5 reports: *Ararat* of London (19, 25, 36, 43, 45)

4 reports: Lord James Bryce (57, 64, 67, 82); *Horizon* of Tiflis (46, 55, 105, 106); Leopold Favre in Geneva (13, 62, 94, 123); *Sonnenaufgang* (12, 18, 142, 145)

3 reports: British Foreign Office (48–50)

2 reports: *Balkanian Mamoul* (83, 99); Rev. F. N. Heazell (39, 147); *Mschak* of Tiflis (56, 58); *New Armenia* of New York (81, 103); *Times* of London (76, 100); *United Press* (1, 146); Mr. Trowbridge (122, 130)

1 report: *Le Journal* of Paris (144); *Arev* of Alexandria (74); *Arev* of Baku (47); *Associated Press* (34); *Assyrian Mission Quarterly Paper* (148); Mr. J. D. Bourchier (75); Rev. I. N. Camp (137); *The Churchman* of Oxford (37); *Egyptian Gazette* (135); *Gazette de Lausanne* (21); *Manchester Guardian* (16); *Messagero* of Rome (73); *Missionary Herald* of Boston (78); Mr. G. H. Paelian (79); *Pioneer Press* of St. Paul, Minnesota (20); Mr. A. S. Safrastian (22); *Van-Tosp* (24); Mrs. Margoliouth of Oxford (40); Miss Grace Higley Knapp (15); Rev. F. N. Heazell (33); Rev. H. J. Buxton (53); Prof. Thoumanian (92); Prof. Xenidhis (95); Miss H. E. Wallis (129).

Appendix B

The following table lists the actual sources which were credited in the publication in 1916. Most of the information in this table comes from *Key to Names of Persons and Places Withheld,* although some of this information was also contained in the main volume.

Table 2

SOURCES/WITNESSES CITED IN THE BRITISH PUBLICATION OF
THE TREATMENT OF ARMENIANS IN THE OTTOMAN EMPIRE 1915–16[39]

Reports Provided by Neutral and Belligerent Nationals: 102 Reports

Sonnenaufgang (12); ACASR (14, 44); Ainslie, Miss Kate (121); Barby, M. Henry (144); Barnard, J. D. (148); BFMPC missionary (Urmia) (35); Birge, Mrs. (108); Bourchier, J. D. (76, 100); Briquet, M. Pierre (123, 124); Buxton, Rev. H. J. (53); Chambers, Rev. William (128); Christie, Mrs. (114, 120); Cochran, Mrs. J. P. (32); Cold, Miss Edith (126, 127); Davis, Leslie A. (Kharpert) (65); Dodd, Dr. William S. (109, 125); Elmer, Prof. Theodore A. (87a, b); Frearson, Miss (137); Gage, Miss Frances C., (88, 89, 96); Geddes, Walter M. (118, 136, 141); German missionary (Marsovan) (91); Gorrini, Commendatore G. (73); Graffam, Miss Mary L. (78); Heizer, Oscar (54, 72)

Holt, Miss (102, 103); Hoover, Dr. (104); Jackson, Jesse (139a, b, c, d); Jessup, Rev. F. N. (30); Johannsen, Miss Alma (23); Knapp, Grace H. (15); Kurd Ali of Aghazade of Faro (58); Labaree, Rev. Robert M. (28, 29); Leslie, Mr. (133); Lewis, Miss Mary E. (31); Marcher, Miss Hansina (64); McDowel, Rev. E. W. (41); Member of U.S. diplomatic service (101); Members of U.S. mission station, Urmia (38); Mohring, Schwester L. (145); Montenegrin *kavass* of Ottoman bank (74); Morgenthau, Henry (2); Muller, Hugo A. (42); Nathan, Edward (115a–d); Nisan, Rev. Y. M. (33); Partridge, Rev. Ernest C. (77); Partridge, Mrs. (79); Peet,

W. W. (10, 90, 150); Post, Dr. Wilfred M. (110–112); Price, Philip M. (45); Riggs, Ernest W. (69, 70, 71); Riggs, Miss Mary W. (66); Rohner, Miss Beatrice (117b, 142); Ryan, Mr. Arthur C. (13); Schafer, Miss Schwester P. (117a, b, c); Sewney, Mrs. (80); Shane, Miss Myrthe O. (26); Shedd, Rev. William A. (27); Shephard, Dr. (116); Sporri, Mr. (18); Stapleton, Rev. Robert (149); Stevens, Mr. (48, 49, 50); Wallis, Miss H. E. (129); White, Dr. George E. (86); Wilson, Rev. S. G. (51, 52); Wingate, Henry K. (85); Wood, Henry (1, 146); Yarlesberg, Miss Flora A. Wedel (62); Young, Greg (143); Young, Mrs. J. Vance (135)

Reports Provided by Armenian and Other Native Sources: 66 Reports

Arev correspondent (47); *Gotchnag* journal (63, 84, 98a–c); *Horizon* journal (60, 106); *New Armenia* journal (81); Aivazian, Mr. (8, 87c); Andreassian, Rev. Dikran (122, 130); ARF Balkan Section (3, 11, 61, 107, 113); Armenian colony in Egypt (119); Armenian Patriarchate in Constantinople (4–7); Armenian refugee in Moush (24); Armenian refugee in Moush (25); Armenian refugee in Harpout (66); Armenian refugees (75); Armenian resident of Aintab (138a, b); Armenian resident of Aleppo (140); Armenian traveler in Kaisaria (83); Armenian victim in Eski Shehir (105); Artounian, Mr. Sampson (46); Baroutjibashian, Mrs. Victoria (59); Comrade Serko (99); Demirdjian, Miss (94); Essayan, Rev. Haroutioun (9); Gazarian, Mrs. (20); Gherberos, Mr. (67); Kedjedjian, Mrs. Maritza (68); Khounountz, B. H. (55); Letter, extract, from Angora (97); Minassian, Dr. Y. (56); Muggerditchian, Tovmas (132, 134); Murad of Sivas (82); Roupen of Sassoun (21, 22); Rushdouni, Y. K. (16, 17); Safrastian, A. S. (19, 57); Sargis, Rev. Jacob (34); Sargis, Mrs. Jacob (43); Shimmon, Paul (36, 37, 147); Surma (39, 40); Thorgom, Mge. of Egypt (131); Xenidhis, Prof. J. P. (92, 93, 95)

Appendix C

The following table lists forty-one reports from U.S. State Department records which were received from the Ottoman Empire and subsequently appeared in the Bryce and Toynbee publication.

Table 3

United States Department of State Records
That Appear in the British Publication
The Treatment of Armenians in the Ottoman Empire, 1915–16[40]

867.00/783 Edward Nathan, U.S. Consul, Mersina, 22 September 1915; 867.4016/72 J. B. Jackson, U.S. Consul, Aleppo, 12 May 1915; 867.4016/92 Mr. Leslie, U.S. missionary, Ourfa, 14 June 1915; 867.4016/95 Miss Hunecke, July 1915; 867.4016/95 A.R.F. communique, 7 June 1915; 867.4016/95 Pierre Briquet, Tarsus, no date; 867.4016/95 undisclosed source, Aintab, letter, 6 April 1915; 867.4016/95 undisclosed source, Aintab, letter, 17 May 1915; 867.4016/95 undisclosed source, Aleppo, memorandum, 18 June 1915; 867.4016/106 Dr. White, Marsovan, 1915.; 867.4016/122 Mrs. Victoria Baroutjibashian, American widow,

Harpout; 867.4016/124 Edward Nathan, U.S. consul, Mersina, August 7 1915; 867.4016/126 J. B. Jackson, U.S. Consul, Aleppo, 3 August 1915; 867.4016/127 Leslie Davis, U.S. Consul, Harpout, 11 July 1915; 867.4016/128 Oscar Heizer, U.S. Consul, Trebizond, 28 July 1915; 867.4016/148 J. B. Jackson, U.S. Consul, Aleppo, 19 August 1915; 867.4016/187 Miss Mary L. Graffam, American missionary, Sivas, 7 August 1915; 867.4016/188 Dr. Post, American missionary, Konia, 3 September 1915; 867.4016/189 Dr. Dodd, American missionary, Konia, 8 September 1915; 867.4016/193 Edward Nathan, U.S. Consul, Mersina, 11 September 1915; 867.4016/200 Edward Nathan, U.S. Consul, Mersina, 27 September 1915; 867.4016/212 Gregory Young, U.S. Consul, Damascus, report, 20 September 1915; 867.4016/220 Mr. Peter, U.S. Consular Agent, Samsoun, August 26 1915; 867.4016/225 unknown author, Harpout [probably Miss Mary Riggs]; 867.4016/226 Armenian Revolutionary Federation, Bucharest, 15 October 1915; 867.4016/226 Dr. Post, American missionary, Konia, 27 October 1915; 867.4016/226 undisclosed source, Konia, letter (resume), 2 October 1915; 867.4016/226 Miss Alma Johannsen, Swedish missionary, Moush, November 1915.; 867.4016/238 Edward Nathan, U.S. Consul, Mersina, 30 October 1915; 867.4016/239 Edward Nathan, U.S. Consul, Mersina, 4 November 1915; 867.4016/240 Edward Nathan, U.S. Consul, Mersina, 6 November 1915; 867.4016/243 Walter M. Geddes, Smyrna-Aleppo-Damacus, November 1915; 867.4016/252 Miss Gage, American missionary, August-September 1915; 867.4016/254 Miss Myrtle Shane, American missionary, Bitlis, 14 October 1915; 867.4016/260 Schwester Schafer, Cilicia, 16 November 1915; 867.4016/260 Schwester Rohner, Cilicia, 26 November 1915; 867.4016/260 Schwester Schafer, Cilicia, 1 December 1915; 867.4016/260 Schwester Schafer, Cilicia, 13 December 1915; 867.4016/285 Rev. Robert S. Stapleton, Erzeroum, 21 March 1916; 867.48/271 J. B. Jackson, U.S. Consul, Aleppo, 8 February 1916.

Notes

The author wishes to thank Stephen Sheehi, Vincent Lima, and Dennis Papazian for their comments, criticisms, and support in preparing this chapter.

1. Lord Bryce was British Ambassador to the United States, an Oxford law professor, and a long-standing champion of Ottoman Armenians. He was also the author of *Transcaucasia and Ararat, Being Notes of a Vacation Tour in the Autumn of 1876* (London: Macmillan and Co. Ltd., 1877). Arnold Toynbee, the editor of this work, was a young Oxford University scholar and Foreign Office clerk, who soon became a prominent historian in his own right. In preparing this work, Toynbee sent out his first letters soliciting documentation for this publication on February 1, 1916. See Public Record Office, Kew, London, file number FO 96/205, 26–29.
2. Arnold Toynbee, ed., *The Treatment of Armenians in the Ottoman Empire, 1915–16: Documents Presented to Viscount Grey of Fallodon by Viscount Bryce* (London: Sir Joseph Causton and Sons, 1916; reprint, Astoria, N.Y.: J. C. and L. Fawcett, 1990). This volume was accompanied, in the same year,

by a confidential publication, *Key to Names of Persons and Places Withheld from Publication in the Original Edition of "The Treatment of Armenians in the Ottoman Empire, 1915–16: Documents Presented to Viscount Grey of Fallodon by Viscount Bryce,"* Miscellaneous no. 31, 1916. The main volume has also been called the "Blue Book," as it appeared in the Parliamentary Blue Book series published by the British government.

3. Bryce and Toynbee divided their materials in the following subject categories: General Descriptions; Vilayet of Van; Vilayet of Bitlis; Azerbaijan and Hakkiari; Refugees in the Caucasus; Vilayet of Erzeroum; Vilayet of Mamouret-ul-Aziz; Vilayet of Trebizond, and Sanjak of Shabin Kara-Hissar; Sivas; Sanjak of Kaisaria; Marsovan; Angora; Thrace, Constantinople, Broussa and Ismid; Anatolian Railway; Cilicia; Jibal Mousa; Ourfa and Aintab; Aleppo; Vilayet of Damascus and Sanjak of Der el-Zor; Documents Received while Going to Press.
4. See Toynbee, *The Treatment of Armenians,* docs. 72–75.
5. See ibid., docs. 59, 62, and 64.
6. Given the chronological scope of the publication, *The Treatment of Armenians in the Ottoman Empire* did not cover the 1916 massacres at Deir-el-Zor. The 1916 massacres were highly significant as they wiped out those Armenians who were still surviving in the ostensible "resettlement zones" in eastern Syria. These massacres demonstrated the persistence of the Ottoman authorities in carrying through the genocidal process started in 1915.
7. Enver Zia Karal, *Armenian Question (1878–1923)* (Ankara: Imprimerie Gunduz, 1975), 18.
8. See foreword to Ismet Binark, *Ermeni Olayları Tarihi* (History of the Armenian incidents) (Hüseyin Nazim Pasha's papers) (Ankara: Turkish Prime Ministry General Directorate of State Archives, 1994), xl.
9. Mim Kemal Oke, *The Armenian Question, 1914–1923* (Nicosia: K. Rustem and Brother, 1988), 106–7. See also Kamuran Gürün, *The Armenian File: The Myth of Innocence Exposed* (Nicosia, Istanbul: K. Rustem and Brother, 1985), 42–43; Salahi R. Sonyel, "Turco-Armenian Relations and British Propaganda during the First World War," *Belleten* 58 (August 1994): 381–449.
10. Şinasi Orel and Süreyya Yuca, *The Talât Pasha Telegrams: Historical Fact or Armenian Fiction?* (Nicosia: K. Rustem and Brother, 1986), 146, 121.
11. For a collection of newspaper articles on the Armenian Genocide as reported in the American, Canadian, and Australian press in 1915–16, see Richard Kloian, comp., *The Armenian Genocide: News Accounts from the American Press* (Berkeley: Anto Press, 1985); Armenian National Committee, *The Armenian Genocide: As Reported in the Australian Press* (Sydney: Armenian National Committee, 1983); Armenian Youth Federation of Canada, *The Armenian Genocide in the Canadian Press,* vol. 1: *1915–1916* (Montreal: Armenian National Committee of Canada, 1985). For documentary accounts, many of which appeared in the periodical press as well, see Committee on Armenian Atrocities, "October 4, 1915 Press Release," New York, 1915; American Committee for Armenian and Syrian Relief, "Latest News Concerning the Armenian and Syrian

Sufferers (January 2, 1916)" (New York, 1916); Comité de l'oeuvre de secours 1915 aux Arméniens, *Quelques documents sur le sort des Arméniens en 1915–1916* (Geneva: Société Générale d'Imprimerie, 1916).

12. This confidential key was printed separately because many documents were provided by sources who were still in the Ottoman Empire in 1916. These sources were obscured in the main publication. Bryce and Toynbee communicated this confidential information to a number of trusted individuals in Great Britain and the United States (xl), and promised to print that same list of names as soon as possible (xxi–xxii, xl–xli). The confidential key was printed that same year, 1916.
13. Toynbee Papers, FO 96/205–11 (six boxes), Public Record Office, London.
14. The archives in question are the United States National Archives (NA) in Washington, D.C., and the Houghton Library at Harvard University.
15. The *Key to Names of Persons and Places Withheld* has also been reprinted several times with the republication of *The Treatment of Armenians in the Ottoman Empire*. See, for example, G. Doniguian and Sons, Beirut, 1988. Original copies of this key also appear in other archives, such as NA, Record Group (RG) 59, General Records of the Department of State, Internal Affairs of Turkey 1910–1929, document 307, Washington, D.C.
16. Sonyel acknowledges the Toynbee Papers in a passing footnote, but does not discuss their content. See Sonyel, "Turco-Armenian Relations," 444n. 168.
17. See Sonyel, "Turco-Armenian Relations"; idem, *Minorities and the Destruction of the Ottoman Empire,* Turkish Historical Society, vol. 7, no. 129 (Ankara: Turkish Historical Society Printing House, 1993).
18. At least forty-one reports in the U.S. State Department archives appeared in the British volume. Most of these reports were signed statements, and all of them were sent from the Ottoman Empire. Fifteen of these reports were written by American consuls, ten by American missionaries, eight by others (four of whom were German nationals), six were undisclosed sources, and two were from the Armenian Revolutionary Federation.
19. Rev. Barton was the Secretary of the American Board of Commissioners for Foreign Missions, an American missionary organization based in Boston with longstanding interests in the Ottoman Empire. Barton was also the secretary of the ad hoc Committee on Armenian Atrocities (CAA) and ACASR, the forerunner of Near East Relief (NER).
20. Prior to World War I, American missionaries enjoyed excellent relations with the U.S. State Department. For a detailed discussion of Rev. Barton's access and dissemination of U.S. consular and diplomatic reports on the destruction of Armenians, see Ara Sarafian, "The Paper Trail: The American State Department and the Report of Committee on Armenian Atrocities," *Revue du Monde Arménien* 1 (1994): 127–60. See also memorandum, September 17, 1915, F. L. Polk Papers, Box 22, Folder 0112, Yale University Library, Manuscripts and Archives.
21. Sarafian, "The Paper Trail," 127–60.
22. Rev. Barton was among the first people to be contacted by Toynbee (February 1, 1916) regarding the situation of Ottoman Armenians. See FO 96/205, 26–29.

23. See, for example, FO 96/205 26, 63, 85, 108, 141, 145, 176, 186, 204, 205, 226, 230. Toynbee and Barton also communicated through third parties such as Lord Bryce and Rev. Barton's aides in the United States. See, for example, Barton to Bryce, March 7, 1916, Houghton Library, ABC 2.1/292, page 339.
24. FO 96/205–206. These two volumes are comprised entirely of Toynbee's correspondence regarding the collection of materials on the destruction of Armenians.
25. See, for example, Toynbee to Barton, April 12, 1916, FO 96/205, 207–8.
26. Toynbee to Barton, February 15, 1916, FO 96/205, 63.
27. Toynbee succeeded in establishing relations with M. Leopold Favre, the Swiss compiler of these records. Favre provided Toynbee with invaluable information and documents that were subsequently included in *The Treatment of Armenians in the Ottoman Empire.* For the Toynbee-Favre correspondence, see Toynbee Papers, FO 96/77–79, 80–81, 114–15, 158–60, 164–65, 198–99, 202.
28. Rockwell to Toynbee, July 1, 1916, FO 96/206, 50–51.
29. Toynbee to Barton, March 8, 1916, FO 96/205, 108–10.
30. Barton to Toynbee, April 1, 1916, Toynbee Papers, FO 96/205, 226.
31. Editor's memorandum, *The Treatment of Armenians,* xli.
32. This insert, "Guide to the Reader," specifically pointed out the following record numbers: 2, 12, 15, 18, 22, 23, 24, 31, 40, 43, 47, 53, 59, 62, 64, 65, 66, 69, 72, 73, 78, 82, 87, 88, 89, 96, 102, 104, 108, 114, 117, 118, 121, 122, 123, 126, 130, 133, 137, 139, 141, 143, 144, 145.
33. See, for example, Statement by Miss H. E. Wallis, May 9, 1916, *The Treatment of Armenians,* doc. 129. This work also provided a number of important translations from Armenian, German, French, and Italian published sources.
34. See, for example, NA RG 59, Internal Affairs of Turkey 1910–1929, Washington, D.C.; The Papers of Henry Morgenthau Sr., Library of Congress, Washington, D.C. Both of these collections are microfilmed and readily available to scholars.
35. Toynbee made minor stylistic changes in the reproduction of these reports, which he discussed in the editor's introduction (xlii). In some cases, Toynbee also withheld some key passages to safeguard his sources. These passages were included in *Key to Names of Persons and Places Withheld.* There are very few cases where some paragraphs or sentences were omitted all together. These passages had no bearing on the subject matter of the Blue Book and their removal was of no consequence to the reports in question.
36. For an unabridged compilation of more reports, see Ara Sarafian, comp., *United States Official Documents on the Armenian Genocide,* 3 vols. (Watertown, Mass.: Armenian Review, 1993–96).
37. See, for example, *Papers Relating to the Foreign Relations of the United States, 1915, Supplement, The World War* (Washington, D.C.: GPO, 1928); NA RG 59, Internal Affairs of Turkey 1910–1929; Henry Morgenthau, The Papers of Henry Morgenthau, Sr.; Armen Hairapetian, " 'Race Problems' and the Armenian Genocide: The State Department Files," *Armenian Review* 37, no. 1 (Spring 1984): 41–145; Rouben Adalian, ed., *The Armenian Genocide in the U.S. Archives, 1915–1918* (Alexandria, Va.: Chadwick-Healey, 1991; microfiche

compilation); Sarafian, *United States Official Documents on the Armenian Genocide.* See also Richard G. Hovannisian, *The Armenian Holocaust: A Bibliography Relating to the Deportations, Massacres, and the Dispersion of the Armenian People, 1915–1923,* 2d ed. (Cambridge, Mass.: Armenian Heritage Press, 1980).

38. The Bryce and Toynbee publication, carefully documented and authenticated by archival evidence, can be contrasted with the Ottoman government's "White Book" published in 1916 to vilify Ottoman Armenians as a seditious minority. There is no indication of who compiled or printed this work; no account of the method by which these materials were collected, authenticated, and printed; and there are no archival collections today that provide substance to this Ottoman wartime publication. Ironically, this "White Book" has been recently republished as a primary source in Turkey.
39. Although Bryce and Toynbee did not rely on "native evidence" when constructing their thesis, as these witnesses could have been "excited" and prone to "exaggerate" points of detail, Lord Bryce underscored the point that "the most shocking and horrible accounts" were corroborated by the "most trustworthy neutral witnesses" and that the removal of "native evidence" would have only changed minor details (xxiv–xxv). The table identifies most of the key informants as American missionaries, such as Mary Graffam and Ernest Partridge at Sivas, William Dodd and Wilfred Post at Konia, Mary W. and Ernest Riggs at Kharpert, Francis Leslie at Urfa, and Edith Cold at Hadjin. A second critical group were American consular representatives in the Ottoman Empire, such as Leslie Davis at Kharpert, Oscar Heizer at Trebizond, Jesse Jackson at Aleppo, Edward Nathan at Mersina, and Greg Young at Damascus. These consular representatives also forwarded many of the missionary accounts to the United States via the State Department. The last category of key informants was nationals of neutral countries or those allied to the Ottoman Turks, such as Giacomo Gorrini, the Italian consul-general in Trebizond, Alma Johannsen, a Swedish missionary in Moush, or Schwester Mohring, a German missionary in Syria.
40. Citations indicate original decimal file numbers in NA RG 59, Internal Affairs of Turkey 1910–1929.

3

The Baghdad Railway and the Armenian Genocide, 1915–1916

A Case Study in German Resistance and Complicity

HILMAR KAISER

The role played by German officers and officials during the Armenian Genocide has not been studied adequately and remains open to varying assessments and interpretations. Imperial Germany was the senior ally of the Central Powers during World War I and could not avoid the implications of its association with a genocidal regime in the Ottoman Empire. An examination of the policies and strategies of German military and civil authorities reveals a considerable degree of internal disagreement on what could and should be done. The matter of the Armenian workers on the Baghdad Railway is a significant case in point.[1]

In 1913, a German military mission under Otto V. K. Liman von Sanders was sent to Constantinople to reform the Ottoman army and secure German influence over Ottoman military affairs. The officers of the mission were given leaves of absence from their regular positions and served as Ottoman officers at their new posts. Thus, they were responsible both to the Ottoman High Command and, through the intermediary link of the head of the German military mission, to the German Supreme Army Command (*Oberste Heeresleitung*). The importance of the German officers was further increased during World War I, when the Ottoman Empire entered the conflict with a surprise naval attack on the Russian Black Sea installations at the end of October 1914, prompting a Russian declaration of war on November 2.

When, in April 1915, the Young Turk government began to exterminate the Armenians within the Ottoman Empire, the presumed participation of German officers and consuls became an issue in the press of Entente countries (Great Britain, France, Russia). In response, the German Foreign Office (*Auswärtiges Amt*) denied any German involvement and maintained, moreover, that reports of persecutions and killings were inventions.[2] This denialist position was in direct contradiction to the information that the German diplomats had on hand. The German consuls reported continuously on the deportation and slaughter of Armenians. They urged their embassy in Constantinople to intervene. The German government, however, carefully avoided any interference and ordered that reports should be prepared so as to show that Armenians were guilty of treason and that measures taken by the Ottoman government were justified.[3] The German press was instructed to publish denials, eliciting a sharp protest by Walter Rössler, the German consul at Aleppo, who knew the contrary to be true.[4]

The Foreign Office's strategy was based on a position of strength. After the German defeat in 1918, this strategy was no longer feasible, and damage control was required in an attempt to whitewash the German role and place the blame entirely on its former ally. As earlier denials had undermined the credibility of the Foreign Office, it invited Johannes Lepsius to publish documentation on the German role during the genocide.[5] As a result Lepsius produced a collection of manipulated diplomatic documents: evidence implicating any Germans and most of the material on the Ottoman politicians was left out or deleted. The statement by Lepsius that he had had full access to the archives of the Foreign Office and that no document had been altered was false.[6] Although the book was a product in keeping with the designs of the Foreign Office, its international reception was not. Even Lepsius's sanitized publication included sufficient material for severe criticism of the German role in the Armenian Genocide.[7] The occupation and destruction of the Republic of Armenia by Turkish and Bolshevik troops at the end of 1920, however, removed the need for any further accommodating of international public opinion.

Since the 1960s research on the German role in the genocide has gained new impetus. Ulrich Trumpener discussed the politics of the German-Ottoman alliance during World War I and came to the conclusion that "the Porte's ruthless campaign against its Armenian subjects in 1915 and thereafter was intended primarily to decimate, and to disperse the remnants of, an 'unwanted' ethnic minority and only incidentally concerned with providing security against uprisings, espionage, sabotage, or any other interference with the Ottoman war effort."[8] On the role of the German officers, Trumpener commented that their freedom of action was circumscribed by Ottoman countermeasures, so that they had to depend on Ottoman goodwill. In sum, the German civil and military authorities had only a limited impact on the internal affairs of the empire.[9]

Recently, Trumpener's conclusions have been re-examined by Christoph Dinkel and Vahakn Dadrian. Dinkel has advanced the thesis that German officers were direct participants in the decision to deport the Ottoman Armenian population.[10] According to Dinkel, "German officers proposed the deportations and also played a large role in ensuring that they were carried out against other German opposition."[11] Thus, Dinkel makes a clear distinction between the actions of German military and civilian officials in the Ottoman Empire.

Dadrian has further elaborated on this issue. Introducing additional materials, he has concluded that German participation in the decision making process on the deportations implicated not only the German military authorities but also the civilian authorities. He writes: "The speedy completion of the Baghdad Railway project was of the highest strategic importance for that war effort, a compelling necessity for winning the war in the Turkish theater of operations. The German authorities, military and civilian, were fully aware of this. Yet, for reasons of their own, they joined the Turks in the decision to deport these craftsmen."[12] Discussing the views of the Foreign Office on this specific decision, Dadrian asserts that its reactions were concerned more about the "foolishness" of a German officer countersigning such a decision than about the actual cooperation of the German officer with his Turkish colleagues.[13]

In his most recent analysis of German responsibility in the Armenian Genocide, Dadrian modified his argument as follows: "The speedy completion of the Baghdad Railway project was of the highest strategic importance for that war effort, a compelling necessity for winning the war in the Turkish theater of operations. The German authorities, military and civilian, were fully aware of this. Yet, for reasons of his own, their representative joined the Turks in the decision to deport these [Armenian] craftsmen."[14]

Dadrian did not introduce any new evidence to substantiate the change in his argument. Regarding the actual deportation of the railway workers, however, Dadrian now maintains that Colmar von der Goltz Pasha, a German general in Ottoman service, played a significant part in this operation: "in an affidavit signed by three Armenians involved in the construction details of the Baghdad Railway, one of whom was a doctor and the other two were railroad master builders, Goltz, with reference to a particular instance, is depicted as the actual instigator of the deportation of 21,000 Armenians."[15]

This study considers these conclusions. It analyzes the policies of the Baghdad Railway Company vis-à-vis the Ottoman authorities, the German military, and the Foreign Office. Throughout the war Armenians worked on the staff of the railway company in various positions. Moreover, thousands of Armenians were employed on railway construction sites. Therefore, the directors of the railway company were radically affected when the Ottoman government initiated its anti-Armenian extermination program, and the administrators of the company undertook initiatives on behalf of their Armenian employees. These steps included top-level representations with the German and Ottoman governments in Berlin and Constantinople, interventions with Ottoman provincial governors, and initiatives with individual local Ottoman officials. Thus, the activities of the Baghdad Railway Company provide insights into the strategies of the administrations concerned at various levels. The reports of the railway company provide a particular perspective on the organization of the Armenian Genocide by the Ottoman government and the policies of German military and diplomatic authorities from a non-governmental point of view. The analysis combines entrepreneurial history and research on the genocide.

It should be kept in mind, however, that the Baghdad Railway did not cross the core regions of Armenian habitation in the Ottoman Empire or the principal killing fields in the area of the Ottoman Third Army and the Syrian desert. Thus, the evidence presented here offers only limited insight into the extent of the extermination and its execution, and is not a full analysis of the Armenian Genocide as such.

The Railway during the First Months of the War

Before World War I, building a railway through the Ottoman Empire to Baghdad was the most important German project abroad and had led to a large de facto German sphere of influence in the area. European railway employees who had worked for years in the Ottoman Empire and spoke its various languages gathered information on general conditions which was forwarded through their own communication network to the general directorate in Constantinople. That office was headed by the delegate of the Deutsche Bank, Franz J. Günther, who was in close contact with the German embassy. In cases of need, German diplomats transmitted Günther's reports by diplomatic pouch or by cipher telegram. In sum, the Deutsche Bank had excellent ways of obtaining information from a large area of the Ottoman Empire.

At the outbreak of World War I, direct rail connections between the Ottoman Empire and Germany were cut by Serbia. The situation was aggravated by the mobilization of the Ottoman army, creating a constant burden on the transport capacities of the railway. After the Ottoman entry into the war the situation became critical. The railway was the most important supply line for the Ottoman capital. After the attack of the Entente at the Dardanelles on February 19, 1915, the limited capacity of the single-track line proved to be an even more serious problem.[16]

The situation had been foreseen by German and Ottoman strategists. To avoid the problems anticipated, a German officer, Major Kübel, was installed in May 1914 as head of the railway department of the Ottoman general staff. His task was to ensure that the capacity for military transport would be sufficient within six months. Kübel concluded that in order to achieve this he would have to be entrusted with the management of the lines. In other words, the lines would come under Ottoman state control. Although the head of the German military mission supported Kübel's objective, the Deutsche Bank and the German embassy in Constantinople opposed it. The ambassador, Hans von Wangenheim, argued that the military mission was an instrument of Germany's Middle East policy and should not be thought of as its object. On the insistence of the diplomats and the bank, Kübel was removed after a bitter struggle in July 1914. This defeat was a slap in the face of the German officer corps and would not be forgotten.[17]

Cooperation between the railway company and Kübel's successor, Lieutenant Colonel Böttrich, turned out to be a complicated business. Böttrich, too, supported the financial interests of the Ottoman government against those of the railway company. This taking of sides was of the utmost concern to the company. If it had previously been worried about the costs of the ongoing construction works, the situation had worsened since the outbreak of the war. The supply of building materials that had to be imported had stopped. As construction costs rose so did the costs of operating the lines. The supply of coal became a crucial question and was only improved slightly by substituting firewood. Thus, the war created a sharp rise in expenditures for the company, coupled with an increase in traffic but without a higher income. Agreements with the Ottoman government stipulated that military transport was to enjoy a sizable discount so that the costs of operating the trains were barely covered. The situation became desperate when the government refused to pay for military transport altogether, while at the same time insisting on continued maximum services. This, however, was not the only surprise. Understanding that military necessity effectively meant free railway tickets, an increasing number of civil officials and other persons presented themselves at the station declaring that they were entitled to free transport. This form of abuse constituted only a minor concern compared with the performance of İsmail Hakkı Pasha, who was charged with the provisioning of Constantinople. The pasha started requisitioning railway cars for this purpose and saw no reason to pay for them. Moreover, he found that this service—for him free-of-charge—provided a lucrative profit through the sale of certificates for railway cars to anyone who would pay.[18]

In sum, all the calculations made by the railway company had become obsolete. Although hoping for a more positive future, for the time being the crucial question was how long the enterprise could stand the drain on its capital. There was no hope that the Ottoman government would honor its commitments, as it maintained that no money was available to pay the company. One possibility for improving the situation was to include financial securities for the company in further agreements regarding new railway sections and those under construction. Negotiations dragged on for some time, however, with no practical results.[19]

By the end of August 1915 the debts accumulated by the Ottoman government had reached 36 million German marks and equaled almost the entire capital of the company. Günther protested at the German embassy when he learned that Böttrich had backed the Ottoman policy, and he denounced the railway company for pursuing "selfish endeavors." He gave a detailed account of the Ottoman abuses and of Böttrich's performance. During a debate Böttrich attacked Günther, adding that the director of the Deutsche Bank, Arthur von Gwinner, had given him unreliable information. On another occasion, Böttrich recommended to Günther some offers by the Ottoman government, although he knew that they were considerably overpriced. Admitting this, he asked Günther to be understanding of his situation.[20] Concluding his protest, Günther hinted at the necessity of removing Böttrich from his post.[21] The conflict was most unfortunate for Günther, because he needed Böttrich's cooperation more than he imagined. The officer would subsequently play a key role in Günther's struggle for his Armenian employees. The company employed about 880 skilled Armenians and a large number of Armenian workers on the construction sites in the Taurus and Amanus mountains, as well as in northern Syria. When the war broke out, these Armenian employees and workers had been left at their jobs to allow for progress of the railway construction.

Railway Deportation and Concentration Camps

In spring 1915, the ruling Committee of Union and Progress (CUP) initiated the annihilation of the Armenians within the empire. The first community to be deported was the Armenian town of Zeitun.[22] While the male population

The Baghdad Railway 1915–1916

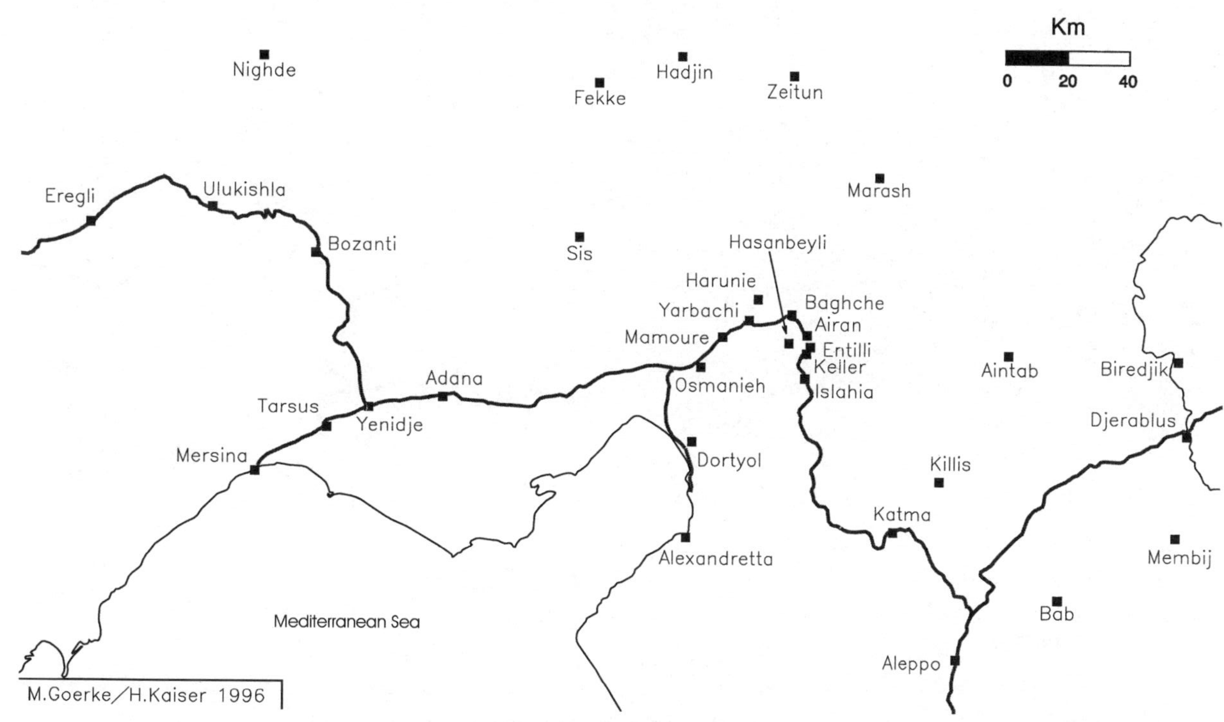

The Baghdad Railway 1915–1916

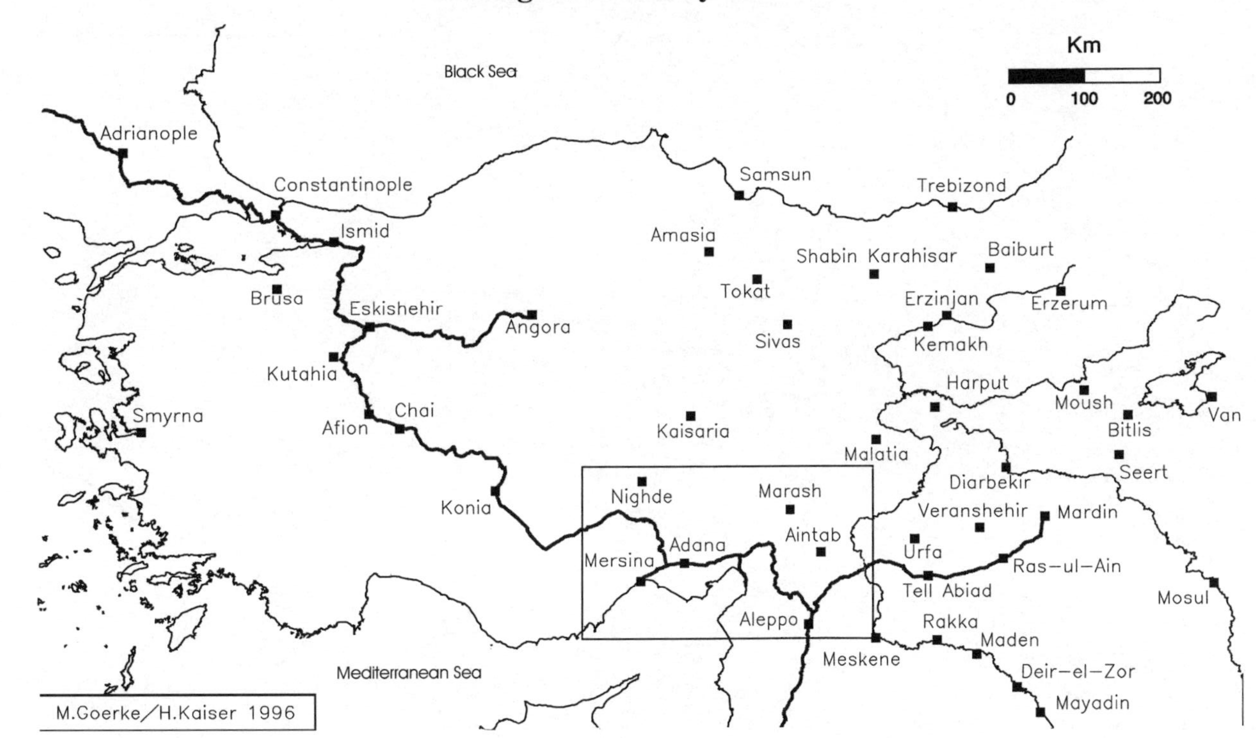

of Zeitun was sent to the Syrian desert, women and children were first deported by and along the railway to the province of Konia, to be sent to the desert later.[23] Thus, the Ottoman government introduced into modern history railway transport of civilian populations toward extermination.

Franz Günther reported that the government was acting with "bestial cruelty." Although freight cars had a standard capacity for the military transport of 36 men or 6 horses, 88 Armenians on average were pressed into sheep cars for deportation. These carriages were two tiered and partly open. Children who were born during the journey were taken from their mothers and thrown out of the carriage. Günther commented that he simply could not justify the lack of action, given that it all happened under the company's eyes.[24] Shortly afterward, Günther sent to Deutsche Bank director Gwinner a photograph of a deportation train, adding that the picture showed the Anatolian Railway as "an upholder of civilization in Turkey."[25] The transportation was performed under the close supervision of the government. Talaat Bey, the minister of the interior, constantly received reports on the numbers of the deportees and their current location. On October 9 and 10, 1915, the authorities at Konia reported that 11,000 Armenians who had been concentrated there had been sent south. Between October 13 and 16, 9,600 Armenians followed. During the following three days, 5,000 Armenians were sent from Konia, and 4,854, during the next two days. When deportation by rail was interrupted because of military needs, the people were marched off along the railway track. On October 23, however, 1,050 Armenians were again packed into fourteen cars from Konia.[26]

Almost all the railway stations became detention camps where thousands died. Beside the railway station in Konia, a large concentration camp had been established.[27] It was one of a series which extended along the railway to the Syrian desert. Deported Armenians remained in these camps until they were sent on to the next stop along this eastward path.[28] The camps were huge: Katma numbered 40,000 persons at the end of October. In November 1915, the Baghdad Railway Company was ordered to transport 50,000 Armenians from Katma to Ras-ul-Ain. The camp near Osmanieh held between 20,000 and 70,000. Thousands died from exhaustion and epidemic diseases. Exhaustion was a consequence of the forced marches and the merciless behavior of the Ottoman authorities. South of Konia at Eregli, Ottoman authorities sometimes withheld water while taxing the entry into the town.[29] Moreover, camps were at times "attacked" and the people butchered.[30]

The camps on the edge of the desert, where the survivors of the caravans from the eastern provinces met the deportees from the railway, became the site of systematic extermination. Two engineers reported how in one day alone 300–400 women arrived completely naked at Ras-ul-Ain. Again on its arrival there, a caravan was plundered by the local Chechens and the gendarmerie.[31] Slaughter and death marching were the principal methods of killing, and those who were not sent south to Deir-el- Zor were starved to death at Ras-ul-Ain or killed in that vicinity.[32] Often living people were buried alive.[33] Hasenfratz, a railway employee at Aleppo, reported slaughters that took place beside the railway track between Tell Abiad and Ras-ul-Ain: "All the bodies, without exception, were entirely naked and the wounds that had been inflicted showed that the victims had been killed, after having been subjected to unspeakable brutalities. A local inhabitant stated that this was nothing in comparison with what one could see a little further down the line."[34] Engineer Spieker reported from Ras-ul-Ain on the arrival of the remnants of the Armenian deportation caravans. All the boys and men over twelve years had been killed. He also gave detailed reports on the systematic mass slaughter and marching to death of women and children. A Turkish inspector told him that this time nine out of ten Armenians had been killed. The fate of those who were still alive was appalling. The engineer described how Muslim railway employees as well as Ottoman officers and soldiers took advantage of the situation. The rape of women by individual or groups of men was frequent, and a slave trade with children and women had developed. The overseer of the camp of Ras-ul-Ain, Sergeant Nouri, boasted of his raping of Armenian children. Killing Armenians had become a profitable business, and a number of Muslim employees left their jobs in order to participate in the slaughter.[35] Near Ulukishla in the Taurus Mountains, railway workers stated that there was nothing wrong in robbing and killing deportees, as the local *kaimakam* had ordered them to massacre the Armenians.[36]

Denial and Evidence

During the summer of 1915, the German Foreign Office made greater efforts to deny the extermination than to intervene with its Ottoman ally to stop the carnage. Talaat nonetheless felt it necessary to reassure Berlin. On September 2, 1915, he communicated to the German embassy the translations of three deciphered telegrams he had sent to various provinces. The telegrams were intended to show that the Ottoman government was protecting the Armenians and supplying them with necessary provisions. The embassy, however, was skeptical about Talaat's honesty.[37] Only one week later it received a report from the German consul in Adana, Dr. Eugen

Büge, who labeled Talaat's telegrams as a "brazen deceit," since an envoy of the Ministry of the Interior had been sent to Adana to countermand the measures stipulated in the telegrams. The local authorities followed the second order. Moreover, the local CUP leader had announced that there would be a massacre if the Armenians were not deported.[38] Büge's report was forwarded to Berlin but mitigated by the comments of Acting Ambassador Ernst zu Hohenlohe-Langenburg, who maintained that the local authorities acted under the influence of irresponsible CUP leaders, ignoring the government's orders. These CUP members were the authors of the outrages against the Armenians and other Christians. Thus, for the time being the German embassy had no proof of intentional deception by the Ottoman government. For such a conclusion to be reached, it would be necessary for Hohenlohe to disregard the fact that the Ottoman government was run by the leaders of the CUP.[39] Büge did not accept his superior's reasoning and collected material to prove that his own assessment was correct.[40]

The Ottoman authorities soon became aware that the railway staff, too, were collecting incriminating evidence. This material contradicted the Ottoman and German propaganda efforts to downplay events and to put the blame on the victims. Djemal Pasha, commander of the Fourth Ottoman Army, issued an order treating the taking of photographs of Armenians as espionage and requiring the railway staff to hand over all photographs and negatives.[41] Nevertheless, photographing continued. Soon it became an established procedure to disobey the Ottoman orders and to act clandestinely in conscious violation of the martial law. Günther, for example, collected intelligence on the extermination of the Armenians and forwarded the material to the Deutsche Bank in Berlin. There, Arthur von Gwinner made the material available to the Foreign Office. Gwinner and Günther were both aware of the risks involved and took precautions against discovery. Thus, Günther wrote special reports that were not registered in the company's files and were sent separately from the official reports. Moreover, no carbon copies of these were kept. Gwinner, for his part, kept the reports in a private file that was deposited in a safe. In addition, Günther and Gwinner avoided direct references wherever possible, and thus some of the reports were kept anonymous in order to protect informants. The material collected stood in complete opposition to official German propaganda.[42]

In August 1915, Günther gave his assessment of events. He recounted the official Ottoman charge that Armenians had massacred Turks in the east but qualified the statement by stressing that he had obtained this information from third parties. After having assured his superior that he was not a pro-Armenian partisan, Günther cautioned Gwinner that his information on the persecutions of the Armenians minimized their true extent, as the government was more guarded in its actions near the railways. The director was sure that the government's policy would result in the complete annihilation of the Armenians. Indeed, he estimated that already 25 percent of the 2 million Armenians in the empire had been killed, and he suspected that the eastern provinces had already been cleared of Armenians.[43]

Between Humanitarian Aid and Resistance

In August 1915, while reassuring the bank director that he was leaving out the worst intelligence he possessed, Günther proposed a secret project. The Ottoman government had demanded reduced transport tariffs, but the company had refused, because only the government would benefit. Besides, a precedent for other reductions would be established. After explaining that the company was paid for the transportation of Armenians, Günther pointed to the opportunity of helping the deportees. Reports from personnel along the lines showed that any support for starving Armenians was prevented by the Ottoman authorities. It had nonetheless been possible to distribute clandestinely some funds from the railway's resources, but the sums were insufficient. Adding a price list of basic foodstuffs to his report, Günther suggested secretly distributing £1,000 (Turkish). Gwinner consented immediately. As a result, Günther overspent the relief budget, although he gained Gwinner's consent for this later.[44]

Soon, the protected status of the company's Armenian workers began to become insecure. Local authorities and CUP circles tried to include the workforce in the deportation scheme. As direct encroachments on the construction sites had to be avoided, other solutions had been found. Although the workers enjoyed some protection, their families did not. For example, the authorities in Killis, a town from which many workers of the Amanus construction sites came, started to deport the families of workers, thereby inducing the men to leave their jobs to be with their loved ones. In Osmanieh, the military authorities threatened to confiscate the property of the Armenian railway workers and to mistreat their families.[45]

Winkler, the engineer responsible for the railway construction in the province of Adana, tried to protect his workers. As the local authorities seemed to act on their own initiative, he appealed to the *vali* (governor) of Adana. The *vali* told Winkler that nothing could be done, as direct orders had come from Talaat and Minister of War Enver Pasha to deport all Armenians in the province to Aleppo and further east. The first to be deported were the

Armenians of Zeitun, Hadjin, Hasanbeyli, Entilli, and Baghche, while their houses and fields were to be handed over to Muslim immigrants. As most of the workers came from these towns, they too had to be deported. Thus, the pledge to leave the Armenian workers on the construction sites was revoked. The *vali* told Winkler that unskilled Muslim immigrants would replace the deportees. Clearly, the company's operations had become a target of CUP chauvinism.[46]

The result of this interference was a temporary interruption of the works, while an ensuing shortage of firewood for the locomotives restricted the transport of military supplies. Winkler, who saw deportation caravans passing the constructions sites, was deeply moved by the fate of the Armenians. He had no idea how the Armenians could survive at their destination. His Armenian workers were in danger, and any chance of stopping deportations locally was unlikely. Moreover, Consul Büge had informed Winkler that the German embassy would not intervene with Enver Pasha on behalf of Armenians. In sum, many engineers felt like abandoning their jobs in protest against the deportations. This, however, would have endangered the company's negotiations with the Ottoman government on the extension of the line. Moreover, an interruption might serve as a pretext for the government to seize the line. Günther instructed Winkler to continue work under all circumstances until instructions had been received from Berlin.[47]

The Struggle for the Armenian Employees and Workers

The deportation of the workers was the start of an attempted expulsion of all Armenians in the employ of the railway. The next group targeted was the company's Armenian staff. Two central demands were put forward by the Ottoman government. First, that the company's correspondence and bookkeeping was henceforth to be in Turkish, thereby removing the major obstacle to the employment of Muslims. Second, that the Armenian staff was to be dismissed and replaced by Muslims.[48] Günther was aware that his adversaries were determined to succeed. In regard to the language question, the company's position was not hopeless. Legally, the company was obliged to use Turkish only in correspondence with the Ottoman authorities. But insisting on its rights did not seem to be advisable, and the company tried to adopt an accommodating line. Günther played for time, pointing to technical problems while stressing his support for the Ottoman government. It was essential to avoid making immediate definite concessions.

Soon, however, playing for time was no longer an option. The Ottoman authorities started to separate the Armenian employees from their families in order to deport the two groups separately. In Angora, the *vali* had arrested nineteen employees. The company demanded that the authorities respect the agreement with the government. As the correspondence brought no results, the company sent an envoy to Angora, but the *vali* told that him that he had come too late: "C'est impossible de les restituer. Comprenez-vous: impossible!—Ils ne reviendrons jamais plus." (It is impossible to restore them. Do you understand, impossible!—They can never return again.")[49]

Thus, it was no longer possible to follow a strategy of stalling. Günther went to Enver and Talaat to defend his other employees. In the language question, a compromise was reached during a discussion with Talaat, who consented that French could be used as a second language for a time. As for his employees, Günther refused to make any concessions. He informed Talaat that in case of deportations, it would be impossible to operate the railway efficiently and the transports would grind to a swift halt. This threat was formidable. The Ottoman armies on the Gallipoli peninsula had enough food reserves for only one or two days. They could not hold out for long without supplies from the hinterland. Thus, Günther was warning that an encroachment on his staff would inevitably lead to the defeat of the Ottoman Empire. A heated discussion ensued, but Talaat had to give up the plan of an immediate full scale deportation. On August 17, 1915, Talaat instructed the authorities at Eskishehir to postpone the deportation of the Armenian railway employees and workers. In a broader order addressed to various provinces and districts on August 29, he temporarily put off the deportation until replacements for the Armenians could be found.[50] This was an initial success for Günther. He had not only saved the permanent staff but managed to include the workers on the construction sites as well.

The postponement of deportations brought only a short respite, and soon the government demanded the removal of 190 porters and unskilled workers and their replacement by Muslims. Instead of deporting all the Armenian employees in the company or a total deportation from a certain location, the government planned the deportation of certain categories of workers. Once more, Günther reiterated his warnings about the effect on the transports and disclaimed any responsibility for the consequences. Again, he was successful; the deportation was postponed. On September 25, 1915, Talaat informed the authorities of various provinces and districts that the deportation of Armenians working for the railway had been put off until a decision had been reached by a special commission on railway issues. The local authorities and CUP circles nonetheless continued to deport the families of workers, thus coercing the men to join their families. It seemed that this was done in a systematic manner. Winkler suspected that Talaat's order had been secretly revoked by a second counter order. The Ottoman army command believed the workers in the Amanus were members of secret Armenian organizations and had ordered precautionary measures. Moreover, the *vali* of Adana informed Winkler that the government's exemption was valid for only four weeks. In short, all the concessions that had been gained resulted only in a temporary respite.[51]

Günther then abandoned his policy of not openly seeking German diplomatic assistance and began to involve the embassy and leading German officers. Having informed Ambassador Hohenlohe that Lieutenant Colonel Böttrich had become a serious problem for his company, Günther bypassed his adversary and directly contacted General Otto von Lossow, the German military attaché, and General Fritz Bronsart von Schellendorf, chief of the Ottoman general staff. Both officers were in touch with Enver. Günther now learned that the decision about his Armenian employees as well as the language question had been delegated to a commission. Thus, the earlier agreement with Talaat Bey was at this point officially a dead letter. Moreover, the German officers had not vetoed the deportation of the employees. The decision was in the hands of a committee whose authority had been acknowledged by German officers. In addition, the commission was staffed with known CUP extremists. Summarizing the situation in a secret report to Deutsche Bank director Gwinner, Günther stated: "In the language question and in the question of the replacement of the employees by Muslims, we are on our own."[52]

When the special commission on railway matters convened, the CUP members proved to be particular active and zealous. It became apparent that the committee was a body to issue fiats and not to investigate the claims of the railway company. It was made clear to Günther that his invitation to meetings was only a matter of politeness. When he attended one of the sessions on October 8, 1915, he was confronted with a decision on the language question. By January 1, 1917, at the latest, all internal company correspondence had to be in Turkish. French would be allowed as a second language until July 1, 1919. Correspondence with the authorities had to be exclusively in Turkish. A positive aspect of the meeting was that the matter of the employees had not been brought up. Günther, however, feared that the plan to deport his employees was imminent; a decision could be announced at any time. Thus, Günther tried once again to secure the support of ranking German officers. Bronsart gave such assurances, and Böttrich, who was a member of the commission, promised to approach Enver to confirm that no employees would be deported during the war. To bolster Günther's moves in Constantinople, Gwinner sought the assistance of the German Foreign Office in Berlin.[53]

The Decision on Deportation and the Company's Reaction

Despite the efforts of officials of the Baghdad Railway Company, the special commission decided that the Armenian employees should be deported. Colonel Böttrich had not only failed to secure Enver's support but had even signed the decision in his capacity as chief of the Ottoman general staff's railway department. The document, dated October 17, 1915, stated that the deportation of the railway employees was an integral part of the general deportation policy of the Ottoman government.[54] No further reason for the order was given. All the Armenian employees, with no exemption for those living in Constantinople, were to be deported. The staff was divided into two categories. The first category was to be deported during a period ranging from one to twelve months, while the second had to leave after one year, up to four years. The vacant places were to be filled by Muslims or men of other nationalities considered trustworthy. In cases where no Muslim replacement was available, the Armenian employee might stay longer. The replacement had to follow the prescribed procedure exactly and was to be supervised by the Ottoman authorities. No reference was made to the workers on the construction sites. In sum, the decision restated the familiar strategy of the Ottoman government. A preliminary measure to prepare for the deportation was to prevent the absence of the Armenian employees. Thus, the Ottoman railway military commissar issued a ban on all holidays and sick leaves for railway employees.[55]

Günther did not give up. Because protests to the Ottoman government had become useless, he contacted the German embassy and General Bronsart von Schellendorf. Explaining once more the dangers of the execution of the deportation order, Günther asked Bronsart to suggest to Enver a postponement until the demobilization of the Ottoman army after the war. Moreover, Günther proposed including a clause that the execution of the deportation have to be sanctioned by the railway company. Bronsart did not reject Günther's scheme but hesitated to become officially involved in the affair. Claiming to be incompetent regarding railway matters, he told Günther that Colonel Böttrich considered the deportation as technically possible. Bronsart stated that he would make his decision based on consultations with the embassy and the military attaché (Lossow) since any decision in this matter involved a high risk of failure, which would force him to resign as Ottoman chief of the general staff.[56] His caution was probably motivated by a desire not to antagonize Enver, with whom Böttrich was cooperating. Enver's goodwill was of vital importance for Bronsart, as without the support of the Ottoman minister of war he would already have been removed.[57]

Thus, Günther did not receive the assistance he sought, but he had obtained valuable information. He knew that Böttrich had deceived him about his personal attitudes and role in the affair. Böttrich was not merely working in a difficult post and trying to get along with CUP circles but was a driving force behind the project. Bronsart's reference to Böttrich as an expert on the running of the railway was a critical revelation. Therefore, Günther came to understand that his own opinions on the consequences of deportation were not undisputed in German circles. Accordingly, success with his adversaries solely on the basis of technical arguments had become unlikely. Thus, Günther modified his strategy. Keeping his principal technical argument, he concentrated his attacks on Böttrich. The railway manager presented Böttrich not only as a problem for the railway and the war effort, but as a threat to German political interests in general.

> Not only, that Mr. Böttrich has made no protest to the [Ottoman] War Office against the decisions of the Commission but also stooped to transmit these decisions with his signature affixed to them.
>
> Our enemies will someday pay a good price to obtain possession of this document, because by means of the signature of one of the members of the Military Mission, they will prove that the Germans have not only done nothing to prevent the Armenian persecutions, but certain orders to this effect have emanated from them, that is, have been signed by them.
>
> The fact that this document, of which much will be said in the future, bears a German and not a Turkish signature, is precious to the Turks too, as the Military Commissioner has caustically smiling pointed out.[58]

Günter's arguments impressed Gottlieb von Jagow, the state secretary for foreign affairs. Having read a telegram addressed by Günther to Gwinner, Jagow remarked that it seemed to him that it was high time to protest very emphatically against the madness of the Armenian persecutions.[59] At the embassy, Günther's earlier complaints against Böttrich had had some effect, too. Arthur Zimmermann, the state undersecretary for foreign affairs, had contacted Ambassador von Wangenheim to inquire about his view on Böttrich. Wangenheim answered in full support of Günther. He explained that he had done everything he could to bridge the differences between the railway company and Böttrich. Unfortunately, the officer displayed a complete lack of understanding of the economic and political importance of the railway. Moreover, the breakdown of railway transport predicted by Günther might very well occur if Böttrich was to remain at his post.[60] Böttrich's signing the deportation decision had disqualified him in the ambassador's eyes. Using General von Lossow's services, the ambassador explored Bronsart's views on removing Böttrich. Bronsart admitted that Böttrich had his shortcomings but thought that his dismissal would be impossible, as no replacement would be available for the duration of the war. Thus, Bronsart avoided opposing Böttrich's critics while supporting the officer on technical grounds.[61]

Because the Ottoman government continued to insist on the deportation and a leading officer of the military mission had identified himself with the order, tacitly supported by Bronsart, an appeal to the Supreme Army Command became necessary. The embassy turned to the Foreign Office in Berlin to secure its intervention. Von Jagow had difficulty in believing that Böttrich had signed the decision. Having been assured that this was so, the foreign minister instructed his representative at the German military headquarters, Carl Georg von Treutler, to attempt to remove Böttrich.[62] The official occasion for the initiative was provided by military attaché von Lossow, who sent a telegram to General Erich von Falkenhayn, chief of the Supreme Army Command, explaining the situation. Lossow stressed the importance of the Armenian personnel and the danger of the interruption to transport. Moreover, he drafted a telegram that Falkenhayn might send to Enver hinting at the delivery of new railway stock and an increase of traffic to Syria. Thus, a change in the general situation would necessitate a postponement of the deportations. The Foreign Office ordered the embassy to take immediate steps at the Sublime Porte, and Jagow recommended Lossow's suggestion strongly to the Supreme Army Command, arguing that the supply of the armies in Arabia, and thus the planned attack on the Suez Canal, was in jeopardy.[63]

General von Falkenhayn dispatched the telegram after strengthening the reference about the Armenian employees. Although the Foreign Office managed to get Falkenhayn to overrule Böttrich's policy, the diplomats failed to get the officer removed. Like Bronsart, Falkenhayn refused to replace Böttrich on grounds of military necessity. In a letter to von Treutler, he cautioned that information obtained from Günther was to be regarded as biased. Problems between the railway company and Böttrich were of a monetary nature, and the Ottoman government had no money. Böttrich was only doing his job and this might easily bring him into conflict with the railway company. Any other officer would end up in the same situation. Falkenhayn referred to the question of the railway employees only briefly at the end of letter, stating that he had done everything he could. Thus,

Falkenhayn avoided commenting on Böttrich's role and implied that the German military's part in the affair had been settled.[64]

On November 22, 1915, shortly before the date of the first deportation, Bronsart informed the embassy that the deportation had been postponed, presumably for the duration of the war. Böttrich, however, seemed to make the deportation of the Armenian employees his personal objective. On December 2, the matter was discussed in a meeting in which Günther and Böttrich took part. Without giving any further explanation, Böttrich insisted on the deportation of the Armenians. He declared that he had explained to Enver that the deportation was technically possible. To abrogate this decision would undermine his authority with Enver. Any interference of the Foreign Office in this military matter was out of place and unimportant, as he was acting in accordance with the German and Turkish general staffs. All opposition against him would be in vain, because he enjoyed General von Falkenhayn's full trust. Günther concluded that the deportation had become a question of Böttrich's vanity.[65]

Böttrich's behavior stood out in blatant contrast with the strategy of the Foreign Office. After the defeat of Serbia in October 1915, and the establishment of a direct land route to the Ottoman Empire, the German government was able to support its ally with equipment and troops.[66] The Foreign Office presumably counted on increased influence and modified its Armenian policy. In harmony with Jagow's view on the persecutions, the new ambassador, Paul von Wolff-Metternich, remonstrated with Ottoman politicians. Officially, however, the German government continued to deny the extermination of Armenians. On December 6, Metternich reported to Berlin that Böttrich was aggravating the already delicate German position in the Armenian Question.[67] On receipt of reports by Günther and Metternich, Jagow contacted Falkenhayn again, this time personally. Reminding Falkenhayn of his initiative to keep the Armenian employees, Jagow added that his move had failed because of Böttrich's resistance. Moreover, Böttrich was thwarting all efforts to mitigate the deportation order. He was also supporting the Turkish side in other cases of diverging interests and was thus damaging the German position. In Turkey, Jagow added, the opinion was widespread that Germany had precipitated the persecution of the Armenians: "For the proof of the correctness of this view, the Turks would be able to refer with a semblance of justification to the conduct of Mr. Böttrich."[68] Jagow, however, failed once more to undermine Böttrich's position.

In the following months the Foreign Office and the military clashed continuously on Böttrich's policies. Falkenhayn went so far as to blame the German ambassador of being partial and strengthened Böttrich's position by declaring that the latter was acting as a Turkish officer who had to look after Turkish interests. As he had not damaged German interests, there was no call to take steps against him. When new disputes evolved, Böttrich continued to back the Ottoman state against the railway company. The Foreign Office kept warning General von Falkenhayn of the possible consequences. Eventually, Wilhelm Gröner, the chief of the German military railway administration, sent an officer to Constantinople to investigate. The only result was that Böttrich was reminded not to forget German interests.[69] Two months later Gwinner warned Günther of new trouble ahead. Gwinner had spoken to Gröner about railway issues and learned that Böttrich had left a bad impression on Günther and Eduard Huguenin, the second director in Constantinople. Nonetheless, Gröner and Falkenhayn were indignant about the complaints made by the embassy which were not taken seriously. Gröner stressed that he had no other officer available for Böttrich's position and that no one else was willing to take the post. Gwinner added that it seemed Bronsart had also taken Böttrich's side. This was important because new agreements were soon to be signed. Böttrich insisted that the new contract be formulated in Ottoman Turkish, even though the language lacked the necessary precision and technical vocabulary.[70]

Notwithstanding the bitter struggle between the railway company and Foreign Office on the one side and the military on the other, the Armenian employees benefited from the unrelenting efforts of Günther and his allies in the embassy. The deportation order was not executed. Almost all the Armenian employees and their families survived under the protection of the railway company.[71]

The Construction Works in the Amanus Mountains

The reprieve was due in part to an effort to speed up railway construction. Thus, at the end of 1915 the Ottoman government was even willing to supply work battalions for the railway company. This cooperation was necessary because the Ottoman government refused to return any of the previously deported workers.[72] The railway company's need for workers quickly became known all over northern Syria. The engineers had even started to recruit deportees, although this was strictly prohibited. As it was illegal to employ Armenians, exposure would have meant their immediate deportation. Therefore, many Armenians were registered under false names and nationalities, and they filled numerous positions: as doctors in railway hospitals, bookkeepers, engineers, and so forth.[73] In short, the construction works depended in large measure on the Armenians. Sometimes, the German engineers hired a person, knowing that he was not trained for the job. In these cases, the motive was to save the applicant from death. A number of Armenian intellectuals and clergymen who were prime targets of the CUP were thus saved by the railway. While working together the railway engineers and Armenian staff often developed friendships. Their mutual understanding had to be hidden from Ottoman gendarmes and spies.[74]

The Armenian workers received regular rations and the company managed to take care of their other needs as well. The construction camps, however, were situated in an area contaminated by malaria; hygienic conditions were terrible.[75] Despite this, an Armenian community life began to emerge. The engineers had employed whole families, and, as a result, men, women, and even children were to be seen working along the line. In addition, the engineers organized an orphanage for the children from the deportation caravans with the help of German missionary sisters. The company hospital at Entilli became a refuge for Armenian women. Köppel, the engineer in charge at Entilli, hid about 200 Armenian girls pretending that the women were needed for breaking stones.[76] Armenians who had reached the camps and recovered soon developed their own initiatives to help others, and staff members advised new arrivals where to find a job. Armenian workers also married women from the passing caravans in order to save their lives. An Armenian assistant in the hospital at Yarbashi supplied medicine to the fugitives and the few who tried to offer armed resistance. In the same hospital another worker took revenge by killing Muslim in-patients who had raped and murdered Armenian deportees.[77]

These developments did not escape the attention of the government. In January 1916, Talaat had been informed that between 15,000 and 20,000 Armenians were in the Amanus Mountains. Many had come from Aleppo. Talaat demanded that this be rectified. He ordered an investigation to determine from where and with whose permission they had arrived, and he asked for a count of the Armenians working along the railway. In February, he received new numbers. About 7,000 Armenians instead of the official 3,130 were working on the construction in the Amanus. Thus, Talaat had proof that Armenians were hired illegally, and he demanded that the illegals be deported to their prescribed destinations.[78] Gendarmes came to take away individuals, but deportation on a larger scale was attempted only occasionally and usually resulted in the engineers intervening. Once again, Talaat ordered a further count. The usual procedure was to ask the railway company to submit lists of their employees.[79] Also, several government commissions worked along the lines registering Armenian workers under the pretext of issuing identity cards to them. These cards were supposed to secure the stay of the workers at their jobs. Nevertheless, the commissions never had enough blank forms to provide for more than a small number. This was not an accident. The real purpose of these commissions was to prepare the deportation of the workers according to secret lists. The Armenians had been subdivided into four categories: intellectuals and young people, strong young men, workers of medium age, and all the rest. Winkler suspected that the people in first three categories were regarded as especially dangerous. On the categorization of women and children, however, he had no information.[80] Engineer Winkler's cautious formulations were not because of a lack of information but rather because he had reasons not to disclose his sources. Armenian officials had opened a safe in which lists had been stored overnight by police officials. The lists contained the name, the father's name, and the marital status of each worker. It was further noted whether the worker was a fugitive from deportation or in what other way the employee had arrived at the construction site. Moreover, various marks had been added to the names. Two zeros indicated that the person was considered dangerous or suspicious. The Armenian staff discovered that the Ottoman officers had telegraphed to the places of birth of these persons in order to find out more about them. Besides this, certain signs earmarked the workers for special deportation destinations.[81] The preparations of the commissions alarmed the engineers. They informed a German school teacher, Martin Niepage, who was on his way to Germany, that the Armenian workers were soon to be deported. Niepage appealed to the Foreign Office to rescue the Armenians in the Amanus. As it turned out, his initiative came too late.[82]

The Deportation of the Armenian Workers

At the beginning of June 1916, the gendarmerie in the construction region was reinforced. Officially, the gendarmes were to hunt Armenian partisans, but it became clear that they had encircled the camps to make flight impossible. On June 13 the deportations began. Armenians were called on and immediately marched off in large groups without being allowed to make any preparations. Complete chaos ensued. Families were separated; children ran around crying. The authorities acted with the utmost of cruelty. A woman suffered an abortion in the streets, but the gendarmes still tried to push her on. The engineers sent urgent appeals to Günther in Constantinople to immediately inform the German embassy and the Deutsche Bank. The remonstrances against the deportation were ineffective, however, for the moment, all the engineers could do was to hide and save a few individuals, but mostly it was only possible to provide the deportees with some food and money.[83]

The operation was supervised by Colonel Avni Bey, the gendarmerie commander of Adana. By June 19, the railway traffic and construction works had stopped on the orders of Winkler. In the hospitals, patients were left without care as the staff were also deported. The spread of epidemics was feared, and cholera in fact did break out.[84] In a survey of the effects of the deportations, Winkler did not give the exact number of Armenians affected, as the operation was still continuing. He estimated on June 17, however, that only 2,900 out of 8,300 workers were left. Many Turkish workers had also fled, fearing the gendarmes. Armenians who had received government identity cards were not exempted. Winkler concluded that according to authoritative information deportations of Armenians working in the Taurus Mountains were also imminent.[85]

The breakdown of transportation threatened the war efforts of the Central Powers on the Arabian fronts. General von Falkenhayn demanded von Lossow's intervention with Enver Pasha. By then, the Turkish minister of war and other authorities understood well the catastrophic effects of the deportations. Böttrich drafted for Enver a telegraphic counter order to the *vali* of Adana. It became clear almost immediately, however, that the telegram would have little effect, because the original text had been modified.[86] Only as many Armenians as absolutely necessary were to be allowed to return.[87] This was crucial, as 1,600 British and Indian prisoners of war arrived in the Amanus in terrible condition on June 25. They were the survivors of a death march from Kut-el-Amara.[88] At Islahia a captured British officer watched the deportation of the Armenian workers. The accompanying guards told him that the Armenians would be sent off to their death and that the prisoners of war would replace them at the construction works.[89] Therefore, the defeat of the British army at Kut-el-Amara decided the fate of the Armenians in the Amanus, for the Ottoman government was able to rid itself of these workers. The interruption of the construction works was therefore more likely the result of bad planning than a lack of consideration for strategic concerns.[90]

At about the same time, Winkler received a request from Böttrich to furnish information on four points: first, on the possibility of continuing work with the present labor force; second, if it was correct that Winkler had demanded the return of the Armenian workers or else the construction would cease; third, if it was correct that the engineers were being prevented from entering the railway tunnels; and, fourth, what the exact number of Armenians had been before the deportation. Böttrich implied that his information was that there had been approximately 15,000. At this point, Böttrich again took sides with the Ottoman government and exerted pressure on the railway company. Although having at first been ordered to stop the deportations, now Böttrich tried to make sure that all Armenians would be expelled. Moreover, he used this opportunity to find out if the company had surreptitiously resisted Ottoman orders, thereby identifying himself even further with the anti-Armenian program of his Turkish superiors. Winkler confirmed Böttrich's information that the engineers were denied access to the tunnels but denied all the other points of the inquiry. In regard to the number of Armenian workers, he accused Böttrich of suspecting him of being a liar and demanded to know the source of his information. Winkler maintained that he did not expect or wish the return of the Armenian workers as they were useless by now. The engineer concluded by stating that he was staying at his post only out of patriotism.[91]

The number of the deportees was a crucial issue as the government had accused the company of sheltering 15,000 Armenians. Other estimates varied between 11,000 and 21,000. Winkler had indeed hired and kept many more Armenians than he was allowed. To defend himself, he ridiculed Ottoman statistical methods, although he himself had participated in the counts. Winkler admitted that about 1,000 Armenians more than the officially stated number had been in the camps, but these had arrived sometime after his initial count.[92]

The apprehension about the modification of Enver's original order to deport all Armenian workers in the Amanus was well justified. By June 29, no Armenian had returned and the few who remained were also being deported.[93] Shortly afterward, a special envoy of the Ottoman general staff, Lieutenant Colonel Refik Bey, arrived in the Amanus to investigate the situation.[94] One tunnel was blocked by fallen rocks, and no personnel was available to repair the damage. Refik promised to bring in specialists from other places.[95] Discussing the issue of Enver's order, Refik denied that any directives for the return of the Armenians had ever been given. Winkler concluded from the contradictions that two orders must have been issued. One had been intended only for presentation to the railway administration, whereas the second was sent to the Ottoman authorities in Adana. Refik informed him that the Council of Ministers had decided on the deportation long ago. The *vali* had received the strictest orders to that effect, and Refik added that the deportation was irrevocable. The return of a single Armenian would be unthinkable. When the order had been given to supply sufficient workers for the construction sites in the Amanus, Armenians had not been included. Thus, Refik confirmed Winkler's suspicions.[96] Although he knew better, Winkler told Refik that several hundred Armenians had returned and wanted to know what the latter would do. Refik answered that he would allow

Winkler to keep the specialists. When Winkler told Refik that he would be acting contrary to the decision of the Council of Ministers, Refik answered: "That does not matter; I can do it."[97]

The Massacre of the Deportees

The outward change in Winkler's attitudes toward the Armenians and their importance for construction of the Baghdad Railway reflected a realistic assessment of the situation. Winkler had to take his own position into consideration, since it had been openly called into question. More important was his realization that he had lost. Within hours of the first deportation, rumors and then definite confirmation arrived about large scale massacres of the deportees.

The extermination units consisted of gendarmes led by CUP members under the command of Avni and Muslims from the surrounding villages.[98] The first slaughters occurred while the deportees were crossing the Amanus chain. In a narrow gorge riflemen opened fire on a convoy of men. During the day, the gendarmes robbed the deportees and at night raped and killed girls and young women. Near the destroyed Armenian village of Fundajak, the gendarmerie stopped convoys and executed blacklisted men.[99]

The later convoys had to pass over the corpses of their murdered colleagues.[100] The authorities tried to remove all traces of the massacres quickly and buried the corpses of the slain in mass graves.[101] One convoy which reached Urfa without any large scale massacre lost 387 out of 1,000 persons.[102] Another convoy was halted in a cholera- and typhus-infected area. In Urfa, Arabs informed the survivors that they would be led to their deaths. The last survivors of the convoy formed by young workers were killed near Veranshehir.[103]

The only aid to the convoys came from the remnants of the Armenian community of Marash, who were the next to be deported, and from the German missionaries stationed there. Not knowing what was taking place, nurse Paula Schäfer went to the Amanus to bring help to the Armenian workers. In the evening she had to leave the road because it was blocked by corpses. She found crying babies four weeks old lying in the fields. People wounded with bayonets were slowly dying along the road. Many people had been cut into pieces or burned. A pregnant woman had been impaled. One nurse in her group lost her mind and started to play with the decapitated corpse of a girl. A couple of hours later Schäfer met two convoys of deportees and bribed the gendarmes to treat the people well. She collected 150 orphaned children, but she believed that several hundred were still dispersed in the mountains. A carriage was sent from Marash southward in the direction of Urfa to collect other children, but it had to return because the road was blocked with corpses.[104]

These massacres and deportations were part of the last large Ottoman cleansing campaign coordinated by Talaat in 1916.[105] On June 20, while Avni was still in the Amanus, Talaat ordered the authorities of Marash to support him in preparing deportations there. Talaat added that the Marash Armenians were to be sent far away from the railway and main roads.[106] Shortly after the deportation of the workers in the Amanus, the Armenians still serving in the work battalions of the Ottoman army were killed.[107] Armenians were also deported from Aleppo and Mardin to Deir-el-Zor. The concentration camp of Ras-ul-Ain had been completely emptied and part of the deportees massacred on their way to Deir-el-Zor. The deportation from the concentration camps at Deir-el-Zor started on July 22. Metternich concluded that the Armenian deportations in the eastern provinces had entered their final phase.[108]

Conclusion

This investigation of the Baghdad Railway Company's reactions to the Young Turk extermination policies allows a number of conclusions to be drawn about the Armenian Genocide in general and the role of the Germans in particular. In 1915–16, a uniform German position toward the Ottoman Armenians did not exist. Competing administrations and individuals shaped German policies with disastrous consequences for the Armenians, as has been demonstrated.

The railway department of the Ottoman general staff was headed by a German officer, Lieutenant Colonel Böttrich, who formulated decisions that were in harmony with the aims of the Ottoman government. By identifying himself with the Ottoman deportation policy, the officer secured his own position and gained sufficient Ottoman backing to enact a policy antagonistic toward the railway company. For Böttrich, the issue of the deportation of the Armenian workers became a tool to assert his will over the railway company. Thus, he not only signed an order for deportation but also took an active interest in its enforcement. Moreover, when the deportation of the workers in the Amanus Mountains had brought about an interruption in the supplies of several Ottoman armies, Böttrich still sided with the Ottoman deportation policy and tried to break any resistance on the part of the railway company. Therefore, Böttrich has to be seen as a dynamic factor in the execution of the Armenian Genocide. Unlike his predecessor, Böttrich was not removed from his post at the demand of the German embassy and the railway company. This highlights the crucial duplicity of Böttrich's position as both an Ottoman and a German officer. He could check opposition from either side by stressing his Ottoman or German obligations. As it happened, however, this was not necessary, as he enjoyed the support of both of his immediate superiors, Minister of War Enver and Chief of the General Staff General Bronsart von Schellendorf. Thus, the German Supreme Army Command under General von Falkenhayn did not take any decisive steps to remove Böttrich; on the contrary, it disregarded Böttrich's critics and reinforced the officer's position.

Regarding the actual execution of the deportation of the railway workers, it is clear that General von der Goltz (Pasha) was not involved. On the way to the Mesopotamian front von der Goltz and his staff crossed the Amanus in early November 1915, that is about eight months before the final deportations started. The general died in Baghdad on April 19, 1916, two months before the Amanus deportations.[109] Moreover, contrary to Dadrian's statement, von der Goltz was not accused of having ordered the deportation of the Armenian workers but of a concentration camp at Osmanieh. No railway construction site existed at Osmanieh. Furthermore, in their affidavit the survivors made a clear distinction between the deportation of this concentration camp and that of the Armenian workers.[110]

The German embassy followed a strategy of public support for the Ottoman ally and echoed official Turkish anti-Armenian propaganda, even as it reported to the German Foreign Office on what actually was taking place. The Armenian Genocide was a secondary issue for the Foreign Office, where the importance of the Ottoman contribution to the war effort was widely appreciated. With the unfolding of the Armenian Genocide, however, German economic interests were increasingly endangered. The increased German influence following the defeat of Serbia provided the basis for a gradual modification of Foreign Office policies. Stronger protests were then voiced against the persecution of the Armenians, yet no practical sanctions were imposed. The remonstrances of the German ambassador apparently made little impression on the Ottoman government. The reasons for this are to be found in the Ottoman determination to exterminate the Armenian community and in the ambassador's inability to win the support of the German army.

The Ottoman government and the ruling Committee of Union and Progress (CUP) were determined to exterminate the company's Armenian employees, just as they were to extirpate the entire Armenian population. They pursued their goal following a double strategy. This strategy combined, on the one hand, a consistent diplomatic effort to gain the railway company's consent and cooperation in the deportation of its employees, and on the other hand, to use subordinate administrators to create a fait accompli at an opportune moment to make it seem that the government was not involved. In dealings with their German partners the ruling CUP members tried to hide the close cooperation of the Ottoman central administration, military officers, and local authorities. Therefore, a system of official orders and secret counter orders was employed. The counter orders reversed the former official orders that had been shown to the Germans. In critical situations, such as the resistance against the deportation program by the governor of Marash in 1916 or the interruption of railway transportation, special liaisons furnished with full executive powers were used to overcome the problems. Deportations and massacres were directed and monitored closely by officials in Constantinople. The principal methods of extermination along the railway were massacre, death marches, forced starvation and dehydration, and systematic exposure to contagious diseases.

The declared aim of the Baghdad Railway Company's policy was the protection of its interests. One of these aims was the safeguarding of its Armenian employees. Thus, conflicts with the Ottoman government were inevitable. The company fought relentlessly and used all the pressure it could bring to bear on the government to give up its plan to deport the Armenian workers. In a decisive moment, Günther warned Talaat that the deportation of his employees would interrupt supplies for the armies at Gallipoli and thus bring about the defeat of the Ottoman Empire. Utilitarian motives were clearly of importance for the company's pro-Armenian policy, but were not the only reasons. Humanitarian considerations stood behind the company's own relief efforts. Supplying the German embassy with incoming reports on atrocities, the company's director worked for a change of official German policies. The company's measures far exceeded mere diplomatic activities. The directors, as well as their staff, engaged in clandestine resistance. Against strict Ottoman orders, deportees were supplied with provisions, and railway construction sites became havens for the persecuted. The actions of individual engineers illustrate a coherent company policy.

Company resistance could not, however, prevent the deportation and massacre of the workers from the Amanus in June 1916. The destruction of this Armenian labor force amply demonstrates how the Baghdad Railway Company and its German allies had frustrated the Ottoman government's attempt to co-opt the company in its deportation scheme. The government therefore resorted to a carefully prepared fait accompli to defeat German resistance. The disastrous consequences for its military supply must have taught the government a lesson. Perhaps, it was this experience that ultimately spared most of the remaining Armenian employees and workers of the railway staff and those on the construction sites in the Taurus Mountains.

The Armenian employees themselves were mainly an object of politics. Nevertheless, they developed their own strategies of resistance. While living on the edge of death, they tried to get as many other Armenians as possible into the "life boat" of the railway construction sites. New arrivals were given false identities, orphans were sheltered, and many deported girls were saved through marriage. Although extermination squads operated in their immediate vicinity, Armenians established families and tried to survive. In spite of all the suffering, they had not given up hope for a better future and negated the deadly logic of the CUP's genocidal policy. Thus, their struggle for survival was a preview of a new beginning by survivors in postwar times.

This study of the Baghdad Railway Company's Armenian policy confirms Christoph Dinkel's thesis that German officers participated in the decision to deport Armenians and tried to ensure enforcement of that decision. Vahakn Dadrian's thesis that both German military and civilian authorities, fully aware of the consequence, "joined" the Ottomans in the decision to deport the Armenian railway workers is not sustained by the evidence presented here. The German embassy, backed by the Foreign Office, supported the Baghdad Railway Company in its struggle against the Ottoman authorities and Lieutenant Colonel Böttrich. The Foreign Office secured the intervention of the Supreme Army Command and prevented the execution of the deportation decision of October 1915. This intervention possibly marked a cautious change in the Armenian policies of the Foreign Office. The case of the German army is, however, more complicated. Böttrich abetted the Turkish genocidal policy, and the Supreme Army Command generally observed a policy of noninterference in Ottoman administrative issues, while also supporting Böttrich in his capacity as an officer of the general staff of the Ottoman army. In general, the Supreme Army Command intervened only when deemed absolutely necessary. Hence, when it became clear that the consequences of the anti-Armenian policies of Böttrich and the Turkish government jeopardized the flow of military supplies, the Supreme Army Command intervened. In the case of the railway staff, it was in time; in the case of the Armenians in the Amanus, it was too late. Thus, the refusal of the Supreme Army Command to yield to the demands of the Foreign Office and the railway company to recall Böttrich seems to have been a factor in the deportation and massacre of the Armenian workers.

In sum, German involvement in the Armenian Genocide covers a spectrum ranging from active resistance to complicity. A uniform German policy did not exist. German military, civilian, and railway officials represented different interests and accordingly followed different strategies. Often, these strategies were in conflict, as were the relations between their proponents.

Notes

Research for this study was partly funded by the Zoryan Institute, Cambridge, Mass., and one of its founders, Kourken M. Sarkissian. I profited from the support of Armenian and Turkish friends and I wish to thank them all. I am especially indebted to George Hintlian, who introduced me to Armenian materials and translated the quoted texts.

1. In this study the term "Baghdad Railway" represents the investments of the Deutsche Bank in the Ottoman Empire. The various companies were formally independent, but all were supervised by a representative of the bank.
2. Ulrich Trumpener, *Germany and the Ottoman Empire, 1914–1918* (Princeton: Princeton University Press, 1968; reprint, Delmar, N.Y.: Caravan Press, 1989), 204–5, 217, 225; Akaby Nassibian, *Britain and the Armenian Question, 1915–1923* (London: Croom Helm, 1984), 70, 75–76, 79, 85–86.
3. Auswärtiges Amt—Politisches Archiv (hereafter AA—PA), Türkei (hereafter TR) 183/37, zu A 22101, Zimmermann to Wangenheim, August 4, 1915.
4. AA—PA, TR 183/40, A 35046, Rössler to Bethmann Hollweg, November 16, 1915, and A 468, Rössler to Bethmann Hollweg, December 20, 1915.
5. During World War I, Lepsius had tried to stop the extermination of the Armenians through representations to Enver Pasha. Later, he published a volume of German documents on the genocide. He had, however, also been a supplier of Armenian-related political and military intelligence to the Foreign Office. Moreover, his patriotism was of the same radical nationalist brand as that of the Foreign Office officials with whom he shared an anti-Republican sentiment. In short, Lepsius was for the Foreign Office the ideal man for the job. AA—PA, TR 183/37, A 18969, Lepsius to Rosenberg, June 15, 1915. On Lepsius's nationalism, see Norbert Saupp, "Das Deutsche Reich und die Armenische Frage 1878–1914" (Ph.D. diss., Cologne, 1990), 229–30.
6. Johannes Lepsius, ed., *Deutschland und Armenien 1914–1918: Sammlung diplomatischer Aktenstücke* (Potsdam: Tempelverlag, 1919; reprint, Bremen: Donat and Temmen Verlag, 1986). On deletions in the published documents, see Trumpener, *Germany and the Ottoman Empire,* 205–6. On the policy behind these manipulations, see AA—PA, TR 183/56, zu A 20906, Göppert to Lepsius, July 26, 1919.
7. Bundesarchiv, Abteilungen Potsdam, Auswärtiges Amt, Zentralstelle für den Auslandsdienst 562, A.N.B. no. 3844, Göppert to Lepsius, September 4, 1919.
8. Trumpener, *Germany and the Ottoman Empire,* 67.
9. "During most of the war period, specifically until the spring of 1918, the majority of the Turkish leaders, and Enver in particular, were prepared to collaborate closely with the Reich in the military conduct of the war, but they vigorously and, on the whole, effectively resisted all German attempts to meddle in the internal affairs of the Ottoman empire." Ibid., 370. See also Frank G. Weber,

Eagles on the Crescent: Germany, Austria, and the Diplomacy of the Turkish Alliance, 1914–1918 (Ithaca, N.Y.: Cornell University Press, 1970), 145.

10. "It is certain, however, that the measures against the Armenians (including the deportation) in the Third Army's region (beginning May 1915) were not a purely Turkish 'solution' but were proposed and demanded by this circle of German officers. The same is probably true for the region under the Fourth Army." Christoph Dinkel, "German Officers and the Armenian Genocide," *Armenian Review* 44, no. 1 (Spring 1991): 120. Ohandjanian formulated independently a similar thesis based on Austro-Hungarian consular reports. Artem Ohandjanian, *Armenien: Der verschwiegene Völkermord* (Vienna: Böhlau Verlag, 1989), 208–21.
11. Ibid., 120.
12. Vahakn N. Dadrian, *The History of the Armenian Genocide: Ethnic Conflict from the Balkans to Anatolia to the Caucasus* (Providence, R.I.: Berghahn Books, 1995), 262.
13. "The case of Lieutenant Colonel Böttrich's indiscretion, and the ensuing panicky reaction of the German Foreign Office, has been examined above. The vehemence of that reaction did not so much attach to the cooperation of Böttrich with his Turkish colleagues at the headquarters on the authorization of the deportation of a particular segment of the Armenian population, but rather to his foolishness to reveal his active role by placing his signature on the respective order." Ibid., 292. In a recent article, however, Dadrian has referred to the German ambassador's resistance to "the unrelenting Turkish onslaught against the remnants of the victim nation." See idem, "Documentation of the Armenian Genocide in German and Austrian Sources," in *The Widening Circle of Genocide: A Critical Bibliographic Review,* ed. Israel Charny (New Brunswick, N.J.: Transaction Publishers, 1994), 3:100.
14. Idem, *German Responsibility in the Armenian Genocide: A Review of the Historical Evidence of German Complicity* (Watertown, Mass.: Blue Crane Books, 1996), 132.
15. Ibid., 125–26.
16. On the railway company's policy, see Trumpener, *Germany and the Ottoman Empire,* 285–316; Gerald D. Feldman, "Die Deutsche Bank vom Ersten Weltkrieg bis zur Weltwirtschaftskrise," in *Die Deutsche Bank 1870–1995,* ed. Lothar Gall et al. (Munich: C. H. Beck Verlag, 1995), 137–314.
17. Kübel could count on the support of his superior, General Liman von Sanders. To overcome the resistance of the army, the bank finally appealed to the German emperor. See Deutsche Bank, Historisches Archiv, Orientbüro 1031 (hereafter DB—HA, Or), Gwinner, Helfferich to Kaiser Wilhelm II, June 13, 1914. One month later the bank learned that Kübel would be soon removed: DB—HA, Or 1031, Zimmermann to Helfferich, July 14, 1914. See also Fritz Fischer, *Krieg der Illusionen: Die deutsche Politik von 1911–1914,* 2d ed. (Düsseldorf: Droste Verlag, 1978), 490. For information on the Ottoman General Staff's railway department, see Mehmet Özdemir, "Birinci Dünya Savaşı'nda Demiryollarının Kullanımı ve Bunun Savaşın Sonucuna Etkisi" (The use of railroads during

World War I and its effect on the outcome of the war) *Dördüncü Askeri Tarih Semineri* (Ankara: Genelkurmay Basımevi, 1989), 369–402.

18. Trumpener, *Germany and the Ottoman Empire,* 303; AA—PA, TR 152/83, A 29586, Günther to Hohenlohe, September 1, 1915; Rafael De Nogales, *Four Years Beneath the Crescent,* trans. Muna Lee (New York: Scribner's Sons, 1926), 169.
19. AA—PA, TR 152/83, A 29586, Günther to Hohenlohe, September 1, 1915; Großes Hauptquartier Türkei, 41c, J.38928 III, Gwinner, Stauss to Günther, July 13, 1916; Trumpener, *Germany and the Ottoman Empire,* 290–300; Feldman, *Die Deutsche Bank,* 154–56.
20. AA—PA, TR 152/83, A 29586, Günther to Gwinner, September 8, 1915, and A 29970, Günther to Verwaltungsrat, October 6, 1915.
21. AA—PA, TR 152/83, A 29586, Günther to Hohenlohe, September 1, 1915.
22. Başbakanlık Osmanlı Arşivi, Dâhiliye Nezâreti Evrakı, Dâhiliye Şifre Kalemi (hereafter: BOA, DH.ŞFR,), 52/93 Talaat to Djemal Pasha, April 24, 1915, Emniyyett-i Umûmiyye Müdîriyyeti (hereafter EUM) Spec. 14; Türkiye Cumhuriyeti, Başbakanlık Devlet Arşivleri Genel Müdürlüğü, *Osmanlı Belgelerinde Ermeniler (1915–1920)* (The Armenians in Ottoman documents [1915–1920]) (Ankara: Başbakanlık Basımevi, 1994) (Osmanlı Arşivi Daire Başkanlığı, Yayın No. 14), doc. 7 (hereafter OBE); DH.ŞFR, 52/286, Talaat to Maraş district, May 9, 1915, EUM Spec.14 (OBE no. 13); DH.ŞFR, 53/312, Talaat to Konia province, June 10, 1915, EUM Spec. 32 (OBE no. 32).
23. BOA, DH.ŞFR, 54-A/278, Talaat to Konia province, August 5, 1915, EUM Spec. 4924; DB—HA, Or 1704, Seeger, Biegel, Janson, Maurer to Embassy, August 16, 1915, encl. in Günther to Verwaltungsrat, August 21, 1915; The Papers of Henry Morgenthau, Sr., Library of Congress (hereafter Morgenthau Papers), reel 22, frame 474–75, Schreiner, May 25, 1915. For the condition of the deportees from Zeitun at Konia, see ibid., reel 7, frame 557–58, Dodd to Morgenthau, May 6, 1915. In August 1915, the Armenians of Zeitun who were in Konia province were told that they might return home. Arriving in Osmanieh they learned that their real destination was the Arabian desert. See AA—PA Konsulat Adana: Armenisches (Dobbeler) to Schuchardt, September 9, 1915.
24. "Wie es einmal vor der Geschichte zu rechtfertigen sein wird, dass dies alles unter unseren Augen geschieht, ohne dass wir uns rühren, weiss ich nicht." DB—HA, Or 1704, Günther to Gwinner, October 14, 1915. A German military epidemologist described the deportations along the railway as a moving "disease transport." See Peter Mühlens, "Vier Jahre Kriegshygiene in der Türkei und auf dem Balkan " *Vor 20 Jahren,* 2. Folge (1935): 158. See also Arnold J. Toynbee, *Armenian Atrocities: The Murder of a Nation, With a Speech Delivered by Lord Bryce in the House of Lords* (London: Hodder and Stoughton, 1915), 41; idem, *The Treatment of Armenians in the Ottoman Empire, 1915–16: Documents Presented to Viscount Grey of Fallodon, Secretary of State for Foreign Affairs.* Preface by Viscount Bryce (London: Sir Joseph Causton and Sons, 1916; reprint, Astoria, N.Y.: J. C. and L. Fawcett, 1990) (Miscellaneous no. 31, 1916), docs. 104, 107, 108. (This Blue Book should be consulted

together with *Key to Names of Persons and Places Withheld from Publication in "The Treatment of Armenians in the Ottoman Empire, 1915–16: Documents Presented to Viscount Grey of Falloden by Viscount Bryce"*). United States National Archives, Record Group 59 (hereafter NA RG 59), 867.4016/307; Morgenthau Papers, reel 7, frames 557–58, Dodd to Morgenthau, May 5, 1915. Most of the reports preserved in Record Group 59 of the U.S. National Archives utilized in this study were published in Ara Sarafian, comp., *United States Official Documents on the Armenian Genocide,* vols. 1–3 (Watertown, Mass.: Armenian Review, 1993–96). On the use of sheep cars, see also Ahmet Refik (Altınay), *İki Komite İki Kıtâl* (Two committees, two massacres), ed. Hamide Koyukan (Ankara: Kebikeç Yayınları, 1994), 34, 37; John A. Still, *A Prisoner in Turkey* (London: John Lane and Co., 1920), 64. In October 1915, 2,700 Armenians were deported from Konia in 36 cars, an average of 75 per car. See BOA, DH.EUM, 2. Şube, 68/100, Governor Sâmih Rıf'at to Ministry of Interior, October 30, 1915 (OBE no. 123). On the standard capacity of railway cars, see DB—HA, Or 1031, (Günther) to Gwinner, Helfferich, May 20, 1914, encl. in Günther to Verwaltungsrat, May 20, 1914; Suzanne Elizabeth Moranian, "The American Missionaries and the Armenian Question: 1915–1927" (Ph.D. diss., University of Wisconsin, Madison, 1994), 23–24, 123–24.

25. "Einliegend sende ich Ihnen ein Bildchen, die Anatolische Bahn als Kulturträgerin in der Türkei darstellend." DB—HA, Or 1704, Günther to Gwinner, October 30, 1915. See also NA RG 59, 867.4016/137, Dodd to Morgenthau, August 15, 1915.
26. BOA, DH.EUM, 2. Şube, 68/88, Judge Nâcî to Ministry of the Interior, October 10, 1915 (OBE no. 124); DH.ŞFR, 57/8, Talaat to Karahisar-ı Sâhib district, October 14, 1915, EUM Spec. 29; DH.EUM, 2. Şube, 68/92, Naci to Ministry of Interior, October 16, 1915 (OBE no. 127); DH.ŞFR, 57/65, Talaat to Eskişehir, Karahisar-ı Sâhib, Kütahya districts, October 17, 1915 EUM; DH.EUM, 2. Şube, 68/95, Sâmih to Ministry of Interior, October 19, 1915 (OBE no. 136); 2. Şube, 68/96, Sâmih to Ministry of Interior, October 21, 1915 (OBE no. 137); 2. Şube, 68/99, Sâmih to Ministry of Interior, October 23, 1915 (OBE no. 139).
27. On August 20, 1915, the German journalist Zabel who had traveled in the interior reported to the German embassy that Armenians were directed first to the large concentration camp of Konia. There, they were allowed to sell their belongings but only to Turks in order to pay for further railway transport. Those who could not pay had to walk. Marginal note in Seeger, Biegel, Janson, Maurer to Embassy, August 16, 1915, encl. in AA—PA Konstantinopel (hereafter: Konst.) 170, J.4857, Günther to Neurath, August 21, 1915. See also Still, *A Prisoner in Turkey,* 64.
28. DB—HA, Or 1704, Hasenfratz to Günther, October 4, 1915, encl. in Günther to Gwinner, October 16, 1915. For other descriptions and estimates of numbers, see AA—PA, Konst. 172, J.284, Hoffmann to Embassy, November 8, 1915; NA RG 59, 867.4016/212/219, Jackson to Morgenthau, September 20 and 29, 1915; *The Treatment of Armenians,* doc. 116.

29. AA—PA, TR 183/39, zu A 30012, record of statement by Paul Kern, September 13, 1915, encl. 1 in Büge to Bethmann Hollweg, October 1, 1915; NA RG 59 867.4016/200/239, Nathan to Morgenthau, September 27 and November 4, 1915. An American traveler estimated the population of the Katma concentration camp at 150,000. Memorandum by Walter M. Geddes, encl. in 867.4016/243, Horton to Secretary of State, November 8, 1915. Friedrich Freiherr Kress von Kressenstein, *Mit den Türken zum Suezkanal* (Berlin: Vorhut Verlag Otto Schlegel, 1938), 132. Kress saw the camp in October 1915. In November, the German consul at Aleppo reported repeatedly on the contamination of the road over the Taurus and Amanus mountains and in the city of Aleppo. Typhoid fever had spread because of the deportation of Armenians. Already several Armenian employees of the railway company had died. German troops along the railway line were in danger, too. See AA—PA, Konst. 409, J.9462, J.9986, Rössler to Embassy, November 5 and 15, 1915. The route between Osmanieh and Islahia was described as being "practically a cemetery." See NA RG 59, 867.4016/268, "Report by an Eyewitness," encl. in Horton to Secretary of State, January 15, 1916. For reports on the camps of Osmanieh, Mamoure, and Islahia, see "Report of Paula Schäfer," November 16, 1915, "Report by Sister Beatrice Rohner on her visit to a tent camp in Mamoure on November 26, 1915," and "Report by Sister Paula Schäfer on a visit in the tent camp of Islahia on Dec. 1, 1915," encl. in AA—PA, TR 183/40, A 2682, Schuchardt to AA, January 26, 1916. These reports were communicated to the British government and published in *The Treatment of Armenians,* doc. 117a–c. For further evidence on the camps close to the stations of Külek and Osmanieh, see Sarah Carmelite Brewer Christie, typed transcript of her personal diary, 1915–19, entries for October 1, 11, 18, 1915, as quoted in Alan Alfred Bartholomew, "Tarsus American School, 1888–1988: The Evolution of a Missionary Institution in Turkey" (Ph.D. diss., Bryn Mawr College, 1989), 114–16. On conditions and various camps in the province of Konia, see NA RG 59, 867.4016/188, Post to Morgenthau, September 3, 1915; 867.4016/189, Dodd to Morgenthau, September 8, 1915; 867.4016/226, Post to Morgenthau, October 27, 1915; 867.4016/251, Post to Peet, November 25, 1915. On Katma, see Archives du la Ministère de Guerre (France), 7 N 1254, Report of Mr. Brewster, encl. in de La Panouse to Painlevé, May 9, 1917, D no. 5037, in *Les Grandes puissances, l'Empire Ottoman et les Arméniens dans les archives françaises (1914–1918): Recueil de documents,* ed. Arthur Beylerian (Paris: Imprimerie A. Bontemps, 1983) (Publications de la Sorbonne) Série Documents—34, 352–53, no. 356. The numbers of deportees match the figure of 40,000–50,000 given by Naim Bey who according to Andonian had been at one point the "secrétaire du Bureau de la Sous-Direction des Déportés à Alep." Although the authenticity of the documents is still debated, the timing, the number of deportees, and the problems these camps produced for military transport are all confirmed by the documention used here. Consequently, the telegram ascribed to Talaat on page 50 of Andonian's book does not pertain to the number of Armenian railway workers but to the concentration camps along

the railway. This imprecision, however, might very well reflect the point of view of the Ottoman authorities, who did not necessarily differentiate between the deportees and those working for the railway construction, as the company had been hiring deportees illegally. See Aram Andonian, *Documents officiels concernant les massacres arméniens* (Paris: Imprimerie H. Turabian, 1920), 48–50; Bibliothèque Nubarian, Paris, Liasse 27, Andonian to Tarzian, July 26, 1937.

30. In the autumn of 1915, the concentration camp at Islahia was for six weeks the scene of continued robberies and slaughters by Kurds. German railway engineers could not protect the deportees. After the personal intervention of Djemal Pasha, who hanged some of the perpetrators, a temporary change occurred. See AA—PA, Konst. 172, J.283, Rössler to Metternich, January 3, 1916, no. 16. The conditions in the camps under which the Armenians survived differed radically from the luxurious lifestyle of local military commanders. See Hasan Cemil Çambel, *Makaleler, Hâtıralar* (Articles, memoirs) (1964; reprint, Ankara: Türk Tarih Kurumu, 1987), 136–37. On death squads operating in the Amanus and the condition of deportees, see De Nogales, *Four Years Beneath the Crescent,* 171–72, 174, 177–78.
31. AA—PA, TR 183/38, A 28019, Rössler to Bethmann Hollweg, September 3, 1915.
32. On the death marches, see AA—PA, Konst. 172, J.283, Rössler to Metternich, January 3, 1916. Rössler reported on oral information obtained from Bastendorff. He added that this information was much more appalling than the details contained in the engineer's written report.
33. AA—PA, Konst. 172, J.284, Report by Flechsig, October 20, 1915, encl. in Hoffmann to Embassy, November 8, 1915; J.283, Bastendorff to Rössler, December 18, 1915, encl. 2 in Rössler to Metternich, January 3, 1916. The Rasul-Ain concentration camp was surrounded by a wall with only one guarded entrance. While people were left to die inside, mass graves were prepared in the vicinity. See Christoph Schröder, "Die armenischen Greuel," *Berliner Stadt Anzeiger,* September 25, 1919, no. 455 Morgenausgabe. See also Archives du la Ministère de Guerre (France), 16 N 2946, War Office, September 25, 1916, annex to La Panouse to Joffre, September 30, 1916, in Beylerian, *Les Grandes puissances,* 250–51; Wegner to Bonin, November 26, 1915, in Armin T. Wegner, *Der Weg ohne Heimkehr: Ein Martyrium in Briefen* (Berlin: Fleischel and Co., 1919), 16–23.
34. DB—HA, Or 1704, Hasenfratz to Günther, October 19, 1915 encl. in Günther to Gwinner, October 30, 1915. The intentional killing of Armenians is further confirmed by the behavior of the military commander of Tell Abiad. The officer blamed Arab Beduins for giving safe conduct to a caravan of Armenians. Two days later he had disappeared without leaving a trace. The Arabs had apparently taken revenge. AA—PA, Konst. 172, J.284, Hoffmann to Embassy, November 8, 1915. On Beduins helping Armenians near Tell Abiad, see Archives du la Ministère de Guerre, British Intelligence Service to Ministère de la Guerre, May 30, 1916, in Beylerian, *Les Grandes puissances,* 208–9.

35. AA—PA, Konst. 170, J.4563, Spieker, July 27, 1915, encl. in Rössler to Hohenlohe, July 27, 1915. For the same statement by Spieker, see the report by a German missionary in Konsulat Adana: Armenisches, (Dobbeler) to Schuchardt, September 9, 1915, and Konst. 172, J.283, Bastendorff to Rössler, December 18, 1915, encl. 2 in Rössler to Metternich, January 3, 1916. In 1917, a German physician recorded that along the railway an Armenian woman was worth less than a goat. The slave trade in Armenian women was a common sight at the railway stations. German and Ottoman officers, too, as well as some German railway personnel, took advantage of this situtation. The engineers repeatedly tried to help, at least in individual cases. See Theo Malade, *Von Amiens bis Aleppo: Ein Beitrag zur Seelenkunde des grossen Krieges: Aus dem Tagebuch eines Feldarztes* (Munich: Lehmann, 1930), 195, 204. The *kaimakam* of Tell Abiad offered German engineers young Armenian girls for the night. Report by engineer Pieper, in Ernst Sommer, *Die Wahrheit über die Leiden des armenischen Volkes in der Türkei während des Weltkriegs* (Frankfurt a.M.: Verlag Orient, 1919), 22–23. For violations of young women by high ranking Ottoman administrators, see Konst. 172, J.284, Hoffmann to Embassy, November 8, 1915; TR 183/38, A 28019, Rössler to Bethmann Hollweg, September 3, 1915; Martin Niepage, *Ein Wort an die berufenen Vertreter des deutschen Volkes: Eindrücke eines deutschen Oberlehrers aus der Türkei* (Berlin: Als Manuskript gedruckt, n.d. [1916]), 8. See also Andonian, *Documents officiels,* 41n. 1. The violators of Armenian women came from the highest classes of Ottoman society. The governor of Aleppo, Bekir Sami Bey, seriously injured an Armenian woman while trying to rape her. See BOA, DH.ŞFR, 55–A/60, Talaat to Ali Münif Bey, September 4, 1915, Kalem-i Mahsus.
36. AA—PA, Konsulat Adana: Armenisches, J.855, Büge to Embassy, September 24, 1915. The information was supplied by railway manager Meier of Mersina.
37. AA—PA, TR 183/38, A 26474, Hohenlohe to Bethmann Hollweg, September 4, 1915. One of the telegrams was dated August 29, 1915, whereas the other two were undated. Hohenlohe, who had doubts about the value of the material, added that Talaat had told him a few days before: "la question arménienne n'existe plus." On August 30, 1915, the Austro-Hungarian ambassador, Pallavicini, saw Talaat. Summing up the substance of the interview, he concluded that the Ottoman government regarded the Armenian Question as settled. Haus-, Hof- und Staatsarchiv, Politische Abteilung (hereafter HHStA PA) XII, 209, Pallavicini to Burián, August 31, 1915, no.71/P.B. The Austro-Hungarian documents utilized in this study were collected by Artem Ohandjanian and published as *The Armenian Genocide: Documentation,* vol. 2 (Munich: Institut für armenische Fragen, 1988).
38. AA—PA, Konst. 170, J.5263, Büge to Embassy, September 10, 1915. Büge's action was most likely agreed on with Winkler. Both men informed their respective superiors about the suspected deceit using identical arguments and on the same day. See Konst. 97, J.8078, Winkler to Günther, September 10, 1915, encl. in Hübsch to Neurath, September 15, 1915. On the role of the special envoy, see also NA RG 59, 867.4016/193, Nathan to Morgenthau, September 11, 1915.

Reporting on the telegrams and the persecution of the Armenians in general, Austro-Hungarian Ambassador Pallavicini also came to the conclusion that Talaat Bey was playing a double game. See HHStA PA, XII 209, Pallavicini to Burián, August 31, 1915, no. 71/P.B; Pallavicini to Burián, September 3, 1915, no.72/P.H. Pallavicini to Burián, September 8, 1915, no.73/P.A.

39. AA—PA, TR 183/38, A 27578, Hohenlohe to Bethmann-Hollweg, September 14, 1915. Hohenlohe's argument that Ottoman local authorities were the real culprits was probably motivated by a wish to show that his previous remonstrances with the Ottoman government had been successful. On this initiative, see A 24507, Hohenlohe to Bethmann Hollweg, August 12, 1915. See also Trumpener, *Germany and the Ottoman Empire,* 218–19.
40. See his report of October 1, 1915 with twelve enclosed eyewitness reports. To preempt doubts about the veracity of the material, Büge notarized the statements. See AA—PA, TR 183/39, zu A 30012, Büge to Bethmann Hollweg, October 1, 1915.
41. AA—PA, Konst. 170, J.5779, Rössler to Hohenlohe, September 27, 1915, encl. 1; Huber, Niepage, Gräter, Spieker to AA, October 8, 1916, in "Die armenischen Greuel: Drei Dokumente," *Die Friedenswarte* 18 (1916): 321–24 (doc. 1). For an earlier order, see *Germany, Turkey and Armenia: A Selection of Documentary Evidence Relating to the Armenian Atrocities from German and Other Sources* (London: J. J. Keliher and Co., 1917), 75n. See also Wegner, *Der Weg ohne Heimkehr,* 169–70.
42. German officers were reported to have stated that the lives of thousands of Armenians did not matter. See DB—HA, Or 1704, Günther to Verwaltungsrat, August 10 and September 14, 1915.
43. DB—HA, Or 1704, Günther to Gwinner, August 17, 1915.
44. DB—HA, Or 1704, Günther to Gwinner, August 17, September 7, and November 1, 1915; Gwinner to Günther, August 26 and 28, 1915. On prohibitions to give food to deportees, see De Nogales, *Four Years Beneath the Crescent,* 173; Morgenthau Papers, reel 7, frame 557–58, Dodd to Morgenthau, May 6, 1915. For a critique of the railway company asking deportees to pay for their tickets, see NA RG 59, 867.4016/189, Dodd to Morgenthau, September 8, 1915. Dodd's colleague Post reported on the abuses of Ottoman officials who sold tickets to deportees at exorbitant rates. See RG 59, 867.4016/251, Post to Peet, November 25, 1915.
45. DB—HA, Or 305, Winkler to Günther, July 7, 1915. For the attempts by the *kaimakam* of Ras-ul-Ain to deport and kill Armenian workers, see AA—PA, Konst. 172, J.283, Bastendorff to Rössler, December 18, 1915, encl. 2 in Rössler to Metternich, January 3, 1916. By October 11, 1915 the Armenians working on the railway were the only ones left in Osmanieh. See BOA, DH.EUM, 2. Şube, 68/89, Governor Fethi to Ministry of Interior, October 11, 1915 (OBE no. 126). According to an author who had access to the Turkish military archives, the plan to remove the Armenians from the railway lines originated from the Ottoman Ministry of War and dated from May 1915. Özdemir, "Birinci Dünya Savaşı'nda," 392–93.

46. DB—HA, Or 305, Winkler to Günther, July 7, 1915; Winkler to Riese, July 7, 1915. See also HHStA PA, XXXXVIII, 366, Dandini to Burián, August 8, 1915, Z.10/P.
47. DB—HA, Or 305, Winkler to Günther, July 7, 1915; Winkler to Riese, July 7, 1915; Günther to Verwaltungsrat, July 12, 1915. By November 1915, the construction works in the Amanus had slowed down considerably because of the deportations of qualified Armenian workers. Hans von Kiesling, *Orientfahrten: Zwischen Ägeis und Zagros: Erlebtes und Erschautes aus schwerer Zeit* (Leipzig: Dieterich'sche Verlagsbuchhandlung, 1921), 22.
48. For further information on the CUP's policy toward the foreign companies, see Zafer Toprak, *Milli İktisat—Milli Burjuvazi* (National economy—national bourgeoisie) (Istanbul: Tarih Vakfı Yurt Yayınları, 1995).
49. DB—HA, Or 1704, Günther to Verwaltungsrat, September 14, 1915. According to an Austrian intelligence report, the employees had been massacred close to the railway station. The killings were part of a larger annihilation program at Angora that was directed by Atif Bey, a government envoy. HHStA PA, XL, 272, Konfidenten-Bericht, December 2, 1915, no. 444; see also NA RG 59, 867.4016/189, Dodd to Morgenthau, September 8, 1915.
50. BOA, DH.ŞFR, 55/64, Talaat to Eskişehir district, August 17, 1915, EUM Spec.13; DH.ŞFR, 55/318, Talaat to Konia, Angora, Hüdâvendigâr, and Adana provinces and districts of Karahisâr-ı Sâhib, Kütahya, Eskişehir, Niğde, August 29, 1915 EUM. AA—PA, Konst. 97, J.8078, Winkler to Günther, September 10, 1915; DB—HA, Or 1704, Günther to Gwinner, September 20, 1915, and Günther to Verwaltungsrat, November 5, 1918.
51. Veli to General Headquarters, August 28, 1915, in Turkey, Prime Ministry, Directorate General of Press and Information, *Documents,* vol. 1, 3d ed. (N.p., n.d.), no. 33; AA—PA, Konst. 97, J.8078, Winkler to Günther, September 10, 1915, encl. in Hübsch to Neurath, September 15, 1915; DB—HA, Or 462, Winkler to Riese, September 16, 1915; and Winkler to Günther, September 16, 1915; Konst. 97, J.7976, Büge to Embassy, September 24, 1915. Büge reported on Winkler's complaints against the *vali*'s interference of the construction works. See also BOA, DH.ŞFR, 56/156, Talaat to Konia, Angora, Hüdâvendigâr, Adana provinces, İzmit, Karahisâr-ı Sâhib, Kütahya, Eskişehir, Niğde districts, September 25, 1915, EUM Spec. 593. Şükrü Bey, a special envoy with the title "deportation commissar" who was coordinating the deportation from Aleppo at that time, received similar orders on September 29 and 30, 1915. See DH.ŞFR, 56/232, EUM Spec. 48 and 56/235, EUM Spec. 85. Talaat was repeatedly involved in the cases of individual Armenian railway employees and their families. See, for example, DH.ŞFR, 55-A/226, Talaat to Kütahya district, September 12, 1915, EUM Spec. 593, and 56/239, Talaat to Karahisar-ı Sâhib district, September 30, 1915, EUM Spec. 20.
52. AA—PA, TR 152/83, zu A 29586, Zimmermann to Wangenheim, October 13, 1915; DB—HA, Or 1704, Günther to Gwinner, October 14, 1915.
53. DB—HA, Or 139, Günther to Verwaltungsrat, October 14, 1915; DB—HA, Or 462, Gwinner to Günther, October 19, 1915.

54. AA—PA, Konst. 97, J.9428, Hübsch to Neurath, October 30, 1915. The enclosed text is not a deportation order but a copy of the decision taken by the commission. It was sent to the military commissar of the Anatolian Railway, who forwarded a copy to the railway company. The text of a deportation order ascribed to Talaat has been published by Andonian. The French edition of the book does not indicate a date. Andonian, *Documents officiels,* 50; Vahakn N. Dadrian, "The Naim-Andonian Documents on the World War I Destruction of Ottoman Armenians: The Anatomy of a Genocide," *International Journal of Middle East Studies* 18 (1986): 316 (no. 23) dates this telegram, January 8, 1916.
55. AA—PA, TR 183/83, A 34059, Vehbi to Anatolian Railway Co., October 31, 1915, encl. in Huguenin to Gwinner, November 6, 1915.
56. Public Record Office, London, Foreign Office 371/5265/E59024, Günther to Verwaltungsrat, October 28, 1915, no. 7702/389, translation.
57. Many initiatives to remove Bronsart had already failed when Enver Pasha and Falkenhayn met in December 1915. Falkenhayn also tried to convince Enver that Bronsart was unqualified for his position, but it was in vain, for as Falkenhayn put it, the pasha was "stuck" to his subordinate. AA—PA, Großes Hauptquartier Türkei, no. 41, Bd. 1, Treutler to Jagow, March 9, 1916; Joseph Pomiankowski, *Der Zusammenbruch des Ottomanischen Reiches: Erinnerungen an die Türkei aus der Zeit des Weltkrieges* (Vienna: Amalthea Verlag, 1928; reprint, Graz: Akademische Druck- u. Verlagsanstalt, 1969), 294; Trumpener, *Germany and the Ottoman Empire,* 80, 85, 91.
58. AA—PA, Konst. 171, A 32610, Günther to Verwaltungsrat, October 28, 1915, encl. in Zimmermann to Metternich, November 18, 1915, J.6866. After the armistice a copy of the report fell into the hands of the British forces occupying Constantinople. See Public Record Office, London, Foreign Office, 371/5265/E59024, Günther to Verwaltungsrat, October 28, 1915, no. 7702/389, translation. It should be noted that contrary to Dadrian's claim Günther did not accuse Böttrich of being "foolish enough" to sign the deportation decision but criticized him for "stooping to" (*herbeigelassen*) the action. The English translation relied on by Dadrian, *The History of the Armenian Genocide,* 262, uses the imprecise expression "has allowed himself." The word "kaustisch," however, was translated correctly as "caustic." Dadrian substituted "ecstatically" for "caustic" without indicating the change to the reader. Both deviations from the original text described here alter the meaning of the document. For another attempt that failed to get a German officer involved in the extermination of Armenians, see AA—PA, Weltkrieg, 11d.secr./10, Scheubner to Schulenburg, December 7, 1915; Paul Leverkuehn, *Posten auf ewiger Wache: Aus dem abenteuerlichen Leben des Max von Scheubner-Richter* (Essen: Essener Verlagsanstalt, 1938), 101–2.
59. AA—PA, TR, 152/83, A 31421, Günther to Gwinner, October 30, 1915, marginal note by Jagow, Berlin, October 31, 1915.
60. AA—PA, TR 152/83, zu A 29586, Zimmermann to Wangenheim, October 13, 1915, and A 30246, Wangenheim to AA, October 18, 1915; TR 152/84, A 36186, Metternich to Bethmann Hollweg, December 8, 1915.

61. AA—PA, TR 152/83, A 30574, Wangenheim to AA, October 21, 1915.
62. Ibid.; AA—PA, TR 152/83, A 31968, Neurath to AA, November 4, 1915; Großes Hauptquartier Türkei 41a–e, Jagow to Treutler, November 8, 1915, no. 201.
63. Lossow's intervention on behalf of the railway employees hints at a serious disagreement among the leading German officers active in Turkey. Unlike Bronsart and Böttrich, Lossow was on good terms with Falkenhayn and was thus not dependent on Ottoman patronage. Lossow drafted the text of the telegram Falkenhayn sent to Enver. AA—PA, TR 183/39, A 31750, Neurath to AA, November 2, 1915; TR 152/83, zu A 31421, Jagow to Neurath, November 11, 1915; Großes Hauptquartier Türkei, 41a–e, zu A 31421, Jagow to Treutler, November 2, 1915. On Lossow as follower of Falkenhayn, see Pomiankowski, *Der Zusammenbruch des Ottomanischen Reiches,* 281. Lossow's action illustrates the power relations within the Supreme Army Command.
64. AA—PA, TR 152/83, A 31884, Treutler to AA, November 3, 1915; A 33741, Falkenhayn to Treutler, November 19, 1915; Chef des Generalstabes des Feldheeres, encl. in A 33741, Treutler to Bethmann Hollweg, November 20, 1915, no. 76.
65. DB—HA, Or 1704, Günther to Verwaltungsrat, December 3, 1915. The change in the attitudes of the Ottoman military might have been a result of the efforts on the part of Djemal Pasha. Djemal had tried to return the deported Armenian workers to the railway construction, but he feared that Talaat would obstruct this initiative. See AA—PA, Konst. 98, J.10365, Rössler to Embassy, November 25, 1915. On December 9, 1915, Talaat ordered the provincial authorities at Adana to report on the situation around Islahia, BOA, DH.ŞFR, 58/223, Talaat to Adana province, December 9, 1915, EUM Spec. 119. It is interesting to note that Böttrich's affinity with Enver even had deadly consequences for German soldiers. When in 1916 German physicians asked for additional precautions against typhoid fever, Böttrich sided with Enver and refused any assistance. See Ernst Rodenwaldt, *Seuchenkämpfe: Bericht des beratenden Hygienikers der V. kaiserlich-osmanischen Armee* (Heidelberg: Carl Winter Verlag, 1921), 207–8. See also Helmut Becker, *Äskulap zwischen Reichsadler und Halbmond: Seuchenbekämpfung und Sanitätswesen im türkischen Reich während des Ersten Weltkriegs* (Herzogenrath: Verlag Murken-Altrogge, 1990), 406–7.
66. The first direct train from Berlin arrived in Constantinople on January 16, 1916. Carl Mühlmann, *Das deutsch-türkische Waffenbündnis im Weltkrieg* (Leipzig: Köhler and Amelang, 1940), 56; Trumpener, *Germany and the Ottoman Empire,* 297; Weber, *Eagles on the Crescent,* 115–28.
67. AA—PA, TR 152/84, A 36186, Metternich to Bethmann Hollweg, December 8, 1915.
68. AA—PA, TR 152/84, zu A 36187, zu 36227, Jagow to Chief of Army Staff, December 21, 1915. Jagow followed Günther's argument.
69. Großer Krieg Türkei, 41c, Gröner to AA, March 22, 1916. Falkenhayn was eager not to antagonize an Ottoman ally that had offered six divisions for the eastern front in Europe. On February 11, 1916, he declared that Germany needed the Ottoman contribution to the war effort. See Gerold von Gleich, *Vom Balkan nach*

Bagdad: Militärisch-politische Erinnerungen an den Orient (Berlin: Scherl, 1921), 73.

70. DB—HA, Or 463, Gwinner to Günther, May 20, 1916; AA—PA, Großes Hauptquartier Türkei, 41a–e, Jagow to Treutler, July 4, 1916. Jagow transmitted a report of Metternich.
71. In 1918, after the fall of the CUP regime, a delegation of the Armenian employees thanked Günther for all his personal efforts. DB—HA, Or 1704, Günther to Verwaltungsrat, November 5, 1918. See also Özdemir, "Birinci Dünya Savaşı'nda," 393.
72. AA—PA, TR 152/84, A 264, and A 2051, Neurath to AA, January 8 and 28, 1916. For problems in the applicaton of the decision, see DB—HA, Or 463, Huguenin to Gwinner, January 21, 1916. The decision that workers must not return was taken after consultations between Talaat and Enver. See BOA, DH.ŞFR, 58/25, Talaat to Şükrü Bey, November 16, 1915, EUM Spec. 148. See also Trumpener, *Germany and the Ottoman Empire,* 297–98. On transportation problems in the Amanus, see De Nogales, *Four Years Beneath the Crescent,* 165–68.
73. Krikoris Balakian (Grigoris Palakian), *Hai Goghgotan* (Armenian calvary) (Paris: N.p., 1959), 2:25, 31–32. Balakian had been bookkeeper to Klaus, the responsible engineer at Baghche. Thus, he was intimately acquainted with the policies of the company. Ibid., 23. The engineers also gave shelter to deserters from the Ottoman army. See Jacob Künzler, *Im Lande des Blutes und der Tränen: Erlebniße in Mesopotamien während des Weltkrieges* (Potsdam: Tempelverlag, 1921), 5. For students of St. Paul's College of Tarsus working in the Amanus, see Brewer Christie, typed transcript of her personal diary, 1915–19, entry January 7, 1916, p. 47, as quoted in Bartholomew, *Tarsus American School,* 127–28. On April 13, 1916, Talaat told the provincial authorities along the railway lines that railway officers giving travel documents to Armenians were to be courtmartialed. See BOA, DH.ŞFR, 62/313, Talaat to Adana, Angora, Aleppo, Hüdavendigâr, Syria, Konia provinces, Urfa, İzmit, Zor, Karesi, Maraş, Kütahya, Karahisar-ı sâhib, Niğde, Eskişehir districts, April 13, 1916, EUM Gen. 45297 Spec. 104.
74. Khoren K. Davidson, *Odyssey of an Armenian of Zeitoun,* foreword by Aram Saroyan (New York: Vantage Press, 1985), 89–122; Teodik, *Amenun Taretsuitse* (Everyone's almanac) (Constantinople: K. Keshishian, 1920), 253–66; Abraham H. Hartunian, *Neither to Laugh nor to Weep: A Memoir of the Armenian Genocide,* trans. Vartan Hartunian (Boston: Beacon Press, 1968; reprint, Cambridge, Mass.: Armenian Heritage Press, 1986), 74–77. Gräter's information that leading officials of the Baghdad Railway Company had forbidden their subordinates to help Armenians contradicts this interpretation. Gräter, Aleppo, July 7, 1916, in "Die armenischen Greuel," doc. 3. The pro-Armenian attitudes of the personnel at Aleppo are documented by their reports.
75. Hartunian, *Neither to Laugh nor to Weep,* 77. According to a German physician the malaria in the Amanus was especially serious. He estimated that up to 100 percent of the workers were infected. Insufficient provisions and inadequate

health care, together with hard working conditions, increased the number of victims even more. The efforts of engineers to improve the conditions were insufficient. See Viktor Schilling, "Über die schwere cilicische Malaria," *Archiv für Schiffs- und Tropen-Hygiene* 23 (1919): 475–98; and his *Kriegshygienische Erfahrungen in der Türkei* (*Cilicien, Nordsyrien*) (Leipzig: J. A. Barth, 1921), 34–35.

76. Köppel told Elmajian: "Now listen, go over and watch them. Just see that they use the hammer, whether they break the stones or not doesn't matter. Never mind how many stones they break or how many pebbles they can prepare. Just see that they move the hammer, hitting the stone." Eflatoon E. Elmajian, *In the Shadow of the Almighty: My Life Story* (Pasadena, Calif.: N.p., 1982), 64; Balakian, *Hai Goghgotan,* 20.

77. Davidson, *Odyssey of an Armenian of Zeitoun,* 98–101; Hovsep Der-Vartanian, *Intilli-Airani Spande, 1916: Mut Mnatsats Ech Me Mets Eghernen* (The slaughter of Entilli-Airan, 1916: A page remaining dark from the Great Catastrophe) (Jerusalem: St. James Press, 1928), 15.

78. BOA, DH.ŞFR, 59/277, Talaat to Aleppo province, January 11, 1916, EUM Spec. 197; DH.ŞFR, 60/45, Talaat to Aleppo, Adana, Konia, Angora provinces, Eskişehir, İzmit districts, January 16, 1916, EUM Spec. 6618 (OBE no. 164); DH.ŞFR, 60/157, Talaat to Adana, Aleppo provinces, January 29, 1916, EUM Spec.1; DH.ŞFR, 60/274, Talaat to Adana, Aleppo provinces, Maraş district, EUM; DH.ŞFR, 61/1, Talaat to Aleppo, Adana provinces, February 14, 1916, EUM Gen. 42564; DH.ŞFR, 61/17, Talaat to Djemal Pasha, February 15, 1916, EUM Gen. 42595 Spec. 150; DH.ŞFR, 61/128, Talaat to Aleppo, Adana provinces, February 27, 1916, EUM Gen. 43128; DH.ŞFR, 63/96, Talaat to Angora, Konia, Aleppo, Adana, Hüdâvendigâr provinces, İzmit, Eskişehir, Karahisâr-ı Sâhib, Kütahya, Niğde districts, April 25, 1916, EUM Gen. 45798 Spec. 135; DH.ŞFR, 63/75, Nazir to Maraş district, April 22, 1916, EUM (OBE no. 174). It is important to note that like in the case of the number of Armenian deportees, previously given, the documents from Ottoman Ministry of the Interior cited here confirm to some degree the contents of two other telegrams ascribed to Talaat in Andonian's book. Thus, the dating of telegram nos. 840 and 860 as January 1916 appears to be correct. Therefore, it seems that Andonian or Naim Bey did not misdate these telegrams as Dadrian supposes. See "The Naim-Andonian Documents," 316–17 (nos. 32, 38), and Andonian, *Documents officiels,* 49–51. Şinasi Orel and Süreyya Yuca, who have argued that Andonian had forged his material, did not consider the sources under scrutiny here. Thus, their thesis is to be put into question and further research on the "Naim-Andonian" documents is necessary. See Şinasi Orel and Süreyya Yuca, *The Talât Pasha Telegrams: Historical Fact or Armenian Fiction?* (Nicosia: K. Rustem and Brother, 1986).

79. BOA, DH.ŞFR, 62/191, Talaat to Aleppo province, April 1, 1916 DH. Kalem-i Mahsusu 17; DH.ŞFR, 63/23, Talaat to Angora, Konia, Hüdâvendigâr, Adana, Aleppo provinces, İzmit, Eskişehir, Karahisâr-ı Sâhib, Kütahya, Niğde districts, April 17, 1916, EUM Gen. 45454; DH.ŞFR, 63/119,Talaat to Konia province,

April 16, 1916, EUM Spec. 644 (OBE no. 176); DH.ŞFR, 63/259, Talaat to Aleppo, Adana provinces, May 9, 1916, EUM Gen. 46469; DH.ŞFR, 64/104, Talaat to Adana province, May 22, 1916, EUM Spec. 41; DB—HA, Or 464, Mavrogordato to Holzmann Co., July 11, 1916, DB—HA, Or 464, Grages to Riese, July 16, 1916.
80. DB—HA, Or 1704, Winkler to Baudirektion, June 19, 1916.
81. Balakian, *Hai Goghgotan,* 31–32.
82. AA—PA, TR 183/43, A 18208, Niepage, Gräter to Bethmann Hollweg, July 8, 1916. The appeal was also printed and circulated privately. See Niepage, *Ein Wort an die berufenen Vertreter,* 13.
83. DB—HA, Or 463, Winkler to Günther, June 14, 1916, and Winkler to Günther, June 15 1916, encl. in Günther to Verwaltungsrat, June 16, 1916; Balakian, *Hai Goghgotan,* 41, 43, 48–49; Hartunian, *Neither to Laugh nor to Weep,* 85–89.
84. DB—HA, Or 463, Metternich to AA, June 19, 1916; Or 1704, Winkler to Baghdad Railway Co., July 3, 1916; Balakian, *Hai Goghgotan,* 50.
85. DB—HA, Or 1704, Winkler to Baudirektion, June 19, 1916; Morf, Winkler to Direktion, June 18, 1916.
86. AA—PA, TR 152/87, A 17235, Falkenhayn to Jagow, June 29, 1916; Großes Hauptquartier Türkei, 41a–e, Jagow to Treutler, July 4, 1916, transmitting report of Metternich. Later, Refik Bey, railway expert in the Ottoman General Staff, told Winkler that Enver had not carefully read the draft before signing it. DB—HA, Or 1704, Winkler to Riese, July 7, 1916; AA—PA, TR 152/87, A 16479, Metternich to AA, June 21, 1916; TR 152/87, A 16478, Neurath to AA, June 21, 1916; Or 463, Neeff, June 16, 1916; Trumpener, *Germany and the Ottoman Empire,* 306.
87. AA—PA, TR 152/87, A 16815, Metternich to AA, June 15, 1916.
88. DB—HA, Or 464, Winkler to Generaldirektion, June 27, 1916, Balakian, *Hai Goghgotan,* 58–59.
89. "The following morning we noticed a crowd of men, women, and children moving off along the road and looking very wretched. Our guards said that these were Armenians who had been working on the line, but were being taken away to make room for our troops, who would be set to work in their place; they also added that these Armenians would be marched off into a waterless spot in the hills, and kept there till they died." Harry Coghill Watson Bishop, *A Kut Prisoner* (London: John Lane and Co., 1920), 70.
90. DB—HA, Or 1704, Winkler to Riese, July 7, 1916. Winkler found that Refik Bey, a railway expert, was quite ignorant of the organization of a railway.
91. DB—HA, Or 1704, Winkler to Riese, June 28, 1916. Winkler's statements were confirmed by Görke, an expert of the German military. AA—PA, Großes Hauptquartier Türkei, 41a–e, A 18132, Görke to Bevollmächtigten Generalstabsoffizier des Deutschen Feldeisenbahnchefs Konstantinopel, July 1, 1916; A 19974, Großer Krieg Türkei, 41c, encl. in Metternich to Bethmann Hollweg, July 7, 1916.
92. The railway directors must have gathered from Winkler's evasive comments that the number of Armenian workers was significantly higher than admitted.

Winkler was obviously depending on a tacit mutual agreement in this matter. DB—HA, Or 1704, Winkler to Baudirektion, June 19, 1916, and Winkler to Riese, June 28, 1916. Balakian, *Hai Goghgotan,* 49, 86, estimated the number of deportees to be 11,000, out of 11,500 Armenian workers. Hartunian, *Neither to Laugh nor to Weep,* 83, estimated the Armenian labor force at 12,000. Schäfer estimated the two convoys she had met at 7,000 persons. See Sommer, *Die Wahrheit über die Leiden,* 32–33. A report of the U.S. embassy in Constantinople estimated the number of Armenian workers at 9,000–11,000. The diplomats had possibly received this information from the Ottoman Ministry of Foreign Affairs, NA RG 59, 867.4016/291, Philip to Secretary of State, July 21, 1916, no. 1973. Other estimates of deportees was to be 21,000 Armenian survivors. Archives diplomatiques du Ministère des Affaires Étrangères, Nantes (hereafter MAÉ/Nantes), Beyrouth, carton 130, Yirekian et al. to Military Governor of Baghche, July 21, 1919, and carton 137, Hovnanian, Kabayan, Gueukdjian, December 20, 1918.

93. Some of the workers had been hidden by German officials. See, for example, Elmajian, *In the Shadow of the Almighty,* 65–66; DB—HA, Or 463, Neurath to AA, June 29, 1916; Or 464, Winkler to Grages, July 7, 1916. The last to leave were the specialists whose families were deported from Marash and Killis. See AA—PA, Konst. 279, J. I 1574, Grages to Metternich, July 20, 1916.
94. Refik had been the second director of the Ottoman military railway department under Böttrich. Therefore, he understood well the company's strategies to save their Armenian workers. Refik labeled these initiatives as "unpatriotic." See DB—HA, Or 1704, Winkler to Riese, July 7, 1916.
95. Talaat ordered the dispatch of workers from Smyrna to the Taurus construction sites. BOA, DH.ŞFR, 66/196, Talaat to Aydın province, August 6, 1916, EUM.
96. Refik's statement is confirmed by an order from the Ministry of War to the province of Adana. No Armenians were to return and during future deportations from the Amanus and Taurus, interruptions in the work were to be avoided. BOA, DH.ŞFR, 65/59, Talaat to Adana province, June 22, 1916, Kalem-i Mahsus no. 52. See also Balakian, *Hai Goghgotan,* 50.
97. DB—HA, Or 1704, Winkler to Riese, July 7, 1916. All evidence contradicts Winkler's statement on the return of deportees. He may have been bluffing to test Refik.
98. MAÉ/Nantes, Beyrouth, carton 137, Hovnanian, Kabayan, Gueukdjian, December 20, 1918. This report contains abundant evidence of single perpetrators. On the participation of CUP members, local administrators, and Muslim clergy, see carton 130, André to Administrateur en Chef, n.d., Sandjak du Djebel Bérékét; on the role of Muslim villagers, see Hartunian, *Neither to Laugh nor to Weep,* 93–94.
99. Der-Vartanian, *Intilli-Airani Spande,* 24, 27, 32–33, 34, 35; Davidson, *Odyssey of an Armenian of Zeitoun,* 106–7; Hartunian, *Neither to Laugh nor to Weep,* 90; AA—PA, TR 152/89, A 19650, Khatschadurian to Rohner, July 9, 1916, encl. in Rössler to Bethmann Hollweg, July 10, 1916.

100. Davidson, *Odyssey of an Armenian of Zeitoun,* 116; Der-Vartanian, *Intilli-Airani Spande,* 24, 27; Hartunian, *Neither to Laugh nor to Weep,* 91. Andonian, *Documents officiels,* 52, estimated the number of Armenian young men who were massacred at the outset of the deportation at 1,800.
101. Der-Vartanian, *Intilli-Airani Spande,* 42; Balakian, *Hai Goghgotan,* 48. A British prisoner of war, however, still saw corpses lying close to the main road over the Amanus. See Edward Herbert Keeling, *Adventures in Turkey and Russia* (London: John Murray, 1924), 40; Bishop, *A Kut Prisoner,* 70.
102. The deportees of this convoy were comparably lucky. "It was made up mostly of widows, old folks, the weak, children, left-overs." The governor of Marash, who resisted CUP extermination designs, was protecting the deportees in his jurisdiction: "The gendarmes who had brought us from Baghtche were now sent back. The good Ismayale Kemal Pasha had appointed new ones and had told them that I was in this group. They had strict orders to take our convoy to Aintab safely. But beyond that, toward Biredjik, toward Der-el-Zor, the slaughterhouse, he had no jurisdiction." Hartunian, *Neither to Laugh nor to Weep,* 89, 98. Hartunian's statement on the governor of Marash seems to be confirmed by an official Ottoman document. In April 1916, Talaat ordered Djemal Pasha to inquire into the governor's performance, as the latter was suspected of helping Armenians. BOA, DH.ŞFR, 63/100, Talaat to Djemal Pasha, April 25, 1916, EUM Gen. 45797 Spec. 24. Survivors estimated the number of deportees murdered between Baghche and Marash to be more than 2,500, out of 21,000 deportees; MAÉ/Nantes, Beyrouth, carton 130, Yirekian et al. to Military Governor of Baghche, July 21, 1919.
103. AA—PA, TR 152/89, A 19650, Khatschadurian to Rohner, July 9, 1916, encl. in Rössler to Bethmann Hollweg, July 10, 1916. Davidson had been warned by a friendly gendarme not to cross the Euphrates if he wanted to live. See Davidson, *Odyssey of an Armenian of Zeitoun,* 120–22; Künzler, *Im Lande des Blutes,* 76–77.
104. AA—PA, TR 183/44, A 21969, Schäfer to Peet, July 13, 1916, in Rössler to Bethmann Hollweg, July 29, 1916; Sommer, *Die Wahrheit über die Leiden,* 32–33; Balakian, *Hai Goghgotan,* 53–54; Hartunian, *Neither to Laugh nor to Weep,* 95–100. Naim Bey and Andonian, too, credit Köppel with special efforts to save his Armenian employees and their families. He hid Armenian orphans in empty dynamite boxes. According to Andonian, *Documents officiels,* 51, 52–53, Köppel was reprimanded by his superiors for his actions a few days later.
105. Talaat's order to deport the Armenian workers was confirmed to the U.S. embassy by the Ottoman Foreign Ministry. On the motives behind this order an American diplomat recorded that "Minister of Foreign Affairs admitted to me that this had been done to prevent the concentrating of Armenians. He added that these people were hiding and thought that employment with the Germans would save them from further molestation." NA RG 59, 867.4016/291, Philip to Secretary of State, July 21, 1916.
106. BOA, DH.ŞFR, 65/38, Talaat to Maraş district, June 20, 1916, EUM. As in the case for the deportation of the railway workers, the Marash deportation

was carefully prepared. On April 17, 1916 Talaat ordered an exact count of all Armenians in Marash, DH.ŞFR, 63/22, Talaat to Maraş district, EUM Spec. 6. Moreover, Talaat wished to know how many Catholics and Protestants were left in Marash, DH.ŞFR, 63/40, Talaat to Maraş district, April 18, 1916, EUM Gen. 45494 Spec. 5. The Catholic Armenians were allowed to remain in Marash, DH.ŞFR, 63/76, Talaat to Maraş district, April 22, 1916, EUM Spec.590. About a month after the deportation, Talaat asked for the exact numbers of deported Armenians before and after Avni's arrival, DH.ŞFR, 66/65, Talaat to Maraş district, July 25, 1916, EUM Spec.1626. Presumably, the mission of Avni had been necessitated by the refusal of the governor of Marash to obey the deportation orders. During the preceding months, the governor had repeatedly assisted Armenians. See Hartunian, *Neither to Laugh nor to Weep,* 73, 99.

107. Raymond H. Kévorkian, "Recueil de témoignages sur l'extermination des amele tabouri ou bataillons de soldats- ouvriers arméniens de l'armée ottomane," *Revue d'histoire arménienne contemporaine* 1 (1995): 289–303.

108. AA—PA, TR 183/43, A 18548, Metternich to Bethmann Hollweg, July 10, 1916; TR 183/44, A 21969, Rössler to Bethmann Hollweg, July 29, 1916. Armenian women who had survived a march from Adana to Mardin were ordered to go to Deir-el-Zor, too. DH.ŞFR, 66/21, Talaat to Diarbekir province, July 18, 1916, EUM Gen.49557 Spec.39. In October 1916 Wegner saw on his journey from Baghdad to Aleppo along the Euphrates the last Armenian survivors. Close to the river near Meskene he found a pile of human bones. See *Der Weg ohne Heimkehr,* 164–67.

109. Kiesling, *Orientfahrten,* 6–7; Oberstltn. a.D. Raith, "Deutschtum in Persien," *Mitteilungen des Bundes der Asienkämpfer* 11 (1929): 107–8.

110. MAÉ/Nantes, Beyrouth, carton no. 137, Hovnanian, Kabayan, Gueukdjian, December 20, 1918. The copy of the affidavit utilized here is deposited at the French Foreign Office archives in Nantes. Dadrian quoted from a copy now preserved in the Nubarian Library in Paris. A full discussion of Dadrian's theses on von der Goltz's role in the Armenian Genocide is beyond the scope of the present article. From the available evidence, however, it seems doubtful that von der Goltz was involved in the events at Osmanieh.

4
Finishing the Genocide
Cleansing Turkey of Armenian Survivors, 1920–1923

LEVON MARASHLIAN

Between 1920 and 1923, as Turkish and Western diplomats were negotiating the fate of the Armenian Question at peace conferences in London, Paris, and Lausanne, thousands of Armenians of the Ottoman Empire who had survived the massacres and deportations of World War I continued to face massacres, deportations, and persecutions across the length and breadth of Anatolia.[1] Events on the ground, diplomatic correspondence, and news reports confirmed that it was the policy of the Turkish Nationalists in Angora, who eventually founded the Republic of Turkey, to eradicate the remnants of the empire's Armenian population and finalize the expropriation of their public and private properties.

Expropriation of Armenian Properties

At the core of the policy to eliminate the Armenian survivors was the question of how to redistribute the enormous wealth that had been expropriated by the old Ottoman government. The nascent Nationalist government of the embryonic Turkish Republic took legislative and physical actions to confiscate even more properties and to hold on to the properties that had been seized during World War I.

Government agencies and individuals had taken possession of large amounts of land, houses, churches and other structures as well as all kinds of goods and personal effects, down to the clothing off people's backs, on the basis of a law passed in May 1915: "The Regulations Concerning the

Management of the Land and Properties Belonging to Armenians Who Have Been Sent Elsewhere as a Result of the State of War and the Extraordinary Political Situation."[2] The thirty-four articles of this legislative fig leaf, commonly known as the "Abandoned Properties Law," specified protective steps the authorities were supposed to take, such as: "Following the evacuation of a village or district, all buildings with furniture and other objects belonging to the Armenians who have been sent elsewhere" will be "immediately sealed" and "taken under protection." The names of "the owners of the goods" and their type, amount, and value, were to be registered in a detailed way. "Later on, these goods will be sent to convenient storage places such as churches, schools, and houses. Care will be taken to catalogue the goods under the names of their owners." The "type and amount of the goods, the name of their owners, where they are found and protected will be included in registration records, the original copy of which will be preserved at the local government and a ratified copy" at the Commission for Abandoned Properties. "Care will be taken to preserve the goods, pictures and holy books found at the churches in their original places after they are registered and listed. Later on, the local governments will send these belongings to the places where the population is resettled."

Compared with all the space devoted to movable goods in several articles, the article pertaining to real estate was among the shortest: "The type, quantity or number and values of goods and land deserted by the population will be registered in a book and the lists of abandoned properties and land will be drawn up for every village and district and they will be delivered to the administrative commission." Future income from Armenian assets was also accounted for: "In the case of a crop to be harvested from an abandoned field, it will be sold at an auction by a council consisting of members appointed by the commission. The money received as a result of the sale will be preserved at the financial office in the name of the previous owner. A record will be prepared and its original copy will be preserved at the local government and a ratified copy given to the administrative commission."[3]

Although an examination of such detailed records of Armenian assets and accrued income would help indicate whether the government succeeded in carrying out the seemingly reasonable provisions of the Abandoned Properties Law, detailed records of the disposition of Armenian properties are not readily available. On the other hand, there is strong evidence from American and European sources that belies the supposedly solicitous spirit of the Abandoned Properties Law. A typical example is a report to the American Embassy in Constantinople from the American consul in Trebizond, Oscar S. Heizer, in July 1915:

> The 1,000 Armenian houses are being emptied of furniture by the police one after the other. The furniture, bedding and everything of value is being stored in large buildings about the city. There is no attempt at classification and the idea of keeping the property in "bales under the protection of the government to be returned to the owners on their return" is simply ridiculous. The goods are piled in without any attempt at labeling or systematic storage. A crowd of Turkish women and children follow the police about like a lot of vultures and seize anything they can lay their hands on and when the more valuable things are carried out of the house by the police they rush in and take the balance. I see this performance every day with my own eyes. I suppose it will take several weeks to empty all the houses and then the Armenian shops and stores will be cleared out. The commission which has the matter in hand is now talking of selling the great collection of household goods and property in order to pay the debts of the Armenians. The German Consul told me that he did not believe the Armenians would be permitted to return to Trebizond after the war.[4]

The German ambassador in Constantinople, Paul von Wolff-Metternich, reported in June 1916 that deportations were continuing, but "the hungry wolves" of the ruling Ittihad ve Terakki party "can no longer expect anything from these unhappy people except the satisfaction of their fanatic rage for persecution." The goods of the Armenians "have long since been confiscated, and their capital has been liquidated by a so-called commission, which means that if an Armenian owned a house valued at, say, £T100, a Turk—a friend or member [of the Ittihad ve Terakki]—could have it for around £T2."[5]

Most of the remaining articles in the Abandoned Properties Law dealt with the process of distributing, rather than registering, the properties of the deported Armenians:

> Migrants [Muslims] will be resettled in evacuated villages and the existing houses and the land will be distributed to the migrants through temporary documents. . . . Following the resettlement of the migrants, the nomads will be resettled in the remaining villages in the region. . . . Vineyards, orchards, olive groves and similar places in towns and villages may be distributed to those migrants. Income providing buildings such as shops, inns, factories, and depots as well as the ones which are not suitable for the resettlement of the migrants and the ones remaining following the resettlement of all the migrants . . . may be offered for sale by the administrative commission or . . . officials under the supervision of the commission. . . . Detailed lists will be prepared in order to show the type, quantity, place, rent, and the names of the tenants or new owners of both the sold or leased property and the land by underbidding. . . . The sum received as a result of the sale will be trusted to

> the financial offices in the name of the original [Armenian] owners and it will be paid to the owner according to the information to be given later.[6]

In the absence of evidence that these protective measures were actually carried out, perhaps the best commentary on the legality and implementation of the Abandoned Properties Law is Senator Ahmed Riza's courageous condemnation on the floor of the Ottoman Senate in December 1915: "It is unlawful to designate the Armenian assets and properties as 'abandoned goods' [*emvali metruke*] for the Armenians, the proprietors, did not abandon their properties voluntarily; they were forcibly, compulsively [*zorla, cebren*] removed from their domiciles and exiled. Now the government through its officials is selling their goods. . . . Nobody can sell my property if I am unwilling to sell it. This is atrocious. Grab my arm, eject me from my village, then sell my goods and properties, such a thing can never be permissible. Neither the conscience of the Ottomans nor the law can allow it."[7]

After the Turkish defeat in World War I, restitution for property losses along with territorial claims were championed in Europe by the representative of the Republic of Armenia, Avetis Aharonian, and the head of the Armenian National Delegation, Boghos Nubar Pasha, who spoke for the surviving Ottoman Armenians and the Armenians in the diaspora.[8] At the Paris Peace Conference in 1919, they submitted a financial claim totaling nearly $3.7 billion, of which $2.18 billion was for various types of properties. Most of the total losses claimed were for Turkish Armenia.[9]

The task of recovering at least some of these losses, as well as rescuing Armenians who had been taken into Turkish homes, was the challenge of the remnants of the virtually destroyed Ottoman-Armenian community. The postwar period saw the re-creation of organized community life in Constantinople by a variety of political, social, and cultural groups. The Apostolic Armenians reorganized themselves on the basis of the Armenian Constitution of 1863, which provided for an Armenian National Assembly made up of religious and secular representatives, and the Political Council. Four informal elections were held from 1919 to 1922, producing national administrations that dealt with a wide spectrum of affairs. Political parties created the League of the Armenian Parties to coordinate political work, while several compatriotic societies cooperated in relief activity. Cultural organizations included the Armenian Women's Association and various theatrical groups, while educational and professional organizations included the Teachers Union, the Educational Council, the Women's Educational Auxiliary, and the Armenian Physicians Union. The Armenian press experienced a brief revival in the postwar years, despite attempts by the government to censor anti-Turkish stories and restrict the number of new publications.[10]

The Armenian Mixed Council, made up of religious and lay members, was organized by the Apostolic, Protestant, and Catholic denominations to represent the whole Armenian community before the Ottoman government and the Allied High Commissioners. The Mixed Council handled a range of internal issues—administration of a national budget, location of missing relatives and restitution of property, and responding to problems in the provinces. An information bureau was established, which briefly published a newspaper called *Renaissance,* released some 290 documents pertaining to Ottoman officials responsible for the wartime deportations and massacres, and prepared 300 reports on Turkish treatment of the Armenians since the Mudros Armistice (October 30, 1918), for use by the Allied High Commissioners and Armenian representatives.[11]

The national administrations also managed relations with the new Ottoman government. Rather than negotiate directly, the majority of the community leadership wished to wait for the Allies' peace settlement, but Turkish leaders hoped to preempt the peace treaty. In early 1919, Grand Vizier Damad Ferid Pasha approached Patriarch Zaven (Eghiayan) twice through an Armenian intermediary for a rapprochement, but Zaven responded that in view of the unrepentant Turkish attitude, this would not be possible unless the government would agree not to oppose the territorial claims Armenians were making at the peace conference.[12]

Although the Armenians reached an accord of sorts with Kurdish leaders, whose claims had an impact on Armenian claims, coming to a direct agreement with the Turks was not considered a serious option in those heady days when newspapers were consistently headlining the Armenian case.[13] Before leaving Constantinople for the Paris Peace Conference, Damad Ferid asked Ottoman Senator Aghopian Efendi to send word to former Ottoman Foreign Minister Gabriel Noradoungian that he would like to see him in Paris. Aghopian informed Noradoungian that the Turkish leader's purpose was to bring about a "rapprochement between the Turks and Armenians, in order to resolve the Armenians Question." Noradoungian recalled that Ferid Pasha wished to meet "particularly if I were to speak to him as an official of the Armenian nation." When the grand vizier arrived in Paris, Noradoungian went to see him "as an old acquaintance, especially since I held pleasant memories of him." Damad Ferid "still was, in fact, a kind and decent man."

Although a member of the Armenian National Delegation, Noradoungian said he had no right to speak "officially" for the Armenian people. He just wanted to let Ferid know "under what circumstance and from whose side the Armenian Question originated; but Ferid interrupted me almost immediately" when the Ittihad ve Terakki party came up. " 'You don't know what mischief they wrought upon the Armenians,' " Damad Ferid interjected. " 'If I were to begin telling you. . . .' "

Noradoungian stopped him. "I know, I know, and much better than you could know." According to Noradoungian, Ferid was surprised at the extent to which the destruction of the Armenians was known to the outside world. Noradoungian explained that since the early part of the war "the whole world press, almost without exception, was preoccupied with the Armenian deportations and massacres. The press is still concerned with it even to the present day, constantly publishing column after column of articles and reports in quite horrifying detail." Throughout "the world, even in the most distant countries, there has developed today a very unfavorable public opinion regarding Turks and their leaders." Those "crimes" had been recounted in numerous books as well as in the press. Noradoungian said he could put together "a small library." Ferid thought "for a long while and said, 'De sene boşuna geldik.' " ("Don't tell me I came for nothing.") Yes, Noradoungian answered, "I'm afraid that's the way it is."

After this exchange, "there was no more talk" of rapprochement. According to Noradoungian, Damad Ferid, "who undoubtedly knew a great deal about the Armenian atrocities," probably thought that "if those dreadful events were really common knowledge—and he did not doubt my assurances on the matter—it would be completely useless for Armenians and Turks to think about a rapprochement. We merely groped for old memories to talk about for a little while, and I bid him farewell."[14]

Placing all their political eggs in the diplomatic basket of the victorious Allies, the Armenians worked on recovering what they had lost in Anatolia. The obstacles confronting the reconstituted community in Constantinople were formidable. In February 1920, Armenian religious leaders submitted to the Supreme Council in Paris a memorandum claiming that Turks had destroyed approximately 2,000 churches and 200 monasteries and related properties. The patriarch of Constantinople demanded restitution of these ecclesiastic properties as well as payment—as stipulated by the Abandoned Properties Law—for four years of accrued income from them. Apparently the Ottoman government did not respond. Meanwhile, a British High Commission report corroborated several related difficulties. They included the Ottoman government's refusal to compel Muslims to return property acquired through intimidation, forcing Christians to buy back their own confiscated livestock, and continued possession of Christian properties by the Agricultural Bank and other official institutions.[15]

The British pressured the postwar Ottoman government to enact a new law concerning properties. Although the British had urged that Armenian and Greek property still held by Turks should be returned to the victims' heirs or to the respective national communities when no surviving heir existed, the Turkish version of the law stipulated that immovable properties for which no heir existed would revert to the state, while only less valuable (and generally untraceable) movable properties without heirs would revert to the national communities. The stipulation that appeals would be heard by the Turkish Ministry of Finance, rather than by a mixed Turkish-Allied-Armenian commission, further diluted the meaningfulness of the Turkish version.[16]

Even these limited provisions were not properly implemented. Although a representative of the Ottoman Ministry of Interior continued coming to the British embassy to sit on the Mixed Commission set up in 1919 to handle property disputes, the British High Commissioner in Constantinople, Sir Horace Rumbold, reported in April 1922 that for "a considerable time" the commission's work had been "hampered at every turn by the unwillingness of the Turkish authorities to recognize or give effect" to the Turkish representative's own decisions.[17]

While the stragglers of the old Ottoman regime were dragging their feet over the return of "abandoned" properties, the leaders of the ascendant Nationalist regime, led by Mustafa Kemal Pasha, were introducing a new set of confiscatory measures. In April 1922, the British Foreign Office confirmed that "the Kemalist authorities were about to decree that the property of Armenians who have fled the country will be confiscated if not reclaimed within three months." Rumbold reported to London that on April 22, 1922, the Grand National Assembly in Angora passed a law concerning the "confiscation of property of absent owners in the liberated districts of Anatolia," which "is in itself an aggravated reproduction" of the Abandoned Properties Law of 1915, "which was declared null and void under Article 144 of the Treaty of Sèvres" signed on August 10, 1920.[18]

In May 1922, the Ministry of Interior in Angora issued a statement that tried to refute the charges made by Americans and Europeans that the government was robbing the Armenians. By issuing this statement, however, the Nationalist government—as distinct from the Ottoman government—actually implicated itself in the question of property confiscation because it accepted responsibility for an accounting of the records: "The Grand

National Assembly by a law which it enacted leases by public auction, through a public custodian the property left by the Armenians and deposits the rents received from such houses to the credit of their owners. No confiscation whatever of any such property has been made. . . . The right of inheritance of the Christians is not restricted. They are on the same footing in this respect as the Mohammedans. This can be verified by consulting the files of the government. . . . No Turkish official is guilty of enriching himself at the expense of the Christians."[19] Angora's explanation bore no resemblance to the reality on the ground as described by third-party observers. Its assurances could not be "verified by consulting the files of the government" since those files were not made available. In the meantime, all the existing evidence indicated that the pattern of confiscation begun in 1915 continued into 1922 and even accelerated up to and through the Lausanne Peace Conference in 1923.

Recovery of Armenian Captives

Whereas attempts at reclaiming properties produced little result, the relief activities of the reorganized Armenian community and American Near East Relief (NER) and other agencies were quite extensive and succeeded in providing for hundreds of thousands of refugees, many of them orphans.[20] Nevertheless, relief workers had to struggle against Turkish government resistance.

The recovery of Armenians who were captive in Turkish households and orphanages was a major problem, and efforts to gain their release met with only partial success. In late 1919, Patriarch Zaven had demanded that the government take measures to secure the release of captive Armenians. In January 1920, the minister of interior instructed provincial authorities to cooperate in releasing Christian orphans and ordered the dissolution of forced mixed marriages. There is no indication, however, that this order was any more effective than similar rulings made earlier. A NER worker charged in a March 1920 report that women were being sold in a slave market near Constantinople. The fate of Armenians in the custody of nomadic tribes was mixed. Large bribes were required to release children, while in some cases Kurdish chieftains willingly offered to release hundreds of Armenian women and children they said they had protected from the Turks during the war.[21]

The Turks denied charges that Armenians were being held against their will. They even countercharged that many of the children recovered by Armenians and Allied personnel were actually Turks. A British High Commission official branded such claims ridiculous in view of the fact that

Armenian orphanages were already incapable of providing for the thousands of Armenian children under their care and therefore had no reason to take in Turkish children. To settle disputed cases, the British instructed the Armenians to set up a neutral house, supported by Americans and staffed with Turks and Armenians, where children of uncertain nationality could be identified. Nevertheless, the Turkish representative, Nezihe Hanum, resigned after three months, charging that Turkish children were being Armenianized.[22] Nezihe, who was also general secretary of the women's section of the Turkish Red Crescent, told the well-known Turkish activist Halidé Edib that her presence on the committee "did not help the Turkish children, who were being Armenianized daily." Nezihe claimed that the children were left in the care of Armenian women who, "either by persuasion or threats or hypnotism, forced Turkish children to learn by heart the name of an Armenian woman for their mother and the name of an Armenian man for their father." When children in large numbers were brought from Anatolian orphanages, wrote Edib, they were taken to the Armenian church at Kum Kapu, "a hot-pot which boiled the Turkish children and dished them out as Armenians."[23]

Yet Edib herself acknowledged that Turkish orphanages had indeed "taken in Armenian children as well and made them Moslems (which was wrong)." The "rest of the Armenian orphans" were taken in by Americans. "Apart from this, some Turkish families had taken Armenian children out of kindness and pity without any desire to make them Moslems: for the Moslem Turks do not have the missionary instincts of the Christians of the West. That Armenians should want their children back from these orphanages, and that the British should help them, was very natural."[24] Halidé Edib's implication that Turkish families who took in Armenian children did not want to convert them is contradicted by the testimonies of survivors. Oral history interviews confirm the fact that Islamization was a routine requirement, and that Armenians who retained any semblance of Christianity or Armenian identity did so largely by stealth and luck.[25]

Edib's accusation that there was a wholesale attempt to take Turkish children is undermined by the fact that there were only a few isolated cases where children were removed from Armenian and Allied custody on the basis of their being Turks. According to the American High Commission, only fourteen Turkish orphans were removed from among the 750 children at the Armenian orphanage at Kum Kapu, while heavier searches by Turkish officials among the nearly 3,000 children in the custody of the Armenian Relief Committee resulted in only ten children removed as Turks. The Armenian patriarch, in the meantime, claimed in late 1921 that half the children in Turkish orphanages were actually Armenian.[26]

According to NER, 10,000 Armenian women were recovered from harems by late 1919. The British High Commission announced that it had recovered 2,300 Armenian orphans by late 1920. These were in addition to the uncounted others voluntarily released by Turks and freed through indirect influence. Armenian authorities reported that in Constantinople, 3,000 of the estimated 4,000 to 5,000 captive Armenian orphans had been rescued by late 1921. They also claimed that approximately 100,000 Armenian orphans were still unrecovered, mostly in the interior *vilayets.*[27] Edib ignored the actual numbers and wrote that although Turkish orphanages "had taken in Armenian children as well," they were mostly "filled with Turkish children whose parents had been victims of the Armenians."[28] Edib's distorted description of the situation may be explained by a confidential American High Commission intelligence report's characterization of the Turkish activist as a "chauvinist" who was "trying to rehabilitate Turkey."[29] The search for captives went on, but Turkish officials continued to hamper the recovery process. In Kharput, in March 1922, for example, the Turkish relief supervisor prohibited American orphanages from accepting children over age 15, which left some Christian girls no choice but to return to Muslim masters.[30]

Resumption of Persecutions, Massacres, and Deportations

Although the Turks tried to hold on to captive Armenian children who had lived under Muslim roofs, the intent of the Nationalists to eliminate the adult Christian population completely became more and more apparent in 1920 and 1921. The Armenians of the Cilicia region along the Mediterranean Sea were the first to feel the brunt of the renewed policy of persecution.

In sharp contrast to the pervasive pro-Armenian sympathies in the United States and the large-scale efforts of numerous Americans to save Armenian lives, the American High Commissioner in Constantinople, Rear Admiral Mark Lambert Bristol, directly and indirectly facilitated Angora's policy—in order to fulfill his obsessive desire to advance commercial interests. Bristol and the State Department received word of renewed atrocities, but the admiral's reports "tended to exonerate the Turks." When C. H. Van Engert, a High Commission representative at Beirut, reported to the State Department in February 1920 that the Turks had massacred some 5,000 Armenians in Cilicia, Bristol quickly cabled the Department that "Armenians are not being massacred by the Turks." This was more than the Department "could comprehend," so Bristol was asked for a clarification: "Last paragraph 'Armenians not being massacred by the Turks' is not clear. Engert's report from Beirut and other reports agree that several thousand have been massacred. Do you mean massacres have now ceased?"[31]

Bristol professed that Engert had not checked his sources; if he had, he would have seen that they were Armenian, and therefore could not be trusted. "Bristol explained that the native races in the Near East could not distinguish truth from falsehood, hence the job of all Americans was to rely only on American sources of information."[32] Bristol chose to distrust native Armenian sources, yet he tended to trust the equally native Turkish sources. He even minimized, downplayed, or completely ignored even American evidence that corroborated Armenian witnesses and European reports that Armenians were again being massacred.[33] Try as he might, Bristol's subterfuge became futile as American evidence of renewed massacres began to mount. In March, Bristol's flagship sent him an ominous radio report: "Trouble" was expected in seacoast towns, there was fighting in the interior, and Christians were being killed "in villages outside Mersena." It was rumored that thousands of Turkish Nationalist troops were assembled at Konia to attack Adana.[34] A radio dispatch from American officials at Adana in April 1920 outlined the pitiful plight of 3,000 Armenian orphans and the necessity for a prompt American response to save their lives. "Immediate action" was imperative: "delay may be fatal."[35]

As American evidence increasingly pointed to more serious and large-scale atrocities, the manner in which Bristol forwarded the information to Washington changed in a subtle way. Bristol no longer tried to hide what the Turks were doing. He simply sent the somber information to Washington verbatim, with no comment at all. One such dispatch, which he forwarded without comment, was a June 12 cable from Beirut in which Bristol's American source summarized a June 1 report by U.S. Consul Jesse B. Jackson on the situation in the Aintab area. The French had offered to transport 15,000 persons to the town of Killis, but Armenians considered this "outrageous and decided to remain and defend" themselves and their property. The Americans in Aintab sent a petition to the French authorities describing the "gravity of the situation," which in effect violated the terms of a recently concluded French-Turkish agreement, which had provided for the protection of Armenians. According to Jackson: "Unless the world is to hear of one of the worst horrors in its history within fifteen or twenty days at the utmost something drastic must be done at once to save the situation. Fifteen thousand souls will surely perish in the most blood curdling terrifying manner if these people are turned over to the Turks."[36]

Another cable from Beirut two hours later cited reports from Marash that the Armenians were in a "precarious situation," being "threatened by Turks who are preventing" the opening of their shops and their work in the fields. There were periodic "disappearances of individuals" and "terrorizing" of the Armenian population. One relief station, Port Royal East, was feeding 5,000 refugees.[37]

Despite all the unmistakable warnings from American observers, and even though Bristol himself acknowledged that conditions in Cilicia were "growing worse," the Admiral remained unmoved.[38] As part of his campaign to promote American economic interests in Anatolia, he adopted a policy of "not interfering for protection of Christians" and instructed American authorities to take no action. "Under existing conditions in Near East I continue to recommend our maintaining strictly neutral position regarding nationalities and races."[39] Three months later, Bristol relayed without comment another cable from Beirut, dated November 20, which confirmed Consul Jackson's prediction: "A report received through American mission sources from Adana indicates confirmation of destruction of . . . [Hadjin] by Turks and the massacre of nearly entire Armenian population of about eight thousand."[40]

The zone of persecutions extended beyond the coastal region of Cilicia. At the end of 1921, a French missionary eyewitness corroborated reports coming in from Americans. According to the French report, the "crisis" of the Armenians in the interior "appears to have reached its maximum intensity." Their situation "is intolerable and can be summed up with two terms: Systematic plunder and extermination of the Christians." The report itemized in detail seven types of administrative and extra-legal methods by which Armenians were being denied the right to keep or reclaim properties. The report provided numerous specific examples of these measures being put into effect, and concluded that the continuation of these practices "tends to substantiate that the goal being pursued is THE SYSTEMATIC PLUNDER OF THE CHRISTIANS."[41]

Union of Prisoners from Malta with Nationalists in Angora

The all-out effort to eradicate the Armenians was related to the recruitment of former Ottoman officials implicated in the wartime deportation and massacres, including some who were released from detention on the island of Malta in April–May 1921, into the ranks of the rulers in Angora. On April 24, High Commissioner Rumbold wired British Secretary of State for Foreign Affairs Lord (George Nathaniel) Curzon that a few days earlier the local press had announced several appointments to administrative posts. They included the appointment of Sabit Bey as *vali* (governor) of Erzerum, Abdul-Halik Bey as *vali* of Konia, and Muammer Bey as *mutassarif* (administrator) of Kayseri. All were former prisoners on Malta who Rumbold noted were implicated in the wartime destruction of the Armenians. He said Sabit Bey had been *vali* of Kharput from 1914 to February 1916, Abdul-Halik had been *vali* of Bitlis from March 1914 to September 1915, and Muammer Bey had been *vali* of Sivas from 1913 to February 1916. "Each acquired notoriety as a ferocious exponent of the policy of deporting and massacring Christians. Each was arrested after the armistice, and they were all three in due course deported to Malta. Their full records will be found in the files relative to the Malta deportations. Their appointment at the present juncture to high administrative posts is of a piece with the election of the notorious Feizi Bey of Diarbekir to a post in the Angora Cabinet. . . . These three appointments illustrate significantly the temper of the Angora Government."[42]

An exchange of comments written by Foreign Office officials clarified that the release of the Malta prisoners was no indication of their innocence. Near East expert D. G. Osborne declared that they "have never been punished (except by confinement at Malta) for their exploits and their present appointment seems to afford clear proof both of the Angora Government's approval of their methods and of its desire to make further use of these methods." If the Kemalists "now demand the punishment of Greeks convicted of atrocities we might well point to the fact of these men being not only unpunished but reinstated for the obvious purpose of repeating their exploits." Unfortunately, Osborne lamented, "we are on weak ground because of the fact that we never brought them to trial." Foreign Secretary Curzon regretted their release: "I think we made a great mistake in ever letting these people out. I had to yield at the time to a pressure which I always felt to be mistaken." W. G. Rendel suggested that it "might be worthwhile getting a friendly question asked in Parliament about these appointments." Parliamentary Undersecretary of State for Foreign Affairs Cecil Harmsworth disagreed: "I think the less we say about these people in Parliament the better. In connection with a recent supplementary Estimate I had to explain why we released the Turkish deportees from Malta, skating over the thin ice as quickly as I could. There would have been a row, I think, but for the staunch belief among Members that one British prisoner was worth a shipload of Turks—& so the exchange was excused."[43]

A parliamentary question eventually was submitted by member of Parliament Aneurin Williams, concerning the wartime record of Hadji Adil Bey—who was reported to have been recently appointment *vali* of Adana. Foreign Office memoranda confirmed his criminal wartime background and acknowledged the probability that Hadji Adil had received a new appointment, "especially as we know that it is the policy of Angora to give these men high administrative posts." The Foreign Office had no definite information on his appointment, though there was ample information pertaining to his official position at Salonika in 1905, to his prominent position in the Ittihadist period, during which he took a "lead in policy of exterminating Armenians in 1915," and to his arrest in 1919 "for his connection with the Armenian massacres & deported to Malta, whence he was subsequently released." All the evidence confirmed the charges made in the press and pointed to an affirmative answer to a rhetorical question by member of Parliament T. P. O'Conner: "Is it not well known to the whole world that several of the worst of these wholesale assassins who were detained for a long time by us have been appointed to high civil and military commands by the Angora Government?"[44]

A cryptic reference to wartime officials and renewed deportations, in a secret communication to Kemal by Nationalist Commissar for Interior Affairs Fethi Bey in February 1921, gives credence to such charges. Spurred by a local Greek uprising in the Samsun area, Fethi Bey had been sent to investigate "areas infested by the brigands of the Pontus," to study "the question of public security," which was "of vital importance" to the Angora government. The countermeasures recommended by Fethi Bey necessitated particular attention to two considerations that "would be of great assistance to Government officials in carrying out their duties." The two points to which Fethi Bey called Kemal's attention seemed to link the legal status of officials accused of participation in past deportations, with the ongoing policy of renewed deportations.

> (1) A law, promulgated under Ferid Pasha at Constantinople after the armistice, stipulates that such officials as have been accused of having taking part in the deportation of Christians are not subject, as are other officials, to be tried by the Tribunal, but are subject to trial by the Public Prosecutor as ordinary individuals.
> (2) I beg to be supplied with the necessary authorization to carry out deportations on a more expeditious and larger scale than hitherto. This would improve the security both of the Army and the nation.[45]

Drawing a connection between the wartime atrocities and the ongoing persecutions, a British "Diplomatic Correspondent" doubted whether "in the annals of the world's history there exists a more hideous record of persecution and murder or a more damning proof of the sinister and pitiless [character] of the modern Young Turks, now masquerading under the Kemalist label." The spirit of wartime Interior Minister Talaat Pasha "still animates his former associates and subordinates, many of whom are to-day in power at Angora."[46]

The Nationalist paper *Yeni Gün* echoed the tenor of Angora's policy, by glorifying Talaat in an effusive eulogy following his assassination by Soghomon Tehlirian in 1921: "Our great patriot has died for his country. . . . We salute his fresh tomb and bow low to kiss his eyes. Talaat was a political giant. Talaat was a genius. History will prove his immense stature and will make of him a martyr and an apostle. Talaat was a revolutionary but he was, above all, a man of justice. . . . Despite all the calumnies Talaat will remain the greatest man that Turkey has produced." If the Turks had erred in the past, *Yeni Gün* declared, it was in being too good to the minorities. "Beware! We have no intention of repeating the same mistake!"[47]

Persecutions in Anatolia and Propaganda in the Media

Attempts to investigate the latest persecutions again put the Turks on the defensive in the press and in international forums. The Turkish representative in Berne charged that the League of Nations Assembly was biased; it had appointed as reporter a "person whose natural sympathies were entirely on the side of Turkey's enemies, a lady, a slave to her feelings and a poetess," who used the league forum as a "pulpit which she mounted with enthusiasm" in order to spout "expressions of hatred" against Turkey, statements that "slandered and cruelly attacked an honest and honourable people, which has been persecuted for centuries and always been vilified as the persecutor." One British official thought this reference to reporter Mademoiselle Vacaresco was "very bad propaganda," and offered trenchant commentary: "Turkish terms of opprobrium: 'a lady, a slave to her feelings & a poetess'! On the other hand the Turks are described as 'an honest & honourable people, which has been persecuted for centuries' (by whom?) & 'a peaceful & peace-loving nation'."[48]

Suppressing news of the resumption of persecutions became more difficult for the Turks and their sympathizers in the West, when fresh American evidence, most notably "Yowell's yowl," reverberated around the world.[49] On May 6, 1922 the *Times* (London) reported that Major Forrest D. Yowell, director of the Kharput unit of NER, chief surgeon Dr. Mark Ward, medical director Dr. Ruth Parmalee, and orphanage director Isabel Harley, were all expelled from their posts because they had protested the increasing persecution of Christians and the new restrictions imposed on relief activity. "All the American relief workers in the Kharput district," Yowell stated, "were consistently treated with utmost discourtesy and injustice, in spite of the fact that they were doing large relief work for Moslem orphan refugees as well as Christians.' " The Armenians in Kharput "are now in a state of virtual slavery," not allowed freedom of movement. "All the property of the Armenians who died in the recent deportations has been confiscated by the Turks. Armenians have no rights in the courts." Men are thrown into jail "for no reason except to extort ransom from relatives," while women "are forced into Moslem houses as slaves without the right to appeal to any tribunal." Turkish officials "frankly state that the only way they can get money is by blackmailing Christians" and they "frankly state it is their deliberate intention to let all" of them "die, and their actions support their statements."[50]

Yowell clarified the basis of his observations: "I have no personal prejudice against any religious belief, I am not a missionary. I was sent to Anatolia purely for relief work and for saving those in need without regard to nationality or religion. I had a long experience in American Relief work in Poland and in Central Europe, and never permitted myself to become involved in any political or religious controversy. I speak of conditions in Anatolia from the view-point of one impartial and unbiased as possible for any red-blooded American."

Yowell noted that the Turks were "encouraged by vacillation and hesitation" on the part of the Allies, and were "getting bolder and bolder in their intolerance toward minority populations." The American hospital Kharput, for example, was operated virtually under the order of the Turks. "We could receive only such patients as were approved by the Turkish authorities. Many Greek and Armenian refugees terribly ill were turned away to die outside our gates. Some time ago we opened a special hospital for babies, but one day this was suddenly closed by the military authorities without explanation, although closing it meant the death of several patients."[51]

Dr. Ward, one of Yowell's colleagues, quoted Turkish officials as saying: "We have been too easy in the past. We shall do a thorough job this time." Another remarked: "Why do you Americans waste your time and money on these filthy Greeks and Armenians? We always thought that Americans knew how to get their money's worth. Any Greeks and Armenians who don't die here are sure to die when we send them on to Bitlis, as we always choose the worst weather in order to get rid of them quicker." In Ward's opinion, the policy of extermination "was directed by the Angora Government" so that when "adequate guarantees for the safety of the Christian population of Anatolia" were written at the peace conference in Lausanne, "there would no longer be any Christian population to require safeguarding."[52]

Not all Turks were as cruel as those quoted by Ward. In addition to the many individual Arabs, Kurds, and Turks who saved Armenian lives during the deportations, there were even Turkish officials who opposed the persecutions. Rumbold reported that according to what Dr. Herbert Gibbons learned during his visit to Trebizond in May 1922, prominent Turks from Jevislik went to Trebizond to protest against the "unparalleled unhumanity," but they were "beaten and sent away" for intervening. The mayor of Trebizond "has no sympathy" with the "extermination policy and has done what he could to protect little boys." The *vali* of Trebizond "is also opposed to massacres and persecutions of Christians, but he is powerless to stop what is going on. His predecessor tried and was removed." The late governor Sami Bey "likewise refused to take action against boys, and was removed last month." Despite such instances of Turkish kindness and moral integrity, widespread attacks on the minorities remained the order of the day. Rumbold learned from Ward that deportees were being led along circuitous routes, resulting in large numbers dying "on the road from hardship and exposure." Therefore, the "Turks can say that they did not actually kill these refugees, but a comparison" may be made with the way "the Turks formerly got rid of dogs at Constantinople by landing them on an island where they died of hunger and thirst."[53]

London urged an Allied investigation of the new persecutions, but Washington resisted. The resistance was rooted in Constantinople, where the American High Commissioner was colluding in a concerted cover-up crafted in Angora. Admiral Bristol was aware of the renewed deportations, but he did not share the outrage or frustration of his English colleagues. Focused almost exclusively on the pursuit of profit for American businesses, and "very pro-Turk" according to Joseph Clark Grew, the U.S. envoy in Switzerland, Bristol imposed "strict censorship" over news coming out of Turkey, and pleaded for stricter censorship in the United States.[54]

Allen Dulles, the Near East Division chief at the State Department (and later CIA director), was often of one mind with Bristol, but in a cable to Constantinople in April, he bemoaned how difficult it was to keep things under wraps: "Confidentially the Department is in a bind. Our task would be simple if the reports of the atrocities could be declared untrue or even exaggerated but the evidence, alas, is irrefutable and the Secretary of State wants to avoid giving the impression that while the United States is willing to intervene actively to protect its commercial interests, it is not willing to move on behalf of the Christian minorities."[55]

To discredit the damning evidence from American observers, an attempt was made to produce American evidence intended to offset the negative publicity which was further blackening the image of Turkey. One tactic was to call attention to excesses committed by Greeks. Without minimizing the tragedy of Turkish victims of Christian excesses, however, Western officials recognized that in terms of number and scope, incidents of excesses committed by Christians were dwarfed in comparison to the overwhelming evidence of excesses committed by Turks. In the words of one official, "the great mass of independent evidence in the possession" of the British government concerning "atrocities on both sides goes to show that the Turkish atrocities, which have clearly been carried out on a systematic plan and under order from superior authorities, have been on an infinitely vaster scale than those attributed to the Greeks which," in any case, the Turkish atrocities "preceded by many years."[56]

Turkish efforts to balance the picture failed because there was a great mass of evidence against the Turks, such as a report on an investigation by Charles P. Grant, American official at Karakilisse, in April 1921. Grant reported that "they found a great number of corpses, mostly of children," all along a river which ran in a deep valley. "The number of victims must have been 12,000, two-thirds of them being refugees from Kars and Alexandropol. . . . The absence of male corpses was particularly striking, the oldest victim being about 14 years old. . . . The victims who were shot must have been shot at close range, after having been lined up on both sides of the valley, inasmuch as the cartridges were found five or six steps away from the river banks. The plateau, which was strewn with scraps of female underclothing, must have been the scene of violent outrages against the women."[57]

Another tactic to counterbalance the incriminating evidence was outright denial. For example, a clumsy propaganda ploy involved an American reporter and a relief official. Correspondent Larry Rue of the *Chicago Tribune* reported that a NER official, Captain Harold C. Jaquith, issued to the official Anatolia Press a "Vigorous denial of allegations of atrocities" made by Major Yowell. Yet even the author of the *Tribune* article raised suspicions, when he revealed that Jaquith had "accepted an invitation by the Turks to go to Kharput to investigate details of the alleged outrages committed against the Armenian and Greek populations there," and that Jaquith "is now in Angora." The *Daily Telegraph* called Jaquith's statement "A Strange Denial."[58]

Jaquith's denial as reported by the Anatolia Press and the *Chicago Tribune* was contradicted by numerous sources. "The Turkish authorities" at Kharput, Dr. Ward recalled, "told me that they had not done their job efficiently during the war, and they were now putting the finishing touches on what they began then." The Turks were taking advantage of "our delay" and "hastening the deliberate process of extinction, hoping that by the time intervention comes," they "will have disposed of the Christian peoples altogether." Dr. Ward thought the presence of Americans "annoys" the Turkish authorities because they "would like a free hand and no witnesses to their bloody deeds.[59]

One of the many witnesses was Edith Woods, a NER nurse stationed at Kharput until November 1921 and in Malatia until spring 1922.

> It was like an endless chain. . . . The children would often be dead before I had taken their names. Forty to fifty of the older women died each day. You see starvation, exposure, exhaustion. . . . Their mouths were masses of sores, and their teeth were dropping out. And their feet, those poor, bleeding feet. The Turks were doing nothing at all for them. In Malatia the dead lay around in the streets and fields. No attempt was made to bury them. . . . Deportation is sure death—and a far more horrible death than massacre. Unless one sees these things it is difficult to believe that such monstrous cruelty and barbarity exist in the world. Making women and children suffer that way until they die seems incredible. But that is Malatia.

Woods also exposed the pro-Turkish atmosphere at the American Embassy. "They receive us coldly" at the U.S. Embassy in Constantinople "when we want to tell what we know for the benefit of our Government, and let it appear very clearly that my story is unwelcome and that I am a hysterical woman exaggerating or falsifying—that is the way it is" at the embassy.[60]

In the face of corroborated information provided by third-party sources, the assurances provided by Angora's Ministry of Interior pertaining to the treatment of the Christian minorities, like the assurances on properties, appear almost surrealistic.[61] Dr. Gibbons thought the Turkish government's excuses were "a calumny upon the good Turks, of whom there are many, even in official" capacities.

> The ordinary Anatolian Turk is a fine fellow, who, unless incited to it by an appeal to his fanaticism, wouldn't hurt a fly. But the great mass of the Turks are unfortunately ignorant and indolent and they can be, despite their instinctive kindliness and tolerance—worked upon to do the horrible things. When mob spirit is aroused, they are capable of unspeakable cruelties. Massacres of Christians in Turkey have never broken out spontaneously: for Christians and Moslems ordinarily get along very well. The massacres have been ordered. So have the deportations. And the killings en route and starvation are the result of a deliberately ordered plan . . . the awful things that are happening to-day . . . under the authority or within reach of the long arm of the Angora Government are intended as a part of the programme to make Turkey truly Turkish. The men in control in Angora intend to do away with the Christians. I am not writing conjecture and hearsay. The proofs of this are indisputable.

Yet, there "are humane and kind hearted Turks," Gibbons stressed, "and there are Mohammedans who fear God, and who are shocked by the impious horrors of the extermination policy."[62]

British Reactions to the Renewed Persecutions

The denial stories the Turkish government planted in the Western press supplied fodder that was rapidly loaded into the political guns of the pro-Turkish forces in Parliament who were arrayed against the prime minister, the Foreign Office, and the members of Parliament who supported the Armenians. A heated debate on the atrocity issue and the whole Eastern settlement was initiated by member of Parliament Major General Charles Townshend on May 30, 1922. He questioned the latest evidence against the Turks. He stated that since the Mudros Armistice the Allies and specifically Prime Minister David Lloyd George and the Foreign Office had been treating the Turks with "the most merciless severity," a "blunder" which had driven the basically reasonable Turkish leaders including Kemal to extremes. Townshend declared, "I know him well and respect him," and if given a chance to negotiate, would tell the Turkish leader: "For heaven's sake, Kemal, moderate your demands. We must have peace." Townshend begged the government to "alter its policy and follow Beaconsfield, Palmerston and that great man Salisbury," who had all wanted "that military race, the Turks, as our friends on the road to India."[63]

Lieutenant Commander Joseph M. Kenworthy followed in the same vein. He wondered whether the government "was going to try to stampede us with the story of Turkish atrocities as Gladstone did three generations ago with much more cause?" Kenworthy claimed that the story of recent atrocities by Turks "that we have been allowing ourselves to believe is open to the greatest doubt," and quoted in full Jaquith's reported rejection of the Yowell/Ward testimonies. But interestingly, even Kenworthy did "not understand" the reference to Jaquith being invited by the Turks to investigate charges that Turks committed atrocities, and he did not understand the reference to Christians of Kayseri protesting those charges against the Turks. Kenworthy sought an explanation in equilibrium. "I neither accepted the original statement in its entirety nor do I accept this denial in its entirety," Kenworthy exclaimed, adding that there are "excesses on both sides, and so long as war continues there will be these excesses." Kenworthy lamented that Lloyd George was always talking about the severe unemployment problem in England but not bringing about one of the conditions needed to alleviate it—peace in Anatolia. He noted that "Asia Minor is a great market for British goods, but if we get ourselves known as the enemies of Islam, we shall alienate our loyal subjects in India."[64] Aubrey Herbert supported the views expressed by Townshend and Kenworthy.[65]

Member of Parliament O'Conner shot back at the "Turkophile" onslaught, accusing Kenworthy of "minimising the massacres by the Turks and maximising the alleged massacres by the Greeks and proclaiming a policy more Turkophile almost than the Turks themselves." Any attempt to call attention to "these abominable atrocities of the Turks on the Christians," O'Conner charged, is met by Kenworthy "with every weapon of raillery and suggestion and doubt and animosity." Kenworthy interjected: "They are exaggerated." O'Conner retorted: "Is it an exaggeration that a million Armenians were killed during the War? Is it, or is it not? . . . I call the testimony of Lord Bryce and the other authorities who examined most carefully into these things and who, having tested the evidence, brought forth that most damning document of the most hideous massacres in history."

O'Conner was "astounded at the refracting perversity of partisanship" in Kenworthy's ordinarily "clear and humane mind," for he had recently succeeded in securing "further protection in regard to performing animals." O'Conner sympathized with that issue and congratulated Kenworthy on his successful efforts in behalf of animal rights, "but am I not entitled to ask from him for human beings, though they happen to be Christians and not Mahommedans, such protection against butchery as he is entitled to ask for protection against the ill-treatment of monkeys, birds, and performing parrots?" Townshend, Herbert, and Kenworthy, O'Conner continued, would "retort by saying: 'Oh, but there were Greek atrocities.' Who denies it?" O'Conner declared that he himself had raised these charges recently with Greek Prime Minister Eleutherios Venizelos, who had acknowledged Greek excesses but had made the "unanswerable reply, 'You must compare the comparable,' " not the "deeds that are done in the savage hours of war with the deeds that are done with the sanction and by the initiative of the Government, and as the Government policy—the massacre of the Armenians" during World War I being an example. O'Conner wondered whether Kenworthy knew any Armenians or Greeks and exclaimed caustically: "Will he say that any English woman in her home is a higher or nobler specimen of womanhood than the typical Greek or Armenian? Yet when these people are ravished and murdered, when their babies are butchered before their mothers' eyes, my hon. and gallant Friend has less sympathy with them than with the performing monkey or the caged canary."[66]

Another MP, Lord Robert Cecil, backed O'Conner's denunciation of attempts to equate Greek excesses with the systematic exterminations ordered by the Turkish government. He could not "conceive how anyone could possibly palliate the conduct of the Turks during the last few years, and during a much longer period." Cecil did not think anyone would do his "cause any good by minimising the atrocious crime or set of crimes committed by Talaat and all of his myrmidons" during World War I: "Unfortunately, similar crimes have been committed both before that time and since, by direct orders from the old Constantinople Government, and not by the casual fury of local people. It has been proved over and over again that the local authorities are not, generally speaking, responsible for these brutalities, but that they have been committed almost always by the orders of the central government."

Even the ardently pro-Turk Kenworthy backed off: "I do not palliate that."[67] Undersecretary of State Harmsworth agreed with Cecil that the charge of massacre "against one of the parties is out of all comparison more serious than that against another," but he saw no advantage in debating the point in Parliament, since American sources already confirmed the information about the latest Turkish excesses that the British had obtained through their own official sources.[68]

The tone of this debate chagrined the Foreign Office. Rendel characterized the speeches by Townshend and Kenworthy as "disgraceful" and a "scandal even for the Turkish party." Osborne remarked that it was "a very unpleasing debate to listen to & it is hard to say which was the more sickening, the fatuous posturing of Gen. Townshend, the venomous misrepresentations of Liet. Commander Kenworthy or the lachrymose generalities of Mr. T. P. O'Conner." Concerning Herbert's discussion of whether Christians or Turks began the excesses, Rendel alluded to the Ottoman conquest of Constantinople in 1453 and fired back a wry rebuttal, pointing out that "atrocities began when the Turks first invaded Asia Minor in the XV century and the latest lot have been going on continuously since long before the Greek landing in Smyrna" in 1919.[69]

Eventually the Jaquith story and another denial attempt, involving Julian Gillespie, a U.S. Commerce Department assistant sent to Angora, were completely discredited. One damning exposé came from American Methodist Episcopalian Bishop James Cannon Jr., who wrote to the *Times* in October that on a recent trip to Constantinople, he had spent a great deal of time on a "careful investigation," which included talking "at length with Mr. Jaquith," who "stated that never at any time had he disowned Dr. Ward and Major Yowell, nor had he ever at any time intimated that they had made any misstatements. It is true that the Turks expelled Dr. Ward and Major Yowell from Anatolia because they had told the truth" about the renewed "deportations and massacres." Cannon stressed that there was "not a single member" among the NER staff of "over two hundred workers who has any doubt as to the truthfulness of the statements made by Major Yowell and Dr. Ward, and the statements attributed to Mr. Jaquith and Mr. Gillespie are not only absolutely false, but show what lengths Turkish propaganda is carried in the effort to deceive the world concerning the real determination to deport and if necessary, exterminate all the Christians."[70]

Corroborating Cannon's account, Rendel wrote in a Foreign Office memorandum that the Yowell/Ward reports "have been confirmed by every American relief worker" familiar with the district in question who was personally interviewed. "Turkish propaganda organizations published denials over the signature of certain other Americans, including Mr. Jaquith," but the British government had since received "conclusive proof of the falsity of these denials and of the fact that Mr. Jaquith's statement was a Turkish fabrication."[71]

Finishing the Genocide on the Road to Lausanne

As the propaganda war was played out in Europe and America, the atrocities continued in Anatolia. Dr. Gibbons described the difference between the wartime experience of the Armenians and the new methods being employed by the Kemalists against the Greeks and Armenian remnants in the Black Sea coastal regions. At Trebizond, for example, it would have been impolitic to have pulled off a repetition of the horrors of 1915.

> The Turks have an expression, "Yiwash-yiwash," which means to go slowly. That is how clearing Trebizond of its remaining Christian population is being managed. . . . Now they are going after the little boys. It used to be conscription that was invoked as an excuse to take the men. When they got down to deporting the boys from 15 to 18, the Turks said it was to give them preliminary training. Now—as I write—they are making a new visitation of the angel of death in Greek homes, and seizing boys from 11 to 14. The poor little kiddies are gathered together like cattle, and driven through the streets to the Government House, where they are put in a filthy dungeon half underground. One could not believe this was possible. It would be more merciful for the victims and their mothers to kill them outright. But that is not the way it is done. It would attract attention, and be difficult to deny or explain. . . . The way it is done is this: the deportees are presumed to have cholera or the plague, and are made to enter the enclosure. No food is given them. . . . Then begins the bleeding of the families of the victims. It is intimated that the loved ones will die if food is not brought. Many a woman has tramped two days over the mountains to bring bread to her husband or son. He is given some to encourage her to return. But a bribe must first be paid, and part of the

> food is stolen before it reaches the lost soul behind the barbed wire. And it is difficult for the women to get to the Jevislik camp and back again without being dishonoured . . . several times a week a Greek girl is shot or stabbed when attempting to escape rape. There is no punishment for this crime. The authorities do not even make an investigation. "The girl got herself into some drunken brawl—a bad lot, these Greeks," you will be probably be told, if you make an enquiry. The women feel that very soon the experience of the Armenian women of Trebizond will come to them—they will be deported into the interior, and—en route—most of them will be "lost"[72]

By autumn of 1922, the forced exodus of Christians reached a scale unmatched since the deportations and genocidal massacres of 1915–18.[73] Several pressure tactics were used to induce Armenians to leave "voluntarily." Armenians were subjected to exorbitant taxation and unofficial persecution in the form of economic boycotts, attacks in the press, beatings, robberies, and even killings by the local populace—all a part of what the American consul in Aleppo described as an implicit understanding between Turkish authorities and the Muslim population.[74] Even Constantinople became increasingly uncomfortable. Armenians and Greeks feared going out at night and so many Christians resorted to wearing the Turkish fez for camouflage, that there was a shortage of fezes.[75]

The policy of expulsion and confiscation picked up momentum just as it became evident that guarantees for minority protection were to be discussed at the peace conference in Lausanne. In October 1922, using its April law on abandoned properties as justification, the Nationalist government demanded that foreign banks in Smyrna should furnish lists of the goods and securities deposited by Greek and Armenian clients, with a view to sequestering these assets.[76] On November 22, 1922, two days after the start of the Allied-Turkish deliberations in Lausanne, the British consul in Aleppo reported that Armenians "driven out" of Cilicia were not allowed to dispose of their property, being "told that the Government alone has the right to dispose of their property and in effect the Government confiscates it."[77] Sometimes the Armenians were told "they were free to dispose of their real property, but of course" they "could find no purchasers, the Moslems knowing" that "they could get the houses for very little" after the departure of the Christians. "I have also heard," the consul continued, that Muslims who "wished to purchase houses from Christians before their departure were either threatened with reprisals by their co-religionists or else effected the purchases at extremely low rates."[78]

An Arabic newspaper reported that Turks in Mardin, learning of the Kemalist victory over the Greeks, "spread a rumour to the effect that the Christians must quit the country within 2 months." Hearing this, "the Christians started selling their property for a trifle," and took flight. Houses worth "1000 Turkish Gold pounds in Mardin are offered for sale for £[T]100, but nobody buys" them. "Obviously," the British consul in Damascus observed, "they can wait a few days and simply take them."[79] The consul in Aleppo reported that refugees from Marash and Aintab stated that "after having left their houses and lands, they were attacked on their way to the Syrian frontier by robbers and relieved of their money and valuables."[80]

When the elimination of the Armenians from Anatolia became an accomplished fact and when the ultimate abandonment of their cause in Europe became a near certainty, the Armenians found the new Turkish leaders impossible to deal with. A meeting between Patriarch Zaven and Nationalist representative Hamid Bey in January 1922 bore no results, and finally, the Nationalists forced Zaven's resignation when he refused to support their proposal in December 1922 that the unofficial Armenian representatives at Lausanne should be withdrawn.[81]

The Armenian representatives were not withdrawn, but they too were forced to resort to direct talks with the Turks. The head of the Turkish delegation in Lausanne, Ismet Pasha, described a heated meeting in early 1923 with Noradoungian of the Armenian delegation, when he and the other Turkish negotiator, Riza Nur Pasha, stuck firm to a severe and uncompromising position. Resigned to the reality that the chances of securing a cession of territory to Armenian sovereignty had disappeared, Noradoungian appealed instead for the creation of an "Armenian National Home" inside Turkey and under Turkish sovereignty. "Where do you want it?" Ismet asked mockingly. "In the east? The north? The west? Where?" Noradoungian was practically pleading: " 'Anywhere; just let us have some place for an Armenian Home. We will gather there to live.' " Ismet retorted that under the rubric of a national home in Turkey, Noradoungian was proposing in effect the separation of a piece of Turkey to create an "artificial country" for the Armenians. Ismet was terse: "We will not think of it, we will not accept it, we will not do it. Do you have anything else to say?"[82]

The possibility of securing something by appealing to Turkish remorse or generosity had vanished over the course of four years. In 1923, recalling his rejection of a direct Armenian-Turkish rapprochement in his meeting with Damad Ferid in 1919, Noradoungian knew that the opportunity had been lost: "Of course how could I have known then, that from one moment to the next, such political conditions would develop that would cause the Allied governments to forget the lavish promises they had made to the Armenian people during the War."[83]

While the final conference to settle the Eastern Question was still in session in Lausanne, the Grand National Assembly in Angora passed yet another law on properties, on April 15, 1923, which was even more severe than the 1922 and 1915 laws. The new law stipulated that ownership of all properties of non-Muslims who had left for any reason prior to the signing of the Treaty of Lausanne (in July 1923) would pass to the Turkish government.[84] This latest law and the other policies and actions of the Grand National Assembly highlight an important dimension of the Armenian Question. There was a clear continuity between the old Ottoman government's policy of deportation, extermination, and property confiscation set into motion in 1915, and the new Turkish government's policy in the 1920s. The founders of first government of the Republic of Turkey finished the Armenian Genocide, by plundering and eliminating the remnants of the Ottoman Armenians, who otherwise might have reclaimed their confiscated property as citizens of the new republic.

Notes

1. Lawrence Cretan, "The Armenian Remnants in Turkey: 1918–1922" (Seminar paper, University of California, Los Angeles, 1976), 2. Cretan's paper is a well-documented study based on American, British, and Armenian archival sources as well as secondary sources in Armenian and Western languages. There is a large body of primary sources and secondary works on the massacres and deportations of 1915 to 1918. See, for example, Vahakn N. Dadrian, *The History of the Armenian Genocide: Ethnic Conflict from the Balkans to Anatolia to the Caucasus* (Providence, R.I.: Berghahn Books, 1995).
2. Turkish Prime Ministry, Directorate General of Press and Information, *Documents* (Ankara: Başarı Matbaacılık Sanayii, 1983), 1:92–98.
3. Ibid., 1:94–95.
4. U.S. National Archives, Record Group 59 (NA, RG 59), 867.4016/126, Oscar Heizer to Morgenthau, July 28, 1915, cited in *Armenian Review* 37, no. 1 (Spring 1984): 106.
5. Wolff-Metternich to Berlin, June 30, 1916, in *Deutschland und Armenien, 1914–1918: Sammlung diplomatischer Aktenstücke,* ed. Johannes Lepsius (Potsdam: Tempelverlag, 1919; reprint, Bremen: Donat and Temmen Verlag, 1986), 277, cited in Christopher J. Walker, *Armenia: The Survival of a Nation* (New York: St. Martin's Press, 1980), 235. The Ittihad ve Terakki, or Committee of Union and Progress, was the party in power during the war.
6. Turkish Prime Ministry, *Documents,* 1:95–97. The quotation encompasses several articles.
7. Senator Ahmed Riza in the Ottoman Senate, December 13, 1915. See Yusuf Hikmet Bayur, *Türk İnkılabi Tarihi* (History of the Turkish revolution), vol. 3, part 3 (İstanbul: Maarif Matbaası, 1957), 48, cited in Dadrian, "Genocide as a

Problem of National and International Law: The World War I Armenian Case and its Contemporary Legal Ramifications," *Yale Journal of Internationl Law* 14, no. 2 (Summer 1989): 269. The French translation of this work is Marc and Mikaël Nichanian's *Autopsie du génocide arménien* (Brussels: Ed. Complexe, 1995).

8. For the negotiations that produced the Treaty of Sèvres, which granted the Armenians much of their claims, see Richard G. Hovannisian, *The Republic of Armenia:* Volume III: *From London to Sèvres, February–August, 1920* (Berkeley: University of California Press, 1996); Levon Marashlian, "The London and San Remo Conferences and the Armenian Settlement: The Belated Decisions, February–April, 1920," *Armenian Review* 30, no. 3 (Autumn 1977): 227–55; no. 4 (Winter 1977–78): 398–414. For a study on the internal debates and policy decisions of the Armenian negotiators, see Houri Berberian, "The Delegation of Integral Armenia: From Greater Armenia to Lesser Armenia," *Armenian Review* 44, no. 3 (Autumn 1991): 39–64.
9. Philip Mason Burnett, *Reparations at the Paris Peace Conference: From the Standpoint of the American Delegation* (New York: Columbia University Press, 1940), 2:590, and *Tableau approximatif des réparations et indemnités pour les dommages subis par la nation arménienne en Arménie de Turquie et dans la République Arménienne du Caucase* (Paris: Imp. P. Dupont, 1919), cited in Richard G. Hovannisian, *The Republic of Armenia*, vol. 1: *The First Year, 1918–1919* (Berkeley: University of California Press, 1971), 456–57. For fuller studies of the property question, see André N. Mandelstam, *Confiscation des biens des réfugiés arméniens par le gouvernement turc* (Paris: Imp. Massis, 1929); Kevork K. Baghdjian, *La confiscation, par le gouvernement turc, des biens arméniens . . . dits "abandonnés"* (Montreal: N.p., 1987). For the *Tableau approximatif,* submitted by Aharonian and Nubar, see Baghdjian, *La confiscation,* 261–69.
10. Cretan, "Armenian Remnants," 34–35. Eight daily Armenian newspapers were published in Constantinople for varying lengths of time up to 1923, 3 were published in Adana, 2 in Smyrna, and 1 in Aintab. Also, more than 40 periodicals and 11 annual publications appeared in the capital, where an Armenian Editors Union was formed.
11. Ibid., 32–33. For more on the activities of Constantinople Armenian leaders in these years, see, for example, the numerous documents containing the minutes of the Greek and Armenian Section of the British High Commission, found in Foreign Office Archives, Public Record Office, London (cited hereafter as FO), 371/7933, especially file 301, which begins with E301/301/44, Rumbold to Foreign Office, transmitting minutes of the December 29, 1921 meeting of the section. These meetings were attended by British officials of the Armenian and Greek Section as well as Armenian and Greek representatives. They contain a great deal of information on the renewed deportations and conditions in Anatolia in general.
12. Cretan, "Armenian Remnants," 30–31. A Turkish historian claims that in February 1919, the Ottoman government attempted to negotiate with Armenians,

"promising them autonomy within the Turkish state, and proposing an exchange of populations in some areas where tension was acute." The Armenians purportedly rejected this overture, evidently hoping "to gain much more by continuing their intrigues with the Great Powers." See Salahi Ramsdan Sonyel, *Turkish Diplomacy from Mudros to Lausanne, 1918–1923: Mustafa Kemal and the Turkish National Movement* (London: Sage Publications, 1975), 5–6.

13. Berberian, "The Delegation of Integral Armenia," 42–45. An agreement was reached with Kurdish representative Sherif Pasha. For more on Armeno-Kurdish relations, see Tessa Hofmann and Gerayer Koutcharian, "The History of Armenian-Kurdish Relations in the Ottoman Empire," *Armenian Review* 33, no. 4 (Winter 1986): 1–45.
14. Gabriel Noradoungian, "Antip Husher: Gabriel Efendi Noradoungiani, Nakhkin Osmanian Artakin Gordsots Nakharar" (Unpublished memoirs: Gabriel Efendi Noradoungian, former Ottoman minister of foreign affairs), *Baikar,* June 17, 1952. Noradoungian left Constantinople before the outbreak of World War I. In the postwar period, he was the vice-chairman of the Armenian National Delegation. For a brief biographical sketch, see Y. G. Çark, *Türk Devleti Hizmetinde Ermeniler, 1453–1953* (Armenians in the service of the Turkish state, 1453–1953) (İstanbul: Yeni Matbaa, 1953), 153–56.
15. Archbishop Zaven [Eghiayan], *Patriarkakan Hushers, Vaveragirner u Vkayutiunner* (Patriarchal memoirs, documents, and testimonies) (Cairo: Nor Astgh, 1947), 332; *Erkir,* February 6 and 7, 1920; FO 371, 3472/27/44, cited in Cretan, "Armenian Remnants," 20.
16. FO 371–704/1334/3472/27/44, cited in Cretan, "Armenian Remnants," 19–20.
17. FO 371/7933-E4693/301/44, Rumbold to Curzon, April 27, 1922.
18. Ibid., 7907-E11825/27/44, Rumbold to Foreign Office, October 24, 1922. See also 7905-E11499/27/44; FO 7874-E5290/18/44, Foreign Office response to Parliamentary Question by Colonel Wedgewood, May 18, 1922.
19. "The Explanation of the Ministry of Interior," May 22, 1922, in "Explanation furnished by the Anatolian News Agency in connection with allegations made by Major Yowell," 6–8. See FO 371/7878-E5692/19/44.
20. Cretan, "Armenian Remnants," 35–42.
21. *Erkir,* November 15, 1919, January 2, 1920; *Times* (London), April 15, 1920; FO 371, E703/27/44.
22. Zaven, *Patriarkakan Hushers,* 291–92; FO 371–E703/27/44, cited in Cretan, "Armenian Remnants," 15–16.
23. Halidé Edib, *The Turkish Ordeal* (New York: The Century Co., 1928), 17. Edib was a graduate of Robert College and a well-known writer. She was an effective activist for the promotion of Turkey's image.
24. Ibid., 16.
25. There are several Armenian oral history collections: Audio tapes collected by the Armenian Library and Museum of America (Boston); audio tapes of interviews conducted by students of Richard Hovannisian (UCLA); audio tapes deposited with the Armenian Assembly of America (Washington, D.C.); videotaped interviews conducted by Zoryan Institute (Cambridge, Mass.); 16 millimeter

film interviews conducted by the Armenian Film Foundation (Thousand Oaks, Calif.). For a summary of the early oral history projects, see Levon Marashlian, "The Status of Armenian Oral History," *Society for Armenian Studies Bulletin* 5 (Spring 1980): 3–7.

26. NA, RG 59, 867.48/1448, and 867.4016/436.
27. *New York Times,* January 9, 1920; NA, RG 59, 867.4016/436; Zaven, *Patriarkakan Hushers,* 292, 296; *Times* (London), April 15, 1920, cited in Cretan, "Armenian Remnants," 17.
28. Edib, *Turkish Ordeal,* 16.
29. Admiral Mark L. Bristol Manuscript Collection, U.S. Library of Congress, Washington, D.C. (cited hereafter as Bristol Papers), "Ships and Shipping, Turkey" file, box 78, undated intelligence report, marked confidential, outlining the backgrounds of several prominent personalities in Constantinople.
30. *Times* (London), June 8, 1922; *New York Times,* June 4, 1922; ibid., June 7, 1922, cited in Cretan, "Armenian Remnants," 51. This was but one of the many restrictions on Armenian and American relief efforts the Nationalists imposed between 1920 and 1923.
31. Peter M. Buzanski, "Admiral Mark L. Bristol and U.S.–Turkish Relations, 1919–1922" (Ph.D. diss, University of California, Berkeley, 1960), 151. For a study of Bristol's personal and economic motivations, see Levon Marashlian, "Economic and Moral Influences on U.S. Policies toward Turkey and the Armenians, 1919–1923," *11. Türk Tarih Kongresi: Kongreye Sunulan Bildiriler* (Ankara: Türk Tarih Kurumu Basımevi, 1994), 5:1873–1944.
32. Buzanski, "Bristol and U.S.–Turkish Relations," 151.
33. For examples of Bristol's manipulative use of evidence on Cilicia, see Bristol Papers, "Syria and Cilicia" file, box 76, Bristol to Sec. of State, March 9, 1920, and NA, RG 860J.4016/29, Dr. William S. Dodd to Bristol, April 9, 1920, and Bristol to Dodd, April 26, 1920.
34. Bristol Papers, "Syria and Cilicia" file, box 76, Dupont to STANAV (Bristol), n.d.
35. Ibid., "From Chambers and Dodd at Adana for Coombs," n.d.
36. Ibid., Bristol to Sec. of State, June 14, 1920, relaying a report from Beirut, June 12, 2 P.M.
37. Ibid., Bristol to Sec. of State, June 15, 1920, relaying a report from Beirut, June 12, 4 P.M.
38. Ibid., Bristol to "FLAG PITTSBURGH," June 23, 1920.
39. Ibid., Bristol to Sec. of State, July 1, 1920.
40. Ibid., Bristol to Sec. of State, November 28, 1920, relaying report from Beirut, November 20, 11 A.M. (Hadjin was presumably mistyped in the report as "Hdkioto"). To a parliamentary question from Colonel Wedgewood, the Foreign Office responded that the "report regarding the siege and destruction of Hadjin and the massacre of its inhabitants in October 1920 is correct." FO 371/7874-E5290/18/44, Parliamentary Question by Colonel Wedgewood on May 18, 1922, FO response delivered by Mr. Harmsworth. The purpose of this chapter is not to determine the particulars of each event in Cilicia or to provide a

comprehensive discussion of the renewed persecutions all over Asia Minor. The intent is to give a general picture of the broad policies of the Angora authorities as reflected in information received by the British and American governments. For more on events in Cilicia, see Stanley Kerr, *The Lions of Marash: Personal Experiences with American Near East Relief, 1919–1922* (Albany: State University of New York Press, 1973); Ruben G. Sahakian, *Turk-Fransiakan Haraberutiunnere ev Kilikian, 1919–1921* (Turkish-French relations and Cilicia, 1919–1921) (Erevan: Gitutiunneri Akademia, 1970).

41. FO 371/7873-E2762/18/44, "La Situation des Chrétiens à l'intérieur," December 17, 1921, "dû à plume d'un missionaire français, témoin oculaire," provided by the Mixed Council to the British High Commissioner, March 3, 1922, and forwarded to the Foreign Office by Rumbold, March 7, 1922.
42. W. L. Woodward and Rohan Butler, eds., *Documents on British Foreign Policy, 1919–1939,* first series (London: Her Majesty's Stationery Office, 1970), 17:791–92, Rumbold to Curzon, April 24, 1922.
43. Ibid., minutes by Osborne, Rendel, and Curzon. Rumbold said Feizi Bey replaced Rauf Bey. Several British prisoners of war were exchanged for the Malta deportees.
44. FO 371/7874-E6954/18/44, Parliamentary Question by Williams, July 12, 1922, and FO minutes.
45. FO 7876–3611/19/44, Fethi Bey (Samsun) to Kemal (Angora), February 4, 1922, translation of the intercepted message in a British intelligence report, included with a parliamentary question pertaining to atrocities in the Pontic region.
46. *Daily Telegraph,* May 29, 1922. See also FO 371/7874-E5516/18/44, May 29, 1922.
47. *Bulletin Périodique,* April 12–May 24, 1921 and April 6–June 6, 1922, quoted in Marjorie Housepian, *Smyrna 1922: The Destruction of a City* (London: Faber and Faber, 1972), 98–99. *Yeni Gün's* article added: "We, the heirs of the great patriots of 1908, shall continue their work in the same spirit, in the same tradition and with the same energy." *Bulletin Périodique,* no. 14 (April 12–May 24, 1921): 9, cited in Housepian, *Smyrna,* 98 and 256n. 98.
48. FO 371/7876-E3820/19/44, Turkish representative Djavid to League Secretary-General, March 17, 1922 (forwarded by league to Foreign Office on March 31), and minutes.
49. *Chicago Daily Tribune,* May 19, 1922, cited in Housepian, *Smyrna,* 96. For more on this episode, see Marjorie Housepian Dobkin, "What Genocide? What Holocaust? News from Turkey, 1915–1923: A Case Study," in *The Armenian Genocide in Perspective,* ed. Richard G. Hovannisian (New Brunswick, N.J.: Transaction Books, 1986), 97–109.
50. "Turks' Insane Savagery. 10,000 Greek Dead," *Times* (London), May 5, 1922; *New York Times,* May 6, 1922 (see FO 371/7877-E4879, E5158/19/44). For similar information from another American eyewitness, see "American's Appeal. A Tragic Record," *Daily Telegraph,* May 16, 1922 (see FO 371/7877-E4980/19/44).

51. FO 371/7877-E5601/19/44, a lengthy report dated May 5, 1922, that was scheduled to appear that morning in the *New York Tribune, Philadelphia Public Ledger,* the *New York Times,* and the *New York World.* Yowell added that during the previous year, "the local government has taken twelve buildings from us without any compensation for the rent we had paid in advance for them."
52. FO 371/7878-E5674/19/44, interview with Dr. Ward, in a secret War Office military intelligence report issued May 22, 1922. Another American, Mr. Knapp, and a British subject, Miss Murdoch, both of whom worked for NER at Arabkir for two years until their departure in April 1922, corroborated much of Ward's information. FO 7879-E5875/19/44.
53. FO 7878-E5466/19/44, Rumbold to Foreign Office, May 27, 1922; and 7876-E4868/19/44, Rumbold to Curzon, May 10, 1922.
54. Dobkin, "What Genocide?" 106, citing NA, RG 59, 867.00/1525, Bristol diary entry, May 12, 1922. For Grew's comment on Bristol, see Joseph Clark Grew, *Turbulent Era: A Diplomatic Record of Forty Years, 1904–1945* (Boston: Houghton Mifflin Co., 1921), 1:539.
55. Bristol Papers, Dulles to Bristol, April 21, 1922, quoted in Dobkin, "What Genocide?" 106.
56. FO 371/7878-E5568/19/44, Oliphant to India Office, June 9, 1922, in response to an India Office telegram (May 30, 1922) regarding the concerns of Indian Muslims with the proposed commission of inquiry.
57. "Turkish Atrocities: Angora and Inquiry, Refusal or Evasion," *Daily Telegraph,* June 8, 1922. Grant had visited the site on April 28, 1921. For a comparison, see "Report on Certain Destroyed Villages in the Turkish War Zone in Anatolia," signed by Annie T. Allen and Florence H. Billings (undated), which the London Muslim League had released to the press, in FO 371/7879-E5739/19/44.
58. FO 371/7877-E5173/E5151/19/44, May 19 and 20, 1922; "A Strange Denial," *Daily Telegraph,* May 29, 1922.
59. "Turkish Atrocities: Eyewitness's Terrible Report, Interview with American Relief Worker," *Manchester Guardian,* June 6, 1922. For yet another interview with Ward, see "Kemalist War on Christians: Hostility to American Relief Work," *Times* (London), June 8, 1922.
60. *Daily Telegraph,* n.d., clipping in FO 371/7878-E584/19/44, Rumbold to Foreign Office, May 30, 1922. Rendel noted that Larry Rue "is clearly hand in glove with the anti-relief concession hunters," and that the Foreign Office had "of course received innumerable reports from a great number of different Americans (e.g., Dr. Crathern, Mr. Hopkins, Mr. Fuller, Mr. Hosford, etc.) which all agree about the magnitude of the atrocities," that were confirmed by Colonel Rawlinson, Signor Tuozzi, the Ismid Commission, and a number of "independent witnesses, so we could if necessary make a strong case even without mentioning names." Ibid.
61. According to the Ministry of Interior in Angora:

> The rights of the Armenians before the courts of law are not restricted . . . Christians have never been imprisoned without due process of law. Our prison files will show the veracity of this. . . .

> Christian women are not employed in Turkish houses without their will . . . those suspected of trying to strike the armies from the rear, have been sent to the interior in an orderly way and have been set free there. No civilized law can prevent a Nation from taking such measures by way of defense. The sick and the feeble of these deported Greeks have been taken care of by the government and in recent times have begun to send money to their families as will be proven by the records of the Post Office and the Agricultural Bank. In view of these facts it cannot be claimed that the Turkish Government is pursuing a policy of extermination. . . . The accusation that Christian women and girls have been used for immoral purposes by the Turks . . . is entirely false. In fact, it does not even call for a denial.

See FO 371/7878-E5692/19/44, "The Explanation of the Ministry of Interior," May 22, 1922.

62. FO 371/7878-E5692/19/44, Herbert Gibbons (Trebizond) to *Christian Science Monitor,* May 21, 1922.
63. *Parliamentary Debates,* Commons, May 30, 1922, 5th Series, vol. 162, 2029–34.
64. Ibid., 2034–38.
65. Ibid., 2038–41.
66. Ibid., 2041–47.
67. Ibid., 2047–51. Cecil also addressed the mandate issue. See James B. Gidney, *A Mandate for Armenia* (Kent, Ohio: Kent State University Press, 1967); Mine Erol, *Türkiye'de Amerikan Mandası Meselesi: 1919–1920* (The American mandate question in Turkey, 1919–1920) (Giresun: İleri Basımevi, 1972); Antranik Masis, *The Question of the American Mandate over Armenia* (Nicosia: Proodos Ltd., 1980).
68. *Parliamentary Debates,* Commons, May 30, 1922, 2052–56.
69. FO 371/7878-E5584/E5591/19/44, minutes by Rendel and Osborne dated June 1, 6, 7, 1922.
70. Bishop James Cannon, Jr., letter to the editor, *Times* (London), October 4, 1922.
71. FO 371/7955-E10952/10524/44, "Notes on Turkish Atrocities from February to September 1922," prepared by Mr. Rendel, October 10, 1922. Rendel's memorandum includes considerable detail on the Yowell/Ward reports and other evidence.
72. FO 371/7878-E5692/19/44, Gibbons (Trebizond) to *Christian Science Monitor,* May 20, 1922.
73. NA, RG 59, 867.4016/702/794/851; *New York Times,* November 17, 1922; ibid., November 30, 1922; ibid., December 1, 1922; *Times* (London), July 16, 1922; ibid., July 19, 1922; ibid., December 7, 1922.
74. NA, RG 59, 867.4016/720/726/736/794/954, and 867.48/1457; Near East Relief, *Reports to the Congress of the United States, 1920–1925* (New York, 1921–26), vol. for 1922, 17–18, 25–26; *Times* (London), November 3, 1922; ibid., December 4, 1922; *New York Times,* December 19, 1922.
75. For more on the circumstances under which thousands of Armenians and Greeks left Turkey in this period, see NA, RG 59, 867.4016/708/718/719/741/767;

Times (London), October 9, 1922; *New York Times,* September 25, 1992; ibid., November 15, 1922; ibid., December 6, 1922, cited in Cretan, "Armenian Remnants," 84–85.

76. FO 371/7907-E11825/27/44, Rumbold to Foreign Office, October 24, 1922. See also 7905-E11499/27/44.
77. FO 7875-E13829/18/44, Morgan (Aleppo) to Foreign Office, November 22, 1922.
78. FO E14548/18/44, Morgan (Aleppo) to Curzon, December 13, 1922.
79. *Alif Ba,* December 3, 1922, in FO 371/7875-E14558/18/44, translation forwarded to London by HMG Consul Palmer (Damascus), December 4, 1922. The newspaper also reported that the "Turkish Government issued an order to the effect that the American schools in Mardin should be closed," that over "1000 boys and girls (Armenian orphans) are now wandering about the streets," that a "rich Armenian woman of Kharpout desired to leave with her daughter (who was 12 years old) for America" but "the Turkish Passport Officer told her that it was forbidden for pretty girls like her daughter to leave the country," that men "between 18–45 are recruited as soldiers" and someone "who wishes to escape military service must pay 300 Turkish banknotes and a baggage animal," that "10 Turkish pounds is the usual charge for each person smuggled out from Mardin to Deir El Zor," and that the Turkish government "has actually issued orders that the Christians must leave the country within 5 months."
80. FO 371/7875-E14548/18/44, Morgan (Aleppo) to Curzon, December 13, 1922. Despite the scope of the expulsions from 1921 to 1923, a few pockets of Armenians managed to cling to several localities. In the fall of 1929, a final exodus of several thousand Armenians was reported by British authorities in Aleppo. Zaven Messerlian, "Turkio Nerkin Gavarneru Hayots Partadir Artagaghte, 1929–1930" (The forced exodus of the Armenians of the interior provinces of Turkey), *Haykazian Hayagitakan Handes* 3 (1972): 105–17.
81. Zaven, *Patriarkakan Hushers,* 308–9; NA, RG 59, 867.4016/780/790; *Times* (London), December 14, 1922, cited in Cretan, "Armenian Remnants," 31–32.
82. İsmet İnönü, *Hatıralar* (Memoirs) (Ankara: Bilgi Yayınevi, 1987), 2:80–81. According to İsmet, Noradoungian said nothing; whereupon İsmet launched into an extremely blunt denunciation of Armenian claims. See also Riza Nur, *Hayat ve Hatıratım* (Life and my memoirs) (İstanbul: Altındağ Yayınevi, 1968), 3:1069–71.
83. Noradoungian, "Antip Husher." Noradoungian dictated his recollection of his 1919 meeting with Damad Ferid on March 24, 1923. His published memoirs do not contain a reference to his meeting with Ismet Pasha in Lausanne.
84. Eventually, between 1926 and 1932, several additional laws were enacted to facilitate the expropriation of Armenian properties. Messerlian, "Hayots Partadir Artagaghte," 102–3. See also Mandelstam, *Confiscation des biens.*

5

The Forty Days of Musa Dagh

Its Impact on Jewish Youth in Palestine and Europe

YAIR AURON

Franz Werfel's *The Forty Days of Musa Dagh* had a considerable impact on Jewish youth in Eretz Israel (Palestine under British Mandate) and in Europe during the 1930s and the 1940s. Little has been studied about the attitude of the "Yishuv" (Jewish community in Palestine before the creation of Israel in 1948) and of the Zionist movement regarding the Armenian Genocide. The relevance of *The Forty Days of Musa Dagh* would be highly significant in any such investigation.

The Forty Days of Musa Dagh narrates the story of the inhabitants of several Armenian villages in the vicinity of Musa Dagh (Mount of Moses) in the district of Cilicia during World War I. The lead character, Gabriel Bagradian, an Armenian living in France for twenty years and far removed from his people, arrived back in the Ottoman Empire with his wife and son on the eve of the war for family reasons. The outbreak of the conflict and the political events soon to follow impelled Bagradian to make fateful decisions, both on a personal and a communal level. The most daring and consequential was the organization of his fellow Armenians to rise up against the Turks rather than to wait hopelessly for certain doom. The tale of that remarkable uprising is also Gabriel's personal story.

In writing the saga, Franz Werfel relied on journalistic accounts, official documents, and oral testimony. The Musa Dagh rising was one of the few instances of successful Armenian resistance to the Turks. Nonetheless, the book is not a work of history but of literature. Werfel completed the manuscript in 1932 after two visits to the Middle East, including Palestine.

He was undoubtedly shaken by the Armenian massacres and upset by the sight of refugees, but most of all he was moved by his encounters in Damascus with Armenian orphans, who were living reminders of the slaughter.[1] When the book was published in 1933, Hitler had already gained power. Soon after, the Nazis added *The Forty Days of Musa Dagh* to the long list of distinguished works banned or consigned to the flames.

On publication the book gained instant literary acclaim, making an impact around the world. It was translated into many languages, dramatized, and adapted into film script. Werfel's account was far more than a literary masterpiece. Its significance must be sought and understood on different levels. Fundamentally, there was a dramatic narration of a tragic historical event. Werfel brought the account of the Armenian Genocide to the awareness of the world public and international community. Most important, however, were the decisiveness and relevance of the issues he treated, related as they were to human nature and human responses.

Werfel's work deeply affected millions of people in many countries. It also touched the Jewish youth of the 1930s, both in Eretz Israel and in Europe, where Musa Dagh became a symbol for them. Eventually, during World War II, it evolved into a model, an example to emulate. Jews, emphasizing Werfel's Jewishness, tend to praise the masterful work greatly. Some go so far as to claim that "only a Jew could have written such a work." When anyone reads this striking historical novel, it is hard to believe that it was written before—not after—the Holocaust. Unquestionably, the book touches on profound issues, generating associations and memories with Jewish contexts, including troubling questions of Jewish identity, that disquieted Werfel himself.

Werfel succeeded in infusing and weaving into his masterful canvas enormously powerful historical and literary symbolism; whether this was intentional or not may never be known. These symbols, however, carry the most profound message, both in ancient and modern Jewish chronicles. Gabriel Bagradian, an assimilated Armenian, came forward, at first reluctantly, to lead his people in a time of distress. Is it not the biblical account of Moses, the founder of the Jewish faith? Is it not the modern story of Herzl, the godfather of the Jewish state? Is it not the prophetic warning of Werfel himself, about the impending Jewish Holocaust? After all, is not Musa Dagh the Mount of Moses, both literally and figuratively? Throughout the book, questions are raised about the significance of life, the inevitability of death, the reasons and purpose of human struggle, the role of the individual and his problematic relationships with one's own community, inquiries concerning responsibility and leadership, and additional transcendent issues. These queries have been the everlasting concerns for the Jews throughout their troubled history and especially in the 1930s and 1940s.

Werfel was born in Prague in 1890. At the age of eighteen, his first poem was published in a Viennese paper. In 1911, his first collection of poems appeared in Berlin. In World War I, he served as a soldier in the German army, participating in battles on the Russian front. After the war he settled in Vienna. In the 1920s, he traveled extensively around the world and visited, among other places, Eretz Israel.

Werfel belonged to a large group of Jewish authors writing in the German language and working in central Europe at the end of the nineteenth and beginning of the twentieth century. Jewish scholars, artists, and writers enjoyed prominence while playing an important role in the flowering of German culture during those years. The question of their identity, however, and their inner confrontations and uncertainties about their Jewishness, troubled many of these artists in various ways. The "Jewish-German" symbiosis reached its tragic conclusion after the Nazis rose to power. After the Nazis seized Austria in 1938, Werfel fled to France, only to escape again when the Nazis occupied that country. After many tribulations, Werfel arrived in the United States, where he died in Los Angeles in 1945. In addition to his poems, he wrote several plays in an expressionistic style and enjoyed much popularity, especially in Europe. But his great literary acclaim was as a novelist, particularly after the publication of *The Forty Days of Musa Dagh.*

Initial Jewish Responses to *Musa Dagh*

The Hebrew version of Werfel's book appeared in 1934. It was translated by Yosef Lichtenbaum and published by Stiebel.[2] (The book generated reactions and critiques, and it is important to emphasize that the following passages do not, and can not, exhaust the subject.) The author Dov Kimhi, whose books, especially his novel *The House of David,* have recently gained renewed attention, wrote an article on *Musa Dagh* in 1933, before the book had been translated into Hebrew. The review article was written after Kimhi had read chapters of Werfel's work appearing in the *Neue Freie Presse* of Vienna.

Kimhi praised Werfel, saying: "The scope which Werfel embraced, this time, is a great and a far moving one; the tragedy of the destiny of that misfortunate people was indeed immense, and it was only fitting that a poetic soul should search into it and draw out its humanity, its eternity."[3] Furthermore, in Kimhi's opinion there was a fundamental idea well beyond the historic settings and the tragic facts, which portrayed the Armenians as

> the people ravaged by "holy" suffering on the Biblical mountaintop, at the pinnacle of tragedy, unparalleled in the twentieth century; but didn't that nation become dedicated to its agony, uplifted, sanctified by a new life, compelled into interpreting all these torments as a reward for suffering? Or, like those who suffer from their weakness, who wither away, their immolation neither shaking the planet nor turning the individuals or the people into Chosen Ones? It is a quintessential Jewish belief in being smoldered and sanctified by fire. A Jewish poet has transposed [that Jewish predicament] into "another zone" and searched for resolutions among the Gentiles, because he did not want to look for answers among us, among his people.[4]

After describing the "Great Assembly," one of the most dramatic highlights of the book, when the Armenians finally decide to mount to the summit of Musa Dagh to make a stand and fight there, Kimhi writes:

> What reverberates in the text is not at all "typically Armenian." Many of these great passages, from the immense cry for life, could also have been voiced by other heroes, closer to Franz Werfel's, the Jewish poet, race. [Werfel] also once climbed a high steep mountain, and experienced a Jewish last trial of life, and viewed from the height of the Eternal Concept [on Massada] the valley of the Jordan River and the Dead Sea, where powerful Roman armies were assembled with lethal weapons and huge catapult stone-launchers, and scorned from that altitude of the Eternal Concept those who gathered in the valleys below, and identified with [the Jews] who slew themselves to prove to [the Romans] the Great Eternal Fact that "all flesh is dust . . . and the Word of our God will reign forever." . . . Werfel, however, chose the Armenians for expressing the theme of human tragedy, even though there was an impending catastrophe closer to him. And since no man can escape his destiny, the Hebrew reader—for whom the dilemma posed by Werfel in his book has been a life's companion, the essence of his communal blood—reads this book on the Armenians as the tragedy of ourselves, the Jews. And that is what is most precious for us in these pages.

Kimhi creates the context of Massada, he thus expressed the Eretz Israel experience which, in those years, nurtured the story of Massada as the myth of heroism.

Kimhi also raised another theme that repeatedly appeared in the various references to Gabriel Bagradian, the Armenian–not-Armenian, the assimilationist leader of the uprising, elements that apply to Werfel himself. "The estranged son who returns to the flock of his people." Beyond that, Kimhi writes, "you listen to our cry of pain, the voice of the Jew—and it does not disappear in the tragedy of others—for only the Jew knows what exile is in the fullest sense of the term."[5]

A review by R. Zeligman, published in the journal *Hapoel Hatzair* (The young worker) in August 1934, mildly criticizes the novel's literary weaknesses but then adds:

> The book so strongly attracts the heart, and its author invests so much love and pathos in his thesis, that we cannot dwell on these weaknesses, and we almost do not notice them. . . . The book is highly interesting for the educated reader in general; and the Jewish reader, in particular, will find a special interest in it. The fate of that Armenian tribe recalls in some important details the destiny of the people of Israel. The Jewish reader will encounter, without surprise, some known motifs, familiar to him from his life and his people's history. Furthermore, it is known to the Jewish reader that the Armenians were persecuted and suffered because of their race. Werfel made Gabriel Bagradian to say it specifically to his French wife: "No, this you cannot understand, Juliette; no one who has not become hated by the world because of his racial origin can understand this." Another "Jewish theme" could be perceived in the following description: "the Armenians eyes are almost always large, eyes with expression of terror at the sight of atrocities committed for a thousand years." The Jewish reader will also not wonder at hearing that the Armenian people are all imbued with the desire for education and knowledge. The book, valuable as is, achieves enhanced value for the Jewish reader through the motifs cited.[6]

The similarity of fate—Jews and Armenians being victims—is a prominent feature in the critiques of the book, alongside the recurrent refrain of complaint: "Why is a Jew writing about the fate of another people, and not the destiny of his own?" These elements stand out bluntly in an article by Moshe Beilinson, one of the foremost leaders of the Jewish workers movement in Palestine. In the article titled "A Monument to the Glory of Israeli Alienation" appearing early in 1936 in the paper *Davar,* Beilinson voiced reservations about the term "Armenian destiny."[7] For Beilinson the term did not seem proper: "this term is not justified." On the other hand, he proceeded to state that

> in truth, this is a Jewish book, and not just because it was written by a Jew, but in a less abstract way, simpler and more concrete, the author is speaking about us, our [Jewish] fate, our struggle. . . . I confess to a strange feeling when I took up this book, for I had already heard of its fame and the role it played and would forever play in extolling the heroic fight of the Armenian people, in setting up a poetic monument to their suffering and tribulations, [the book] in this superb way avenges their destruction. . . . It was a mixture of envy and anger, jealousy of that most wretched of peoples who thus won some reward, and anger that a fellow-Jew erected that monument to an alien people.

Haven't we suffered? Haven't we been persecuted? Has the sword of destruction not been wielded over our heads innumerable times? Have we not struggled against our bitter fate? But, behold, a great poet arises among us, with a worldwide reputation, at the height of his powers, but his epic is not for us. . . .

The book opens with a picture of the misery of the refugee children, wretched-looking and starving, who worked in the carpet factory [in Damascus] and this gave the decisive push to draw out from the historic abyss the inconceivable fate of the Armenian people. Weren't the author's eyes blinded? Had he traveled the face of the Earth and not seen the "picture of misery" of "wretched children" who were not Armenian refugees in Damascus? Did he search in the depths and could not find "an inconceivable fate" other than that of the Armenian people? This, indeed, is an unfortunate product of an assimilation, his readiness to serve others.

Perhaps the unsavory feeling, that of despondency, engulfed me totally and I could not share it with another; let me confess that there was such a feeling. But, as one reads on, it dissipated. It is a great and powerful book, one for generations, and no sense of unsavoriness will persist.

And then, another feeling prevailed with the passing of each additional page, replacing the envy and thrusting out the anger. Even if the book glorified strangers, admired the heroic war of the Armenian people, and caused readers to identify themselves with the suffering of that people, that was only the [superficial] exterior, for in truth, this is a Jewish book, and not just because it was written by a Jew, but in a less abstract sense, simpler and more concrete, the author wrote about us, [allegorizing] our destiny, our struggle.

The "Armenian destiny" as Franz Werfel perceived it and as he repeatedly stressed this concept in his universalism, his almost metaphysical mode, has no justification. Terrible persecutions befell this unfortunate people, both in Turkey and in Russia; but that was essentially the fate of a national minority under the heel of the oppressor. No hatred of generations accompanied the Armenians wherever they turned; no inescapable abyss, which separated them from other nations they encountered.

They were not an accursed monster, neither in the eyes of the Christians nor of the Muslims. No blood libel hovered over them. The world's children did not absorb hatred for them with their mothers' milk. They were not condemned to a life of wandering. They did not rove from land to land, country to country. They did not taste exile. They lived on their land, even though it was divided up among foreign states. They contributed to their culture. They were rooted in their soil. Their blood was, indeed, spilt by attackers.

But this fate, lamented by Werfel in a tragic-heroic epiphany, is not the Armenian fate—it is the Israeli fate! Those "eyes" of despair beyond all history, about which Werfel speaks, are not Armenian, but Israeli eyes. The boy standing suddenly in the middle of the road and asking his comrade "Why are we in fact Armenians?" is asking the question of an Israeli child of the disoriented generation. And the old man who asserts "to be an Armenian"

> is truly an Israeli saying that. This intercessor, a German priest, pure of soul, naïve and wise, unhappy, grievous, covered in sweat, whose feelings and his senses have been blunted through grievous emotions, who runs to his nation's rulers to persuade them to prevent the disaster and to Turkey's rulers to get them to stop the slaughter, is none other than "a Righteous Gentile."[8]

Beilinson turns the phrase "the Armenian destiny," that he regards as unjustified, into "Israel's fate." The sad eyes of the Armenian refugee children which so affected Werfel were none other than "Israelite eyes." He chooses to say "Israeli eyes" and "Israeli fate" and not "Jewish eyes" or "Jewish destiny." Beilinson does not end with that:

> Indeed, a book totally Armenian does not mention Jews; in fact, a Christian spirit pervades it, and every epigram and quotation before each chapter is precisely from the New Testament, a book glorifying the heroic war of the Armenian people, a book singing a mourning dirge and ennobling Armenian ordeals. That is how the world perceives it. . . . But that could not be the result, whether the poet knew and wanted this, or whether he did not want or know what he was doing, it is an Israeli book; nay, more than that, a Zionist one! And yet, without question, it is a book of Israeli assimilation, not just one written by an assimilated Jew, but a book of alienation.[9]

Gabriel Bagradian is a Herzl-like figure, with Herzl's fate. According to Beilinson, Herzl was a fairly assimilated person in a Jewish context, but "there is no justification, in the Armenian reality," he writes, "for this figure of an assimilated person returning to his people in time of danger." Beilinson interprets the theme of "Israeli alienation"—assimilation, in essence—and draws an analogy between Herzl and Bagradian, who of all Musa Dagh's people remains behind and alone on the mountain of rebellion. Despite all his efforts and sacrifices, Bagradian does not succeed in returning to his people. "Who can know if ultimately Bagradian was not a Herzl-like figure? For it was only at the start of the 'Forty Days' of our uprising and resurrection that Herzl lived among us. Musa Dagh is the Mount of Moses. Indeed, every man has his Mount Nebo [where Moses left his community and this Earth—never arriving at the promised land]. This was the Nebo of the man who returned to his people, yet remained a stranger amongst it."[10]

Accompanying the article were remarks apparently added by the journal's editors titled: "Our Demand from the Jew and the Zionist." After listing the requirement of physical labor and the introduction of the Hebrew language and Hebrew culture, the statement concludes: "In sum, the Movement demands from the Jew and from the Zionist his life, his heart, all his soul.

And it should not be accused of exaggeration nor of cruelty: the nature of the Movement requires this affliction, this great demand."[11]

Although it is beyond the scope of this discussion to analyze Werfel's attitude in regard to Judaism or his Jewishness. Meyer Weisgal, who knew Werfel well in the 1930s and considered himself to be his friend, wrote in his autobiography that in *Musa Dagh* Werfel expressed through the Armenians: "his consciousness of the Jewish tragedy (he told me the Armenians were his substitute for the Jews) but he never consciously reconciled himself with his Jewishness."[12] Werfel was perceived by many Jews, and certainly by many Zionists, as "an assimilated Jew." Those belittling Werfel's Jewishness, however, did not look into the full significance of that charge. The reaction to his book in Eretz Israel in the 1930s, from that viewpoint, was ambivalent: "Why did he write on the Christian Armenians' travails and not his people's suffering?" On the other hand, it was being said that "only a Jew could have written such a work."

Werfel visited Palestine twice, in 1929 and 1930. At that time, he expressed reservations and opposition toward Zionism, a feeling which he reversed, however, during the 1940s. Werfel's visits—during the second of which he encountered the Armenian tragedy—were evidently not made as a tourist. His motivations may have included a wish to examine the situation of "the new Jew" in Eretz Israel.[13] Werfel admitted he was attracted to certain elements of the Christian faith. But he rigorously rejected any possibility of conversion while Jews were suffering and being persecuted. It appears that in the 1940s he considered writing a novel dealing with the Holocaust but did not live long enough to follow through. In any event, *Musa Dagh* influenced the crystallization of the consciousness of many young Jews in Eretz Israel and the Diaspora in the 1930s and 1940s. For many of them, reading that book was an overwhelming emotional experience.

Musa Dagh and Eretz Israel during World War II

In 1942, the Yishuv went through a period of terror in light of the possibility that the Nazi army would invade Palestine. The Jewish community and its leadership were not united in their strategy of what needed to be done. Side by side were thoughts of surrender, defeatism, and powerlessness, as well as voices of courage, determination, and readiness to fight. With the arrival of General Erwin Rommel's Nazi army near the Egyptian border, posing a threat to Palestine and its Jewish community, plans were made to "turn Mount Carmel into the 'Musa Dagh' of the Jews of Eretz Israel." It evolved into a comprehensive plan to gather the Jewish defense forces in Eretz Israel into the Carmel region, and to conduct against the German invaders the fight from those heights. The plan was given several names, such as "the Northern Plan," "the Carmel Plan," "the Massada Plan," and a few called it the "Musa Dagh Plan."

The command of the operation was handed over to Yitzhak Sadeh, the Palmah (the special commando-like units) chief, and the planning was entrusted to Yohanan Rattner, a senior Haganah (the Yeshuv's leading military force) commander. The core of the group would comprise the Haganah and Palmah forces, the main military power available to the Yishuv in those years.

Haviv Kenaan's book, *200 Days of Fear,* relates the testimony of Meir Batz, one of the founders of the Palmah and the Haganah, a commander who was asked by Rattner to take a leading role in organizing the forces. Batz was summoned by Rattner, who then asked him if he had read *The Forty Days of Musa Dagh.* To his affirmative reply, Rattner reacted: "We want to turn the Carmel into the Musa Dagh of the Jews of Eretz Israel. Our comrades are trying to locate suitable places in the mountains for defense and for launching [guerrilla] attacks. Maybe we'll turn the Carmel into Massada."

One evening, the two went on a reconnaissance mission in that sector. Batz recalled: "I shall never forget that patrol for the rest of my life. We marched from Ahuza along the Carmel ridges. The moon smiled at us from the sky with its round face. I saw the Jewish Musa Dagh in my mind, which would ensure the Yishuv's future, especially its honor."[14] Batz adds: "We put our faith in the power of resistance of the Jewish Musa Dagh, and were determined to hold out for three or four months."[15] The memories which were associated with the plan were of Massada, Tobruk, and Musa Dagh. Some regarded "Musa Dagh as a more cogent model than Tobruk—Musa Dagh was conceived and planned by a man. It was an actual imperative, and therefore, it had to be possible."[16]

Another reference to names and symbolism aroused by the plan appears also in a letter from Yisrael Galili, another Haganah senior commander, to his wife Zippora, on March 24, 1942:

> I returned from my journey to "Ashdoti" [Davidka Nimri] with Yitzhak "S" [Sadeh]. On the way, we again turned over and discussed the idea of Haifa/Tobruk. Perhaps Haifa/Massada/Musa Dagh? In any event, it had a gripping notion. It has the elements of preparation, political work and imagination to rely on; there are extenuating topographical aspects; there is, for Britain, a military and political interest in holding Haifa; this idea is susceptible to enthusiastic response, and could mobilize a large force of Hebrew fighters.

> The political and historically symbolic meaning has great value and possible glory for the war of the Jews [together] with the British, in the defense of Haifa. It will be a fortified, island-like, in the event of an invasion. It is not easy to reject such a proposal. The idea is worth turning into a cause for a political campaign in London [and] America and for mobilizing allies.
>
> We shall supply the human material, who will give its life for the war for defending this land; from our allies we shall demand the required huge fortifications, the equipment (especially artillery) and support from the sea.[17]

The Impact in Europe during World War II

The recollections aroused in Eretz Israel, in connection with the struggle against a possible German invasion of the country, were of Massada, Tobruk, and Musa Dagh. In the ghettoes of Europe, Musa Dagh was cited more frequently, and Massada much less. A non-comprehensive evaluation corroborates the fact that, for the members of Jewish youth movements in the ghettoes, Massada was less of a relevant and appropriate symbol. It magnified and even glorified suicide. Musa Dagh's meaning was struggle, uneven odds to be sure, yet still with a chance. It symbolized the faint hope of salvation. The overwhelming communal consensus was appropriately voiced in Białystok Ghetto in 1943: "Nothing is left for us but to regard the ghetto as our Musa Dagh."

The Jewish underground movements operating in the ghettos debated bitterly their choice of direction, the purpose of their struggle, its meaning, the significance of their lives, and their likely deaths in the harsh reality in which they were ensnared. From those shattering and gripping discussions, which raised moral, existential, and Jewish dilemmas, some records were found after the war. They were written as the discussions were going on. One of these debates was disclosed in a gathering of Kibbutz Tel Hai by members and activists of the Dror branch, a Zionist-Socialist youth movement; the debate had taken place in Białystok on February 27, 1943.

The document was buried in Białystok and was found after the war. It was published under the heading *Pages from Fire*. The discussion represented an important record for understanding the dilemma faced by the Jewish underground groups in the ghettos. It had to be decided whether to stay in the ghetto or to take cover in the forests. During the debate three positions emerged: to stay in the ghetto and resist the Germans at any price; to save themselves by escaping; to move to the forests and to conduct armed resistance from there.

Herschel Rosenthal was the main advocate of "counteraction," that is, remaining in the ghetto. He declared, among other things: "Our fate is decided. There is, therefore, nothing left for us but one path, which is to organize a collective resistance in the ghetto at all cost; to regard the ghetto as our Musa Dagh, and to add a chapter of honor to the history of Jewish Białystok and to our movement."[18] A diary entry (February 19, 1943) in this stirring book, from Mordechai Tannenbaum, the commander of the Jewish underground in Białystok, describes a meeting to resolve the differing positions among the members of another youth movement, the "Zionist Youth" group and their comrades, whose dominant viewpoint was to leave the ghetto. In Tannenbaum's view, abandoning the ghetto represented "national betrayal." He added:

> Your task is to fulfill the national mission within the ghetto (and not leave the elderly on their own!) And should you stay alive, then arm yourselves and go into the woods. For the moment, search for connections [of both options] and establish a route. But first and foremost is the acquisition of weapons.
>
> The opposing argument was that it is better to be a living dog than a dead lion. They recalled that statement in "Musa Dagh." The old people wanted to fight on the thresholds of their homes, while the younger ones wanted to leave, etc. They wanted Aryan documents. Finally, after another clarification, everyone agreed to join my viewpoint.[19]

In a comment on this passage, the editors of *Pages from Fire* wrote that "because of the similarity in the fates of the two peoples, the Armenians and Jews, 'Musa Dagh' gained much popularity among the ghetto youth."[20]

In a letter from Tannenbaum (May 25, 1943) to Bronka Klibansky, the Jewish liaison with the Byałistok anti-Nazi Aryans, he wrote: " 'Musa Dagh' is now in fashion among us. If you read it, you will remember it all your life. It's by Franz Werfel."[21] Klibansky added that she read the book in Polish, perhaps even in German. She believed Tannenbaum had read it before the war, and reflected on it during the ghetto period. He and others recommended that the book be read.[22]

Activists of "Hashomer Hatzair" in Białystok, another Zionist-Socialist youth movement, also sought the book. Haike Grossman, a leading member of "Hashomer Hatzir" and of the Jewish underground in Poland, explained that the books read in that period by the active members were those whose content and themes were relevant to the realities of the time. "They educated themselves, thereby strengthening themselves; their challenge and their task impelled them to become both strong and human at the same time. That is what the movement and the nice books they read taught them. During that period, they read *Musa Dagh.* The book was passed from hand to hand."[23]

We find a similar corroboration in the memoirs of Inka Wajsbort, titled *Together and Yet Alone in the Face of the Terror.* She describes the events of the summer of 1941, when she was less than 16 years old. She was a member of "Hashomer Hatzair" in Sosnowice in lower Silesia area of Poland, which was annexed by Nazi Germany in 1939. For the Jews in that zone, it was relatively easier at the beginning than for those elsewhere in Poland. She wrote:

> Among the members of my group in the youth movement, Franz Werfel's book *The Forty Days of Musa Dagh* was passed from hand to hand. It totally captivated me. For four full days I was immersed in it and could not take my eyes away. I did not leave the house nor looked after my sister, I did not speak with Mother, nor joined at the table [at meal times]. Mother looked at me, her daughter, pityingly as though I had fallen ill with the "disease" of *Musa Dagh*. . . . I myself was in Musa Dagh, I was under siege; I was one of the Armenians doomed to die. If I raised my eyes from the book it was only to let out a cry, Mother! How could this be? The world knew and stayed silent? It is not conceivable that children in other countries went to school during that period, women put on makeup, men carried on their businesses, as though nothing had happened. . . . And a whole people was wiped out there.
>
> My mother knew nothing of Musa Dagh. That, also, appeared awful to me. I was totally shaken by the tragedy. When I finished reading the book, and for the first time went out into the courtyard, it was on a summer's day, flooded with the afternoon sun. I was struck, immediately, by a feeling of happiness at my existence on Earth. I was grateful to the Creator for the brilliance of the sun, the blue of the sky, the sight of two girls with pigtails skipping over a rope and counting their jumps in laughing voices—and that the world still was there. . . . At the time, I was not yet comparing it with the Holocaust, that summer of 1941; I did not yet feel the approach of a new Musa Dagh. That came later.[24]

In May 1942, before the expulsion of the Jews from Sosnowice, Mordechai Anielewicz, the commander of the Jewish underground in the Warsaw Ghetto, came to their ghetto. He reported to the adult members of the movement on what had happened in other areas of Poland where a large proportion of the Jews had already been annihilated. "Was that, then, Musa Dagh again!? And wasn't the world silent again!?"[25]

Additional evidence from that era is to be found in the *Vitlle Diary* by Yitzhak Katznelson, a poet and author, a teacher and educator, and a principal eulogizer of the Holocaust. He was connected with the Jewish Pioneer Organization and, when the war broke out, moved from Łódź to Warsaw. He published his writings in the underground journals of the "Dror" organization. During the Warsaw Ghetto Uprising, he was with the

"Dror" battalion of fighters in the city. In May 1943, he was transferred as a Honduran citizen to the French detention camp at Vitlle where he wrote his last works, including the *Vitlle Diary.* He died at the age of sixty in Auschwitz in May 1944.

Mourning the killing of the Jews, Katznelson asked (August 8, 1943), "Who will avenge us from this bestial and loathsome people?" He wrote "with his heart's blood" to his younger brother: "Where are you? Shall we indeed never see each other again on earth?"[26] Katznelson added:

> The Turkish Army (not the people, only the army) under the auspices then of the Germans, who had the same destructive spirit toward all nations, as they have today—except they did not intend then to direct their war only against Israel—those Germans were guilty of the blood of the Armenians which the Turks spilled, even though a German priest went to the Turkish regime and pleaded for mercy for the Armenians. [The reference is to the Protestant pastor Johannes Lepsius].
>
> Among the many vermin not a single priest has asked those accursed ones among humanity: Why are you murdering Jews? Why do you spill all that blood? The Turks killed the Armenians, a rival people with whom they had accounts to settle—more than a million individuals. The Armenian people found someone to expose their suffering, someone to mourn them, to avenge their blood, in an author of Jewish origins, the Jew Werfel, whose people, Werfel's people, are not a rival of this criminal nation; a people without a land, without claims or complaints, a quiet, poor people, an abandoned people, dispersed and separated among many, when it was slain and lost six millions and more, when its victims were its children and its elderly—who will mourn for them?
>
> The Werfels will mourn for any people, but not for their own . . . . The pseudo-Jews who have survived will not learn a thing from the loss of their people, did not see the blessing in their lives, will not acknowledge their martyrdom and death at all. . . . Who will mourn for us? Who will set up a memorial for us? Who will relate in detail to many others about this great people, this people of Levites among others, of the sons of prophets, of the children of their God in lands which killed them, all of them, leaving not a child, not a fetus in its mother's womb—more than six million in a brief; who will write the Jewish saga of Musa Dagh? When the Armenians were killed, they were mourned in a Jewish book; but when the Jewish People was killed, who will mourn for them?"

Yitzhak Katznelson's writings were published by Yitzhak Zuckerman and Shlomo Even-Shushan. A bibliographic comment apparently by Zuckerman about Franz Werfel confirmed: "His well-known book on the massacre of the Armenians, *The Forty Days of Musa Dagh,* was widely read by young people in the ghettos."[27]

Yitzhak Zuckerman (Antek) was the deputy commander of the Jewish revolt in the Warsaw Ghetto. The tremendous impact of *Musa Dagh* on him was recalled by Zvika Dror, a member of Antek's kibbutz named "the Ghetto Fighters," who testified that Antek "was a kind of tutor to me concerning the Holocaust, in conversations, in giving ideas what to read, etc."[28] Dror added: "When he wanted to explain to us, he said the Warsaw Ghetto uprising could not be understood without reading *The Forty Days of Musa Dagh* by Franz Werfel. And added, incidentally: 'This Jew understood the soul of the Armenians better than he understood the Jewish soul'."[29]

Another reference is given by Dov Ben Ephraim (Lutek), one of the leaders of the Jewish underground in Tchenstokhova, who writes on how he was sent into the Konyestopol forest "with the purpose of organizing a 'Musa Dagh'."[30] Among the underground members of the socialist youth movements in western Europe, the book also made a strong impression. Members of the underground in Holland read it in German. "It was a 'textbook' for us. It opened our eyes and spelled out for us what could happen, without our knowing, in fact, what would happen."[31] The book was probably read in Yiddish (there were at least two Yiddish editions), in Polish, and in German. In *Hunger for the Printed Word: Books and Libraries in the Jewish Ghettoes of Nazi-Occupied Europe,* author David Shavit found that the most widely read books among adults were *The Forty Days of Musa Dagh* and Tolstoy's *War and Peace,* and among younger readers *The Heart* by Edmond de Amicis.[32]

Conclusion

These few instances cited—and there are others like them—indicate the great significance youth movements attributed to the book, already before the war and especially after it started. *Musa Dagh* was an example, a point of reference, and to a certain degree, a model to be esteemed, admired, and imitated.

There is much attractiveness and interest in the speculation that Werfel was really dealing with Jewish destiny, and through the hero of the novel, Gabriel Bagradian, Werfel was relating his own difficulties and identity dilemmas. Bagradian, like Werfel, was cut off from his people. Bagradian went to visit his home "after twenty-three years of Europe, Paris! Years of complete assimilation!" In Paris, "He had been allowed to live as scholar, a bel esprit, an archeologist, an historian of art, a philosopher." Bagradian was "more French than ever, Armenian still, but only in a sense—academically."[33]

Jewish symbolism was clearly manifest in the narrative; Musa Dagh is the Mount of Moses. The fighting on the mountain, according to Werfel, continued for 40 days (the biblical flood lasted 40 days, Moses stayed on the mountain 40 days, etc.). In reality, according to the documents Werfel used, the fighting lasted for 24 days, while other documents speak of 36 days. Yet other calculations make the entire saga of the uprising 53 days.[34] There are also clear analogies between Bagradian, who died on the summit of Musa Dagh while French vessels were miraculously rescuing his people, and Moses, buried on Mount Nebo and never reaching the Promised Land. Some would want to draw an analogy also between Bagradian's visit to his homeland, for which he felt no closeness, and Werfel's visit to Eretz Israel. These, of course, are only few of the symbols.

It is evident, though, that *Musa Dagh*'s magnetism—destined to become a symbol for the Jewish fighters—was derived from the great power residing in the text, which aroused so many people in Europe in the 1930s. For the people living during that brutal wartime period, and especially for the Jewish youthful combatants of the ghettos' underground groups, the book contained three additional vital elements. First and foremost in importance and symbolism was the existential setting, the tragic realization of an imminent sacrifice, of being an intended victim. In addition to the victim's identification with another victim, there was a real fear that the Jewish fate was sealed. In the ghettos, more than anywhere else, the reality of total devastation became more apparent, at least for the members of the underground.

Secondly, the young Jewish readers and the Armenian characters shared a self-perception of themselves as Promethean victims who struggle, righteous rebels who aspire to freedom, not ready to surrender their lives and honor even if their fate was already pre-determined. Even the dilemma so widely posed in the past in the context of the Holocaust—"going like sheep to the slaughter"—appears numerous times in *Musa Dagh.* That self-examination constantly appeared in Werfel's book: "I know how I mean to die—not like a defenseless sheep . . . not in the filth of a concentration camp." Furthermore, "even if there's no such good fortune in store for us, there'll still be plenty of time for dying. And then at least we shan't need to despise ourselves as defenseless sheep."[35] From that viewpoint, reading the book strengthened the spirit of the members of the youth movements, the future fighters, as Mordechai Tannenbaum and other underground leaders suggested.

There may have been, however, a difference in interpretations given to *Musa Dagh* by the members of the underground groups in eastern Europe and in western Europe. The emphasis in eastern Europe, because of very different conditions and perhaps because of differences in mentality, was "the question is how we will die!" Death appeared inevitable, the matter to consider was its execution, and the honorable demise was: "Not like a defenseless sheep" (a quotation from the priest Ter Haigasun, in the chapter on The Great Assembly). By contrast, in Holland and perhaps elsewhere in western Europe, the story of Musa Dagh left the door open for at least a chance of salvation. Resisting the Germans and victory over them would mean staying alive. They identified, in culture and spirit, with Gabriel Bagradian, the "assimilated" Armenian, who later led the rebellion, and who interrupted the priest's words, by saying: "Why death!"[36]

Thirdly, momentous moral questions arise from Werfel's book. It prominently expresses humanistic values, to which the members of the youth movements were sensitive, as well as the moral uncertainties by which they were beset. The story of the defense of Musa Dagh became, indeed, a source of inspiration, an example for the underground members to learn, a model to imitate. They equated their fate with that of the Armenians. In both cases, murderous and evil empires conspired to uproot entire communities, to bring about their total physical extinction. In both cases, resistance embodied the concept of death and national honor on the one hand, and the chance of being saved as individuals and as a nation on the other.[37]

All in all, *Musa Dagh* was relevant because it dealt, in the most penetrating manner, with the existential and moral questions that preoccupied young Jews in those difficult years. Werfel's book broke away from what was defined in that period as the narrow scope of literature. *The Forty Days of Musa Dagh* influenced many members of the youth movements who extolled it and regarded the Armenian uprising as an example to emulate. It is with deep regret that I must point out that the young generation in Israel today has heard nothing of *Musa Dagh,* and, shamefully, know nothing about the genocide of the Armenian people.[38]

Notes

1. Werfel's biographer, Peter Stephan Jungk, claims that Werfel was wrong when he added a note at the beginning of his book: "The miserable sight of some maimed and famished-looking refugee children, working in a carpet factory, gave me the final impulse to snatch from the Hades of all that was, this incomprehensive destiny of the Armenian nation." In his opinion the visit was in the first months of 1930. See Peter Stephan Jungk, *Franz Werfel: Une vie de Prague à Hollywood* (Paris: Albin Michel, 1990), 339.

2. A new edition of *Musa Dagh,* translated by Zvi Arad, was published by Am Oved in 1979. A comparison of the two Hebrew translations, before and after the Holocaust, could be an interesting subject for research.
3. Dov Kimhi, *Massot Ketanot* (Jerusalem: Reuven Mass., 1938), 226.
4. Ibid., 228.
5. Ibid., 230.
6. R. Zeligman, "The Forty Days of Musa Dagh," *Hapoel Hatzair,* no. 41 (August 1934).
7. Moshe Beilinson, "A Monument to the Glory of Israeli Alienation," *Davar,* January 22, 1936. The article also appeared in the collection *Dovrut: For Reading Circles and Study Groups, A: Beilinson Selections* (Ein Harod: Hakkibutz Hame'uhad, 1936).
8. *Dovrut,* 91–92.
9. Ibid., 93–94.
10. Ibid., 95.
11. Ibid., 96.
12. Meyer Weisgal, *Ad Kan* (So far) (Jerusalem: Weidenfeld and Nicholson, Ma'ariv Library Publishing Press, 1971), 93.
13. See Jungk, *Franz Werfel,* 52, 264. See also the unpublished correspondence between Weisgal and Werfel, dealing openly with Werfel's Jewishness, his attitude toward Zionism, and his rejection of a possible act of conversion, allegedly because of the persecutions of the Jews and because of Christian anti-Semitism. Central Zionist Archive, Z5/702.
14. Haviv Kenaan, *200 Days of Fear* (Tel-Aviv: Mol-Art Publisher, n.d.), 244–45. Yehoshua (Josh) Palmon was, at that time, engaged in training the units of the undercover Palmah groups. These units were intended to be employed behind enemy lines in the event of an invasion by Rommel. According to Kenaan, Palmon and his colleagues were fearful of the possibility of a terrifying mass slaughter if the Germans entered the country and that the Jews of Eretz Israel would meet the same fate as the Armenian minority faced in the Ottoman Empire in World War I. Ibid., 253.
15. Uri Brenner, *Facing the Threat of German Invasion of Eretz Israel in the Years 1940–1942,* Yad Tabenkin, Research Booklets, 3 (1981), 154–55. Brenner also relied, in addition to Kenaan, on the radio program "Musa Dagh on the Carmel," broadcast by Kol Yisrael on June 3, 1971. See also Yoav Gelber, *Massada: The Defense of Eretz Israel in World War II* (Ramat-Gan: Bar-Ilan University, 1990).
16. Emmanuel Markovsky-Mor, in Galili Files, File no. 8, Haganah Historical Archive (HHA).
17. Galili Files, File no. 8, Letters to Zippora, HHA.
18. Mordechai Tannenbaum-Tamaroff, *Pages from Fire,* rev. ed. (Jerusalem: Yad Vashem and Beit Lohamei Hagettaot, 1984), 79. Herschel was one of the central figures in organizing the Białystok underground and Tannenbaum's closest friend. He was killed in the August 1943 uprising, at the age of twenty-four. Ibid., 283 (annotated index).
19. Ibid., 50.

20. Ibid., 238. The editors Bronka Klibansky and Zvi Shener were, through their personal experiences, very familiar with details of the period and with the mood prevailing among the members of the youth movements in the ghetto.
21. Ibid., 138.
22. Bronka Klibansky, interview by the author, July 1, 1990.
23. Haike Grossman, *The People of the Underground* (Tel-Aviv: Sifriyat Poalim, 1965), 125; Levy Aryeh Sarid, "The Fighting Jewish Underground in Byałistok," *Moreshet,* no. 55 (October 1993): 68.
24. Inka Wajsbort, *Together and Yet Alone in the Face of the Terror* (Tel-Aviv: Moreshet, with Beit Lohamei Hagettaot, 1992), 33–34.
25. Ibid., 60.
26. Yitzhak Katznelson, *Last Writings, 1940–1944,* new ed. (Beit Lohamei Hagettoat: Hakkibutz Hameu'had, 1956), 211.
27. Ibid., 259.
28. Zvika Dror, letter to the author, June 28, 1990.
29. Zvika Dror, "Life with Kushmar" (under the auspices of Yitzhak Zuckerman), *Davar,* June 8, 1990. Dror conducted interviews and edited the book *Dapei Edut* (Pages of testimony) (Beit Lohamei Hagettoat: Hakkibutz Hame'uhad, 1984).
30. Dov Ben Ephraim, *Edut* (Testimony) (Jerusalem: The Center for Oral History, Institute of Contemporary Judaism, Hebrew University). The author is grateful to his colleague Dr. Ariel Horowitz who directed him to this testimony.
31. Yigal Binyamin, interview by the author, November 22, 1994. Binyamin was a member of the socialist underground in Holland.
32. David Shavit, *Hunger for the Printed Word* (Jefferson: McFarland, 1997).
33. Franz Werfel, *The Forty Days of Musa Dagh* (New York: The Modern Library, 1934), 5–6.
34. Jungk, *Franz Werfel,* 176. According to the testimony of one of the uprising's leaders, published in the American weekly *The Outlook,* on December 1, 1915, there were 53 days of self-defense.
35. Werfel, *Musa Dagh,* 205–8.
36. Ibid., 206. The author is grateful to Yigal Binyamin, who drew his attention to this distinction, which needs additional confirmation.
37. Ra'ya Cohen-Adler, "Franz Werfel's The Forty Days of Mussa Dagh as Investigative Literature," in *State, Government and International Relations* (Jerusalem) 32 (Spring 1990).
38. For a broader discussion of the issues raised in this chapter, see Yair Auron, *The Banality of Indifference: Attitude of the Jewish Community in Palestine and the Zionist Movement towards the Armenian Genocide* (Tel Aviv: Dvir Publishing House, 1995; English version forthcoming from University of Toronto Press).

6

Survivor Memoirs of the Armenian Genocide as Cultural History

LORNE SHIRINIAN

By the end of World War I, almost half of the Armenian nation had been destroyed in the Armenian Genocide. After the war, the survivors of the genocide were gathered in orphanages in Greece and in various places in the Middle East, or they went to the new Republic of Armenia, a greatly reduced territory in the Caucasus. Despite stated intentions, the international community did little to help Armenians politically. Resurgent Turkish nationalism under Mustafa Kemal Ataturk and growing Soviet strength in the Caucasus, combined with the Allied pull-back from the region, dashed all hope for an Armenian homeland encompassing its historic territories. By 1922, the Armenian republic had been incorporated into the Soviet Union; Western Armenia remained devastated and practically devoid of Armenians. Many of the survivors were then taken from the orphanages and refugee camps to begin new lives in various parts of the world. The modern Armenian Diaspora had begun.

The Armenian nation has never had any meaningful official recognition of this crime against humanity; indeed, the world has not made itself ready to hear the testimonies of the survivors. Nevertheless, this deliberate silence has not prevented Armenian survivors from telling their stories. Elie Wiesel wrote, "If the Greeks invented tragedy, the Romans the epistle, and the Renaissance the sonnet, our generation invented a new literature, that of testimony."[1] Wiesel referred to the Holocaust generation, but forgot the generation of Armenians who suffered the genocide of 1915 and who began to bear witness soon after.

The twentieth century has seen the birth of a new literary genre, the survivor memoir. The focus of this essay is on the abundant literature, memoirs, and autobiographies recording the fate of those Armenians who survived the 1915 genocide and its aftermath. Survivor memoirs may take many forms and deal with a variety of subject matter such as living through a war or a natural catastrophe. Memoirs present certain problems, for they are literary in nature with a strong narrative element, yet they are also history and are historiographic in nature. Both of these areas raise questions as to truth, fictionality, and representation. Some of the texts studied are clearly memoirs, while others cross the line between autobiography and memoir. I have excluded works of poetry and drama, which can also contain elements of memoir writing. In some cases, a memoir may have been dictated or told to another person who then wrote down the story. I have excluded texts that are too obviously biographical in nature; that is, they have been dictated to a second party who then writes the narrative. The problem is that the biographer can embellish and edit the text without proper input from the survivor. Short stories, diaries, and letters as well will not be considered, neither will works of journalism. Donald Miller and Lorna Touryan Miller have done excellent work on the oral testimony of the survivors in their book, *Survivors: An Oral History of the Armenian Genocide.*[2] Oral histories are, however, developed from a different dynamic and very different processes from those of written texts. For example, there is a performative aspect that is part of the oral testimony given by a survivor. In addition, in such interviews the interviewer stimulates a response from the interviewee through direct questioning. Finally, oral testimony is not edited. In contrast, however, written survivor memoirs are usually revised and edited before publication. Consequently, oral histories will not be considered in this discussion.

The texts I will study have been written in English. I recognize that a great deal of material exists in Armenian both in the Diaspora and in Armenia. I am interested in the Diaspora as the site of production of these texts as well as in English, a new and acquired language for the survivors, as the mediation of the genocide experience and the lingua franca of Armenian Diaspora culture in North America. The fact that a great many survivors of the genocide have chosen to write their memoirs in English in North America is telling; their texts are an integral part of the Armenian experience in the Diaspora and thus are important elements of its cultural history.

The Armenian Genocide is a large field of study that has been actively researched by historians, political scientists, sociologists, and literary scholars. If there is one area related to the genocide that has been virtually ignored, however, it is survivor memoirs. When Armenians arrived in North

America to settle and gather the remnants of their nation in Diaspora, among their first cultural creations was the survivor memoir. One of the first important questions these texts pose for researchers is to whom is given the guardianship of the Armenian Genocide? To the historian? To the political scientist? To the writer of poetry, fiction, and drama? To the survivor? Each in his/her own way attempts to recreate the event in written texts. This act, remembering and writing, is yet another reminder that in such texts, whether they be historical or literary in nature, we are given reality that is represented. In either case, in the narration, the telling transforms what is being told. This essay will look at Armenian survivor memoirs from the 1915 genocide and will concentrate on three related fields: the form of the genre, the responses of the authors to their experiences, and the survivor memoir as cultural history.

Survivor Memoirs

Memoirs are prose stories written by real persons about their own life. The recounter acts as a witness, and the individual point of view is emphasized. Nevertheless, a memoir has a broader dimension than just the individual life. A text that merely focuses on the individual life and the personality of the writer is autobiography. A memoir, on the other hand, contains elements of the history of the times and the social group to which the writer belongs. We understand the genocide through the various ways it is passed down to us. For example, we comprehend what the survivors went through from the way the genocide is represented, not only from archival documents and historical texts but also from memoirs and autobiographies. The narrative forms of these literary genres contain historical memory. Thus, what is remembered of the Armenian Genocide depends on how it is represented. We can say that because survivor memoirs are part literature and part history, they are a form of literary historiography. They take the form of a historical document as well as a literary text with strong narrative and fictional elements. In the preface to her memoir, *Daughter of the Euphrates,* Elizabeth Caraman writes

> I do not tell this, the story of my life as I remember it in the interior of Turkey during and before the massacre years of 1915–1919, because it is the most harrowing, but because in the twenty years that have elapsed, no other survivor of that affliction has arisen to perpetuate the personal experiences of one who lived it. My account merely rounds out, in part, the story of the tragedy of the Near East which has elsewhere been copiously told by "observers," by Near East Relief workers, by impassioned but impotent statesmen, and by platform lecturers. . . . The names of all the characters except those of my immediate family are fictitious.[3]

Here, the historical perspective of an eyewitness participant in the events of the genocide, combines with an element of fictional characterization as part of the narrative structure of the story. The survivor memoir retains various literary conventions besides characterization such as chronological time, description, dialogue, and most importantly, a narrative voice that is capable of linking and binding together the chaotic events of the catastrophe, thereby imposing order. The way historical events are configured depends on the way plot structures are developed, and this is a literary process. The encoding of such events is culture specific in that the way a culture makes sense of personal and public pasts will depend on paradigms that are culturally provided.[4]

In North America, we can recognize two ways in which the genocide has been used in the plot strategy of culturally recognized forms. The first is in historical romance, romantic adventure novels, and plays with tragic elements. Some examples are Albert S. Apélian's *The Antiochians,* Jack Hashian's *Mamigon,* Marie Sarrafian Banker's *Armenian Romance,* H. H. Haig's play, *The First Genocide,* and Bedros Margosian's *Of Desert Bondage.*[5] Typically, one finds statements on the dust jacket or in the introduction which indicate a claim to factuality as well as fictionality. In the introduction to Banker's *Armenian Romance,* she writes, "A true story, partly under fictitious names." Apélian writes before his novel begins: "*The Antiochians* is a work of fiction. With the exception of historical names, events and dates, any similarity to the names of persons living or dead or to actual events is coincidental and unintentional." What these additions do is to posit their fictionality, yet at the same time contradict it to some extent by positing their factuality in that writers were in many cases a witness to and participants in the events that they have now partly fictionalized in their narration. On the dust jacket of Haig's play, one finds, "*The First Genocide,* his first published play . . . stems from his own memories of the Armenian tragedy." In this way the literary and the historical complement each other, so that the reader is placed in a position where the enjoyment and appreciation of the fictional nature of the text is enhanced by belief in the historical accuracy of the narrative.

In North America, the second way the genocide has been used as plot material in culturally recognized forms is in the memoir, the survivor memoir—specifically, having a strong set of culturally provided categories such as Christianity and the American Dream. Much of the language of these texts describes the tragedy in religious terms. In addition, many of the survivors who live in the Diaspora in North America are very grateful to their new country, which has permitted them to prosper and practice their culture and religion in peace and stability. In Elise Hagopian Taft's memoir, *Rebirth,* these two elements come together clearly in the following excerpt: "One finds it so different in America, where one can live in dignity and honor and achieve the respect of one's fellow man regardless of one's origin and language or creed. Dishonored and disinherited, uprooted and crucified in the old country, we are here regenerated as human beings and reborn. This is the essence of the American Dream, reaching out to the farthest shores."[6] Thus, elements of religious discourse, "crucified" and "reborn," are combined with the ideals of the American Dream.

These memoirs have a status and function in Armenian culture as well as in Armenian collective memory and form a layer of Armenian social imaginary life. The writing of these works indicates a faith in memory and history in that the author believes that the text will be significant. The hope must be that as time passes and the events of the genocide become a distant and vague rumor, the memoir will be a substitute for memory and that as a document it will be able to give a credible representation of the unimaginable.[7] Memory, which is always susceptible to alteration and disappearance, can become a factor of social cohesion in the written memoir, for it is through other people's memories that the individual completes his own experience, which in the end attaches him to the community to which he or she belongs.[8] The memoir, therefore, has an important social function.

The survivor memoir is a highly complex genre. As historical and fictional narrative, it is a product of the individual imagination, yet there is inherent in the genre a claim to the truth. In proceeding to an understanding of these texts, we must ask what the survivors' responses are to their experiences as they translate knowing into telling. The survivor memoir is born from the time when culture and violence collide, leaving the survivor with a fragmented sense of life. Because these texts are testimonial in nature, they very often contain a prologue or an introduction in which the author writes an apologia, a justification for writing, a statement of intentions. In these sections, one senses the author has gathered these fragments together as part of the process of healing to make life whole again, to release himself or herself even momentarily from the burden of surviving. Taft writes: "I did it for my three sons so they would know something of their roots, the mass deportations, the atrocities perpetrated by the Turkish government in 1915 and thereafter."[9]

Even distanced in time, the effect of the events is still chilling. However, because the survivors feel compelled to write their story, often without ever having written a lengthy text before, the very act of writing is a curiosity for these people, who express their feelings openly and without pretension.

Ramela Martin says in her memoir, *Out of Darkness:* "Writing makes me an observer, and I can examine my life without giving gloss or glamor. I find I am frightened of a future filled with the past, filled with memories of terror. And where shall I seek my beginnings? In Armenia, where I witnessed brutality on a scale my people, 70 years later, still speak of in hushed voices? Where is the beginning? . . . But I have survived and will share those events that marched relentlessly through me to become part of my existence."[10]

The survivors are willing to explore and expose their deep pain to teach family members of a new generation their modern history through lived experience; however, in many cases, the desire moves beyond the personal and places the specificity of the Armenian tragedy, in a larger human context. Taft writes: "May the world get to know through these pages the true meaning of Genocide and what it does to the human spirit, and resolve never to let the Holocaust happen again to any people on earth."[11] By referring to both the Armenian Genocide and the Holocaust, Taft joins the two catastrophes as a problem confronting all of humanity.

Kerop Bedoukian, in the preface to his memoir, *The Urchin: An Armenian's Escape,* also connects his personal experience to a larger human condition as he describes his intentions in writing his memoir. "The organized massacres of the Armenians by the Turkish nation during the first world war is a memory that the survivors cannot forget. This book is my story of when, as a young boy, I experienced these events from the beginning to the end: therefore, they are vivid in my recollection. Although much has been left out, nothing has been added or exaggerated. . . . My attention was directed outward—to *see* what was going on around me. [With] naïve objectivity to the perception of experiences which, in all truth, were full of horror and terror. . . . I have chosen to remain true to the memories of a young boy who, in the manner of a child, was curious as to the nature of the world around him."[12] What is emphasized here is not only the survivor's need to unburden himself of his memories of the tragedy but also his ability to observe events that were taking place around him. He places his life in a broader social and historical context, which is a defining feature of the survivor memoir.

In survivor memoirs, we witness through the eyes of the writers a sudden and absolute change from a normal existence to an all-pervasive meeting with death.[13] Through the survivors' testimony, their bearing witness, they make the past intelligible and meaningful for us in the present. The narrative account moves from the individual experience to the communal. The crucial function of these texts as cultural and social history comes from the fact that Armenians (like many other peoples) view the past through their collective experience in history. Survivor memoirs are key texts of Armenian identity;

they force individuals to re-evaluate their commitment to their identity and their community. Survivor memoirs, then, are part of the process that leads Armenians to validate the social and personal boundaries that identify them.

Survivor Memoirs as Cultural History

For the survivors, living in the Diaspora in North America is seen as a mixed blessing; they are grateful to have been able to begin a new life here. Dirouhi Kouymjian Highgas remembers her arrival in 1929: "For the first time in my life, I no longer felt like a refugee girl. I had the strangest feeling—as if I had been away for a long, long time, and had just arrived home."[14] The survivor memoir is a response to exile and represents the home reached through a voyage of self-realization. Nevertheless, the memory of the genocide is never forgotten, and the commitment to speak out remains strong. Elizabeth Caraman's memoir, *Daughter of the Euphrates,* ends with a bitterness that is softened by what her new home has offered her: "As a family we were no more, in Turkey or in the world. The Turk, truly, had exterminated us from the face of the earth."[15] In the end she asks: "If I was deserting my homeland, what was I leaving behind . . . a land in which I had helped to bury too many brutally killed, too many heartlessly starved into a voiceless death, too many in the grip of disease. A land of awful memories, of lifelong nightmares. I was escaping it all—escaping all except that thing called Memory. . . . I was seeking AMERICA!"[16]

Although America may be a haven and the survivor may feel integrated and even assimilated into American life years after the genocide, there is an overriding sense of loss and perhaps even guilt that survival in the New World entails the loss of centuries of Armenian identity. In *Rebirth,* Taft writes: "If I grieve in a nostalgic sense at the loss of the Armenianism in my grandchildren, I do so because I survived by remaining Armenian in a world which had sought to destroy me. *I would not let it destroy me.* And it was only my "Armenianism" and all that it implies in terms of survival—that saved me as a human being."[17]

The passing on of Armenian culture, then, is the key to survival for many of the writers. The impossible story that their memoirs represent is written to combat loss of identity, community, and home. For Armenians, 1915 is always in the background. It forms, to a great extent, the particular tragic vision of life many first and second generation Diaspora Armenians have. At the same time, Armenians have developed a resounding response to this vision—survival. Part of the cultural importance of these texts simply lies in their encoding the thoughts and feelings of the first generation of

Armenians in North America after 1915, which provides a reference point with which to compare the evolution of Armenian identity in the Diaspora in the second and third generations. Survivor memoirs inform us about the Armenian Genocide and its aftermath in a way that objective history cannot.

Ultimately, as a response to immense tragedy, the survivor memoir documents the search for home and for self-discovery. On this journey, an historical vision emerges in which the meaning of the self is anchored, and for survivor-memoir writers, this clearly resides in remaining Armenian against the odds. Genocide is the attempt, not only to eradicate a people from the face of the earth but also to destroy any record of their existence so that it appears that their culture was never a motif in the human tapestry. Survivor memoirs of the Armenian Genocide affirm presence and affirm that even after catastrophe, Armenians have survived and have learned to adapt their culture in a new world. Armenian culture in the Diaspora has been changed perhaps irrevocably; nevertheless, despite the immense sadness in these texts, one senses great strength and energy in the personal and cultural affirmation of the survivors.

Armenians have to a large extent failed to have their recent history inscribed into the Western world's master narrative despite the overwhelming mass of historical evidence and eyewitness testimony. What they have been able to do is to absorb the genocide into the main events of their collective life with the result that catastrophe, wandering, exile, diaspora, and rebirth have formed new cognitive and discursive archetypes and paradigms for them. Ultimately, however, the overwhelming importance of survivor memoirs of the Armenian Genocide as cultural history resides in the fact that they contribute to and form a major component of the collective memory of the Armenian nation.

To return to the question posed at the beginning of this essay as to whom the guardianship of the genocide is to be entrusted, I will answer by saying that all, of course, have a responsibility. Nevertheless, survivor memoirs are without question the specific and authentic literature of the Armenian Genocide. They form an immense reservoir of Armenian literature, history, feeling, and thought. To understand the human dimension of the catastrophe, one must read the testimony of the survivors.

Notes

1. Elie Wiesel, "The Holocaust as Literary Inspiration," quoted in Barbara Foley, "Fact, Fiction, Fascism: Testimony and Mimesis in Holocaust Narrative," *Comparative Literature* 34, no. 4 (1982): 334.

2. Donald E. Miller and Lorna Touryan Miller, *Survivors: An Oral History of the Armenian Genocide* (Berkeley: University of California Press, 1993).
3. Elizabeth Caraman, *Daughter of the Euphrates* (New York: Harper and Brothers, 1939; reprint, Paramus, N.J.: Armenian Missionary Association of America, Inc., 1979), xiii.
4. Hayden White, *Tropics of Discourse: Essays in Cultural Criticism* (Baltimore: Johns Hopkins University Press, 1978), 85–86.
5. Albert S. Apélian, *The Antiochians* (New York: Vantage Press, 1960); Jack Hashian, *Mamigon* (New York: Coward, McCann and Geoghan, 1982); Marie Sarrafian Banker, *Armenian Romance* (Grand Rapids, Mich.: Wm. B. Eerdmans, 1941); H. H. Haig, *The First Genocide* (New York: Vantage Press, 1967); Bedros Margosian, *Of Desert Bondage* (Boston: The Van Press, 1940).
6. Elise Hagopian Taft, *Rebirth* (Plandome, N.Y.: New Age Publishers, 1981), 141.
7. Sidra DeKoven Ezrahi, *By Words Alone: The Holocaust in Literature* (Chicago: University of Chicago Press, 1982), 23. Ezrahi makes this point with reference to Jewish Holocaust literature. It is equally applicable to Armenian survivor memoirs.
8. André Bridoux, *Le Souvenir* (Paris: Presses Universitaires de France, 1956), 26.
9. Taft, *Rebirth,* vii.
10. Ramela Martin, *Out of Darkness* (Cambridge, Mass.: The Zoryan Institute, 1989), v.
11. Taft, *Rebirth,* viii.
12. Kerop Bedoukian, *The Urchin: An Armenian's Escape* (London: John Murray, 1978).
13. Robert J. Lifton, *Boundaries* (Toronto: CBC Publications, 1969), 3.
14. Dirouhi Kouymjian Highgas, *Refugee Girl* (Watertown, Mass.: Baikar Publications, 1985), 178.
15. Caraman, *Daughter of the Euphrates,* 274.
16. Ibid., 274–75.
17. Ibid., 141.

7

Problematic Aspects of Reading Genocide Literature

A Search for a Guideline or a Canon

RUBINA PEROOMIAN

The Premise

Hagop Oshagan, a prominent post-genocide Armenian writer-critic, was the first to attempt the segregation of the genocide literature. He believed that the genocide literature is a special genre in itself deserving a special approach. He searched for a methodology that could unravel the impact of the Great Catastrophe (Մեծ Աղէտ) on the writer and his work. Very often, both in his critical and creative writings, he talked about the problems of writing in this genre and of judging this genre aesthetically. After Oshagan, other Armenian critics, too, discussed the literature of catastrophe as a separate category, and gradually the idea of the genre of genocide literature took shape. Genocide literature, thus, is understood to encompass that unique body of artistic creations triggered by a traumatic, unprecedented collective experience in the history of the Armenian people. Today, when we speak about Armenian Genocide literature, there is a general understanding of its meaning and scope, although defining boundaries remains problematic, and the definition of the genre still lacks precision.

The study of Armenian Genocide literature has taken many directions. In my own studies I have concentrated on the works of first-generation survivor-writers, such as Zabel Esayan, Suren Bartevian, Hagop Oshagan, Aram Andonian, Vahan Tekeyan, and those who fell victim to that atrocity they described so well, such as Siamanto and Varuzhan. I have tried to fathom the depths of the wound inflicted on the Armenian collective psyche and to find answers to questions arising from these works. I have analyzed the treatment of key recurring themes such as self-criticism or internalization of catastrophe, the inability or unwillingness to grasp the reality of events, the image of the Turk, the manifestation of self-defense, and the role and duality of God. Through this typology of genocide literature, I have tried to reveal the victims' and survivors' perception of the catastrophe and the psychological impact of that catastrophe on future generations. In the knowledge that this unique Armenian experience has strong grounds for comparison with Jewish sufferings, I have ventured into the scholarship on Jewish Holocaust literature and incorporated the comparative dimension in my work.

In this essay, I work with a different inquiry which, unlike my adopted literary approach, is not controlled by questions arising from within the texts. The questions that I pose to the texts of the Armenian Genocide, to the critics, and potential readers are devised a priori, and arise from a concern about the problems of genocide literature. These questions, I contend, will lead to a better understanding of genocide literature and, what is more important, of the facts of the Event itself. I base my contention on the hypothesis that the genocide literature is a means to explain the genocide. I express, *imprimis,* my indebtedness to Alvin Rosenfeld's *A Double Dying,* which inspired some of key insights in this discussion.[1]

Baffling Questions

Why read genocide literature? Is there anything to gain by reading it or to lose by not reading it? How should we read genocide literature and what should we look for in it? When does genocide literature stop being a fictional artistic creation and become a historical recording of events? Can literature contribute to our finding of the truth of the genocide?

Many readers may, consciously or unconsciously, avoid genocide literature because of its depressing and heartrending nature. When mere survival in today's world involves such an intense and consuming struggle, why engulf ourselves in the sufferings of others who came before us and deny ourselves a lighter, more comfortable literary diversion? A romanticized answer to this question would be that generations of the survivors of a national catastrophe should always remember the victims of that catastrophe and relate to it for inspiration and determination. Therefore, Armenians likewise owe it to their martyrs to read about their suffering, their ordeal, their doleful victimization. Sentimentalism aside, however, as Kafka says, we should choose books that ask more of us than we are willing to give. "We must have those books," he wrote, "which come upon us like ill-fortune and distress us deeply like the death of one we love better than ourselves, like suicide. A book must be an ice-ax to break the sea frozen inside us."[2]

Books such as Hagop Oshagan's *Kaiserakan Haghtergutiun* (Imperial song of triumph) and *Mnatsortats* (Remnants), Aram Andonian's *Ain Sev Orerun* (In those dark days) and *Mets Vojire* (The great crime), and Zabel Esayan's *Averakneru Mech* (Amidst the ruins) do to us just what Kafka suggests. Nevertheless, can an ordinary reading of these books introduce the reader to the depths of the Armenian Genocide, to grasping its meaning and its expression in literature? Furthermore, these books are neither readily available nor accessible to non-Armenian readers and in some cases to Armenian readers as well. Here, the critic can play a role as mediator or facilitator. Is it not true that the most fundamental role of the critic is to introduce readers to a particular work or body of literature or, as Lawrence Langer states, "to lead readers back to the literature under discussion"?[3] Beyond this basic function, critics must devise guidelines to help the reader to comprehend and appreciate genocide literature, for conventional literary approaches can only produce questionable results. Indeed, it is doubtful if adopting canons and inquiries of a particular school of literary criticism, such as the structuralist, formalist, Marxist, psychoanalytic, and feminist could work to explain the enormity of Armenian suffering and Turkish atrocity. It is doubtful if a search for the expression of class struggle, covert psychological drives, gender differences, or the deconstruction of sophisticated metaphors and complex grammatical structures could help the critic to fulfill this difficult task. Clearly, an appropriate critical method has yet to be devised.

In spite of its inherent tendency to reject conventional literary forms, the literature of atrocity is still based upon form and language. Very often, however, the forms have been revolutionized, taboos obliterated. A strong negation of tradition is intended when Suren, a protagonist of Shahan Shahnur's *Nahanje Arants Ergi* (Retreat without song, 1929), calls "Narek" (the popular title given to Grigor Narekatsi's Book of Lamentation, tenth to eleventh century) the most disgusting, sick, deceiving, and immoral Armenian book, an enemy, who poisoned the Armenian nation.[4] Vahé Oshagan, likewise, breaks the tradition, overcomes the taboos, and in order to shock the indifferent community and the reader, describes an act of sacrilege in an Armenian church in America. Three Armenian terrorists enter the church in the middle of the Mass, proceed to the altar, and begin their "performance" of the planned profanity before the eyes of dumbfounded parishioners.[5] Aside from negating norms and conventions of the past, these authors and still others are expressing a bitter outcry against the tragic lot of the nation. In their writings, they both reverse literary norms and rebel against the fate of their people. This is in itself a unique response to the Catastrophe which tends to become a technique in the literary expression of genocide, as we will see.

Descriptions of harrowing scenes of brutality and powerful eyewitness accounts are abundant in Armenian Genocide literature. One can hardly control the torrent of emotions that Aram Andonian's account of the execution of a boy in the concentration camp arouses. The boy is caught trying to escape. The gendarmes torture him to death in front of the eyes of the dumfounded inmates to set an example of the punishment awaiting them if they ever think to flee.[6] Hagop Oshagan's depiction of the slow and torturous beheading of a man while his wife is forced to watch can provoke nightmares. Reading these alarmingly vivid and graphic descriptions of barbarism, one can hardly help cry out with Oshagan, No! "It was not the outbreak of war that made the Turks so much Turk."[7] Yet these works cannot have their full impact on the reader if there is no familiarity with the entire context of the atrocities. In the same vein, Siamanto's *Mahvan Tesil* (The vision of death) cannot have its full impact unless the reader is aware of the poet's tragic fate in the atrocities he ventured to depict. This is where the critic assumes an important role and where the enormous contribution of Jewish scholarship to understanding Holocaust literature lies. Armenian scholarship on genocide literature lags far behind, although the richness and plethora of the Armenian Genocide literature are indisputable. The fact of the matter is that the Armenian Genocide literature has not been properly studied and effectively introduced to the world. In contrast, the role Jewish scholars play in enriching and disseminating Holocaust literature is remarkable. The consciousness of the importance of this role reverberates in the studies of Holocaust literature. Edward Alexander's analysis of Isaac Bashevis Singer's *The Family of Moskat* is an example. On this novel, depicting events prior to the Holocaust, Alexander infers that the impact "gains its tremendous force less from the events within the novel than from the reader's knowledge of what will befall the Jews after the novel ends."[8] The critic's role here is building the historical context, adding to what Rosenfeld calls the reader's "interpretive frame of reference" to complete the narrative of the atrocity.[9] Rosenfeld builds on this hypothesis by exemplifying the case of Anne Frank's diary, a classic in Jewish Holocaust literature. He asserts that Anne Frank's diary exerts its greatest power when the reader realizes the little girl's fate in Auschwitz. The diary alone, without Ernst Schnebel's *Anne Frank: A Profile in Courage,* is not the same.[10] Supplemented with historical background and information, genocide literature approaches the realm of factual narrative.

Conventional Methods Incapacitated

The critic tries to help the "reality" of the tragedy to come across as clearly and thoroughly as possible. Since the reality is human loss and suffering as well as the victimization of humanism in a man-made catastrophe and since the norms of artistic creation have also fallen victim to that catastrophe, no tool or method developed in all the schools of criticism combined can work. Confronted with the dilemma, Hagop Oshagan complains, "The generation of the Constitution had handed down no oracles to face up to such unplaceable acts. That is what also makes possible the destruction of our soul."[11] Obviously, Oshagan expected a tradition of dealing with catastrophe to have been transmitted to his generation to enable them to grasp the meaning of these "unplaceable acts," to explain them, to ensure collective survival. Oshagan's expectation was probably based on his conviction that the Catastrophe of 1915 was not unprecedented but only the culmination of the previous ones. In an interview with Beniamin Tashian he is quoted as saying, "For two thousand years (sometimes five to ten times in one century) our people have experienced their 1915s."[12] According to Oshagan, with a history studded with massacres and persecutions, Armenians should have devised the means to cope with them, to explain them, to respond to them. According to Oshagan, such tools have not been devised, and thus the transmission has not occurred. Nichanian digs into the depths of this statement by Oshagan and hits different cords. I would suggest that the ancestors of the Armenian people surely built a paradigm of responses to catastrophe throughout history, but this paradigm was disrupted by the enormity of the genocide of 1915. The "oracle" was certainly transmitted but was not enough to help to deal with such magnitude of devastation. Souls were destroyed; speech was incapacitated.

For the Holocaust, in the same vein, Rosenfeld writes: " 'Reality' underwent so radical a distortion as to disarm and render no longer trustworthy the normal cognitive and expressive powers. As a result, reason seemed to give way to madness, as language did time and again to silence. When those thresholds dissolve, literature—a product of the composed mind and senses—is reduced to screams and whimpers."[13]

Examples of this transformation are abundant in the literature of Armenian Genocide. Many times the author helplessly halts the narrative, witnessing the painful disruption of the paradigm of literary forms. Language becomes inadequate; metaphors, similes, and symbols cannot do justice to the realistic representation of the reality. The writer is incapacitated. Art is strangled, rendered inarticulate before it is born; the outcome is silence or fragmentation, as in Siamanto's *Mahvan Tesil:*

> Massacre! Massacre! Massacre!
> In the cities and outside the cities in our land.
> And the barbarians, with booty and blood,
> Return leaving the dead and the dying.
> Flocks of ravens hover above.
> Bloody is their mouth; they chortle like drunks . . .
> Listen! Listen! Listen!
> The sound of storm in the waves of the sea . . .
> O! close your windows and your eyes too,
> Massacre! Massacre! Massacre!

Siamanto cries helplessly, unable to find meaning or even metaphor in that catastrophic event.[14]

Others demonstrate the same dilemma actually by spelling it out in prose. Zabel Esayan confessed, "What I saw is beyond all imagination. . . . It is difficult for me to present the entire picture. Words are incapable of expressing the dreadful and unspeakable sight that my eyes witnessed." Nonetheless, she persists in recording the "confused and perplexed expressions" of the survivors of the Cilician massacres, "their sighs and tears, the incoherent words" that they stutter, "saying nothing of the reality."[15] Suren Bartevian lamented his inability to find "words accurate enough, dramatic and tragic enough, to describe the depressing, suffocating scenes of misery." In another instance, he confesses, "This is the first time that I discover so brutally the impotence of the painful struggle of my pen, the inadequacy of all meanings of the word to capture the scenes around me . . . the horrifying reality that crushes my soul."[16]

Similarly, in Jewish Holocaust literature, Khaem Kaplan lamented over and over again, "It's beyond my pen to describe the destruction."[17] Abraham Lewin, writing in the Warsaw Ghetto conceded: "It is hard for the tongue to admit such words, for the mind to comprehend their meaning, to write them down on paper."[18] As Samuel Beckett wrote: "There is nothing to express, no power to express . . . together with the obligation to express."[19]

Despite the incapacitating effect of witnessing catastrophe, as Beckett suggests, there still exist both the paradoxical urge and the obligation to express what one sees. Rosenfeld calls this paradox the "phenomenology" of Holocaust literature, which he expounds as the "contradiction between the impossibility but also the necessity of writing."[20] In a broader context,

I suggest, this tendency can be seen as the phenomenology of the literature of atrocity.

Writers of atrocity attempt to recreate the dark, inexplicable side of human nature. We the readers, on our part, share the author's experience, but we only grasp a small corner of the reality of the catastrophe. Lawrence Langer is right in saying, "Our vision of it may never be complete, but the composite portrait offered by these texts does much to rescue it from obscurity and to light up its dreadful features with the deciphering rays of language."[21]

Through the act of language and the creation of art out of atrocity, thus, writers eternalize their morbid experience. In so doing, they seek a more or less cathartic deliverance and the securing of their own survival. One can surmise, then, that some genocide writers have thus triumphed over death and exemplified the human spirit of survival, making a new beginning possible.

In other cases, however, the undeniable outcome is the triumph of silence over language and of death over survival. Some critics and writers reject the possibility of literature of atrocity and find the term self-contradictory, the undertaking immoral. "There is no poetry after Auschwitz," Paul Celan declared. According to Michael Wyschogrod: "Art takes the sting out of suffering. . . . It is therefore forbidden to make fiction of the holocaust. . . . Any attempt to transform the holocaust into art demeans the holocaust and must result in poor art."[22] Holocaust survivor and writer Elie Wiesel finds the attempt to create Holocaust literature an act of irreverence toward the event itself: "Auschwitz negates any form of literature," he wrote. "A novel about Auschwitz is not a novel. . . . The very attempt to write such a novel is blasphemy."[23] It is as if by recasting the Holocaust as fiction, a writer is denying its reality and dishonoring all those who suffered and died.

Hagop Oshagan did not deny the possibility of creating art out of the Armenian Genocide. He realized, however, that Western Armenian literature, being a product of social, political, and cultural determinants reacting on an artist's individuality, intellect, and creative mind, died with the genocide of 1915. It is, thus impossible to continue to create art in the same pre-1915 tradition.[24] He struggled throughout his life to find the right approach to it, and his unfinished novel *Mnatsordats* speaks of his inability to forge art out of such great suffering and horror. Suren Bartevian, likewise, tried in vain to find the strength and inspiration to create "the great elegy, the splendid epic poem . . . the divine and eternal 'Book of Blood' " (Նուիրական եւ յաւիտենական «Մատեանը Արիւնի») that would embody his idealized response to the Catastrophe.[25] The contemporary Armenian poet Krikor Beledian does not think it feasible to write poetry with the pre-1915 norms, traditions, and spirit: "The Catastrophe closed the chapter on poetry" (աղէտը փակեց պատմութիւնը քերթուածին), he declares, echoing Celan.[26]

In spite of these doubts, none of the writers mentioned above stopped writing about the Jewish Holocaust or the Armenian Genocide. The attempt to write after the Catastrophe, in spite of the Catastrophe, became the source, the beginning of the Armenian Diasporan literature. A new concept of Diaspora was born, a concept that was generated from the Catastrophe, which preconditioned the literary milieu with a set of factors entirely different from the pre-1915 era. Hagop Oshagan defined the Diaspora as an elongated catastrophe, in which decades of hope and aspirations had come to a tragic end, and despair, frustration, and fragmentation had become a way of life.[27] The agonizing reality of an inexplicable tragedy and an unsolved mystery influenced outlooks and perceptions and drove some writers, Jewish and Armenian alike, to make negation and repudiation the key to the technique they devised to write post-Genocide or post-Holocaust poetry. In the case of Paul Celan, the technique consists of the denial of, ironical allusions to, and reversal of traditional concepts from the Bible and other established works.[28]

Shahan Shahnur also used this technique of repudiation and denial of old, traditional concepts that were held sacred by the Armenian people. This technique was especially effective in his novel *Nahanje Arants Ergi* and a collection of essays, titled *Tertis Kiraknoria Hamare* (The Sunday edition of my paper). Shahnur subtitled his novel "The Illustrated History of the Armenians" and began with the most provocative sentence to describe his protagonist, Petros or Pierre. "But he was a mature lad, the proof being that he could not delimit the words whore and God."[29] Then, a graphic description of a lovemaking scene between Petros and the French girl follows. In his various works, essays, short stories, and novel, Shahnur portrays the assimilation and alienation of Armenian youth, survivors of the genocide, who have found refuge in Paris. Sorrowful episodes in their difficult struggle succeed one another and the blame for their failure to adapt to the new life, their alienation from the Armenian community, their sad ending in an asylum or in dark corners of the streets goes to the Armenian forefathers. Suren the bold and outspoken character in *Nahanje Arants Ergi* attacks them ruthlessly: "Armenians are sterile, senseless, and shallow. They have no right to live because they have not given birth. . . . Our forefathers are eunuchs; they have not been able to sculpt anything out of flesh. There is a great lack in us that they have not been able to fill. . . . The succeeding generations of our forefathers have not been able to rescue us, give us that great love."[30] Curiously, throughout the novel, there is no criticism of the Turk who perpetrated the Catastrophe and caused the aftermath. The blame is always laid on the institutionalized Armenian values and ideology, which were not able to withstand the calamity. Denying the past and attacking the older generation was not unique to Shahnur. That was a common trait among the members of the "Menk" group—of which Shahnur was a member—formed in Paris in 1931 of young Armenian writers, mostly orphans of 1915 massacres. Hagop Oshagan, also a target of their staunch criticism, attributes this phenomenon to foreign influences and the frustration of this generation of orphans to keep pace with the present.[31]

In his same novel, Shahan Shahnur launched another technique to remedy the Catastrophe very much similar to that of Zareh Vorbuni in *Sovorakan Or Me* (An ordinary day, 1956). The technique consists of touch-up and repair, according to Marc Nichanian. By trying to repair the wound, these two post-genocide Armenian writers tried to make up for the destruction and to reinstate the obliterated canons (Օրէնք). The novels of both writers symbolize the search to find proper norms for post-genocide literature.

The technique of contemporary writer Krikor Beledian consists of reversal and refutation. He keeps the language, the words and, at the same time, rebels against them. He refutes and negates the pre-genocide connotations of words and concepts with a negative prefix, as in poetry/anti-poetry (քերթուած/հակաքերթուած), language/anti-language (լեզու/հակալեզու), meaning/anti-meaning (իմաստ/հակաիմաստ). In his collection of poems titled *Vayrer* (Loci), in which this prefix is frequently used, Beledian talks about anti-*matière* (հականիւթ). It is significant, however, that he moves from meaning to anti-meaning and not to meaninglessness; similarly, from language to anti-language and not to speechlessness or silence. The author desires to remain in the world of meaning and language, in spite of negating them: «բայց ենք լեզուին մէջ հակալեզուին ».[32] In his critical work, in an analysis of Nikoghayos Sarafian, Beledian strives to find the traditionalism of the perception of the end or terminus, «Վախճանի ընկալումի աւանդականութիւնը» . His reference is, of course, to the Catastrophe, or more precisely to the eschatology of the Catastrophe «Վախճանը , որ աղէտն է ստեղծեր».

To Read and Write about Genocide: A Must, an Affliction

As with Jewish writers and the Holocaust, writing about the Armenian Genocide has become more than a vocation or a calling for Armenian writers.

It is rather an affliction, a predicament. The Jewish writer asks, "how to write about Holocaust, yet how not to write about it?" Avoidance and denial are overcome, and the urge to write about it becomes an affliction that absorbs the writer. Art is born, albeit fragmented or incomplete, which then casts its spell over the reader. The reverse of the question is: "how to read Armenian Genocide literature, yet how not to read it?"

What is the value of genocide literature in the realm of hard facts? We know that historical facts conveyed by historians are less affected by the author's imagination than genocide narratives such as eyewitness accounts, memoirs, and novels. Nevertheless, historians are not immune to artistic imagination and pictorialization. In the Armenian classical era the boundary between the two genres of history and artistic creations was fuzzy, almost nonexistent. Classical Armenian historiography is primarily an artistic representation of historical facts, a form of literary art. The issue is, therefore, not the existence but the extent or essence of "digressions." In other words, as James E. Young put it in *Writing and Rewriting the Holocaust:* "In what way do historians fictionalize and novelists historicize?"[33] We have to agree that with the generations of the survivors of a historical catastrophe the overall portrait and the indelible impression of that catastrophe are shaped not so much by the hard facts but with the strokes of the artist's brush fictionalizing the event.

In posing this question I do not favor one approach over the other. Neither do I equate scientific historical discourse with subjective representations of an event. I simply wish to demonstrate the intrinsic value of genocide fiction to a complete understanding of the Armenian Genocide. Just as historical knowledge of the event is essential for a clear interpretation of genocide fiction or symbolic poetry, genocide literature reveals the universal truths that lie at the roots of historical fact and puts inconceivable realities into human perspective. Thus the two genres are mutually complementary and indispensable aids to our grasp of the meaning of atrocity.

Today, when we look back on the Armenian Genocide, the distance of over eighty years has dulled our perceptions and colored our judgment. In order to be able to absorb the meaning of the Armenian Genocide as both a terminus and a beginning for the Armenian people and for Armenian art, in order to make it work as the touchstone of the Armenian national consciousness in the Diaspora, Armenian Genocide literature must be read and written about. Armenians owe it not only to their victims but to themselves to liberate their psychological, emotional, and creative responses to the Catastrophe. Their word may not be the last on genocide; others have suffered and will continue to suffer as survivors of other world atrocities. Nevertheless their outcry against genocide should continue to echo as Armenians and citizens of the world in the endless struggle to perpetuate both humanity and humanism.

Notes

1. Alvin Rosenfeld, *A Double Dying: Reflections on Holocaust Literature,* 2d ed. (Bloomington: Indiana University Press, 1988).
2. Ibid., 18.
3. Lawrence Langer, *The Holocaust and the Literary Imagination* (New Haven: Yale University Press, 1975), xiii.
4. Shahan Shahnur, *Nahanje Arants Ergi* (Retreat without song), 4th ed. (Beirut: Sevan Press, 1981), 120. This flagrant attack on sacred values of Armenian tradition is common with Suren, who vents Shahnur's own unconventional views on Armenian life and reality.
5. This outrageous scene of sacrilege is described in a short story titled "Otsum" (Consecration), published in the collection of short stories *Takartin Shurj* (Around the snare), 1988 by Vahé Oshagan. One of the terrorists slowly and disgracefully strips the priest of his holy attire, while he resolutely continues the mass. The other two, a boy and a girl, get on the front row pew and put on an obscene kissing scene. Amid all this the tape recorder they have brought in is playing loud and wild music stifling the holy liturgy, the *patarak.*
6. For the discussion of this episode, see Rubina Peroomian, *Literary Responses to Catastrophe, A Comparison of the Armenian and the Jewish Experience* (Atlanta: Scholars Press, 1993), 163–64.
7. Ibid., 203.
8. Edward Alexander, *The Resonance of Dust: Essays on Holocaust Literature and Jewish Fate* (Columbus: Ohio State University Press, 1979), 149.
9. Rosenfeld, *A Double Dying,* 24.
10. Ibid., 17.
11. This sentence is the opening of one of Hagop Oshagan's important remarks on Armenian Genocide literature expressed in volume 7 of his *Hamapatker Arevmtahay Grakanutian* (Panorama of Western Armenian literature), in the chapter on Suren Bartevian. Marc Nichanian analyzes this remark in "The Style of Violence," *Armenian Review* 38, no. 1 (Spring 1985): 6. By the generation of the Constitution, Oshagan means the Western Armenian *literati* of the 1850s who initiated the Armenian National Constitution to govern Armenian community affairs in the Ottoman Empire.
12. B. Tashian, *Mairineru Shukin Tak: Grakan Zruits H. Oshakani Het* (In the shade of the cedars: A literary discussion with H. Oshagan) (Beirut: Altapress, 1983), 19.
13. Rosenfeld, *A Double Dying*, 28.
14. See Peroomian, *Literary Responses,* 78.
15. Ibid., 94.
16. Ibid., 125.
17. Rosenfeld, *A Double Dying,* 7.

18. See Lawrence I. Langer, ed., *Art from the Ashes: A Holocaust Anthology* (New York: Oxford University Press, 1995), 3.
19. Rosenfeld, *A Double Dying,* 8.
20. Ibid.
21. Langer, *Art from the Ashes,* 3.
22. Ibid., 14.
23. Ibid.
24. Hagop Oshagan, *Spiurke ev Irav Banasteghtsutiune* (Diaspora and the true poetry) (Jerusalem: St. James Press, 1945), 2–3.
25. Peroomian, *Literary Responses,* 136, 138.
26. Krikor Beledian, *Vayrer* (Loci) (Paris: N.p., 1983), 149.
27. Hagop Oshagan, *Vkayutiun Me* (A testimony) (Aleppo: Nayiri Press, 1946), 93.
28. Rosenfeld, *A Double Dying,* 30.
29. Shahnur, *Nahanje Arants Ergi,* 7.
30. Ibid., 100–102.
31. Oshagan, *Spiurke ev Irav Banasteghtsutiune,* 63.
32. Beledian, *Vayrer,* 121.
33. James E. Young, *Writing and Rewriting the Holocaust: Narrative and the Consequences of Interpretation* (Bloomington: Indiana University Press, 1988), 6.

8

The Role of Historical Memory in Interpreting Events in the Republic of Armenia

DONALD E. MILLER

Historical memory always plays a role in interpreting contemporary events. Theoretically, this assertion draws on the sociology of Alfred Schutz, who argues that events, in themselves, never possess meaning.[1] Meaning is something attributed to events or objects and, in his view, meaning is based on two things operating in a constant dialectic: the sedimentation of past experiences and one's intentionality toward the future. Together, these two elements interact to constitute what he calls the system of relevances or apperceptive schema that provides the interpretive lens by which one makes sense out of current events. I believe that Schutz's theory is useful in understanding why 350,000 Armenians (out of a total Armenian population of some 400,000) fled Azerbaijan after pogroms in Sumgait and Baku in 1988–90. Of these, some 200,000 sought refuge in the Republic of Armenia. The pogroms, while horrific, did not justify in themselves the mass exodus that occurred unless viewed as the precursor to an actual genocide, because the people who fled, in many instances, left behind well-established homes, all of their household furniture and possessions, jobs, and often a relatively affluent lifestyle. My thesis is that these pogroms, which had strong parallels to the massacres in Turkey of 1894–96 and 1909, were viewed as indicative of a much more cataclysmic event in which the lives of all Armenians living in Azerbaijan might be threatened by "the Turks." In this regard, Schutz's theory would imply that the sedimentation of past events (that is, the various massacres and genocide which constitute the collective memory of all Armenians) played a role in the interpretation of the pogroms that occurred in 1988–90.

My reference point for this paper is two substantial archives of oral history interviews: one hundred interviews that my wife and I did with elderly survivors of the genocide and over three hundred interviews that our research team did in the Republic of Armenia in 1993–94.[2] These latter interviews focused on four populations: refugees from Azerbaijan, survivors of the 1988 earthquake, individuals affected by the war in Nagorno-Karabagh, and citizens of Yerevan who have struggled for survival since blockade was imposed.

Genocides and massacres never occur in a political vacuum, and certainly the Sumgait and Baku pogroms were no exception. The complementary principles of *glasnost* and *perestroika* had been announced by Gorbachev, and Armenians interpreted this new openness as an invitation to explore the possibility of uniting Nagorno-Karabagh with the Armenian Soviet Socialist Republic. A petition drive was organized by an informal group that called itself the Karabagh Committee, and on September 18, 1987, there was a massive demonstration in Yerevan. Five months later, on February 13, 1988, substantial crowds took to the streets in Stepanakert, the capital city of Nagorno-Karabagh, and within a week there were a half million people gathering in the Theater Square in Yerevan to support the call for unification.[3] It was a nearly carnival-like atmosphere in which strangers talked freely with each other on the streets, and photographs of these mass demonstrations filled the front pages of newspapers such as the *Los Angeles Times*.[4]

On February 22, 1988, a counter-demonstration of Azeris living in the border town of Aghdam (Agdam) headed toward Stepanakert. According to one version of the story, this group of counter-protesters wreaked havoc on Armenians and their property along the way, but it is also clear that they met resistance and two Azeris were killed by Armenians in the village of Askeran. As the crowd from Aghdam fled back to their homes after the confrontation, rumors of Armenian brutality circulated and several days later, on February 27, massacres against the Armenian population of Sumgait erupted. Although the Sumgait pogroms received some press coverage and at least one book has been written on the events that transpired, I want to turn directly to our interviews with eyewitnesses—individuals who were living as refugees in the Republic of Armenia when our research team interviewed them in 1993–94.[5]

The Sumgait Massacres

An Armenian we interviewed from Baku went to Sumgait shortly after the massacre to help his friends evacuate, and he reported the following sight:

"When we arrived, what happened was impossible to believe. There were dead bodies on the floor, some had been burned alive, some had their chests pierced with a crowbar, some had their ears or heads cut off. It was something unexplicable." When our interviewer asked whether he had actually seen these things or just heard of them, he insisted: "All that I just told you about I saw with my own eyes." Other eyewitness accounts verified this testimony of the sadistic brutality that occurred. Another of our interviewees described a sixty-year-old woman who, she said, "they pierced with metal through her anus, raped her, and [then] killed her." This survivor also knew of a girl who had been gang-raped in front of her parents. Still another interviewee cited an acquaintance, six or seven months pregnant, who was raped and then killed.

A Sumgait survivor told our interviewer that she first became alarmed on February 27 when she saw a crowd of teenagers and young adults running around shouting, "Death to the Armenians!" She also observed individuals in this same crowd marking Armenian homes with crosses, based on an address list that they were carrying. By February 28, the massacres were in full swing. A resident of Sumgait said that she observed a large crowd of about 300 Azeris. Her mother returned from church and reported having seen an Armenian water vendor who had been killed, and her husband, who was out buying bread, witnessed a storeowner being beaten and his shop looted. Our interviewee said that at about 4:30 P.M. she left her husband and children and went downstairs from their fourth story apartment to telephone the police, because by this time there were shouts in the streets and multiple rumors of violence. When she called military headquarters, however, they assured her that everything was okay, in spite of her insistence that they send someone to investigate. As the noise and sounds of celebration in the streets continued, she again left their apartment and went back downstairs to call the police, and this time they told her that the Russian army was coming to quell the violence.

Having made her call, she immediately headed back upstairs to her apartment only to encounter several men carrying her husband down the steps. He was dripping with blood. She rushed past him to her children, and as soon as she entered the apartment she discovered that it was occupied by several Azeris. Many things were missing from the house, but she found her three children unharmed, huddling together in one of the bedrooms. She rushed them downstairs and recognized a military friend on the street who offered to take her and the children to his own home. By March 2 things had quieted down and all of the Armenians were told to gather for transport out of Sumgait. Before leaving, however, she ventured back to her house to salvage some things to take with her, but in her words: "They had taken everything away. All I did was close the door." Her husband died as a result of the injuries sustained on February 28 but her father, who was also beaten severely, survived.

Another survivor of the Sumgait massacres offered a similar account of the events of February 28: "Our building was surrounded and they started breaking our windows and doors. I told my son, 'Run for your life. Run for your life my dear son.' And he took off. They had cut our electricity, but not that of the Turks. The killings had begun. . . . I hid in my neighbor's house and I gave away all my jewelry. Had I not, they would have killed me, too. But the soldiers came. As soon as they came, my neighbor, my Turkish neighbor that was hiding me, said: 'You've got to go, because the soldiers are here.' I found out that the soldiers were carrying the injured, the sick, the hurt to the hospital. I came out and I saw bodies everywhere. They had poured benzine on them and burned them." She went to the hospital, and when she returned there was nothing left of her apartment: "Windows were all broken, the doors were broken, the house was destroyed, and they had killed my husband." Later she discovered her son had also been killed and his body burned.

At this point in her account, she began to cry, but then went on to describe the perpetrators of the violence. She said they were 16 to 30 years of age and appeared to be intoxicated, which matched the description offered by other survivors whom we interviewed. In assessing the toll on human life, she said that out of ten Armenian families living in their building, eight people had been killed. Another survivor cited a similar number: "In our block there were three big apartments: 4, 5, and 6. Out of those three apartments, twelve people were killed. I can name them one by one."

More than one survivor said that the violence stopped because Russian troops arrived to quell the massacres. Repeatedly, survivors also stated that the death rate would have been much higher except for the fact that Azeri neighbors protected them. A survivor we interviewed said, "There was one kind Azeri. This particular man, I saw with my own eyes, he had 25 to 30 Armenian employees and he saved every one of them. He gave them bread, drinks, and with his own car, he hid them and took them to safety." Many individual acts of kindness were reported in our interviews in which Armenians were hidden by neighbors during the peak hours of the massacres, and then assisted in escaping to safety. One survivor said, "if it wasn't for those kind Turks who hid many Armenians, I don't think that many Armenians would have been left alive. That's what I believe."

Based on the limited sample of refugees that we interviewed, it appears that Armenians and Azeris had peacefully coexisted for a number of years.

Indeed, they felt secure enough that when the rallies for independence occurred in both Karabagh and Armenia, according to one survivor, "Young [Armenian] men with bands on their heads would walk around on the streets shouting: 'Karabagh is ours, Karabagh is ours, Karabagh is ours. It's not the Azeris!' Yes, they did march and they did shout these words." From one perspective, such rallies might be viewed as provocative; on the other hand, in the light of Gorbachev's announced policy of *perestroika* the right to self-determination was perceived to be consonant with a shift in Soviet policy. At least this was the interpretation by many Armenians of a February 26, 1988 televised speech by Gorbachev.

Whatever the actual source of the massacres in Sumgait— hooligans as Gorbachev claimed or a more organized political strategy to quiet dissent— there is no moral justification for the carnage that resulted. Officially, 31 were killed, although estimates range as high as two hundred. According to Samvel Shahmuratian, drawing on 150 interviews with Sumgait survivors, the following occurred: "For a period of three days in February of 1988, virtually all of Sumgait, a city of over 250,000, became an arena of mass, unimpeded pogroms of the Armenian population. There were dozens of deaths; in a significant number of cases, the victims were burned alive after beatings and torture. There were hundreds of wounded, many of whom became invalids. There were rapes, including rapes of underage girls. More than 200 apartments were ravaged, dozens of automobiles were burned or smashed, and dozens of studios, stores, kiosks, and other public property incurred damage. There were thousands of refugees."[6]

The 200,000 Armenians living in Baku heard reports on television of the events that were transpiring in Sumgait which was only a short distance away. In addition, many of them had relatives living in Sumgait who were eyewitnesses to what occurred. For example, one Baku resident stated to us: "My husband's relative was living in Sumgait and he saw everything from his balcony. He saw how a girl was stripped and forced to dance on the street and how they were extinguishing cigarette butts on her skin. He saw it all with his own eyes. When he was telling us about it, he was nervously shaking and crying."

A student from Baku told us that she had a classmate who frequently visited a friend who was studying in Sumgait. One day this girl was not present in class and she discovered that she was in the hospital. When she went to visit her the next day, she said that the girl was "all beaten up, all black and blue and she couldn't move from her bed." For nearly two weeks this student went to visit her friend and gradually the girl's story unfolded: She was on the bus going to visit her friend in Sumgait when some Azeris stopped the bus and requested everyone's passport. Discovering this girl was Armenian, a woman pulled her by the hair into the aisle of the bus and started to kick and beat her. At this point she fainted, was thrown out of the bus, and apparently a Turkish couple who witnessed this event took pity on her and put her on a bus going back to Baku, where she was then hospitalized. This girl remarked to the student we interviewed: "It's interesting, a Turk beats me up, almost to death, and another Turk, with a good conscience, saves my life."

While this student was visiting her friend in the hospital, she encountered other casualties of the Sumgait massacres. One person, in particular, affected her: "There was this little boy. His name was Vitalig, I'd say he's about eight grade level. His mind was totally gone. I found out that in front of him, the Turks had mutilated his mom and his sister and killed them." She also encountered a woman who was recovering from stab wounds to the waist, and another woman whose story deeply troubled her: "There was this young lady and she told me that she was raped right in front of her dad and beaten up. Right in front of her dad. She said some of those Turks that were watching were neighbors and they wouldn't do anything. Instead they laughed." There was a little girl, six or seven years of age, who kept crying, "Mom, they're coming." She repeated this over and over again and could not be comforted.

Hence, Armenians in Baku were very aware of what occurred in Sumgait, but it is also true that many of their Azeri neighbors expressed shock and outrage at what had happened to the Armenians living there. For example, a student reported coming to class shortly after the events of late February and her Azeri professor asked, "How many Armenians do I have in this class?" Six woman students stood up, and he then told them what he had personally observed: "A beautiful Armenian [girl] like one of you was burned in Sumgait in front of a building. I still can hear her shouts of agony." According to this student, the professor started to cry and then said, "I don't understand why Armenians are being killed." This student said: "He took his books and his notes and he just put them on the desk and he said, 'You know, I cannot lecture today because I am too upset about what is going on in Sumgait.' So he just let us go that hour."

The Baku Massacres

By November and then intensifying in December 1988, pogroms started to spread to Baku. One of our interviewees described what she witnessed on December 7, the day of the earthquake in Armenia: "There is a student housing complex near us, dorms, and when their news program announced about the earthquake in Armenia, you won't imagine what they started doing. They started jumping up and down and screaming [in celebration]. And that was the youth. They did not seem human. We have many dorms there and all of them celebrated, they had fireworks." When queried as to whether she had actually witnessed this, she said: "We could see that from our window. And we could hear their screams." Another survivor said that Azeris were butchering sheep and barbecuing them right on the streets, singing songs and celebrating that so many Armenians had been killed by the earthquake.

According to Baku refugees that we interviewed, the attitude toward Armenians rapidly began to deteriorate after the Sumgait massacres, with only intermittent assistance coming from the Soviet army. One interviewee stated: "The situation changed drastically. The relationships changed. Azeris became very rude and started treating us with disrespect. Only a few of them were compassionate and even tried to help. The majority was set against us. Everything was different, even at work. It was terrifying. Sometimes it was hard even to leave home. At that time, Armenians were not going anywhere. They could be killed or raped. Anything could be done to them. Some started to get prepared to leave, some did not want to believe that it was serious and that it will last."

Civil disturbances against Armenians continued into 1989. The Armenian cathedral in Baku was burned, and intimidation and hostility toward Armenians intensified. A number of vicious rumors began to circulate about how Azeris who lived in Armenia were being treated. This disinformation stirred the passions of the general population. An Armenian who worked at the train station in Baku described the evolution of one such rumor: "Once, when we were waiting for a train, in June of 1989, a very awful rumor started spreading. They were saying that now a train will come from Yerevan and bring refugees, which were injured or cut into pieces, some had their noses cut off, or ears cut off, or their legs, or heads. The whole city panicked and everyone went to that platform waiting for 'the train' to come. I went to look, too. The train came and we saw absolutely healthy people coming out of it. None of them was even scratched." On his way home he was waiting at a bus stop, and people were talking about the "the train" which had just arrived. According to this interviewee: "One person was even swearing in the memory of his deceased relatives that he saw how the injured people were brought out of the train, put into the emergency cars, and so on. I couldn't take it anymore and I told him that he is lying and he is influencing people with his lies. I don't think that they thought of me as an Armenian, because I speak the language [Azeri] very well. I said that I work on the platform and that I was there when the train arrived. Yes, there were refugees, older people, children, but I have not seen any injured ones."

On December 5, 1989, crowds of Azeris began to threaten Armenians. One of our interviewees said that a group was heading towards his house shouting, "Show us some Armenians, where are the Armenians?" but they turned on another street before reaching his house. This crowd was stopping buses and pulling out people who were Armenian and beating them. One observer of these actions said that a "crowd instinct" had taken over. In his view, "it was worthless to look for a sense of justice or decency in those animals," even though some Azeris were protesting what was occurring. More than one interviewee told us that the youth in these crowds seemed to be either drunk or on drugs: "They were carrying the Turkish flag—Azerbaijan did not have its own flag at that time. They were walking, yelling, and insulting Armenians. They were like some jungle savages."

Beginning on January 13, 1990, a repetition of the pogroms of Sumgait were carried out in Baku against the Armenian population that remained. Armenians were pulled out of buses and beaten brutally. One observer of this violence said that multiple individuals would gang up on a single Armenian: "Not one-on-one, about ten or twenty people would attack one person and play with him or her like with a soccer ball. You can't get close to them and you can't help. They use whatever they can to torture that person. They use their hands, legs, chains. If a person is lying there all alone, what is he able to do to protect himself? After murdering, they would just turn around and leave. Often the strangers would ask them, 'Why are you beating him or her? It is enough.' "

Such sadism is difficult to comprehend, particularly given the rather harmonious relations that had existed between Armenians and Azeris in Baku. However, the civil anarchy that evolved against Armenians seemingly was fueled by implicit approval from respected individuals. For example, one interviewee remarked: "There was a writer who wrote mainly for children and all of his works were nice and kind. Suddenly, once, he appeared on television and declared that all people whose last names ended in 'ian' must leave and be fired from their jobs." Another interviewee similarly noted the affect of the media on fueling the carnage against Armenians: "The Azeris, in a group of 5–6 people, were going into houses where they knew Armenians lived. When they found a women there, they raped her; when they found some men, they beat them almost to death. No one could protest against them. No one defended Armenians because they had heard on TV that they are free to do anything they want to Armenians. They would stop some cars and, if the driver was an Armenian, they turned the car over, beat the driver, killed him, and burned the car. In the stores, if the sales person suspected that the buyer was an Armenian, she refused to sell any bread to that person."

Specific examples of the foregoing generalizations can be offered from our interviews, although many of them are rather graphic. For example, a woman surgeon from Baku summarized the event that triggered her own decision to emigrate to Armenia: "I remember the last thing that disgusted me and forced me to leave. I had a patient, a young girl, six months pregnant. She lived on Krylov Street. She was at home with her parents-in-law when a group of men broke into their house. They robbed the house and beat the old couple, who were later transported to the surgical department in our hospital. Their neighbors hid the girl, but somebody told them that there is another member of the family, a young girl. They went in and I don't know how many men raped her, a pregnant woman. She was brought to me. When I examined her, I was horrified. Right after she left, I moved my granddaughter out of Baku." This same physician also encountered a woman in an Armenian church in Baku who had been raped: "When I got there, I saw a 50-year-old woman lying down with her head wrapped in a cloth and with a big bruise under her eye. I asked what had happened. Somebody said that she is insane. The priest and his wife were there. I was told that she was raped and that the rapists inserted a bottle into her vagina." This doctor ended her account saying, "I feel embarrassed telling you all this."

As Armenians attempted to flee the pogroms, they continued to be assaulted. A survivor of these events observed the following from the window of a train bathroom, in which he had locked himself. "I waited there for the train to leave. I could see how the Azeris were literally burning people. They were pouring benzine over them and burning them. They were going into the train, dragging out people, checking their passports. I have no idea who gave them the right to do so. All of them were dragged out without any regards for their age or gender. Women, older people, younger people were all dragged out of the train. The Azeris beat them up, burned them and their belongings. There was one big fire into which everything was thrown. I saw that fire with my own eyes. People were pushed into it after being beaten." When asked whether Soviet soldiers were there, he replied that the crowds were so "mad" that they did not dare get close to what was occurring. In his view, the scene was analogous to animals tearing apart a prey that they have captured.

On January 19, 1990, a state of emergency was declared and 20,000 Soviet troops were sent in to ostensibly quell the riots against the Armenians, but also to quash the Azeri independence movement. According to one report, 93 Azeris and 29 Russian soldiers died in street skirmishes.[7] After the

Baku pogroms, Armenians from all over Azerbaijan fled—some to Armenia and others to Moscow and other places that they could find work. Ironically, some of the Sumgait refugees who left after the February uprisings ended up in Spitak, Gumri, and Vanadzor, cities that were hard hit by the earthquake. These individuals thus faced two major traumatic events within a single year.

The Current Plight of Refugees

It is important to note that some of the individuals who left (even after the Baku pogroms) were able to return and take some of their household belongings that they had left in the care of Azeri neighbors. On occasion, they found that their apartment or house had already been occupied by Azeris (including individuals who had fled Armenia as refugees). Very few Armenians were able to sell their houses for full value, and many individuals simply abandoned everything that they had spent a lifetime accumulating. People who were professionals and well established in Azerbaijan arrived in Armenia, oftentimes not knowing the language (many only spoke Russian and Azeri) and feeling very much like second-class citizens. Because of the earthquake, housing was extremely scarce and while doing interviews we visited many apartments where entire families were living in one or two rooms.

As a result of the blockade and the general state of the Armenian economy, most of the refugees we interviewed were unemployed and were living at a mere subsistence level. One person said that their current existence resembles prehistoric times. They survive on bread and water and occasionally a little cheese. One of our interviewees said that her younger children do not know what meat is, since it has never been a part of their diet. After living in comfortable homes in Azerbaijan, it has been an enormous strain to go through the last several winters without heat, only an hour or two of electricity a day, if that, and little prospect of diminishing their plight. When we asked one interviewee what her worst moment had been since arriving in Armenia, she said that it was when her son came to her, reminded her it was his birthday, and she had nothing to give to him. More than one refugee said that the only hope they have is for their children; they do not see circumstances getting any better for themselves.

Conclusion

In asking refugees to reflect on the pogroms they had experienced, several individuals made a direct comparison to the Armenian Genocide of 1915. Others referred to the slaughter of 15,000 Armenians who were put to the sword in Baku in 1918. I suspect that genocide comparisons would have been even more overt in our interviews except for the fact that many Armenians living in Baku and Sumgait were highly assimilated. Intermarriage with Azeris was not uncommon; nearly all upwardly mobile parents sent their children to Russian schools. Consequently, Armenian history was known through family memories more than through formal teaching.

I do not think one can explain the response of 350,000 Armenians leaving their homes, possessions, and childhood memories except that they feared a repetition of events that only too frequently had marked them as a survivor people. However horrific the pogroms were, it is also true that a relatively small number of people were killed: 31 in Sumgait and 160 in Baku, according to official counts (although these may be considerable underestimates). Thus, in trying to understand such a massive reaction by the Armenian population, one can certainly ground much of their fear in the reality of their situation. But I strongly suspect that deep in their historical memory is a conviction, articulated in the words of one interviewee, that never again will Armenians be "lambs for the slaughter." The social and political conditions faced by Armenians living in Azerbaijan paralleled too closely the context of previous massacres and genocides for Armenians not to be alarmed when the pogroms in Sumgait broke out. I see the following parallels between the pogroms against the Armenian population and the previous threats to their existence:

> Armenians were a minority population in both Azerbaijan and Turkey, thus clearly identifiable for persecution.
>
> Armenians were more upwardly mobile than the majority population, hence creating the possibility of potential social conflict.
>
> The overarching political conditions were unstable in both the Soviet Union and the Ottoman Empire—revolutionary change often being a prerequisite of genocide.
>
> Armenians were scapegoated for political events outside the borders of the country in which they were residing.

It is only speculation, but I have wondered what the fate of the Armenian population would have been had there still been Armenians living in Baku and Sumgait during 1993 and 1994 when the war in Nagorno-Karabagh began to turn against the Azeris. Ironically, the massacres of 1988–90 and the resulting mass emigration of Armenians from Azerbaijan might have avoided a new genocide against the Armenian population.

I do not want to exaggerate the parallels between the 1915 genocide and more recent events, but I cannot ignore noting the suffering caused by the blockade against the Republic of Armenia and the parallel to the inhumane conditions created by the deportations. Also, the sadistic brutality against the Armenians, including rape, physical disfigurement, and torture occurred in both the Sumgait-Baku pogroms and the genocide. In addition, the festive celebration of Armenian deaths is common to both the events of 1915 and 1988–90. Furthermore, there are other parallels, such as being forced to abandon or sell at a fraction of their real value household articles (for example, in the case of the genocide) and homes (for example, in the case of the Sumgait-Baku pogroms).

In spite of the parallels I have noted, there are also substantial differences between the two events. During the genocide, news of the massacres and deportations in various provinces spread rather slowly, by word of mouth, and so it was not immediately apparent that a coordinated plan of extermination was unfolding. In contrast, technology allowed almost instantaneous communication and linkage of events in Sumgait, Baku, Yerevan, Stepanakert, and so on. Technology had other effects: both airplanes and trains facilitated refugees in fleeing Azerbaijan in a way that was not possible during the genocide. A further difference is that refugees had a host country to which they could go (that is, Armenia), which was not the case in 1915. And another difference is that whatever role the Soviet government may have played in fostering the Sumgait-Baku pogroms, it also had the power to stop them, which was not true of any single power during World War I except for, perhaps, Turkey's ally Germany.

In conclusion, although there are parallels between the genocide and the recent pogroms in Azerbaijan, I think there may be a more direct parallel between the massacres of 1894–96, as well as those of 1909, and the pogroms of 1988–90. For one thing, the events in Baku and Sumgait cannot technically be called genocide, but, even more importantly, the methodology of the 1988–90 pogroms bears greater similarity to the pre-1915 period. The 1894–96 massacres were typically rather localized and were only a day or two in duration, paralleling the Sumgait and Baku pogroms. The intent seemed to be to send a message to the Armenians about their role and place as a minority population, rather than to actually exterminate the entire population. The 1909 massacres in Adana had some of the same qualities, viciously reacting to Armenian claims for equal treatment and rights but not attempting to kill all Armenians living in the region. In the case of the Sumgait-Baku pogroms, the motives may have been more complex, depending on whether the reference point is the Soviet government—which may have used the massacres to send a message to the Armenian SSR regarding independence and the unification of Armenia and Nagorno-Karabagh—or whether one is looking at the intentionality of the perpetrators of the direct violence, which seemed to reflect an older spirit of nationalistic racism.

Finally, I would note that the refugees we interviewed repeatedly commented on the good relationships that they had experienced with many of their Azeri neighbors prior to 1988, and that the reason many Armenians survived was because of the intervention of these people on their behalf. I would also remind us that many orphan children survived during the genocide because of the intervention of Turks in their lives. There is little doubt but what the demonic and the heroic exist side-by-side in all human beings. What defines our humanity are the day-to-day choices that we make in negotiating this dual nature.

Notes

1. Alfred Schutz, *The Phenomenology of the Social World* (Evanston, Ill.: Northwestern University Press, 1967).
2. The interviews with Armenian Genocide survivors are described in Donald E. Miller and Lorna Touryan Miller, *Survivors: An Oral History of the Armenian Genocide* (Berkeley: University of California Press, 1993). The interviews conducted in the Republic of Armenia in 1993–94 were done by graduate students associated with the Haigazian College, and averaged an hour in length. The interviews were translated by Arpi Haleblian.
3. The population of Yerevan was about 1.2 million people at that time.
4. See Peter Rutland, "Democracy and Nationalism in Armenia," *Europe-Asia Studies* 46, no. 5 (September 1994): 839–61.
5. Samuel Shahmuratian, ed., *The Sumgait Tragedy: Pogroms against Armenians in Soviet Azerbaijan,* vol. 1: *Eyewitness Accounts* (New Rochelle, N.Y.: Aristide D. Caratzas and Zoryan Institute, 1990).
6. See Shahmuratian, *The Sumgait Tragedy,* 1.
7. Rutland, "Democracy and Nationalism in Armenia," 850.

9

Denial of the Armenian Genocide in Comparison with Holocaust Denial

RICHARD G. HOVANNISIAN

Deniers and rationalizers of the Armenian Genocide during World War I and of the Holocaust during World War II may not be acquainted with one another and may not even have read each other's publications, yet there are striking similarities in their methodologies and objectives. In the Armenian case, denial is far more advanced and has gained a foothold in the mainstream of the historical profession. Nevertheless, in time the strategy has changed from one of absolute negation of intentional mass killing to that of rationalization, relativization, and trivialization. These forms of denial are intended to create doubts and cloak disinformation by appealing to a sense of fairplay and of giving a hearing to the other side of a misunderstood and misrepresented issue. Prejudice and stereotyping, the deniers maintain, are residues of historical scapegoating or wartime propaganda and the machinations of the alleged victims to enrich themselves personally and collectively at the expense of others.

The same strategy is applied in the case of the Holocaust, although almost all the principals have been identified as belonging to anti-Semitic fringe elements and figures of the political extreme right. Yet, even the Holocaust has entered the phase of historical debate, notably in Germany. A side effect of this debate has tended to create a tension among some scholars of the Holocaust, inasmuch as those who place the Holocaust in the context of human victimology trivialize the enormity of the event by pointing to the repeated violence and mass destruction in the twentieth century, the annihilation of the Armenians in the Ottoman Empire being a primary example. This attempted trivialization of the Holocaust has strengthened the proclivity of certain Jewish scholars to differentiate between the scope of the Holocaust and the Armenian calamity, from which the label of "genocide" is withheld or at least qualified.

The following discussion will not entail an in-depth analysis of the history and methodology of negation, rationalization, relativization, and trivialization of the Armenian and Jewish experiences. Rather, the common threads that link the approaches of the deniers will be outlined to indicate how much ground is shared by those who seek to hide the truth. There are, of course, also significant differences. In the Armenian case, for example, there were no gas chambers, and the debate that has raged about the use and purpose of poison gas and the crematory ovens is specific to the Holocaust. Yet, this very debate is linked with intent, and it is the aspect of intent that is paramount in the apologies of the rationalizers and relativizers of the Armenian Genocide.

It has been said that denial is the final phase of genocide. Following the physical destruction of a people and their material culture, memory is all that is left and is targeted as the last victim. Complete annihilation of a people requires the banishment of recollection and the suffocation of remembrance. Falsification, deception, and half-truths reduce what was to what may have been or perhaps what was not at all. History becomes "something that never happened, written by someone who wasn't there." Senseless terror gives way to reason, violence adapts to explanation, and history is reshaped to suit a contemporary agenda. By altering or erasing the past, a present is produced and a future is projected without concern about historical integrity. The process of annihilation is thus advanced and completed by denial.[1]

Denial under the guise of historical debate is an oft-used strategy. The rationalizers pretend to pose a plausible, scholarly viewpoint, and a reasonable proposal. Emphasis is directed away from the planned, systematic process of mass murder, and genocide is explained in the context of general wartime civilian casualties, the numbers of victims are minimized, and doubt is cast upon the reliability of the eyewitness testimony and documents relating to the mass killings. Historical deception replaces absolute negation, but the objectives remain unchanged.

Denial and rationalization as attack on true and honest representation of the past have been institutionalized in the Armenian case. In an introduction to his study on the Holocaust, Michael Marrus states contemptuously: "I have had no difficulty excluding from this book any discussion of the so-called revisionists—malevolent cranks who contend that the Holocaust never happened."[2] Those who study and write about the Armenian Genocide cannot be so unequivocal, because the denial has been institutionalized by a government, its supportive agencies, its influential political and academic collaborators, and by extension, its powerful military allies and trading partners. Kurt Jonassohn has aptly observed that a major difference in the treatment of the Armenian Genocide and the Holocaust is that

> the Holocaust literature is directed at remembering, understanding, and preventing a recurrence by emphasizing the role of human rights, while much of the literature on the Armenian genocide still addresses matters of historical fact—almost three-quarters of a century after the events of 1915. Another difference is that German authors are participating in the examination of what happened, whereas Turkish authors are still trying to deny that a genocide occurred.[3]

This is largely the result of the unrelenting campaign against the actuality and factuality of the Armenian Genocide. Unfortunately, some members of the academic community have been co-opted into this offensive by denying the premeditated, organized nature of the Armenian destruction and lending their names to advertisements and circular letters to that effect. Such individuals avail themselves of the principle of academic freedom without heeding the equally fundamental principle of academic integrity and responsibility.

As the central characteristic of genocide is the calculated, intentional decimation of the targeted group, refuting the factor of intent is foremost in the denier's brief. Negators and rationalizers of both the Armenian Genocide and the Holocaust emphasize the following points:

1. Stories about alleged genocide are based on wartime propaganda.
2. Armenians in the Ottoman Empire and Jews in Europe were perceived as posing very real security threats, and their actions demonstrated that these concerns were not imaginary.
3. There was no intent to annihilate either group, only to relocate its members.
4. The deaths that occurred were primarily from the same causes that carried away even more Turks and Kurds, in the Armenian case, and Germans in the Jewish case.
5. The number of Armenian and Jewish dead is much less than claimed, and most of the alleged victims actually ended up in other countries.
6. The myth of genocide was created in both cases for economic and/or political motives.
7. Those who believe and promote the myth have been the willful or unwitting abettors of communism and Soviet expansion and the destabilization of the NATO alliance and the West.

8. The proponents of truth—that is, those who do not accept the reality of genocide against the Armenian people—are struggling against powerful political lobbies to rectify negative stereotypes and historical misconceptions as persons brave and bold enough to champion free speech and inquiry.[4]

The strategies of denial are not always parallel. In the Jewish case, for example, it is critical to show that the Jews constituted a distinct cultural-racial group—that is to acknowledge their separate existence in Germany and the rest of Europe—in order to deny their victimization. In the Armenian case, the deniers manipulate statistics, history, and culture in order to minimize the significance of the Armenian presence in the area once called Armenia and now known as Eastern Anatolia. In this effort, it is necessary to obscure all evidence of that presence by changing toponyms, destroying historical monuments, and making Armenians disappear from the written record. Proudly proclaiming a cultural heritage that includes ancient civilizations from the Hittites to the Romans and even the Byzantines, Turkish spokesmen, buttressed by their foreign collaborators, eliminate most of the three millennia of Armenian history in the region. The destruction of a people has been followed by the destruction of its material culture and now even a campaign to eliminate its very memory.[5]

The constant repetition of rationalizations and the mixture of half-truths with falsehoods have had a more telling effect than absolute and unequivocal denial. Even a person believing himself to be knowledgeable about the Armenian Genocide can be shaken by the seeming rationality of relativist arguments. *Washington Post* correspondent Richard Cohen, writing that he believed there was such overwhelming evidence of the Holocaust that it could not be denied, then added:

> That, at least, is what I had thought until recently. But then not too long ago, I found myself sitting at the end of an enormous table in the embassy of Turkey. At the other end was the ambassador himself and what he was telling me was that the crime [Armenian Genocide] I had always thought had happened had not . . . [and] what the world persisted in calling a genocide was actually a civil war—one with atrocities on both sides and one in which the central government in Constantinople lost control over its own troops and could not protect the Armenians. There never was a policy to exterminate the Armenians.
>
> I had mentioned this genocide in a column—and mentioned it thinking that it was a given—that no one could possibly dispute that it happened. . . . But the ambassador said this had not happened. Sure, there were "incidents" and, yes, the Armenians had been banished. . . . And so I sat there at the table unable to prove that one of the great crimes of history had actually been

> committed. . . . None of this would matter—certainly not to the Armenians of 1915, the Jews of the 1940s, or the Cambodians of just yesterday—if it was not for the fact that to control the future, you have to first alter the past—take possession of it and rob it of its lessons.

Cohen concludes that truth is the last victim of genocide: "And so year by year, person by person, the genocide blurs, doubt corrodes it, and the easy word 'alleged' creeps in to mock the Armenian anguish."[6] As yet, no German ambassador or other government official has recited like declarations regarding the Holocaust, but the forces of denial are nonetheless pressing hard to make their way to center stage.

Wartime Propaganda

Stories about intentional mass killing, say the deniers, are founded on wartime propaganda for the purpose of turning public opinion against the enemy, which is made to seem so odious as to be worthy of merciless punishment. Among early disseminators of this position were French negators Maurice Bardèche and Paul Rassinier, followed by Robert Faurisson, British popular historian David Irving, and American professor Arthur Butz, all of whom have pointed to the myth of extermination camps as being a part of Allied propaganda to demonize the other side. Writing in different styles and varying gradations of denial, this group and others who share their view emphasize that the supposed Holocaust and its 6 million Jewish victims is a hoax, a big lie, created and exploited by Jews and international Zionism to establish and consolidate the state of Israel and reap great sums of money as indemnity.[7] The victorious side intentionally distorted the actual conditions in the concentration camps to paint the defeated adversary as so evil as to necessitate just—that is extreme—punishment. Such negators have built on the foundations laid by American revisionist historians such as Harry Elmer Barnes who explain the rise of Hitler and the Nazi regime as the logical outcome of the unfair treaties imposed on the defeated powers at the end of World War I and who have asserted that stories of German excesses in World War II have been politically motivated. There is enough guilt to go around to all the parties in conflict, and it is therefore underhanded to single out just one government or country.[8]

Such an approach is no less explicit in the Armenian case. Turkish diplomat Kamuran Gürün shows the Turkish side to be the victim of its own lack of aggressiveness: "We can easily state that propaganda is one of the weakest points of Turks. This was so in the Ottoman Empire, as well as in the Turkish republic. The propaganda activity of Turks has been restricted to refuting articles and erroneous assertions; thus it has been nothing more than a passive effort to defend the Turkish position. This attitude enabled the opposite side to act freely in portraying the Turks continuously as being guilty."[9] American deniers such as Stanford Shaw and Justin McCarthy have labeled accounts of more than a million Armenian victims as the work of the "Entente propaganda mills." McCarthy, apparently drawing freely from Gürün's book, *The Armenian File,* maintains that the prevailing anti-Muslim attitudes in the West, the biased accounts of American missionaries, and the operation of the Allied Powers' "propaganda machines" were utilized to perpetuate and intensify negative views of the Turks. Deniers always have explanations. In his manual for students and teachers titled *Turks and Armenians,* McCarthy writes:

> The English propaganda machine churned out atrocity stories against both Germany and its ally Turkey to aid in its war effort both at home and abroad. Several European states coveted Ottoman territory, and the massacres and atrocities for which the Ottoman government was said to be responsible were used as the justification for breaking up the Ottoman Empire and for taking all or nearly all lands away from Ottoman rule. The Western nations needed to believe and promote Ottoman and Turkish atrocity stories in order to excuse their own plans to annex Ottoman lands.[10]

He adds that propaganda was simply a weapon for fighting the war "and the Armenian Question was one of the main battlegrounds in which the propaganda war was fought." Although such propaganda against the Germans was subsequently studied and exposed, no such postwar investigations were conducted regarding Turkey. "Instead, the deceptions and distortions of propaganda on the Turks and Armenians have survived, so the legacy of hatred and prejudice remains."[11] Thus the mission of McCarthy, Shaw, Heath Lowry, and others of like mind, is "to set the record straight."

Deniers are keen on discrediting survivor testimony. In the case of the Holocaust, they insist that such untrustworthy accounts as are given by survivors are full of inconsistencies and exaggerations and were intended to swindle the German government out of billions of dollars and to win sympathy to create and bolster the state of Israel at the expense of other peoples. Similar claims are made in a Turkish denial booklet published in the 1980s.

> Carefully coached by their Armenian nationalist interviewers, these aged Armenians relate tales of horror which supposedly took place 66 years ago in such detail as to astonish the imagination, considering that most of them

> already are aged eighty or more. Subjected to years of Armenian nationalist propaganda as well as the coaching of their interviewers, there is little doubt that their statements are of no use whatever for historical research.[12]

What belies such a pronouncement is the fear that eyewitness accounts may have a great deal of use, even though it seems to be argued that eighty-year-old survivors cannot possibly retain a detailed memory of what happened to them and those around them.

Provocation of the Alleged Victims

The deniers and rationalizers of genocide try to show that the alleged victims were not free of guilt and that the security measures taken by the state were no different from what other beleaguered governments have done before and after. Bardèche, Rassinier, Faurisson, and other deniers of the Holocaust assert that the Jewish victims were in most instances partisans, saboteurs, spies, and enemy collaborators—a virtual fifth column. They point to the declaration of Chaim Weizmann in 1939 that Jews everywhere would support the Allied cause against Nazism and argue that it was only natural that the Jews should be perceived as a threat. Bardèche went so far as to assert that World War II was actually provoked by the Jews. Desperate acts of resistance, such as the Warsaw Ghetto uprising, are offered as evidence of Jewish hostility, seriously jeopardizing the war effort by forcing the diversion of regular armed forces to cope with the insurrections. They posit a certain affinity between Jews and communists and therefore the Soviet Union—the greatest enemy of the Reich.[13]

In the guise of a balanced, objective investigator, American Arthur Butz presents various forms of evidence to demonstrate that "Jews did, in fact, pose a security menace to the German rear in the war."[14] Most Jews in concentration camps were there for specific punitive or security reasons, not because they were innocent members of a targeted group. "The various political organizations—Socialist, Communist, Zionist, Agudist—were connected with the resistance organizations, whose activities ranged from active sabotage to propaganda and, on occasion, to armed resistance."[15] Butz is quick to rationalize and relativize: "It is an unhappy fact that partisan, irregular or guerilla [*sic*] warfare, together with the measures taken to suppress such operations, is not only the dirtiest business in existence but has also been a regular feature of twentieth century history."[16]

Another publication uses a favorite argument of deniers of the Armenian Genocide by showing that all governments, including the United States of America, acted against suspected minorities, so the relocations undertaken by Germany or by Turkey should not be considered extraordinary or as war crimes: "The United States and Canada had begun to intern Japanese aliens and citizens of Japanese extraction in internment camps before this became a German policy toward many German and other European Jews. There was no tangible evidence of disloyalty, not to mention sabotage or espionage, among these people of Japanese extraction. The Germans at least had a somewhat more plausible basis to press for the internment of Jews."[17] The anonymous writer concludes: "The internment of European Jews, like that of the Japanese in the United States and Canada, was carried out for security reasons."[18] Moreover, most of the Jews who were moved during the war were simply relocated to provide useful labor in agricultural and industrial enterprises in lieu of service in the armed forces. They were, after all, merely being returned to their lands of origin in eastern Europe.

These propositions are echoed in the Armenian case by Turkish government publications and authors such as Gürün and by their Western collaborators, especially Americans Stanford Shaw, Justin McCarthy, and Heath Lowry. Gürün explains:

> The Armenians were forced to emigrate because they had joined the ranks of the enemy. The fact that they were civilians does not change the situation. Those who were killed in Hiroshima and Nagasaki during the Second World War were also civilians. Those who were killed during the First World War in France, Belgium, and Holland were also civilians. Those who died in London during the Battle of Britain were also civilians. . . . Turkey did not kill them [Armenians], but relocated them. As it was impossible to adopt a better solution under the circumstances, it cannot be accepted that those who died because they were unable to resist the hardships of the journey were killed by the Turks.[19]

Gürün has embellished the rationalization of a key architect of the Armenian Genocide, Minister of the Interior and Grand Vizier Talaat Pasha, who from his postwar place of hiding in Germany in 1919 wrote: "These preventive measures were taken in every country during the war, but, while the regrettable results were passed over in silence in the other countries, the echo of our acts was heard the world over, because everybody's eyes were upon us."[20] Decades later, a Turkish official in Washington tried to draw a parallel for Americans: "Turkish response to the Armenian excesses was comparable, I believe, to what might have been the American response, had the German-Americans of Minnesota or Wisconsin revolted on behalf of Hitler during World War II."[21] Ambassador Şükrü Elekdağ wrote in 1982:

"What took place was a complex tragedy which claimed Turkish as well as Armenian lives. Indeed, it was a civil war within a global war stemming from an armed uprising of the Armenian minority at a time when the Ottoman state was fighting for survival during World War I. Many more Turks than Armenians perished."[22]

The rather transparent excuses for the Turkish deniers were refined by their Western collaborators. Years before he was challenged in the French courts in the 1990s for his denial of the Armenian Genocide, Bernard Lewis cautiously advanced the cause of revisionism by couching the Armenian calamity in terms of mutual warfare threatening the very existence of the Turkish state. In *The Emergence of Modern Turkey,* published in 1961, Lewis explains:

> For the Turks, the Armenian [nationalist] movement was the deadliest of all threats. From the conquered lands of the Serbs, Bulgars, Albanians, and Greeks, they could, however reluctantly, withdraw, abandoning distant provinces and bringing the Imperial frontier nearer home. But the Armenians, stretching across Turkey-in-Asia from the Caucasian frontier to the Mediterranean coast, lay in the very heart of the Turkish homeland—and to renounce these lands would have meant not the truncation, but the dissolution of the Turkish state. Turkish and Armenian villages, inextricably mixed, had for centuries lived in a neighbourly association. Now a desperate struggle between them began—a struggle of two nations for the possession of a single homeland, that ended with the terrible holocaust of 1916 [*sic*], when a million and half Armenians perished.[23]

Stanford Shaw, in a volume coauthored with his wife and published by Cambridge University Press (*History of the Ottoman Empire and Modern Turkey*), engages in many more egregious distortions and deceptions. He makes it seem, for example, that in ordering the Armenian deportations the Turkish authorities were simply following a precedent already established by the Russians.

> In the initial stages of the Caucasus campaign the Russians had demonstrated the best means of organizing a campaign by evacuating the Armenians from their side of the border to clear the area for battle, with the Armenians going quite willingly in the expectation that a Russian victory would soon enable them not merely to return to their homes but also to occupy those of the Turks across the border. [Minister of War] Enver followed this example to prepare the Ottoman side and to resist the expected Russian invasion. Armenian leaders in any case now declared their open support of the enemy, and there seemed no other alternative.[24]

Ascribing sinister motives to the Armenians, Shaw would have his readers believe that there was "no alternative" to deportation: "It would be impossible to determine which of the Armenians would remain loyal and which would follow the appeals of their leaders. As soon as spring came, then, in mid-May 1915 orders were issued to evacuate the entire Armenian population from the provinces of Van, Bitlis, and Erzurum, to get them away from all areas where they might undermine the Ottoman campaigns, against Russia or against the British in Egypt."[25] Concealing the fact that the Armenian population was deported and massacred throughout the width and breadth of Anatolia, Shaw claims that the Armenians were "evacuated" only from the war zone along the Russian frontier and from the Cilician countryside but not the cities in that region near the Mediterranean Sea.[26] The assertion is, of course, so grossly inaccurate that it raises justifiable questions about the academic integrity of its author.

Like Arthur Butz among Holocaust revisionists, Justin McCarthy, a student of Stanford Shaw, tries to show that he is more balanced, yet his underlying motives are as obvious as those of Gürün, Shaw, and other negators. McCarthy may also be beholden to Gürün in his reiteration of the claim that Armenian rebellions flared all over Anatolia, requiring the diversion of entire army divisions to suppress the conspiratorial risings. McCarthy prides himself on being a demographer, yet he apparently does not see the untenable contradiction between his minimalization of the number of Armenians in the Ottoman Empire and his repetition of Gürün's figure that from the province of Sivas (Sebastia) alone there were 30,000 Armenian guerrillas, half of whom had already made their way to the Russian lines to fight against the Turkish armies while the other half were prepared to strike those armies from the rear. McCarthy adds unabashedly: "No one accurately counted the numbers, but unquestionably there were more than 100,000 Armenian guerrillas or other fighters from Anatolia or the Russian territories fighting in Anatolia."[27]

For McCarthy and all other negators and rationalizers, the desperate efforts at self-defense in a few isolated places—Van, Shabin-Karahisar, Urfa, and Musa Dagh—are sufficient proof of Armenian disloyalty and conspiracy. Deportation, a word McCarthy grudgingly uses instead of his preferred term—relocation—became the Turkish government's response to the menace posed by the Armenians:

> The principle of the deportation was based on one of the few known ways to defeat a guerrilla insurgency and has been used from ancient up to modern times. Because guerrillas depend on local villages for supplies, support, and recruits,

> the guerrillas must be separated from the populace. . . . The Ottomans had for centuries deported groups who threatened civil order, including rebellious Turks. . . . Deportation of civilian populations because of real or imagined guerrilla threats has been practiced by many modern governments.[28]

McCarthy then leads the reader to the question of whether such seemingly extreme measures might actually have been the least of all possible evils: "Can one cause real suffering to deportees in order to ultimately save more lives by ending a war (an argument analogous to that of bombing of civilians in World War II)?"[29]

The negators and rationalizers thus allege that the Young Turk regime in World War I and the Nazi regime in World War II understandably were forced to take security measures. The Armenians and Jews were not simply innocent victims, as they have frequently been portrayed. In each case, the government had to relocate certain numbers of the offending group but without any wish to harm them. The measures were certainly far more justified than those taken by other governments in wartime, among them the accusers of Turkey and Germany. Moreover, without intent, there can be no genocide.

The Question of Intent: Rationalization and Relativization

It is imperative for deniers to make it seem that there was no intent to eliminate the targeted group. Intent underlies the United Nations Genocide Convention and broadly accepted definitions of genocide. As unqualified denial has not achieved the desired objectives, modern-day negators have adopted the strategies of rationalization and relativization. The horrors of war affect all elements of the population, not just one group, they say. Far more Muslims than Armenians died during World War I, and many more Germans than Jews perished in World War II. Differences in motivation and means of death are obscured in favor of the thesis of indiscriminate death during the general chaos and calamity of a world war complicated further by civil strife and a certain breakdown of control. Thus, in time of such massive upheaval, there can be no distinction between purported victim and perpetrator.

In the case of the Holocaust, American historian Harry Elmer Barnes created a model to exonerate Germany by emphasizing that it is meaningless to assign guilt, because war is evil as a phenomenon and creates universal suffering. If blame has to be established, however, then there is no doubt that the Germans suffered far more from Allied bombings of civilian populations, starvation, forced removal from vast territories after the war, and vengeance than did any other people. Barnes set the stage for later rationalizers to assert that the Allied Powers were primarily responsible for World War II and that Hitler was driven to resort reluctantly to extreme measures, and for relativizers to declare that the Allied bombings of civilian targets such as Dresden and Stalin's treatment of the peoples of the Soviet Union and eastern Europe were far worse than anything perpetrated by the Germans.[30] If it is not possible to persuade the public that the Holocaust is a complete hoax, the negators can still be successful by making people believe that all sides were equally at fault and that it is unjust to single out one party for the imposition of moral guilt and punishment. Such arguments find a certain receptiveness especially in the United States, where the debate about the necessity of bombing Hiroshima and Nagasaki has become increasingly intense and where the dictum that there are two sides to every story is widely accepted. Pretending to engage in academic inquiry, deniers make quantitative comparisons to obscure qualitative comparisons, aiming to remove the specific features of systematic annihilation and to reduce the culpability of the genocidal government or even fully to exonerate it.

American apologist Austin App advanced the arguments of Barnes by insisting that Hitler's solution to the Jewish problem was emigration, not annihilation, and that gas chambers did not exist, whereas the crematoria were used to dispose of those who died from sickness and disease and other causes.[31] British writer David Irving and American Arthur Butz are somewhat more circumspect and do not deny that large numbers of innocent people were killed, but they contend that such excesses took place without the knowledge or authorization of Hitler, who was preoccupied with the conduct of the war. Among the hundreds of thousands of relevant documents, no direct order for genocide from Hitler has been uncovered. Hence, any blame that exists must fall on Hitler's lieutenants, such as Heinrich Himmler, and on middle-level bureaucrats, who were unable to manage affairs at the local level. This explanation echoes the argument that the unfortunate Armenian deaths were not the result of any plan of the central authorities but rather of disease and epidemic, unruly tribes, and other particular causes. The negators know that if the truth about intent can be dismissed, then the entire genocide can be put in question. This objective is fundamental in denial and relativization of both the Armenian Genocide and the Holocaust. An early denier, John Beaty, labors to show that Jewish deaths in the concentration camps had nothing to do with government policy and then follows Barnes and App in deflecting blame: "The hunger at Dachau was war-time inhumanity by people who themselves were desperately hungry because their food stocks and transportation systems had been largely destroyed by American air bombardments." This contrasted to the "peace-time inhumanity" practiced by the Allied Powers for vengeance after the war by intentionally bringing the German people to the verge of starvation.[32]

Such arguments are also used by the small chorus of French deniers, who allege that stories of mass killings and gas chambers are gross exaggerations and highly suspicious. Paul Rassinier writes: "Gas chambers? Perhaps, but the proof is far, very far, from being established. With the exception of one, in all cases the opposite is proved. In the one remaining case, contrary proof has not been made because it is a question of a camp (Auschwitz-Birkenau . . .) located on the other side of the Iron Curtain where nothing can be verified, and where fabrication of false documents is raised to the level of an institution."[33]

Disclaiming intent is also fundamental to the Armenian case. As early as 1919, Talaat Pasha, from his hiding place in Berlin, wrote: "I admit that we deported many Armenians from our eastern provinces, but we never acted in this matter upon a previously prepared scheme. The responsibility for these acts falls first of all upon the deported people themselves."[34] A publication of a Turkish governmental agency seven decades later repeats the argument that all humanity suffers during wartime and that no one group can be viewed as particular victim in periods of such universal affliction. "Certainly some lives were lost, as the result both of large scale military and bandit activities then going on in the areas through which they [the deportees] passed, as well as the general insecurity and blood feuds which some tribal forces sought to carry out as the caravans passed through their territories." The "tribal forces," of course, has reference to the Kurds, frequently the agents of death mobilized by the Young Turk "Special Organization" but currently a serious problem for the Turkish government and therefore a convenient scapegoat for past excesses, just as at present. Denying any intent of genocidal killings by the Turkish authorities, the publication admits that the problems of the relocated population were compounded by "severe shortage of fuel, food, medicine, and other supplies as well as large-scale plague and famine." It should be remembered, however, that "as many as three to four million Ottoman subjects of all religions died as a result of the same conditions that afflicted the deportees. How tragic and unfeeling it is, therefore, for Armenian nationalists to blame the undoubted suffering of the Armenians during the war to something more than the same anarchical conditions which afflicted all the Sultan's subjects."[35] Relativization neatly explains away the Armenian Genocide.

Turkish denier Gürün, predictably seconded by American apologist McCarthy, maintains that the term "deportation" is incorrect, intentionally misconstrued by the British and French for propaganda purposes. Actually, it was relocation, as the Turkish term carries the connotation of "have to emigrate" or "changing one's location" rather than deportation to a specific place or a concentration camp.[36] Gürün then makes an unusual plea, even for negators and apologists, to exclude from the count of Armenian victims the tens of thousands who died during the "relocation."

> Various deaths occurred for various reasons during the relocation. Some of the deaths were due to epidemics, some were due to climatic factors, some were due to the hardships suffered during the journey, some were due to attacks, because officials did not protect them or because some officials engaged in illegal acts. . . . Who are the ones who can be pointed to as "murdered" in these deaths? Certainly not the ones who were killed while fighting, nor those who died of epidemics of typhus, typhoid fever, cholera, and variola, which were then widespread in Turkey, or of famine. It cannot be claimed that they would not have died if they had stayed in their homes, because the epidemics spread to the areas of their residence and took hundreds of thousands of lives. . . . Should we include in this group those who died because of climatic factors and the hardships of the journey during the emigration? We do not think so.[37]

Gürün conveniently ignores one of the five specific acts that constitute the crime of genocide according to the United Nations Convention: "deliberately inflicting on the group conditions of life calculated to bring about its physical destruction in whole or in part."[38]

Stanford Shaw pushed denial of the Armenian Genocide to unprecedented depths. After portraying the Armenians as long-time rebels and treacherous terrorists, Shaw alleges that the orders for deportation involved only the actual or potential zones of war and that the Young Turk government acted in good faith in instructing that the Armenian exiles should not be harmed. He cites documents that were created for deception without offering the reader even a hint that what happened in fact was the exact opposite of the author's description. As to intent, Shaw gives the false impression that he has investigated all the relevant documents and come to the following conclusion: "Careful examination of the secret records of the Ottoman cabinet at the time reveals no evidence that any of the CUP leaders, or anyone else in the central government, ordered massacres. To the contrary, orders were to the provincial forces to prevent all kinds of raids and communal disturbances that might cause loss of life."[39]

Ignoring the overwhelming evidence of wholesale deportation and massacre, Shaw states brazenly that the Armenians were removed only from strategic war zones and this with the utmost care for their safety and well-being.

> Specific instructions were issued for the army to protect the Armenians against nomadic attacks and to provide them with sufficient food and other supplies to meet their needs during the march and after they were settled. Warnings were sent to the Ottoman military commanders to make certain that neither the Kurds nor any other Muslims used the situation to gain vengeance for the long years of Armenian terrorism. The Armenians were to be protected and cared for until they returned to their homes after the war. A supplementary law established a special commission to record the properties of some deportees and to sell them at auction at fair prices, with the revenues being held in trust until their return. Muslims wishing to occupy abandoned buildings could do so only as renters, with the revenues paid to the trust funds, and with the understanding that they would have to leave when the original owners returned. The deportees and their possessions were to be guarded by the army while in transit as well as in Iraq and Syria, and the government would provide for their return once the crisis was over.[40]

This is not the full extent of Shaw's uncritical recitation of Turkish professions of innocence. He insists that there was no wish to harm the Armenians and that most of their losses occurred while they were retreating with the Russian army into the Caucasus, "not as the result of direct Ottoman efforts to kill them." Relativizing the Armenian decimation, he asserts that "about 200,000 perished as a result not only of the transportation but also of the same conditions of famine, disease, and war that carried away some 2 million Muslims at the same time."[41] Representation of genocide is redirected away from organized, intentional killing to an unplanned, undesired, and not disproportional loss of life.

In his student-teacher manual, Shaw's protégé, Justin McCarthy, pleads the denier's case: "Orders were indeed sent from Istanbul ordering local administrators to protect lives and property of the deportees, and there was no reason to send out such orders if they were not meant to be enforced." Unfortunately, the shortage of regular armed forces, he asserts, constrained the local governors to choose between protecting Muslim villages from Armenian bands or protecting Armenians from Muslims. "They chose to protect their own, as people usually will."[42] As in the case of Holocaust denial, McCarthy dismisses intent by posing the following false questions:

> Why was there no genocide of tens of thousands who lived in Istanbul, Izmir, the European section of the Empire, or other areas, and who survived the war unmoved and unharmed? Many in the columns of deported Armenians were attacked by tribes and bandits and did indeed die from murder, starvation, and disease, but how does one explain the columns that arrived intact and the more than 200,000 Armenian deportees who lived out the war in Syria? If genocide had been ordered why were they not killed?[43]

One may wonder if McCarthy is really unaware of the massacres of thousands and thousands of Armenians after they had straggled into Deir-el-Zor and other locations in the Syrian desert.

Advancing a favorite argument of the rationalization-relativization school of deniers, McCarthy suggests the following teaching objective. "The lesson of war in Eastern Anatolia is not that Turks massacred Armenians. . . . The lesson is that all the inhabitants of the Ottoman East suffered. They suffered such terrors that to try to choose whose torment was greater is absurd."[44] McCarthy sees no inequity between a state-funded, armed military establishment and a largely unarmed, untrained civilian population. Instead, he comes to the following conclusion:

> A government-ordered genocide did not exist in Eastern Anatolia, but there is a wider definition of genocide that applies. If genocide can be the action of one people against another, then genocide was definitely present in Eastern Anatolia. Both Turks and Armenians were its victims, and both were its perpetrators. Armenians killed Turks because they were Turks. Turks killed Armenians because they were Armenians. They had little choice. After the first days of the war, Turks and other Muslims knew that there could be no neutrality in the civil war with the Armenians. They would be killed because they were hated as Turks, not because of any political or tactical reason. Armenians were in the same situation. The extermination was a mutual extermination.[45]

McCarthy's caveat is aimed at appealing to the sensitivities of students and teachers and formed within a humanistic context: "Genocide is a word of great power and vast value as propaganda. It is also a word with many imprecise definitions. . . . It would seem to be far better to study the history of the Armenians and the Turks as a great human loss, and to abandon propagandistic terms."[46]

The transformation of the Soviet Armenian Republic into an independent state in 1991 and the concerted attempts of its leaders to normalize relations with the Republic of Turkey created optimism that the intensity of the denial of the Armenian Genocide would wane and that perhaps a new era in Armenian-Turkish relations might eventually lead to a Turkish admission of wrongdoing and at the very least a formal apology. Such hopes have been clouded, however, by the unbending attitude of the Ankara government, as reflected in the publication in 1995 of a multivolume work of the prime ministry's state archives titled *Armenian Atrocities in the Caucasus and Anatolia According to Archival Documents.* The purpose of the publication is not only to reiterate all previous denials but also to demonstrate that it was in fact the Turkish people who were the victims of a genocide perpetrated by the Armenians. "These documents show that it was not the Turks who slaughtered Armenians, as the Armenians insist, but rather just the opposite, the Armenians slaughtered Turks, and this truth is shown clearly in the documents." Turkey, it is explained, had maintained an "honorable silence" for decades, but unfortunately that noble gesture has been interpreted by some as acceptance of guilt. What has to be made clear, therefore, is "that the truth is exactly the opposite of what is being said by Armenians and that it is time to put an end to the one-sided claims which have characterized this issue thus far."[47] With this development, the strategy of denial proceeds beyond the bounds of rationalization and relativization to a complete role reversal, making the victim the perpetrator.

Numbers

A common feature in the denial of genocide is the manipulation and questioning of statistics by the rationalizer-relativizers. Their skewed calculations are aimed at minimizing the numbers of potential victims inhabiting the areas controlled by the indicted government in order to diminish and relativize the gravity of the crime, and, if possible, to exonerate the accused entirely. After juggling statistics to claim that there were far fewer Armenians and Jews in the affected regions than is generally cited, the rationalizers insist that the Turkish and German regimes simply wanted to relocate the untrustworthy elements, not eliminate them. Holocaust deniers admit that perhaps as many as 750,000 Jews, excluding those of Poland and Romania, were resettled in eastern Europe but argue that the figure of 6 million victims is beyond all reason and possibility.[48] In France, Maurice Bardèche and his followers have claimed that the 6 million figure is not only a wild exaggeration but that it was maliciously invented by Jewish sources for selfish economic and political gain. Paul Rassinier, who himself had been an inmate in Nazi concentration camps, challenged the view that they were actually extermination camps. Asserting that it would have been technically impossible to kill such a great number of Jews, he lowers the probable number of victims to between 500,000 and 1,500,000.[49]

Arthur Butz draws on statistics to assert that there could not have been a real Holocaust, because at the end of the war the Jews "were still there." Most had either emigrated or could be accounted for in various camps. The 6 million figure was "pure demographic speculation." Butz adds: "There is no way a Western observer can check the plausibility, let alone the accuracy, of such figures. He must either be willing to accept Jewish or Communist (mainly the latter) claims on Jewish population for Eastern Europe or he must reject any numbers offered as lacking satisfactory authority."[50] Butz's conclusion is predictable: "In the final analysis the difficulty is that the figures available amount to nothing more than statements, from Jewish and Communist sources, that millions of Jews were killed."[51]

There have been deniers who have gone so far as to allege that the majority of those supposedly killed in the gas chambers and cremated in the ovens were actually living in great comfort in New York City and elsewhere. Jewish leaders knew this to be the case when they lobbied against including questions about religion on the United States census forms in order to prevent the hoax from being exposed. Some revisionists virtually eliminate Jewish victimology altogether: "The losses claimed by the Jews are a myth, for most of the Jews survived the war and found haven in the countries of the Grand Alliance. Their casualties did not exceed 200,000, far fewer than those suffered by most European nations, and these, too, were due exclusively to diseases and other natural causes."[52] The rationalizer-relativizers challenge the reliability of the sources, in order to challenge the reliability of the statistics, in order to challenge the purported intent of the perpetrators, in order to expose the so-called genocide as a hoax.

The manipulation of statistics is no less blatant in the denial and relativization of the Armenian Genocide. Gürün and other Turkish nationalist writers, using various formulas and scenarios, reach the conclusion that the total number of Armenians who died could not be more than 300,000, and quite possibly no more than 100,000. "It is obvious that among these casualties the number of deaths which occurred for whatever reason during the emigration will be less than this figure, and the number of those who can be considered as having been killed will be even less."[53] It follows, therefore, that the number of Armenian victims was not disproportional to the losses of other elements during the war.

American authors Stanford Shaw, Justin McCarthy, and other negator-relativizers have refined the statistical manipulations to lower the number of Armenian victims almost out of sight. Shaw produces the following statistical contortions:

> The Entente propaganda mills and Armenian nationalists claimed that over a million Armenians were massacred during the war. But this was based on the assumption that the prewar Armenian population numbered about 2.5 million. The total number of Armenians in the empire before the war in fact came to at most 1,300,000, according to the Ottoman census. About half of these were resident in the affected areas, but, with the city dwellers allowed to remain, the number actually transported came to no more than 400,000, including some terrorists and agitators from the cities rounded up soon after the war

> began. In addition, approximately one-half million Armenians subsequently fled into the Caucasus and elsewhere during the remainder of the war. Since about 100,000 Armenians lived in the empire afterward, and about 150,000 to 200,000 immigrated to western Europe and the United States, one can assume that about 200,000 perished as a result not only of the transportation but also of the same conditions of famine, disease, and war action that carried away some 2 million Muslims at the same time.[54]

The falsehoods contained in this paragraph have become institutionalized and have been used repeatedly in various publications, petitions, letters to the editor, and speeches in the U.S. Congress and other forums. Merciless deportation becomes "transportation" and the indiscriminate torment to death of men, women, and children becomes a relatively small loss caused by the "famine, disease, and war action" that afflicted the entire population. Planting reasonable doubt about intent and numbers through relativization of suffering is one of the most potent weapons of the deniers.

The Trial of War Criminals

After both World War I and World War II, special tribunals gathered evidence and tried leaders of the defeated regimes for war crimes. A relatively small number of Nazi officials was brought before the Allied Tribunal as a symbolic process against the entire Nazi regime. Some of the accused did not deny the Jewish persecutions but feigned ignorance or helplessness in the matter. The confessions are damaging to the case of the deniers and therefore must be accounted for. It was initially asserted that the confessions resulted from torture or threats of torture. Moreover, the accused hoped to escape harsh punishment by admitting that the Holocaust had occurred but that they were personally not guilty. With the prevailing anti-German hysteria that had been stoked by the Allied Powers, it was deemed better to confess than to insist on the truth. Barnes and other critics of the trials label them as the height of hypocrisy, inasmuch as the leaders of those powers sitting in judgment of the defeated Germans would themselves have been on trial had the other side won the war. There was no validity in trials for war crimes held in the court of the victors, especially as much of the testimony from German witnesses was coerced and that from Jewish witnesses was invented. What was more, most of the evidence submitted emanated from Soviet-held territories and was therefore unreliable.[55]

The deniers regret the fact that the German government acknowledged the guilt of Hitler's regime, considering that act as shameful and even cowardly, yet they explain that it was understandable under the circumstances.

The world wanted to believe in the demonic guilt of Germany, and the postwar government understood that if there was any hope to lessen the heavy losses that were being prepared for Germany by the victorious Allied Powers it would be necessary to accept guilt and show remorse. There would be more sympathy for a repentant defeated side than a defiant one. Rejecting the hoax of the Holocaust would only add to the anticipated punishment. Acceptance of guilt and expressions of remorse could alone pave the way for Germany's reentry into the family of nations. The war crime trials, therefore, were a farce and a parody on justice.

In the Armenian case, a special tribunal was created by the postwar Turkish government to try leading members of the Young Turk regime for war crimes. All members of the central triumvirate—Enver, Talaat, and Djemal—were sentenced to death in absentia, since all had fled the country in the final days of the war. One district governor was actually hanged, but the process of justice halted abruptly. The rise of the Turkish resistance movement headed by Mustafa Kemal had the effect of first stalling and then suspending the trials.[56] The British transferred many of the accused offenders to the island of Malta, but as the Allied Powers prepared to recognize and make their peace with Mustafa Kemal the men were ultimately released in a prisoner exchange. Nonetheless, a large corpus of incriminating evidence had been gathered and the proceedings of the Turkish extraordinary tribunal were published as supplements to a semiofficial journal. Although justice miscarried, the evidence remains. It is also significant that the Treaty of Sèvres between the Allied Powers and the official Turkish government in Constantinople in August 1920 included provisions for the restoration of Armenian exiles, the rescue of Armenian women and children forcibly held in Muslim households, and the obligation of the Turkish government to cooperate in the gathering of evidence of war crimes and apprehending of accused criminals.[57] There was no question at the time about the atrocities committed against the Armenian population.

The success of Mustafa Kemal's Turkish Nationalist movement and subsequent revision of the Treaty of Sèvres through negotiation of the Lausanne treaties in 1923 did away with these provisions, but the relevant documents stand as reminders of the culpability of the Young Turk regime and require an explanation by the deniers of the Armenian Genocide. They advance the same logic as those who dismiss the validity of the Nuremberg trials. Constantinople, they point out, was under Allied control, making the sultan's government nothing more than a helpless marionette. The postwar government of Damad Ferid Pasha was filled with enmity toward the Young Turks and wanted to be rid of the popular and powerful wartime leaders.

The release of most of the accused criminals by the British is offered as proof of their innocence.[58] The extensive incriminating evidence contained in the repositories of Germany, an ally of Turkey during World War I, is explained with the assertion that German reports about Turkish plans to exterminate the Armenians were simply meant to divert attention away from Germany's own excesses against civilian populations in Belgium and other occupied territories. As Pierre Vidal-Naquet has pointed out, the deniers have an answer for everything that contradicts their interpretations.[59]

The Cold War and National Security

The subversion of memory, especially when associated with perceptions of security interests, has been used to redefine the past by individuals and governments alike. Terrence Des Pres has termed the creation of desired images at the price of historical integrity as "the narrative of power."[60] Established power structures guide and ultimately determine accepted versions of the past. Negators and rationalizers take advantage of these structures to advance their cause. Thus, throughout the existence of the Soviet Union and especially the years of the Cold War, any association with Russia or any information emanating from the Soviet Union was regarded with suspicion. It was not difficult for deniers in the West to extend this aversion by claiming that anyone who upheld the "myth" of an Armenian Genocide or a Holocaust was a willful or naïve abettor of the "evil empire," whose goal was the destabilization of the Western security system and especially key NATO partners, in the one case Turkey, and in the other, Germany.

This common feature of denial is immediately apparent in the related literature. Paul Rassinier and the other French deniers cast doubts on the depth of Jewish suffering by pointing out that nearly all of the alleged extermination camps were on the other side of the Iron Curtain where nothing could be verified and where the fabrication of false documents had become institutionalized. Any linkage with communism or the Soviet Union was in itself sufficient evidence of the unreliability of the information. The deniers repeatedly associate Jews and communism, both in showing that the Third Reich had every good reason to feel threatened by the Jews and in implying that an unholy alliance of the two elements produced the myth of the Holocaust. Some even assert that the defeat of Hitler's Germany had the calamitous effect of allowing Stalin's murderous regime to expand throughout eastern Europe and to swallow up half of Germany.[61] These arguments are clearly aimed at the susceptibilities of public opinion shaped by Cold War fears and concerns. Deniers hope to make it seem that insistence on the truth of the Holocaust is playing directly into the hands of the enemies of the free world.

Cold War considerations are even more intrinsic in the negation and rationalization of the Armenian Genocide. Successive Turkish governments have used the geopolitical position of the country to suppress memory of the Armenian Genocide. Pointing to its democratic, secularist, Western-oriented character and its long, strategic border with the Soviet Union, Turkey has exerted inordinate political and economic pressures, sometimes entering into the realm of blackmail, to discourage official recognition and even discussion of the Armenian Genocide.

The strategy of Mustafa Kemal was to propagate the new image of Turkey and to avoid public discussion of the Armenian Question. It was believed that with the passage of time the survivors and eyewitnesses would pass from the scene and their children would become acculturated in foreign countries, thereby resolving the problem without the need of any reparation, compensation, or even acknowledgment of wrongdoing. The Ankara government used diplomatic and economic channels to prevent activities that might keep alive international memory of the Armenian tragedy. As an example, in the 1930s when Metro-Goldwyn-Mayer studios bought the film rights to Franz Werfel's celebrated novel, *The Forty Days of Musa Dagh,* depicting the struggle for survival of several Armenian villages near the Mediterranean Sea, the Turkish government protested to the Department of State, which interceded with the Motion Pictures Producers and Distributors of America to have MGM shelve the project. Quiet diplomatic pressure and the threat of suspending the showing of American films in Turkey were sufficient to keep the Musa Dagh film from the American and world public.[62]

By the outbreak of World War II, the Armenian Genocide had faded from the memory of most contemporaries, while many governments were quite willing to leave the issue in the closet in view of the failure of the world community to live up to the promises to repatriate and rehabilitate the Armenian survivors and to punish the guilty parties. With the Cold War evolving as soon as the world war ended and with the vaulting strategic significance of Turkey, pursuing the question of the Armenian Genocide would threaten the security interests of the West. Terrence Des Pres has observed: "Governments have always required short-term memory, but never more than now. The historical record either enhances or it hinders the ongoing process of propaganda, and the Free World doesn't need ugly events to question its virtue." In the narrative of power, words such as "state security" and "national interest" take on exaggerated meanings given them by the military complex, and "truth is at best a reckless element, a sort of wild card in a deck that otherwise is tightly stacked."[63]

It was not difficult to draw on American academics sympathetic to Turkey, especially those engaged in Turkish studies or those who had lived in the country, to elevate denial and rationalization to the university level by placing the violent past into the perspective of current needs and the role of Turkey as a vital ally. Already in 1951, Princeton professor Lewis V. Thomas admitted that the Turks may have overreacted to any real Armenian threat and that much of the Armenian population had been "slain on the spot or converted to the Moslem faith and assimilated . . . or expelled beyond the frontiers," adding, however, that the Turks did view the Armenians as an "active fifth column." He then reached the following chilling conclusions:

> By 1918, with the definitive excision of the total Armenian Christian population from Anatolia and the Straits area, except for a small and wholly insignificant enclave in Istanbul city, the hitherto largely peaceful processes of Turkification and Moslemization had been advanced in one great surge by the use of force. . . . Had Turkification and Moslemization not been accelerated there by the use of force, there certainly would not today exist a Turkish Republic, a Republic owing its strength and stability in no small measure to the homogeneity of its population, a state which is now a valued associate of the United States.[64]

Thomas began a process that was refined by a generation of his students, including Shaw, and the latter's students, McCarthy and Lowry.

In the efforts of the Armenian-American community in 1985, 1987, and 1990 to have Congress adopt a commemorative resolution designating April 24 as a day to remember man's inhumanity to man, with particular reference to the Armenian Genocide but without casting any blame on the current Republic of Turkey, the Ankara government, its various agencies, its hired public-relations firms in the United States, and its sundry supporters all played the security card once again. The Department of State, the Pentagon, and the National Security Council were pressured into lobbying against passage of the resolution. During the Senate debates, opponents of the resolution rose to speak about the NATO connection, the affront to a critical ally, and considerations of trade and business. There were also a few who questioned the reality of the Armenian Genocide, maintained that there are always two sides to every story, argued that Congress (which adopts hundreds of commemorative resolutions annually) should not make judgments on historical controversies, and warned that passage would encourage the forces wishing to destabilize the West. What was new about these statements resounding in the chambers of Congress was that they came straight out of the denial literature produced by the Turkish embassy, the Institute of Turkish Studies, which was funded by the Turkish government and established in Washington D.C., and by the Assembly of Turkish American Associations.[65]

The Institute of Turkish Studies and its director, Heath Lowry, were instrumental in securing the signature of sixty-nine academics in Turkish studies, many of whom had been awarded grants by the institute, for an open letter published as an advertisement in the *New York Times* and the *Washington Post,* and read more than once into the *Congressional Record.* The advertisement and its use by several Senators and Representatives brought rationalization and relativization of the Armenian Genocide to the halls of Congress. The statement reads, in part:

> As for the charge of "genocide": No signatory of this statement wishes to minimize the scope of Armenian suffering. We are likewise cognizant that it cannot be viewed as separate from the suffering experienced by the Muslim inhabitants of the region. The weight of the evidence so far uncovered points in the direction of serious inter-communal warfare (perpetrated by Muslim and Christian irregular forces), complicated by disease, famine, suffering and massacres in Anatolia and adjoining areas during the First World War. Indeed, throughout the years in question, the region was the scene of more or less continuous warfare, not unlike the tragedy which has gone on in Lebanon for the past decade. The resulting death toll among both Muslim and Christian communities of the region was immense.[66]

On one occasion, the decision of the Senate Judiciary Committee to report the commemorative resolution out to the full Senate for debate elicited an immediate response from the Turkish government. American military aerial operations in Turkey were curtailed and the threat was made of more drastic measures. Nearly every major firm doing business with Turkey or having signed contracts for the delivery of aircraft and other kinds of hardware was recruited into the campaign against the resolution. Senator Robert Byrd of West Virginia led the charge against the resolution, threatening to filibuster for as long as it would take to prevent passage. Unlike other opponents who professed sympathy for the Armenian suffering but regarded American military and economic interests more important, Byrd and a few other senators reiterated the arguments of deniers, insisting on the impropriety of using the term "genocide" to describe a "human tragedy" that affected all the unfortunate peoples caught up in the strife of World War I.[67]

The pressure and even blackmail of the deniers and the government behind them have extended to Jewish groups and the state of Israel as well. In efforts to divide and broaden the breach between victim groups, negators of the Armenian Genocide uphold the truth and criminality of the Holocaust and make the appeal to keep it uncontaminated by confusing it in any way with the hoax of a so-called Armenian genocide. Such commingling, they caution Jewish audiences, would dishonor the memory of the innocent victims of the Holocaust and advance the designs of the Armenian deceivers. McCarthy is aware that parallels might be drawn between persons like himself who reject the Armenian Genocide and the deniers of the Holocaust and therefore strives to dismiss such a comparison:

> It is important to note that those who question the "Armenian Genocide" are very different from those who question the Genocide of the Jews by Hitler and his Nazis. No reasonable historian of Germany questions that the Nazis killed millions of Jews in their death camps, but there is a fringe group who does so. The "69 Scholars" who have questioned the use of "genocide" where Armenians are concerned are no fringe group. They are the foremost experts on the history of Turkey in the United States. Thus no one can rightly ignore their questions, as has been done in the past, by saying that "a fringe group of fanatics are the only ones who doubt that there was an Armenian Genocide."[68]

The Turkish government's interference in the International Conference on the Holocaust and Genocide, held in Tel Aviv in 1982, is one example of its blackmail of Israel on the issue of the Armenian Genocide. When the Turkish authorities learned that a handful of papers out of nearly 200 would have some reference to the Armenian Genocide, progressively intensifying levels of coercion were exerted to prevent any discussion of the Armenian case. The threats became so severe as to endanger Jewish lives, causing first the resignation of Elie Wiesel as honorary chairman of the conference and ultimately the withdrawal of sponsorship by Yad Vashem Institute and Tel Aviv University.[69] Many prominent scholars were pressured to withdraw their participation. Although the conference took place, a pallor had been cast, making it clear to what lengths the perpetrator side would go to prevent even discussion of the Armenian calamity. This scenario unfortunately has been repeated many times, underscoring the difference between institutionalization of the Armenian Genocide, on the one hand, and the non-governmental and non-official character of Holocaust denial.

Academic Freedom and the Warriors for Truth

A favorite ploy of negators and rationalizers is to portray themselves as the champions of truth standing outside the established power structure but with the courage to challenge the influential forces that for decades have misrepresented the historical picture. They appeal to a sense of fairplay and emphasize the importance and justness of learning about the other side of a legitimate debate. As soon as deniers manage to thrust genocide into the category of a controversy, they have become successful, for from that position they can make even greater inroads through the processes of rationalization, relativization, and trivialization.

Freedom of speech is a cherished principle in many countries, and the deniers often seek cover under this ideal to propagate their falsehoods. What is disconcerting is that the champions of academic freedom often do not uphold the equally important principle of academic integrity based on reasonable inquiry and the use of standards of evidence and tolerate instead the gross violation of academic responsibility. This has become apparent in resolutions of academic bodies defending the academic freedom of denier Stanford Shaw without expressing any opinion about the abject disregard for standards of the profession. The decision of a French court in 1995 holding Bernard Lewis accountable for his denial of the Armenian Genocide in *Le Monde* elicited a chorus of complaints, some in major United States newspapers, regarding academic freedom and historical controversies. The *Wall Street Journal* wrote: "A court applying the Holocaust denial precedent to a bona fide expert taking one side of a bona fide controversy shows how quickly restrictions on speech can spread. It also serves to obscure why France and Germany needed to enact such laws in the first place."[70]

Like the *Journal of Historical Review,* which tries to dismiss the Holocaust by efforts "to correct the historical record in the light of a more complete collection of historical facts, in a more calm political atmosphere and a more objective attitude," deniers of the Armenian Genocide try to show that they are engaged in an honest endeavor to reveal the truth and do away with distortions and myths that are barriers to peace and goodwill among peoples and nations.[71] McCarthy appeals to teachers, scholars, and politicians to "ask themselves if it is fair to do other than present both sides of the story," noting that in the name of fairness educators have changed much of the "traditional wisdom" once taught to students. The time has come therefore to revise the traditional wisdom relating to the so-called Armenian Genocide:

> The American Drive Westward is no longer taught as a purely noble quest, forgetting its effect on Native Americans. The history of slavery is no longer taught with suggestions that many slaves were happy with their fate. Imperialism is no longer taught as The White Man's Burden. On those matters, the quest for fairness changed the teaching of distorted history. It should also be applied to the Armenian Question.[72]

Hence, revisionism becomes fair and just, and the purveyors of deception hope to attract the uninformed and the naïve to their web.

The call for justice has also been made by negators and rationalizers of the Holocaust. Harry E. Barnes complains of a "blackout" when it comes to this subject. Anyone who might question German guilt is subjected to a conspiracy to silence him and to deny him a reputable forum. There is no doubt that German atrocity stories are politically motivated. Paul Rassinier decries the powerful groups that have succeeded in distorting what actually happened and as an inmate himself takes advantage of his status to challenge the "traditional wisdom." The right of Faurisson to air "controversial issues" has been defended by such noted scholars and scientists as Noam Chomsky in the name of freedom of speech. Even legislative and judicial prohibitions on denial stir the uneasiness of civil libertarians and bring to the deniers a level of notoriety and celebrity that otherwise may not have been theirs.

Trivialization

Although there is a great difference in the personnel and stages of denial as they relate to the Armenian Genocide and the Holocaust, in recent years rationalization and relativization of the Holocaust have managed to advance beyond the anti-Semitic fringe of scholars and writers into mainstream historical discussion, especially in Germany. Unlike the case of the Turkish government in state sponsorship of denial, the German government has not directly aided or abetted this attempt of conservative German historians to diminish German guilt by placing the Holocaust squarely within the context of the history of the twentieth century, a century of extraordinary violence. This so-called Historians' Debate, involving such reputable writers as Ernst Nolte, has as its object what has been termed as "comparative trivialization." Without whitewashing the Nazi regime, Nolte and his collaborators reiterate certain rationalizer arguments, such as the 1939 declaration of Chaim Weizmann, and point to comparative instances of inhumanity such as the Armenian deportations and massacres, Stalin's terror and Gulag camps, American saturation bombings in Europe and atomic bombings in Japan, the excesses during the Vietnam war, the Cambodian "auto-genocide," and other instances of mass killing during the century. It follows, then, that the blame for such behavior should not focus on the transgressions of a single people or single regime.[73]

Comparative trivialization has contributed to a backlash from some scholars engrossed in Holocaust studies. The threat posed by trivialization has reinforced their need to differentiate between the Jewish experience and the tragedies of other peoples. For example, without denying the terrible victimization of the Armenians, several Holocaust scholars, among them Deborah Lipstadt, Michael Marrus, and Steven Katz, write that the Armenian tragedy is incomparable to the Holocaust in scope and intent. Lipstadt reacts to the trivialization by these German historians as follows:

> The historians' attempt to create such immoral equivalencies ignored the dramatic differences between these events and the Holocaust. The brutal Armenian tragedy, which the perpetrators still refuse to acknowledge adequately, was conducted within the context of a ruthless Turkish policy of expulsion and resettlement. It was terrible and caused horrendous suffering but it was not part of a process of total annihilation of an entire people.[74]

The problem with Lipstadt's statement is that the Young Turk policies regarding the Armenians were directed toward a degree of annihilation no different from the Nazi solution to the Jewish question. It is untrue, as some scholars have thought, that the Young Turks were disinterested in the fate of Armenians living beyond the borders of the Turkish empire. The massacres of Armenians in northern Iran in 1914–15 and in the Caucasus, from Kars to Baku, when the Turkish army invaded the region in 1918 provide ample evidence of the scope and intent of the Armenian Genocide. Fortunately, Lipstadt herself has come to accept these facts and to speak out boldly against denial of the genocide.

Marrus describes the Armenian massacres as horrendous and qualifying as genocide in terms of an assault on the essential foundations of Armenian life with the ultimate aim of eliminating it. Nevertheless, he maintains, this is different from the policy of literal extermination practiced by the Nazis. He argues that "however extensive the murder of Armenians within the Ottoman Empire and however thorough the work of the executioners in particular localities, killing was far from universal." After all, "many thousands of Armenians survived *within* Turkey during the period of the massacres." But does the fact that many thousands of Jews still were alive in Nazi-occupied Europe at the end of World War II indicate that the Hitler regime was not bent on eliminating the Jewish element entirely? Marrus is clearly convinced of the victimization of the Armenians, but he inadvertently leaves the door open for deniers by implying that the survival of some thousands of Armenians in Turkey at the end of the war casts doubt on the intent to annihilate the Armenians physically. "However atrocious the results, therefore, the killing process of 1915 lacked the machinelike, bureaucratic, regulated character as well as the Promethean ambition that we have come to associate with the Nazi Holocaust."[75] He also maintains that unlike the Nazis, the Young Turks were not gripped by an all-consuming ideology. But in fact that ideology was so overriding in the persecution of the Armenians that it actually imperiled the war effort of the Central Powers and ultimately elicited sharp protests and threats from the allied government of Germany.

In the first volume of what promises to be a monumental, albeit highly controversial, historical analysis of the Holocaust in comparative perspective, Katz defines the Armenian Genocide as a "tragedy." After stating that it was a "profoundly disturbing, barbaric massacre," he adds:

> Yet, while in no way denying the Armenian tragedy, my understanding of its causation, unfolding, and consequences, not least in terms of its demographic proportions, does not support a fully genocidal reading of this event. . . . To distinguish is not necessarily to disparage. The fact that I choose for specific reasons of definition to deny the term genocide to the Armenian case is not meant to entail any diminishment of Armenian suffering or death.[76]

Such attestations aside, this approach does diminish and will lend no little satisfaction and comfort to deniers, some of whose works Katz has drawn on and apparently been influenced by in his attempt to be as thorough and objective as possible.

Yehuda Bauer, who previously expressed reservations similar to those of other Holocaust scholars deeply troubled by trivialization, has written:

> The proportion of Armenians killed by the Turks in World War I out of the general number of Armenians in the Ottoman Empire was no less than that of the Jewish victims out of the total Jewish population in Europe. Nor are the methods of killing unique. . . . The type of murder committed by the Germans in the USSR—mass machine-gunning—was the traditional method of mass murder in our century, and the death marches of Jews in the closing stages of the war had their precedent in the Armenian case as well. Nor is the fact that in the case of the Holocaust it was a state machine and a bureaucracy that was responsible for the murder unique, because there, too, the Young Turks had preceded the German Nazis in planning the execution of a population with such means as were modern at the time. Indeed, as I have pointed out elsewhere, I would view the Armenian massacres as a parallel, or Holocaust-related event.

Conclusion

It has been said that denial aims to reshape history, to rehabilitate the perpetrators, and to demonize the victims. It demonstrates the fragility of memory, truth, reason, and history. Israel Charny labels deniers as the arrogant killers of truth who try to write the final chapter of the original genocide by murder of recorded memories of human history. The denial of genocide is to celebrate its destructiveness, minimize the significance of human life, and subordinate people to unquestioning obedience to government and authority.[77] Yisrael Gutman adds that refusal to acknowledge the very facts of genocide is a brutal attack on morality and fosters distrust in the historical record.[78] The process becomes increasingly sophisticated through rationalization, relativization, and trivialization. The deniers are more interested in justifying the present and shaping the future than they are about an honest portrayal of the past. By concealing the truth, they become defenders of and accomplices to the great crime.

Yet, there is hope. Growing numbers of students are becoming acquainted with the lessons of the Armenian Genocide and the Holocaust. Many scholars concerned about the insidious denial of the Holocaust are coming to understand the importance of upholding the truth of the Armenian Genocide. In February 1996, more than a hundred scholars and literary figures subscribed to a statement denouncing denial of the Armenian Genocide. The petition, published in the *Chronicle of Higher Education,* reads in part:

> Where scholars deny genocide, their message is: murderers did not really murder; victims were not really killed; mass murder requires no confrontation, but should be ignored. Scholars who deny genocide lend their considerable authority to the acceptance of this ultimate human crime.
>
> The denial of genocide is the final stage of genocide: it murders the dignity of the survivors and destroys the remembrance of the crime. Denial of genocide strives to reshape history in order to rehabilitate the perpetrators and demonize the victims. The Turkish government's denial of the Armenian Genocide encourages—by its very nature—the current programs that deny the Jewish Holocaust and the Cambodian genocide; it encourages genocidal episodes that are currently occurring in Africa, the Balkans, and elsewhere. The Turkish government's tactics pave the way for state-sponsored Holocaust and genocide denial in the future.[79]

Among the signatories to the declaration are noted Holocaust scholars Yehuda Bauer, Israel Charny, Helen Fein, Raul Hilberg, Steven Katz, Robert Jay Lifton, Deborah Lipstadt, and Robert Melson, and among the prominent literary figures are Allen Ginsberg, Norman Mailer, Arthur Miller, Henry Morgenthau III, Harold Pinter, Susan Sontag, John Updike, and Kurt Vonnegut. This salutary expression of solidarity inspires guarded optimism in the ongoing struggle against the manipulators of truth.

This comparative analysis shows that the strategies of negators, rationalizers, relativizers, and trivializers of the Armenian Genocide and of the

Holocaust have crossed many common thresholds. Denial of the Armenian Genocide has penetrated far deeper within academic and political circles than has rejection of the truth of the Holocaust, but the arguments used are nonetheless the same. These include the assertions that the "alleged" genocides were actually invented as wartime propaganda; that the presumed victims were mainly provocateurs and enemy collaborators; that legitimate preventive measures are taken by all governments; that there never was the intent to victimize either group; that the numbers of dead have been grossly exaggerated and are in fact not out of proportion with the overall wartime casualties; that the postwar trials of indicted organizers of the genocides were rigged and meant to gain vengeance against the defeated powers; that a definite connection existed between the supposed victim groups and Russia or the Soviet Union; that the attempts to exploit the genocide issue are really aimed at destabilizing the NATO alliance and countries aligned with the "free world"; and that the very fundamental principle of academic freedom—the right to unfettered investigation and expression—is at stake and requires an active defense against those who cannot tolerate the view that there are two sides to every story.

The arguments are spurious and contorted and their goal is to deceive and to confuse. Any success in raising doubts or appealing to a sense of "fair play" provides enormous satisfaction and motivation to the deniers. The ongoing, concerted campaign of repudiation of the Armenian Genocide may be taken as a preview of things to come regarding remembrance of the Holocaust. This lesson has begun to be heeded by Holocaust scholars and human rights activists. Although an initial reaction of some scholars and public figures to trivialization of the Holocaust was to set apart and even diminish the scope of the Armenian Genocide, this trend seems to be changing and concerned researchers and writers about both crimes are being drawn together by the common threat posed by the four-headed hydra of negation, rationalization, relativization, and trivialization. The underlying motives of all these aspects of denial are deep-seated and range from historic prejudices to current political agendas. In face of this ugly reality, it is incumbent on people of good conscience to unite in combating the bigotry and upholding the precept that academic integrity is an inseparable part of academic freedom.

Notes

1. Elie Wiesel, "Understanding Eyes," *Hadassah Magazine,* March 1987, 24. I wish to acknowledge the contributions to this chapter of Michael Blacher, who

made a comparative study of genocide denial in a graduate seminar under my direction at UCLA.

2. Michael R. Marrus, *The Holocaust in History* (Hanover, N.H.: University Press of New England, 1987), xiv.
3. Frank Chalk and Kurt Jonassohn, *The History and Sociology of Genocide: Analyses and Case Studies* (New Haven: Yale University Press, 1990), 328.
4. See Deborah Lipstadt, *Denying the Holocaust: The Growing Assault on Truth and Memory* (New York: The Free Press, and Toronto: Maxwell MacMillan, 1993); Richard G. Hovannisian, "The Armenian Genocide and Patterns of Denial," in *The Armenian Genocide in Perspective,* ed. Richard G. Hovannisian (New Brunswick, N.J.: Transaction Books, 1986), 111–34. For bibliographic essays on this subject, see Erich Kulka, "Denial of the Holocaust," and Roger W. Smith, "Denial of the Armenian Genocide," in *Genocide: A Critical Bibliographic Review,* ed. Israel W. Charny (New York: Facts on File, 1991), 2:38–62, 63–85.
5. See, for example, Clive Foss, "The Turkish View of Armenian History: A Vanishing Nation," in *The Armenian Genocide: History, Politics, Ethics,* ed. Richard G. Hovannisian (New York: St. Martin's Press, 1992), 250–79.
6. Richard Cohen, "Killing Truth," *Washington Post,* May 31, 1983, B1.
7. See, for example, Maurice Bardèche, *Nuremberg: Ou, la terre promise* (Paris: Les Sept Couleurs, [1948]), and *Nuremberg II: Ou, les faux monnayeurs* (Paris: Les Sept Couleurs, [1950]); Paul Rassinier, *The Real Eichmann Trial: Or the Incorrigible Victors* (Chapel Ascote, U.K.: Historical Review Press, 1979); Robert Faurisson, *The "Problem of the Gas Chambers"* (Rochelle Park, N.J.: The Revisionist Press, 1979); *Mèmoire en dèfense: Contre ceux qui m'accusent de falsifier l'histoire. La question des chambres à gaz* (Paris: La Vieille Taupe, [1980]); Arthur R. Butz, *The Hoax of the Twentieth Century* (Torrance, Calif.: Institute for Historical Review, 1976); David Irving, *Hitler's War* (New York: The Viking Press, 1977).
8. See Deborah Lipstadt, "The Evolution of American Holocaust Revisionism," in *Remembering for the Future: The Impact of the Holocaust and Genocide on Jews and Christians,* supp. vol. (Oxford: Pergamon Press, 1983), 269–76.
9. Kamuran Gürün, *The Armenian File: The Myth of Innocence Exposed* (Nicosia, Istanbul: K. Rustem and Brother, 1985), 36.
10. Justin McCarthy and Carolyn McCarthy, *Turks and Armenians: A Manual on the Armenian Question* (Washington, D.C.: Assembly of Turkish American Associations, 1989), 85–86.
11. Ibid., 88.
12. Assembly of Turkish American Associations, *Setting the Record Straight on Armenian Propaganda against Turkey* (Washington, D.C.: Assembly of Turkish-American Associations, 1982), 11.
13. Lipstadt, *Denying the Holocaust,* 49–64, 103–21.
14. Butz, *Hoax of the Twentieth Century,* 197.
15. Ibid., 221.
16. Ibid., 204.

17. *The Myth of the Six Million* (Los Angeles: Noontide Press, 1969), 87.
18. Ibid., 104.
19. Gürün, *The Armenian File,* 216.
20. [Talaat,] "Posthumous Memoirs of Talaat Pasha," *Current History* 15 (November 1921): 295.
21. Altemur Kiliç, *Turkey and the World* (Washington, D.C.: Public Affairs Press, 1959), 18.
22. United States Congress, 97th Congress, 2d sess., *Congressional Record,* 128, pt. 7 (Washington, D.C.: Government Printing Office, 1982), 8679.
23. Bernard Lewis, *The Emergence of Modern Turkey* (New York: Oxford University Press, 1961), 350.
24. Stanford J. Shaw and Ezel Kural Shaw, *History of the Ottoman Empire and Modern Turkey,* vol. 2: *Reform, Revolution and Republic: The Rise of Modern Turkey, 1808–1975* (New York: Cambridge University Press, 1977), 315.
25. Ibid.
26. Ibid.
27. McCarthy and McCarthy, *Turks and Armenians,* 48. Cf. Gürün, *The Armenian File,* 200.
28. McCarthy and McCarthy, *Turks and Armenians,* 52.
29. Ibid.
30. Harry Elmer Barnes, *Revisionism and Brainwashing: A Survey of the War Guilt Question of Germany after Two World Wars* (N.p., 1962). See also the analysis of Barnes by Lipstadt, *Denying the Holocaust,* 67–70, 73–83.
31. See Austin J. App, *History's Most Terrifying Peace* (San Antonio: Austin J. App, 1974); idem, *The Six Million Swindle: Blackmailing the German People for Hard Marks with Fabricated Corpses* (Tacoma Park, Md.: N.p., 1973). See the analysis of App by Lipstadt, *Denying the Holocaust,* 85–102.
32. John Beaty, *The Iron Curtain over America* (Dallas: Wilkinson Pub. Co., 1951), 78.
33. Rassinier, *The Real Eichmann Trial,* 20.
34. Talaat, "Memoirs," 294.
35. Turkey, Foreign Policy Institute, *The Armenian Issue in Nine Questions and Answers* (Ankara: Foreign Policy Institute, 1982), 25.
36. Gürün, *The Armenian File,* 201–2; McCarthy and McCarthy, *Turks and Armenians,* 52.
37. Gürün, *The Armenian File,* 214–15.
38. *Convention on the Prevention and Punishment of the Crime of Genocide,* Article II, United Nations, December 9, 1948.
39. Shaw, *Ottoman Empire and Modern Turkey,* 316.
40. Ibid., 315. Several years after the publication of Shaw's volume, the Turkish Policy Institute copied this deceptive approach by publishing the following purported order of the Ottoman council of ministers:

> When those of the Armenians resident in the aforementioned towns and villages who have to be moved are transferred to their places of settlement and are on the road, their comfort must be assured and their

> lives and property protected; after their arrival their food should be paid for out of Refugees' Appropriations until they are definitively settled in their new homes. Property and land should be distributed to them in accordance with their previous financial situations as well as their current needs; and for those among them needing further help, the government should build houses, provide cultivators and artisans with seed, tools, and equipment.

Excerpts of other cited disinformation read as follows:

> Make arrangements for special officials to accompany the groups of Armenians who are being relocated, and make sure that they are provided with food and other needed things, paying the cost out of the allotments set aside for emigrants.
>
> The camps provided for transported persons should be kept under regular supervision; necessary steps for their well being should be taken, and order and security assured.
>
> Make certain that indigent emigrants are given food and that their health is assured by daily visits by a doctor. . . . Sick people, poor people, women, and children should be sent by rail, and others on mules, in carts or on foot according to their power of endurance.
>
> Each convoy should be accompanied by a detachment of guards, and the food supply for each convoy should be guarded until the destination is reached.
>
> In cases where the emigrants are attacked, either in the camps or during the journey, all efforts should be taken to repel the attacks immediately.

See *The Armenian Issue in Nine Questions and Answers,* 24–25.

41. Shaw, *Ottoman Empire and Modern Turkey,* 316.
42. McCarthy and McCarthy, *Turks and Armenians,* 53.
43. Ibid., 54–55.
44. Ibid., 46.
45. Ibid., 55.
46. Ibid., 66.
47. Turkey, Prime Ministry, *Armenian Atrocities in the Caucasus and Anatolia According to Archival Documents* (Ankara: Prime Ministry State Archives, 1995), introduction.
48. See, for example, Butz, *Hoax of the Twentieth Century,* 32.
49. Paul Rassinier, *Debunking the Genocide Myth: A Study of the Nazi Concentration Camps and the Alleged Extermination of European Jewry* (Torrance, Calif.: Institute for Historical Review, 1978), 214–20; Aimé Bonifas, "The French Revisionists and the Myth of Holocaust," *Remembering for the Future* (Oxford: Pergamon Press, 1988), 2:2194–95. For a discussion of the "numbers game" played by the deniers of the Holocaust, see Lipstadt, *Denying the Holocaust,* 55–64.
50. Butz, *Hoax of the Twentieth Century,* 10, 15.
51. Ibid., 17.

52. See Randolph L. Braham, "Historical Revisionism and the New Right," *Remembering for the Future* (Oxford: Pergamon Press, 1988), 2:2094. See also Lipstadt, *Denying the Holocaust,* 66.
53. Gürün, *The Armenian File,* 219.
54. Shaw, *Ottoman Empire and Modern Turkey,* 315–16.
55. Lipstadt, *Denying the Holocaust,* 55–56, 63–64, 76–80, 129–32; Braham, "Historical Revisionism," 2094–95. See also the cited works of Barnes and Butz.
56. See Vahakn N. Dadrian, *The History of the Armenian Genocide* (Providence, R.I.: Berghahn Books, 1995), 303–43. See also Dadrian's bibliographic essay, "Documentation of the Armenian Genocide in Turkish Sources," in Charny, *Genocide,* 2:86–138.
57. "Treaty of Peace between the British Empire and Allied Powers . . . and Turkey, Sèvres, August 10, 1920," in *British and Foreign State Papers,* vol. 113: *1920,* ed. Edward Parkes et al. (London: His Majesty's Stationery Office, 1923), 681–83, 706–7.
58. See, for example, Gürün, *The Armenian File,* 229–39; McCarthy and McCarthy, *Turks and Armenians,* 87–94; *The Armenian Issue in Nine Questions and Answers,* 26–28.
59. Pierre Vidal-Naquet, *Assassins of Memory: Essays on the Denial of the Holocaust* (New York: Columbia University Press, 1992), 40–41; idem, preface to the Permanent Peoples' Tribunal, *A Crime of Silence: The Armenian Genocide* (London: Zed Books, 1985), 3–5.
60. Terrence Des Pres, "On Governing Narratives: The Turkish-Armenian Case," *Yale Review,* 75, no. 4 (October 1986): 517–31.
61. See, for example, Carlos Whitlock Porter, ed., *Made in Russia: The Holocaust* (N.p.: Historical Review Press, 1988). See also the cited works of Beaty, App, Rassinier, and Butz.
62. See the file on the Musa Dagh film in U.S. National Archives, Record Group 59, File 861.4061. See also Hovannisian, "Patterns of Denial," 120–21.
63. Des Pres, "On Governing Narratives," 523, 527.
64. Lewis V. Thomas and Richard N. Frye, *The United States and Turkey and Iran* (Cambridge, Mass.: Harvard University Press, 1951), 60–61.
65. On this issue, see Vigen Guroian, "The Politics and Morality of Genocide," in Hovannisian, *The Armenian Genocide,* 311–39.
66. *New York Times,* May 19, 1985; *Washington Post,* May 19, 1985. On the role of Heath Lowry and the Institute of Turkish Studies, see chapter 12 of this volume.
67. See Richard G. Hovannisian, "The Armenian Diaspora and the Narrative of Power," in *Diasporas in World Politics,* ed. Dimitri C. Constas and Athanassios G. Platias (London: MacMillan, 1993), 192–97. For the Congressional debate, see 101st Congress, 2d sess., *Congressional Record* 136, February 20–22, 27, 1990 (Washington, D.C.: GPO, 1990), 1208–36, 1312–57, 1416–48, 1692–1716, 1731–32.
68. McCarthy and McCarthy, *Turks and Armenians,* 97.
69. See the detailed account of conference organizer Israel W. Charny, "The Conference Crisis: The Turks, Armenians and Jews," in *The Book of the International*

Conference on the Holocaust and Genocide, vol. 2: *The Conference Program and Crisis* (Tel Aviv: Institute of the International Conference on the Holocaust and Genocide, 1983), 270–330.

70. *Wall Street Journal,* August 28, 1995, A11. See also responses to the editorial, ibid., September 11, 1995, A21.
71. Lipstadt, "American Holocaust Revisionism," 279.
72. McCarthy and McCarthy, *Turks and Armenians,* 100–101.
73. On the Historians' Debate, see Peter Baldwin, ed., *Reworking the Past: Hitler, the Holocaust and the Historians' Debate* (Boston: Beacon Press, 1990).
74. Lipstadt, *Denying the Holocaust,* 212.
75. Marrus, *The Holocaust in History,* 20–23.
76. Steven T. Katz, *The Holocaust in Historical Context,* vol. I: *The Holocaust and Mass Death before the Modern Age* (New York: Oxford University Press, 1994), 22.
77. Israel W. Charny, "The Psychology of Denial of Known Genocides," in Charny, *Genocide,* 2:22–23.
78. Yisrael Gutman, "The Denial of the Holocaust and Its Consequences," *Remembering for the Future,* 2:2116, 2121–24.
79. *Chronicle of Higher Education,* February 2, 1996, A30.

10

Freedom and Responsibility of the Historian

The "Lewis Affair"

Yves Ternon

In a democracy, historians have a right to intellectual freedom. They are free to choose the subject of their research and to gather information. They are free to express their opinion and to interpret facts. They are free to state arguments for and against a position, to profess doubt, and to expound on hypotheses. They are free to seek further data before reaching a conclusion. There is, however, a counterpoint to this freedom. The freedom of thought and speech entails responsibility; historians elaborate on the past and help to record it. Their readers take for granted that they have done the research honestly, that they have not jumped to conclusions in the absence of solid evidence, that they have not disguised truth or, even worse, resorted to forgery in order to distort the truth. Seventy years of Soviet historiography, not to mention Turkish historiography, have shown that historians serving the state, which propagates its own views and interpretations of events, lose their independence and thus fall out of the company of respected scholars. Objectivity is not only a virtue; it is a prerequisite for all historical research.

Historical truth always calls for the presentation of established facts, such that the results stand above all reasonable doubt. Such truth may be subject to review only in the event that one can show that the sources are unreliable or forged or that new evidence invalidates the previously accepted proof. The weight of the converging evidence is usually so great that it is not often that historical truths can be denied unless, of course, there are other motivations. Historians who have studied the denial of the Holocaust well know how this method functions. The practitioners of denial call it "revisionism." But "negationism" is its real nature. How do they go about it? They take a collection of irrefutable evidence and seek out some little detail to be subjected to scrutiny and dispute. They then blow up this detail and try to cast doubt on the entire work and to topple the whole edifice. This insidious process carried on by the "Assassins of Memory," as Pierre Vidal-Naquet calls them, is a sham.[1] As far as the deniers are concerned, the domain of bonafide historians is beyond their limits and becomes their undoing. Their lies and bad faith bar them from honest historical debate.

It is quite another matter when a scholar esteemed for his prominence in the scientific community uses the tools of the craft, not to revise history, but simply to reject established truth. This type of "negationist" knows that he is speaking to professional doubters. There is nothing easier than to put people in an awkward position by denying obvious facts. The technique consists of fostering doubt with the elementary element of skepticism, bringing the audience to wonder if they have not acquiesced too quickly in acceptance of the evidence without requiring further proof, and finally demanding additional evidence which they know does not exist. Unfortunately, this has been the tactic of Professor Bernard Lewis.

The Crime of Genocide and the Historian's Responsibility

Before tackling what in France is called "the Lewis Affair," I must revert to the matter of the historian's responsibility when dealing with something of such gravity as genocide. Genocide is a crime, the absolute crime, the gravest form of crime against humanity. It is an offense against international law, defined by the United Nations Convention on Genocide in 1948. In order to sustain the charge of genocide, several conditions have to be met: the victim is necessarily a human group, such as is categorized by the convention; the members of the group "as such" have been killed or subjected to conditions that have resulted in death or inability to perpetuate the group. Intent is a critical element. Proving criminal intent to destroy the group in whole or in part is the wellspring of accountability for genocide. Such a crime entails a combination of extraordinary, far-reaching operations, involving an entire country or even a continent. It is infinitely complex, so much so that only the state, with all the power and means at its disposal, is capable of conducting the operation. Genocide is a premeditated crime. This means that its perpetrator has anticipated a line of defense so as to claim non-culpability. The perpetrator has planned the crime with great secrecy, has contemplated the smallest detail, and has tried to eliminate all incriminating evidence. In due time the perpetrator will deny everything and call on the accusers to furnish hard evidence. Finally, the charade will be reversed and the victim group may be accused of killing large numbers of the perpetrator group.[2]

Therefore, in all historical inquiry, especially in the matter of genocide, the freedom of the historian is only relative because it is modified by a fundamental responsibility. One may view the denier of the crime as an accessory to it. The denier will explain, of course, that the available evidence falls short of proving the charge of genocide, and he may suggest another term, different in scope and character, such as massacre, tragedy, or, better yet, reciprocal violence in the course of a civil war exacerbated by "inherited hatred." Even if many of the ingredients of genocide are present but one may be lacking, deniers use this as an escape hatch. They particularly like to insist that intent cannot be proved and that the charge therefore is void.

Ambiguities in and differing interpretations of the definition of genocide are unsettling. Some scholars and activists have broadened the definition to include many groups subjected to human-rights abuses. Others tend to keep the scope of definition within narrow limits for fear that the term might become something trivial and obscure the exceptional gravity of the crime. Some scholars, for example, refuse to classify the crimes of the Khmer Rouge in Cambodia in the 1970s or of the Soviet regime in Ukraine in the 1930s as genocide. They have given their reasons based on statistics or interpretation of the United Nations Genocide Convention. Their arguments are admissible within the limits of scientific debate. The additional evidence they request is based on legitimate skepticism. The independence and good faith of such scholars seems to be beyond question.

When it comes to the Armenian Genocide, its reality stands above the shadow of a doubt. All the requisite components of genocide were present and there is no room for doubt as to the characterization of the victims as a group, as to the killing of members of the group "as such," as to perpetration of the crime throughout the Ottoman Empire, and as to the criminal intent of the perpetrators. Intent, a fragile but by no means missing link, is undeniable, even though everything was done to deny it. The central committee of the Committee of Union and Progress (CUP), from the spring of 1915 to the autumn of 1916, enacted its plan to eliminate the Armenian citizens of the Ottoman Empire. It is inconceivable that this crime could have been executed without a carefully coordinated plan. The testimony of eyewitnesses and survivors alone is so abundant, diverse, and precise as to establish the facts and discount the allegation of an Armenian plot or the claim that deportations or "relocations" were necessitated for reasons of military security. All the evidence points to the fact that the orders for massacre emanated directly from Constantinople and that the deportations were merely a pretext for annihilation.

Although most of the direct evidence, such as the orders to kill, have been destroyed, the residual evidence was great. Some of it was produced at the time of the postwar trials in Constantinople in 1919, when the crime was shown to have been planned and organized by the Ittihad party through public and military agents and the "Special Organization," which had been created specifically for the purpose. According to one scholar "the documents which exist and which prove the case of genocide are more authentic, more profuse and more various than the evidence for most facts accepted as such by historians."[3] In this context, denying that the genocide occurred takes the historian beyond the outer threshold of scholarship and make him or her an agent of the state.

The issue of the Armenian Genocide is the chosen ground for futile debates, in which by dint of fighting over the form, the content is no longer considered. For more than twenty years, I have borne as a millstone the obligation of such legal haggling, the object of which is not to convince a jury, whose duty it is to express reasonable doubt, but rather to convince the attorney for the defense who constantly shies away from the evidence. Denial, especially when adorned with the prestige of the university, can wear out the resilience of the most dedicated scholar. Though scholars have proven to a fault *flagrante delicto* and its premeditation, their dialectical arguments are ever questioned. Rather, the deniers deem each and every exhibit unsatisfactory or label it a forgery. All this is reiterated interminably, beyond all intellectual honesty. One starts by granting deniers further inquests—first one, then another—until it becomes clear that the most indisputable evidence and the absence of any reasonable doubt are of no avail. The adversary is of bad faith, has not the slightest respect for the basic rules of controversy, and will under no condition ever acknowledge the guilt of the defendant. A plea of guilty would in fact be advantageous to both sides. It would put an end to the vain alibis and deceptions. It would then be possible to scrutinize the motives of the crime, not in search of mitigating circumstances—there can be none for genocide—but in order to understand who, in the end, shares responsibility.

The "Lewis Affair"

I wish to repeat once more that established truth should not be challenged in the absence of new evidence. Base politics or other repugnant motives cannot disprove truth. Truth cannot be adapted to a desired end, and it cannot be bartered. That, however, is just what Bernard Lewis and a few others are attempting to do. Dedicated to Turkish studies, they put their talent and their reputation at the disposal of the state, determined to deny the Armenian Genocide in order for the state to preserve the benefits of the crime.

The "Lewis Affair" began in the United States on May 19, 1985, with the publication, both in the *New York Times* and in the *Washington Post,* of an advertisement addressed to members of the House of Representatives. The statement was signed by sixty-nine academics in Turkish studies and sponsored by the Assembly of Turkish American Associations. Among the signatories was the name of Bernard Lewis, the Cleveland E. Dodge Professor of Near Eastern History at Princeton University. The statement reads in part: "The undersigned American academicians who specialize in Turkish, Ottoman and Middle Eastern studies are concerned that the current language embodied in House Joint Resolution 192 is misleading and/or inaccurate in several respects. Specifically, while fully supporting the concept of a 'National Day of Remembrance of Man's Inhumanity to Man,' we respectfully take exception to that portion of the text which singles out for special recognition 'the one and one half million people of Armenian ancestry who were victims of genocide perpetrated in Turkey between 1915 and 1923'."

The reservations of the signatories focused on use of the words "Turkey" and "genocide." The advertisement's claim is true that "the area currently known as Turkey, or, more correctly, the Republic of Turkey, was part of the territory encompassing the multi-national, multi-religious state known as the Ottoman Empire." Is should be noted that those who complained about the use of the term Turkey in place of Ottoman Empire were not so rigorous in their own works. Bernard Lewis, for example, used the term Turkey to refer to the Ottoman state eleven times in a single chapter in his widely used *The Emergence of Modern Turkey.*[4] Moreover, the arguments used to challenge the label of genocide are unsustainable. Indeed, the signatories of this statement, maintaining that "statesmen and politicians make history and scholars write it," further explained that "for this process to work, scholars must be given access to the written records of the statesmen and politicians of the past. To date, the relevant archives of the Soviet Union, Syria, Bulgaria and Turkey all remain, for the most part, closed to dispassionate historians."

Following the appearance of the advertisement, Gerard Chaliand wrote to Bernard Lewis to express disappointment at seeing his signature on this political statement.[5] Lewis responded with a long letter in which he explained his reasons for subscribing to the statement: "The only sure result of the resolution would be the disruption of U.S.–Turkish relations. . . . On the question of archives, in our statement we strongly urged the Turkish Government to open its archives to international scholarship."[6] Chaliand replied: "Don't you think it is uncharitable if not unfair to blame the supposed absence of evidence proving the case of genocide against Armenian populations in Anatolia during World War I, when what is in fact feared is some kind of attempt to destabilize NATO."[7]

That the signatories of the advertisement were of bad faith is obvious. They refused to admit "the case of genocide," while, as Chaliand wrote, "a cursory review of them as historians and linguists will reveal that they have accepted as facts events and policies based on much less evidence than what is available to prove the case of the genocide during the First World War." Gerard Libaridian also wrote Lewis:

> The advertisement also did a disservice to the Turkish people. The advertisement's attempt to equate the genocide with a civil war can only serve to spread the guilt of a government, the Ittihad ve Terraki government, to the whole Turkish population. . . . The Ittihad government, in organizing the genocide, did not care about the consequences of such an act on the Turkish and other peoples; the government of Turkey today seems not to care who is blamed, as long as the authority of the state is not weakened. It is unfortunate that your name was lent to this immoral strategy of a government which has shown little respect for its own people.[8]

In the initial phase of the "Lewis Affair," it seemed that the denial of the Armenian Genocide was part of a policy to support Turkey as a member of NATO and that the stand of American scholars of Turkish studies augured the spectacular opening of the relevant Ottoman archives. Acting as he did, Bernard Lewis became the active accomplice of a political fraud. The Armenian Genocide had already been recognized in 1984 by the Permanent Peoples' Tribunal, in 1986 in the Whitaker Report received by the United Nations Human Rights Subcommittee, and once again in 1987 by the European Parliament.[9] A shift in Bernard Lewis's position at about the same time deserves notice. In the first edition of *The Emergence of Modern Turkey* in 1961, he characterized the Armenian-Turkish conflict as "a struggle between two nations for the possession of a single homeland," which is tantamount to transforming a fictitious threat into a real one. He nonetheless recognized that the clash "ended with the terrible holocaust of 1915, when a million and one half Armenians perished." In the French translation of his book, published in 1988 under the title of *Islam et Laïcité* (Islam and secularism), the translation for which he took full responsibility,

Lewis altered the passage as follows: "and thus a desperate struggle broke out between them, a struggle between two nations for the possession of a single homeland which ended with the terrible slaughters of 1915, when a million and a half Armenians perished, according to certain evaluations, as well as an unknown number of Turks."[10] How many errors and inaccuracies are contained in these few lines. Already, one could question whether Bernard Lewis was just writing nonsense or was taking such liberties with history in order to serve political interests.

The Paris Phase

While in Paris in November 1993 for the publication of two of his books translated into French, Bernard Lewis was interviewed by journalists Langellier and Peroncel-Hugoz of *Le Monde* concerning the relations between Islam and politics and about Islamic fundamentalism. In his response, Lewis praised the Turkish regime, which he characterized as a rampart against Muslim fundamentalism, and called for the admission of Turkey into the European Union. Knowing that in 1987 the European Union had requested Turkey to acknowledge the Armenian Genocide, the journalists then asked: "Why do the Turks still refuse to recognize the Armenian Genocide?" Lewis answered: "You mean recognize the Armenian version of the story?" He again set forth the view of a Turkish-Armenian conflict of two nations fighting over a single homeland and explained that the deportations of the civilian population had been a necessary wartime security measure. He then added: "Both sides agree that the repression was geographically limited. Armenians living elsewhere in the Ottoman Empire, for example, were hardly affected." He drew the following conclusion: "If we talk of genocide, it implies there was a deliberate policy, a decision to blot out systematically the Armenian nation. That is quite doubtful. Turkish documents prove an intent to banish, not to exterminate."[11]

The statement by a scholar, rightly considered as one of the most prominent Islamicists, was all the more astonishing to French intellectuals. At the time, most scholars were unaware of Lewis's previous denials. Given the circumstances, it seemed logical to consider that he had jumped to a hasty conclusion in a field that was really not his strength and that if properly informed he would recognize his error. With Michel Marian and Claude Lefort, we composed a firm but courteous rejoinder, signed by thirty intellectuals and academics. In it we reiterated that scholar of his standing should not countenance "the lie of yesterday's criminals" and lend credibility to the excuse that the deportations were necessitated by military exigencies.

"Such acts are characteristic of a genocide. It is precisely because it is dangerous to abuse this term that genocide must be recognized as such when it is unquestionable. Indeed, the deliberate destruction of the Armenians of the Ottoman Empire has furnished jurists of the thirties with a point of reference, when their alarm over the rise of Nazism grew. And the Pole, Lemkin, used this precedent to fix the concept of genocide."[12]

The matter could have gone no further if Bernard Lewis had not persisted, justifying himself in *Le Monde* on January 1, 1994. His response was inconsistent on several accounts. Not only did he get entangled in unjustifiable argumentation, asserting the deportation of Armenians had been partial and selective in nature and invoking the harsh conditions and the responsibility of bandits attacking convoys, but on top of all that trying to validate the idea of "an Armenian betrayal" in the "context of a struggle, no doubt unequal, but for material stakes." He concluded: "There is no serious proof of a plan of the Ottoman government aimed at the extermination of the Armenian nation."[13]

What was to be done? The problem at hand was that of the responsibility of the historian. The reputation of Bernard Lewis and his adamant insistence could not go unanswered. It was no longer possible to engage in an academic exchange when one party refused to accept the validity of the evidence. Lewis had obviously left the field of scholarship and entered the arena of politics.

Truth, once established, is not negotiable. The Armenian Genocide is not a hypothesis but a certainty. Moreover, by resorting to the already invalidated arguments put forward during eighty years by successive Turkish governments, Lewis became an accomplice to the prolongation of the effects of the genocide by its denial. It is on this account that Armenian associative groups in France mobilized, in spite of their political divisions. On February 14, 1994, the Forum of Armenian Associations of France instituted a civil procedure against Bernard Lewis. The legal action was based on article 1382 of the French Civil Code, which states: "Whoever is guilty of causing harm must make reparation for it." The plaintiffs considered that Lewis had committed "a fault causing very grievous prejudice to truthful memory, to the respect and to the compassion due to the survivors and to their families." After several postponements, the case was heard in mid 1995, culminating in the verdict that Bernard Lewis has not fulfilled his responsibilities as a conscientious historian, for which a token fine was imposed.[14] Although the punishment in this civil case was only symbolic, it was nonetheless regarded as a significant vindication for the Armenian victims and for those who continue to struggle against "negationism."

On February 14, 1994, the Committee for the Defense of the Armenian Cause (CDCA), along with three survivors, brought a separate suit for damages and instituted criminal proceedings against Bernard Lewis based on the Gayssot Act. That law is a 1990 supplement to the Press Act of 1881 stipulating that punishment should be imposed on those "who call into question the very existence of one or several crimes against humanity committed either by members of an organization recognized as criminal or by a person judged guilty of such crimes, whether by French or international jurisdiction." The procedure was complex. The Gayssot Act only takes into account crimes against humanity as defined by the Nuremberg Tribunal, which is to say crimes committed by the Nazi regime between 1939 and 1945. It was promulgated in haste shortly after the desecration of a Jewish cemetery in the city of Carpentras. But this is precisely what the freedom of the historian as pertaining to the "Lewis Affair" is all about. It was to be expected that the suit would not qualify under the strict letter of the law, but the court did hear the case and did recognize the historical validity of the Armenian Genocide.

The trial took place on October 14, 1994, before the 17th Division of the Parisian Magistrate Court. There, I was called on to testify as an expert witness, along with Israel Charny, director of the Institute of the Holocaust and Genocide in Jerusalem. We merely set forth before the court the unquestionable evidence on which was based our certainty that the Armenians of the Ottoman Empire had been the victims of genocide beginning in 1915. The trial also came to grips with the heart of the question—the limits of freedom of the historian. As Lev Forster, one of the counsels for the plaintiffs declared: "Freedom is a fundamental right of the historian as well as of the individual. But does the freedom of the historian permit denial? No! It does not! To be a historian means being capable of acquiring scientific methods of work and analysis, to be truthful, which means to rely on and to produce evidence. . . . In these [*Le Monde*] articles Bernard Lewis has not acted as a historian but as a propagandist working for the admission of Turkey into the European Community."[15]

On October 21, Lewis addressed a memorandum to the president of the 17th Division of the Magistrate Court explaining the circumstances of the newspaper interviews. He admitted that the expression, "the Armenian version of this story," was inappropriate inasmuch as this version is accepted as truth by non-Armenians. With regard to the certain changes in different editions of his book, *The Emergence of Modern Turkey,* Lewis commented that the meaning of words change. Not only had the meaning of "Holocaust" evolved over a period of thirty years, which is correct, but also the word "genocide" had evolved in the opposite direction, which is incorrect, because it is dishonest to confuse the careless application of the term by certain elements in the media and interest groups and the rather precise definition acknowledged by scholars and jurists.

Lewis vigorously rejected the accusation of culpable neglect of his professional obligations or of having deliberately falsified history and instead asserted: "The question to be discussed is the one of knowing if there was or was not a decision taken by the Turkish government to exterminate the Armenians, as well as orders given in that sense. The question is still discussed among historians specializing in that matter."[16]

If such were the case, there would never have been a "Lewis Affair." Quite obviously, if Bernard Lewis demands that a document be produced, signed by Talaat, Enver, or other leaders of the Ittihadist ruling clique before recognizing the reality of the Armenian Genocide, he and others like him can continue in their deceptive ways because it is unlikely that such documents still exist and will surface. No one is in possession of a document signed by Hitler ordering the destruction of the Jews, but the absence of such a written order does not negate the fact that the Holocaust occurred. Requiring such orders is a devious and dishonest maneuver.

Conclusion

Most of the evidence concerning genocide can be established only indirectly through the accumulation, authentication, and cross-checking of documents and other relevant materials in such a way as to remove any doubt and establish with unwavering conviction the absolute truth. Three different and complementary sources help to establish the reality of the Armenian Genocide: witness testimony, victim testimony, and perpetrator testimony, both direct and indirect. The documentation that has been accumulated over the past three decades should convince even diehard skeptics, but this has not been the case. When the legitimate doubt of the scholar is converted into denial, when he refuses to bow to reason, little hope remains and he leaves the realm of scholarship. The question at hand concerns no longer the freedom of the historian. It concerns the right of a scholar to lie. The liar is not always aware that he is lying because, at some point, his whole outlook brings him to a position where the lie is not seen as such but becomes imperative in obedience to a cause higher than that of scientific inquiry. In short, the freedom of the historian ends where, fundamentally, he relinquishes the attitude of the scholar, even as his language and dialectical tools may still give the appearance of science.

The Armenian Genocide is proven in all its components—among them intent. The converging evidence is well in excess of that generally judged abundant in establishing other historical truths. We can follow Aristotle's example by showing that when one moves forward along the road, there comes a time when hypothesis becomes certainty, when the object hazily perceived until that point is recognized unmistakenly as a tree.[17] Only the shortsighted will remain skeptical. Only the blind or the blindfolded will need to touch the tree to make sure it exists. Even then, such persons may doubt its true nature. Jesus has existed. Assuredly, Napoleon led the campaign into Russia. World War I took place. The Nazis built gas chambers to kill Jews. Requesting proof of reality is a perverse act. This demand does not express a reasonable doubt but rather a relentless refusal of the obvious if it does not fit into a predetermined scenario or scheme. The refusal is equivalent in terms of chess to the sacrifice of a pawn. Truth regarding the Armenian Genocide is the pawn sacrificed in order to protect an essential position when the stakes are considered, really or fictively, as critical for Turkey. The ruses are many. One day it may be the importance of a vital NATO ally; another, the role of Turkey as a rampant against Islamic fundamentalism. The negationist, at present, will do his utmost to refute the evidence, just as, yesterday, the perpetrator tried to justify the crime. Even if the truth is unwelcome, however, it can neither be suppressed nor negotiated. The exact designation stands—genocide.

These are the considerations pertaining to the "Lewis Affair." I am not unaware of the reputation of Bernard Lewis. I feel I have expatiated sufficiently on the freedom of the historian and on his responsibilities, as well as the tarnish awaiting those who venture into support of nonscientific political agendas that have penetrated the academic community. I am aware that in several countries new legislation regarding sanctions against denial is being considered and that proponents of academic freedom are uneasy with this development. In turn I would like to speak up for those who have been traumatized and in mourning for the past eight decades not only because of the genocide itself but also because of its denial and negation. When I add the deep grief of that group with my exasperation as a historian at the seeming impossibility, even with abundant proof, to have the truth acknowledged, I am forced to declare that the time is up. The history of the genocide is written and our sole task now is to explain its circumstances and to continue to research and document it. We must cease the debate with persons of bad faith. It is my feeling that the time has come to put an end to our fear of not being credible. The genocide was a horrendous crime. The evidence is all there—province by province, city by city, village by village, hamlet by hamlet, with its countless variations according to time and place yet all the same in the vast process of extermination—genocide. A deliberate plan, carefully organized and brutally executed. The deniers and rationalizers offend the dignity of the historian and of all humanity.

Notes

1. Pierre Vidal-Naquet, *Les Assassins de la mémoire* (Paris: La Découverte, 1987).
2. On the crime of genocide, see Yves Ternon, *L'État criminel: Les génocides au XX*[e] *siècle* (Paris: Ed. du Seuil, 1995).
3. Letter of Gerard Libaridian to Bernard Lewis, July 8, 1985. Gerard Chaliand has provided me with these documents.
4. Ibid.
5. Letter of Gerard Chaliand to Bernard Lewis, June 30, 1985.
6. Letter of Bernard Lewis to Gerard Chaliand, August 14, 1985.
7. Letter of Gerard Chaliand to Bernard Lewis, October 2, 1985.
8. Letter of Gerard Libaridian to Bernard Lewis, July 8, 1985.
9. United Nations Sub-Commission on the Prevention of Discrimination and the Protection of Minorities, *Revised and Updated Report on the Question of the Prevention and Punishment of the Crime of Genocide,* prepared by Benjamin Whitaker, UN Document E/CN.4/Sub.2/1985/6, July 2, 1985.
10. Bernard Lewis, *The Emergence of Modern Turkey* (New York: Oxford University Press, 1961); idem, *Islam et Laïcité: La naissance de la Turquie moderne* (Paris: Fayard, 1988).
11. *Le Monde,* November 16, 1993.
12. Ibid., November 27, 1993.
13. Ibid., January 1, 1994.
14. The affair was tried on June 21, and Bernard Lewis was required to pay "un franc de dommages et intérêts" to the Forum des associations arméniennes de France and to LICRA. See ibid., June 23, 1995.
15. *Internet on the Holocaust and Genocide,* nos. 54–56 (April 1995): C7–C10.
16. Translated from the French original.
17. See Patrice Loraux, "Consentir," *Le Genre humain* (1990): 151.

11
The Truth of the Facts
About the New Revisionism

MARC NICHANIAN

The Trial

The annihilation of the Armenians in the Ottoman Empire during the years 1915–16 has recently been brought to the fore, eighty years after the events.[1] Of course, for the survivors and their descendants it had never ceased to be at the forefront. It was placed on the order of the day for "civilized humanity" in 1994 and 1995 because of a suit, a trial, and a verdict. The suit was brought before a French civil court against Bernard Lewis, a renowned historian of the Islamic world and the Ottoman Empire. He was called before the court for having "contested the reality of the Armenian Genocide or, at the very least, for having banalized the persecutions and the sufferings inflicted on the Armenian deportees."[2] In an interview published in *Le Monde,* he replied to the question, "Why do the Turks keep on refusing to recognize the Armenian Genocide?" as follows: "You mean the Armenian version of this story?"[3] A few weeks later, in a detailed response to the "keen reactions" elicited by this extemporaneous declaration, Lewis, while regretting the Armenian suffering, "an awful human tragedy that has branded until today this people's memory, as the memory of the Jews has been branded by the Holocaust," consistently reduced the tragedy's dimensions to those of a natural catastrophe ("starvation," "disease," "abandonment," "cold"). Even worse, he added: "There exists no serious proof of a decision and a plan by the Ottoman government aimed at exterminating the Armenian nation."[4] This was, of course, the climax of his argument. All in all, the events constituted only a deportation that took a bad turn.

Bernard Lewis has been condemned by the Tribunal de Grande Instance de Paris, and it would be logical to suppose that he was found guilty on the count of the indictment brought by the plaintiff; that is, precisely for negationism. Closer scrutiny of the verdict, however, will show that this is not the case. Such an examination illustrates the literally insane situation in which the survivors are caught when they have to confront an enterprise of systematic, universal, and repeated denial. The examination will be useful as well in order to point out the limits of any court action directed against negationism, in particular of any court action occurring within the context of domestic law. In contrast, now that an international tribunal has been set up to judge the crimes against humanity in Bosnia and a permanent international tribunal has at last been announced, nearly fifty years after the United Nations Genocide Convention of 1948, a critical assessment of the limits of law as well as the necessity and conditions of its implementation may not be superfluous.[5] We have to keep in mind that each genocidal project in this century has been, among other things, but perhaps in its very essence, a challenge to law.[6] This is the perspective in which I want to examine here the legal reaction to the new negationist tide relative to the Armenian Genocide. Because the neorevisionism is largely the product of professional historians, my inquiry relative to the role and the limits of law must be paralleled by another question, that on the essence and functions of history and historians in our world. Who ultimately is in charge of the "truth of the facts?"[7] The historians or the tribunals?

A State of Belligerency

Bernard Lewis's negationist intervention was far from an isolated phenomenon. It was part of a new wave of negationism, with well-defined, albeit extremely subtle, borders. Throughout 1994, several prominent historians and political scientists and a few philosophers who apparently did not want to be left out harked back to the same arguments. The thesis of a quasi-natural catastrophe and of a deportation that took a bad turn in conditions of total war has been developed by American historian Jay Winter in the same newspaper, *Le Monde.* In a strange article, Winter accepts the treatment of the Armenians as a crime and once again relates the facts of the genocide in their entirety, while also beginning with the qualification: "This deportation was not a decision of genocide, although it was tantamount to death for those who were old, sick, and disabled. . . . What transformed the crime of war into genocide was the context of total war, which inexorably changed the deportation into extermination, as a consequence of maltreatment and deprivations."[8] Every reasonable reader can see that there is a serious flaw here. There was a genocide but no genocidal decision, asserts the author; what started as a war crime changed into a genocide. Everybody knows that the term "genocide" supposes and implies, precisely, before any mass murder, the intention and the decision to exterminate. How then can a crime of war be transformed by itself into a genocide? This inconsistency does not seem to cause the author and the newspaper that published his views much chagrin. Winter summarizes his argument in this way:

> The criminal nature of the deportations was proved after the war. . . . The crime was the systematic deportation, the humiliation, and the murder of an entire collectivity. The massacre of children shows that the crime had the purpose of erasing the forthcoming Armenian generation as well as the present one. However . . . it was a somewhat "artisanal" extermination. . . . The ideological preparation of this extermination was superficial. . . . Consequently, the deportation was not a genocide as such. . . . The treatment that the Turks imposed upon the Armenians in 1915 was not motivated by criteria of race.[9]

That is exactly what Freud would have called the argument of the kettle.[10] The crime is recognized in all its aspects, in its totality ("the purpose of erasing the forthcoming Armenian generation as well as the present one") and, in the next proposition, it is reduced and assimilated to the "movements of population . . . that are unavoidable in time of war." All the elements of the genocidal thrust are there, yet it is not a genocide. Why, exactly? Because, according to Winter, the extermination displayed an "artisanal" character, the ideological preparation was only superficial, and there was no racial hatred.

It is not my purpose or my duty to show that these are biased arguments, which recur again and again in the negationist literature. Once and for all, refutation is useless. What is much more interesting is the set of contradictions this and other scholars put forth. The principle is that all the alleged facts of the genocide will be recognized and accepted, except for the essential intention.

Bernard Lewis's arguments are similar, although he concedes less: there was "no campaign of hatred," the deportation "was not total," and, in any event, deportation had always been "a common practice" among the Ottomans. Nevertheless, the most important argument runs as follows: "These events must be seen in the context of a struggle, certainly unequal but for real stakes, and of an increasing concern among Turks—probably most exaggerated but not totally unfounded."[11] To summarize the argument, there was a ground for concern and consequently there was an incentive and a motivation, real or imaginary. All rhetorical precautions and circumvolutions will not change the thrust of the argument that we often encounter in this kind of literature: there was a state of belligerency, therefore the crime was motivated. This is a new kind of denial. The "reality" of the events is not denied as such. There seems to be only a question of interpretation. The historian is the master interpreter. It cannot be ignored, however, that all the interventions of recent years whose purpose has been to demonstrate that the catastrophe that befell the Armenians of the Ottoman Empire either was not a genocide or was not comparable to the Holocaust (and these interventions have been legion) are based, in the final analysis, on the powerful (and irrefutable) argument of the absence of logical motivation for the crime perpetrated by Nazi Germany. All other cases were *therefore* "motivated": they had a recognizable cause, their "intent" or "purpose" was "known, though criminal," as Hannah Arendt said.[12] Or they represented a "systematic project subjected to an ideology" as stated more recently by Philippe Lacoue-Labarthe.[13] The reader may ask what is the use of these arguments, what do they tend to demonstrate precisely, which interests do they serve, to what end are they advanced? "They" did not want to annihilate. To be sure, "they" did not annihilate, but "they" had the motives and the motivation for annihilating.

This argument of the kettle, to which the above-mentioned authors are condemned, may seem entertaining. It may seem offensive as well, when one knows that this new wave of negation does nothing other than protract and refine eight decades of Turkish denial and that it uses, in so doing, an argumentary relay with far-reaching implications: that of the singularity of the Jewish catastrophe. In Winter's intervention (representative in this respect of the new subtle negationist approach), the reference to the singularity is explicit: the small-scale extermination (*l'extermination artisanale*), the superficial ideology, the lack of racial hatred, have their symmetrical opposite in Auschwitz, while it remains unclear whether these arguments are used to establish the singularity or whether it is the singularity that provides their justification, their intimate and ultimate spring.

The same holds true for Lewis, who marshals his arguments in order to prove that "the comparison with the Holocaust is biased in several essential aspects," as if anyone disputes the distinctiveness of each such instance of mass destruction.[14] We must record here an aggravated perversion of the denying and negationist approach, which corrupts the incomparable term of its own comparison. This perversion should attract the attention of those who believe in the absolute singularity of the Shoah, which is here weighed down and undermined by the immoral use of its paltry upholders.

It is a considerable stake. It is one of the greatest moral stakes of our epoch.[15]

Law and the Reality of Facts

Now what does the verdict of the Tribunal de Grande Instance de Paris have to say? In the reasons adduced to the judgment, it declares expressly that it is outside the tribunal's competence to "determine whether the massacres carried out between 1915 and 1917 constitute or not a crime of genocide, as the latter is currently defined by the article 211–1 of the New Criminal Code." The reason is that it is up to the historians and not the courts to arbitrate these issues and to decide how an event has to be qualified or characterized. Consequently, the tribunal would not pronounce any judgment about qualifying the event. It probably has an opinion or an inward conviction on this issue, but it is not this opinion or conviction on which the verdict is founded. If that is the case, however, why does the tribunal pronounce its sentence? Why does it not grant the historian the right to portray the facts as he wishes? The tribunal answers: "It is only by concealing the elements that were contrary to his thesis that the defendant has been able to affirm that there was no 'serious proof' of the Armenian genocide." With such an assertion, the historian had consequently failed in his "duties of objectivity" and had revived the "pain of the Armenian community." In reality, the pain he causes cannot be used as a criterion for a historian's declarations and judgments. The tribunal mentions it only in addition to the principal argument. The latter can be summarized in one sentence: the defendant did not prove the absence of proof. The tribunal has no competence to express an opinion on the nature of historical events. Nevertheless, it does fall within its competence to judge a man's irresponsibility in "such a sensitive matter," be this man a historian or a simple citizen.

It must be said that the idea of a historian concealing "elements contrary to his thesis" is astonishing and not quite convincing. It is possible to infer from this that it would be sufficient for the historian not to conceal these elements in order to be legally authorized to uphold an opinion that differs from that of the plaintiff. This is literally what the verdict of the court says. The "contrary elements" it enumerates are three in number: the conclusions of the U.N. Subcommission on Prevention of Discrimination and Protection of Minorities (1985) and its parent body, the U.N. Commission on Human Right; those of the Permanent People's Tribunal, heir to the Russell Tribunal (1994); and those of the European Parlement.[16] All of these recognize the reality of the genocide. The tribunal nonetheless states clearly: "Bernard

Lewis had the right to contest the value and the purport of such affirmations." Consequently, he had the right to pursue his enterprise of denial, without the court finding fault with it. Nothing in the verdict permits us to think that we are dealing with a denying enterprise. The tribunal is very cautious on this point. The extant law does not allow it to take any other attitude. Must we then infer that the law does not establish facts, or, rather, must we conclude that a fact is never established (and that no verdict by a court can rely on it) as long as right has not said its word? As a preliminary, a fact has to be validated in whatever way it can be done.

If this is the case, it seems quite legitimate to ask what are the current procedures for validating facts. The genocidal thrust in this century has had at least one positive effect. It obliged men of good will to confront this question, perhaps excessively philosophical in nature, but which is nonetheless the most pertinent question in this context: how, generally speaking, does a human community proceed to validate facts? The reader knows perhaps that a book as important as J. F. Lyotard's *Le Différend* turns precisely around this issue and that its argument is based on the phenomenon of denial, with the paradigmatical instance of the Holocaust and the occasional denial of it.[17] Nevertheless, I am not sure that this author provides himself with the adequate means of understanding why the basic question in regard to the procedures that permit the validation of facts for a human community intervenes in the wake of genocidal events. I will come back to this issue. In order to be quite fair with the Tribunal de Grande Instance de Paris, I must add that the court shows a real hesitation as to the "validation" of facts. It seems to admit that the convergent approaches of the "international bodies" have a certain weight not only as elements that contradict Lewis's thesis but also as legitimate validations of the facts themselves. Nevertheless, it does not express this tendency in an explicit manner (that would run counter to the initial principle according to which the capability of qualifying the event is beyond its competence). Here is the exact formulation of the provision I have been commenting on:

> Although Bernard Lewis had the right to contest the value and importance of such affirmations, he had to make note of and analyze the circumstances that could have convinced the readers of their lack of pertinence . . . he should not, in any case, have remained silent about convergent elements of valuation, notably those that had occupied the attention of the international bodies and revealed that, to the contrary of what the criticized utterances are suggesting, the thesis according to which there existed a blue-print for the extermination of the Armenian people is not upheld by the latter alone.

Narrative and Archives: The Validation of Facts

Where and when, then, does the validation of facts take place in human society? When my father died, I was not there. I did not see him die. I did not know that he was dying. Only much later did an inscription on a tomb assure me of his death. When, forty years earlier, my grandparents were put to death with their relatives at the very beginning of their deportation (my family did not go all the way to the deserts), nobody else saw them die; I mean, nobody who has remained alive. Nevertheless, I know how one of them succumbed under the blows of a hatchet or the butt of a gun, how another was pulled from a group of women where he was hiding, how one aunt was traded to a Muslim dignitary so that her sisters could survive. (There is also the question of shame; who has ever talked about the shame among the survivors?) Yes, I know approximately the place where each of them died; I know how he or she was raped or murdered. During my entire childhood, the great oral narrative inside the family assured me, with all appropriate decency, of these events. Yes, they are dead. The narrative is their tomb and will be their tomb forever. I am persuaded, incidentally, that each tomb, in reverse, is a narrative in this sense. I shiver at the idea of families where a deadly silence reigns instead of a narrative serving as a tomb, but this question of mourning is a different issue.[18] My concern, here, relates to the validation of facts. Sometimes, silence is also the best narrative. The narrative validates the closest facts. As to the more distant ones, it seems that they have always been validated by media of all sorts, by the archives, by history. In any case, validation supposes a consensus. The human community is aware of a "fact" as such only because the latter has been borne and established by narratives which, in turn, are supposed to be true. This validation by narration, benefiting from the consensus of veracity, is duplicated in our modern era by the recourse to the archive in the most general possible meaning of this term. As long as this modern duplication of narrative by the archive has not been analyzed, it will be impossible to understand anything about the phenomenon of genocide as such.[19] All the philosophical digressions regarding the function, meaning, and process of validation, those of J. F. Lyotard as well as many others, will fall flat. There exists, in fact, a single case (labeled "genocide" or whatever one wishes) where the consensus no longer plays a role, where the current mechanism for position and validating of facts does not work. This was an open door to madness for those who found themselves at the center of a murderous event that has not been registered in human memory as a commonly validated fact. There is a "genocide" only where the scene of validation, the scene on which the facts acquire a reality, is dominated by the archive. This is why I believe there have been "genocides" only in the twentieth century. This is also why historians today are under a twofold responsibility. Not only are they responsible for the characterization or interpretation of facts; they are also responsible for their very *reality*. This should not be read as a paradox. There is a modern duplication of the narrative by the archive, one heavy with consequences of all kinds. Hagop Oshagan denounces its possible perversion when he writes: "After all, history is nothing but a succession of denials."[20]

I know the exact circumstances of the death not only of my relatives but also of hundreds and thousands of people. For decades, the survivors have recounted, written, and published. They have elicited and collected the testimonies of men and especially women who were often illiterate, who would not have written in any case, and yet "every single one of them had a tragic and atrocious story to tell."[21] However, even if I knew all the details of all deaths, there would still be, in spite of all this knowledge, a fact which would never find validation through this device: the "crime of genocide." We can deal with individual deaths, deaths in groups, or deaths in great masses. We can even deal with the Catastrophe.[22] We never encounter the "genocide." In addition, there is never any memory by the survivors, never any testimony, direct or indirect, from the victims or third persons which could provide indisputable proof of genocidal intention and action. In the case of the Armenians we know that the executioners did not leave official or unofficial documents behind that would reveal their intentions and decisions. The perpetrators did even better: from the beginning, they made the genocidal machinery work as a machinery of denial, in accordance with the modern requirements of validation by the archive.[23] Of course, these requirements have been twisted and perverted, but by the same token they have been for the first time confirmed and revealed.

No work by a historian can counter this, because everything has started with this perversion of the archive. The historian's work, proceeding by means of description, cross-checking, and finally displaying a bundle of convincing and converging arguments, can, de jure, always be questioned. This is approximately what the verdict by the Tribunal de Grande Instance de Paris says. It therefore seems to be natural that historians can decide to advance "a different opinion." This is also the only case, however, where they should not have the *right* to advance such an opinion, because the genocidal machinery is essentially a machinery of denial and those who invented it already understood perfectly that the burgeoning reign of archives would not permit the genocide to become a fact, in face of which there can be no "different opinion." There cannot even be a question of opinion. Thus, the machinery of genocide and denial is destined to destroy the very notion of fact. This is its most radical purpose. All in all, it was the first philosophical machinery of the twentieth century.

When, in 1918, the first survivors came to see Aram Andonian in Aleppo and tell him their horrible experience, they did not do so in order to add their contribution to the great oral narrative that was to constitute the Armenian memory over a period of eight decades.[24] One can be sure as well that these survivors, reduced to the state of living corpses, were not in the mood to philosophize. They all knew perfectly well, however, that in the wake of this planned extermination, the validation of the fact as such would become the primordial question and an object of endless discussion. They knew that the machinery which had crushed them was not only a genocidal machinery (they had no doubts about that: the goal was the complete extermination of their people) but also a "philosophical machinery." On this side of the black box, it was the reality of the fact that became a problem.

They did not know, to be sure, that the Young Turk leaders, as well as the leaders of the Special Organization, would destroy all their archives before their arrest at the end of 1918 or beginning of 1919. They did not know that the 1919 trials in Istanbul, held before a Turkish court-martial under pressure from the British government, would actually return a verdict affirming the "existence of a plan aiming at the extermination of the Armenian people." Nor did they know that, as early as 1922, the issues of the official Turkish journal covering the period of the trials would disappear from circulation, and, together with them, many of the transcripts of these trials.[25] They did not need to know these details; they did not need to be aware of the denial that was organized in masterly fashion after the event had taken place, based on the original denial situated at the very heart of it. Subsequently, they showed a haughty ignorance and carelessness about this chain of consequences. They knew, however, that they had been put through the mill of the philosophical machinery of genocide and denial. They wanted their testimonies to be *archived* so that the word "fact" might still have some meaning for civilized humanity. But they had miscalculated. They were powerless. Their obsession, which aimed at an archival recording of testimonies, had but one consequence, and this consequence was catastrophic. The final result was a disappropriation of their memory, through a serious and, without any doubt, irreparable transformation of memory-generating narrative into a discourse of proof. They had to provide the proof of their own death.

The "Truth of the Facts" and the Essence of Genocide

The fact being "unreliable," merely an object of opinion, there is nothing left but interpretations, or even worse, subjective characterizations of the event. This is also the message of the modern discourse of denial, which meshes with the genocidal machinery. Any characterization is subject to revision and examination. All historians have the right to express their opinions. There are no archives extant. The counterposed theses are antagonistic. What can the historians do other than to defer their judgment? This is how the genocide of the Armenian people has become a case study for historians, a typical situation of undecidability regarding the labeling of events.

Let me attempt to summarize what has been said so far: on this side of the black box, there is no fact, no "reality" of the fact. No master narrative, no political consensus at all will be able to establish or retrieve the reality. At this point, when the historian's responsibility goes beyond the characterization, when it regards essentially the "reality" of facts, that is, their validation, only the law (*le droit*) can establish facts; only the law can decide that the fact is a fact. French jurisprudence has drawn the consequences from this state of affairs by implementing a law (loi Gayssot) which punishes any denial of crimes against humanity committed during World War II. Only jurisdiction and jurisprudence can cut short the contradicting opinions of historians. In this regard, I said at the beginning that all genocidal projects over the course of this century have been first and foremost a challenge to law. In certain exceptional circumstances, law has taken up the challenge.

In order for the reader to measure the stakes of this discussion which concerns the attitude of justice and law toward the "task of the historian," and also the stakes involved in my somewhat philosophical and paradoxical conclusion (only the law can establish facts, only the law can decide that the fact is a fact), I will quote some lines from Robert Maggiori which once again and very clearly delineate the problem in question: "It can seem shocking that an historian of the caliber of Bernard Lewis, proposing his reading of the massacre of the Armenian people by the Turks, be called before the court as if courts were able to estimate the pertinence of a vision of history or an interpretation of historical facts."[26] Maggiori expresses indignation. Any "reading" of historical facts must be examined calmly, within the framework of the discipline concerned. Hence, there is a scandal in this wish to settle by means of jurisdiction a debate that should be settled among specialists.

Subsequently, Maggiori explains this indignation, which does not stem, he says, from the idea that research must be "completely free." Here is his explanation: "To write that the Nazi genocide is not an historical reality and to deny the existence of the gas chambers is a crime. Refusing to qualify the massacre of the Armenian people as a genocide, does this come under the provisions of criminal law?" It is clear that, for the author, this is a matter of "qualifying" the facts, of "interpreting" them. Maggiori shares this opinion with the Tribunal de Grande Instance and the modern discourse of denial. I believe that the real issue is not the "qualifying" but the factuality of the fact. Maggiori continues: "It is necessary to come to a decision about the intention. The intentions of those denying the Nazi genocide are clear. Those of Bernard Lewis are not as clear: do we have to assume that his work as a historian is overdetermined by political or ideological concerns which are capable of giving credit to lies?" This sentence clearly expresses the actual reason for Lewis's denying attitude, even if it does not state its essence. Nevertheless, the sentence is ironic. We cannot believe this, it implies. I do not see in what sense the intentions of a Faurisson are clearer than those of a Lewis (not to speak of their respective interests).[27] Moreover, the civil court has concluded that certain concerns, which we need not take up here, have indeed given "credit to lies." Now the rest of the quotation: "Who pronounces the verdict? A *Historikerstreit,* a dispute among historians, whose aim is the truth of the facts [*la vérité des faits*] or a tribunal which is in fact authorized to sanction the 'offenses against the victims'?" The same civil court has expressed its judgment in regard to this matter: yes, it is up to the court to judge the historian's responsibility, but it is up to the historian to pronounce a verdict as to the "truth of the facts."

We can see here the whole difficulty of the matter. The issue, as defined by Maggiori (and by the civil court) is correctly expressed only if one sticks to the "labeling" of events, if the "truth of the facts" is a question of interpretation. But to repeat: for the genocidal and denying will, the labeling and historical interpretation of events is not a primary issue. Today, one would have us believe the contrary. As a last resort, the stake is the factuality of the fact, its reality as a fact. The stake is the universal process of validation. The events have been invalidated, in regard to their very nature as events, from the beginning. The genocidal fact consists in this very invalidation. Today, historians play with this original invalidation, they count on it, repeat it, and thus prolong it. What court will ever be able to judge such a perversion? It is thus necessary to correct the paradox as initially formulated. In such a situation, to be sure, only law can establish the fact but it can only do so on the condition that it include the full extent of denial in the genocidal act itself. The essence of genocide is denial. Genocide is destined to erase itself as a fact. This is the greatest challenge addressed to historians: how will they reveal the truth of a fact that was nothing less than the removal of any truth?

Meaning and Reality

The extermination of the Armenian people of the Ottoman Empire has become, for some historians, a case study in indecidability concerning the characterization of events and thus a model for a "raw fact." In February 1994, during the wave of denial instigated by Lewis, the journal that had accepted his declarations also published a paper by Eric Hobsbawm on the task of the historian. This paper contains a passage that sums up the entire thrust of the present discussion. It is Hobsbawm's intention to make his audience (apprentice historians of east European studies) accept that it is the task of the historian to be critical of all constructions and all fictions which support, in particular, nationalist positions: in a word, to be critical of all "forgers of history." This task consists precisely in taking a position for "fact" and against "fiction." It is in this context that Hobsbawm engages in a reflection on the very notion of "fact." He says:

> We have a general responsibility in regard to historical facts and a critical responsibility in regard to the politico-ideological abuse of history in particular. There is no need to elaborate on the first of these responsibilities. . . . The other pertains to this intellectual current called "postmodernism," which is all the rage in the universities of the Western hemisphere . . . and which demands that any "fact" claiming an objective existence is but a construction of the intellect. . . . In short, that there is no clear-cut distinction between fact and fiction. However, this distinction exists.[28]

Who would not subscribe to these statements, on the condition that we put aside for a moment the blunder of this "old school" historian, who lightheartedly confuses the "construction of the intellect" with the meaning given to the event by the totality of the narratives that constitute its reception and consequently its reality. In any case, Hobsbawm sees the need to illustrate his remarks further:

> We cannot invent our facts. Elvis Presley is dead, or not. One can answer this question unambiguously by relying on evidence to the degree that such evidence exists, something that happens from time to time. The Turkish government, which denies the existence of an attempted genocide against the Armenian people in 1915, does or does not speak the truth. For most of us, a serious historical discourse will reject the negation of this massacre, even though any conclusion remains ambiguous as to the different versions of the event or as to its integration into the larger context of History.

A long time has passed since I first read these lines, and I am still suffocating from the perversity of the argument. To reject "the negation of this massacre" means without doubt to accept the raw fact which is, in any case, irrevocable. But to accept the raw fact does not at all mean that we are dealing with a universally validated fact; quite the contrary. The entire context, from the distinction between fact and fiction to the death of Elvis Presley, indicates that the problem for Hobsbawm is precisely the problem of the validation of facts. For this, there are evidence, proofs, and archives. The historian is the guarantor of this validation.

Hobsbawm, however, slides surreptitiously from the validation to the characterization or interpretation of facts since there exist, it seems, "different versions of the event." One can immediately recognize here the heavy shadow of denial. It is not possible to decide anything whatever in regard to the characterization of the event. Would this mean that the historian's task suddenly evaporates? When proofs and archives are lacking, everything is left in the sway of ambiguity. Ambiguity is attached to the labeling and possible interpretation of the raw fact and, by way of consequence, to the "genocidal" intention. The raw fact is certainly not a fiction. But is it still a fact? Do the facts still possess a historical reality if one can say nothing, in the strict sense of the word, about their place in history? Logically, the raw fact does not have a place in History, in the "larger context of History." One cannot do anything with it, say anything about it, draw any conclusion from it. In this sense, Hobsbawm pronounces the true (but hidden) statement of the discourse of denial: a raw fact is not really a fact. While pronouncing the truth and while asserting the disqualification of the facts, this discourse escapes even from any suit before a court. It escapes any judgment that could admonish it for not providing the proof of the absence of proof. Hobsbawm carries out this forced takeover, which consists of an invalidating a priori of all judgment, all judicial pronouncement. The facts having been disqualified, how can we provide the proof for anything?

The judgment passed by the High Court of Paris could obviously not cut short this very powerful discourse of denial; it could only confirm it. The discourse of denial is even capable of saying its own truth: in such a situation, there is no fact, no historical factuality, for the basic validation did not play its role. Or even, and this is worse, there is only a raw fact, beyond any possible characterization, to which one cannot assign any meaning and consequently any place in history. The raw fact is a random fact. This is a new category invented in 1994 by a few historians during a campaign which will remain a model in the genre and which no court could in fact refute. A raw fact is a fact that has not been validated, has not found its "place in the context of history" and thus does not make sense.

What I have described is a new sort of revisionism, against which the observer, victim, or survivor—whatever one chooses to call him, is entirely helpless. This is revisionism of the last hour, the historian's revisionism, the worst kind of all. It does not attack the facts, which cannot be revised any more than the death of Elvis Presley. It attacks the significance of the facts, doubtless in the full knowledge that, in so doing, it is undermining the reality of the event. The reason for this is simple, albeit infinitely profound: there is reality only where there is meaning. Revisionism thus proves, perversely but most elegantly, that a raw fact and a real fact are two different things. The perverse historian claims to deal only with facts. Conversely, it is obvious that the usual (Armenian) way of approaching the Catastrophe, which tends, now as always, to establish or to demonstrate the facts over and over again (while entirely ignoring the relation between "meaning" and "reality") is quite helpless in the face of this perversion. It only plays the perverse historian's game and ultimately sanctions it. This revisionism of the last hour, this historian's revisionism, unveils at last the secret, dreadful weapon: the random facts. Yes, the facts are the facts. So what?

In the Name of Ethnic Cleansing

"Meaning" does not wait in the heart of events in the moment when they take place. It can occur only as the result of an interpretation, that is, of a labor directed against other interpretations or the lack of interpretation. One of the most current approaches among acknowledged scholars in the case of the Catastrophe is that Armenians fell victims to "oriental barbarism," to an uncivilized violence that merits no particular commentary, no single reflection or account, as it was situated outside the realm of meaningful or spiritualized historical events. But have the Armenians themselves ever thought otherwise about their own Catastrophe? I doubt it. Have they ever thought about it, have they ever transmuted it into a object of thought, for themselves and then for others? If not, how can they wonder why people do not want to listen, to respect their memory? Today, as a natural consequence of this state of affairs, they are unable to understand that a revisionist interpretation bars for them any access to meaning and therefore to comprehension. The last stratagem of this general bias (and the last feature of the 1994 French campaign) is the use of "ethnic purification" as a tool to comprehend the past events.

In an interview, again in *Le Monde,* Jean-Luc Nancy once more needs to define the limits of "similar events" or "other genocides," and among them the Armenian one, in order to define and conceptualize the uniqueness of the Shoah.[29] His definition makes use of the recently forged notion of "ethnic purification." Nancy states:

> It might be said that the crime, in this case, resides more in the project that gives rise to it than in the murder itself. Nazism called into question the right and possibility of existence for specific categories of human beings. . . . The same holds for "ethnic cleansing" in ex-Yugoslavia (or, not long ago, the Armenian Genocide). Yet Nazism has an additional dimension, which characterizes the "total" crime, if I may put the matter that way, against humanity.

At this point, Nancy is asked if it is necessary, in his view, to maintain the uniqueness of the Shoah over and against all the other tragedies of history. "Yes. This assertion is emphatically not meant to reduce the other massacres to insignificance. But [the Shoah] is unique; its uniqueness lies in the plan to remake or recreate man. The Western world loosed his fury on itself. The history of antisemitism is in many respects the history of the West's terrible relation with itself." This history, and only it, makes it possible then to understand what the West "is" or "will have been"—"the civilization of the production of itself . . . as veritable, absolute, total subject." One finds here a "historial" view of the Holocaust as the culminating point of the "disfiguration" of the West.[30] This should not prevent us from asking whether the "other tragedies" of the twentieth century are not a part of the same "history of the West" and whether they did not occur for the same reasons "at the heart of the West." However profound Jean-Luc Nancy's explanation may be, here as elsewhere uniqueness appeals for a comparison, which in turn calls for a criterion. We see in this concrete example how the argument works in all cases, without exception. It necessitates a "motivation" or an "incentive" for the "other tragedies of the century." Here, the incentive is provided by the idea of "ethnic purification." This labeling, directly derived from the theory the Serbs themselves offered to characterize their actions, is a godsend for this sort of argument and its upholders, who prefer to suppose that one already knows, before making any inquiry into the matter, what happened during similar tragedies.

The irony of this affair is that the Armenians themselves think (and have, moreover, never ceased to think, however they have formulated it) that they fell victim in 1915 to a campaign of ethnic purification. This becomes obvious in another interview with two distinguished Armenian scholars, published in *Le Monde* in the same year, 1994, not long after the one with Nancy.[31] This interview had a long and explicit subtitle, "The Genocide of the Armenians Was a Case of 'Ethnic Purification' Carried Out in the Name of

Territorial Nationalism," probably chosen by the editor, but it was a quotation from the distinguished scholars' thoughts. Ethnic purification in the name of territorial nationalism? This was precisely what was going on in Bosnia at the time. The scholars did not realize that their reference to the political events of the day was playing against them from the very beginning. They had fallen into their own trap, with, of course, their host's baiting. Their view was not wrong, to be sure. But it was not wrong to the extent that the Catastrophe was there reduced to what the executioners wanted. The executioner's logic was still all-powerful eighty years after the events. The scholars' view was not wrong to the extent that "territorial nationalism" was seemingly the unique criterion available to them as a contextual explanation able to confer a meaning on the events.

The proponents of this ill-advised approach had probably not read the interview with Raul Hilberg, published a month or so earlier, in the Parisian weekly *Globe Hebdo*.[32] Perhaps the world's most renowned historian of the Jewish Holocaust made use of the Armenian Catastrophe and the ethnic purification in a splendid demonstration, which deserves to be quoted at length. The question addressed to Raul Hilberg bore on the events taking place in Yugoslavia. Hilberg understood this question as an invitation to state firmly the difference between these events and the Holocaust, which is quite other, and "those who think the contrary have never understood anything about History." The first stage in Hilberg's argument was really unexpected: he said that he had recently read Robert Melson's book, *Revolution and Genocide: On the Origins of the Armenian Genocide and the Holocaust.*[33] Why this strange way around, this reference to the Armenian events at the beginning of the century? Here is the answer: "When the Turks began to deport the Armenians in 1915, they did it in the name of 'ethnic cleansing'; they did not kill them in a systematic way. They wanted to create an ethnically pure Turkey. This is what is going on today in Bosnia."[34] Had not deportation and "ethnic cleansing" always been a "common practice" in the Ottoman Empire? This is word for word what Bernard Lewis has said. But were not, in fact, the Armenians killed in a systematic way between 1915 and 1917? To be sure, Hilberg failed to discern this "truth" from Melson's important study. Do I need to explain any further the current use of the terms "ethnic cleansing" in the context of a general demonstration addressed to those who have never understood anything about history? Is the quotation not sufficient to make it clear how "ethnic cleansing" can be used as an argument by the new revisionism that I have tried to describe?

Notes

1. A French version of this discussion appeared in "Le droit et le fait: La campagne de 1994" in the French quarterly *Lignes,* September 1995, based on a series of lectures on revisionism in France.
2. The sentence appears in the verdict of the trial, returned on June 21, 1995, by the Tribunal de Grande Instance de Paris. The quotation is from an unpublished transcript of the trial.
3. J. P. Langellier and J. P. Péroncel-Hugoz, "Un entretien avec Bernard Lewis," *Le Monde,* November 16, 1993.
4. "Les explications de Bernard Lewis," *Le Monde,* January 1, 1994.
5. This announcement was made during an important conference that took place in Paris, at the Institut des Hautes Études sur la Justice, on June 16 and 17, 1995. The topic of this conference was the genocide in Rwanda "in the light of the other exterminations of this century." It was initiated by Raymond Verdier and, among others, by the Centre d'Études de Droit International of Nanterre. The proceedings appeared in book form, *Rwanda: Un génocide du XXᵉ siècle,* ed. R. Verdier, E. Decaux, and J. P. Chrétien (Paris: Ed. l'Harmattan, 1996).
6. Here as elsewhere in this essay, originally written in French, "law" is the somewhat inadequate translation of *droit. Droit* means "law" in the sense of "principle(s) of justice," and contrasts with *loi,* which refers to a specific manifestation of *droit,* a codified rule. It is occasionally translated "right." Thus the usual English translation of Hegel's classic work on the law is *The Philosophy of Right.*
7. Quoted in Robert Maggiori, "Lewis, tête de Turc," *Libération,* April 28, 1994.
8. Jay Winter, "Le Massacre des Arméniens," *Le Monde,* August 3, 1994.
9. Ibid.
10. See Sigmund Freud, "Jokes and Their Relation to the Unconscious" (1905), in *The Standard Edition of the Complete Psychological Works of Sigmund Freud,* trans. James Strachey (London: Hogarth Press, Ltd., 1960), 8:206.
11. This unbearable argument of "belligerency" has been invoked recently by Marthe Robert (one of the most celebrated literary critics in France, the author of several trail-blazing studies on Kafka's work) in an article titled "Les Génocides ou la dernière trouvaille d'un révisionnisme plus subtil," in the monthly *Passages,* (April–May 1995). The Armenians were belligerants. The Gypsies were thieves. If one contemplates the possibility of genocides other than the one suffered by the Jews, one displays "a more subtle negationism." The same argument of "belligerency" was already upheld by Lewis thirty years ago, at a time when he still spoke of an Armenian "holocaust." See Bernard Lewis, *The Emergence of Modern Turkey* (New York: Oxford University Press, 1961), 356. Robert Melson provided a critique of this argument that was both ironic and harsh in *Revolution and Genocide: On the Origins of the Armenian Genocide and the Holocaust* (Chicago: University of Chicago Press, 1992), 152–59. See the short bibliography of the revisionist literature that relies on the

theme of belligerency (289). This work by Robert Melson is one of the first books entirely devoted to a comparison between the Holocaust and the Catastrophe. The American school of comparative studies has no equivalent in France. In France, a comparatist approach was attempted for the first time at the 1993 conference of Cerisy, inspired by psychoanalysts (J. Gilbert and P. Wilgowicz) and not by historians. The proceedings of this conference have been published under the title *L'Ange exterminateur,* ed. J. Gillibert and P. Wilgowicz (Brussels: Éditions de l'Université de Bruxelles, 1995). In the same vein of comparative reflection, see Yves Ternon, *L'État criminel: Les génocides au XX*[e] *siècle* (Paris: Ed. du Seuil, 1995).

12. To present the full argument, I quote the following passage from Hannah Arendt, *Eichmann in Jersusalem,* 2d ed. (New York: Penguin, 1966, 275):

> What had been mentioned at Nüremberg only occasionally and, as it were, marginally—that "the evidence shows that . . . the mass murders and cruelties were not commited solely for the purpose of stamping out opposition" but were "part of a plan to get rid of whole native populations"—was in the center of the Jerusalem proceedings, for the obvious reason that Eichmann stood accused of a crime that could not be explained by any utilitarian purpose; Jews had been murdered all over Europe, not only in the East, and their annihilation was not due to any desire to gain territory that "could be used for colonization by Germans." It was the great advantage of a trial centered on the crime against the Jewish people that not only did the difference between war crimes, such as shooting of partisans and killing of hostages, and "inhuman acts," such as "expulsion and annihilation" of native populations to permit colonization by one invader, emerge with sufficient clarity to become part of a future international penal code, but also the difference between "inhuman acts" (which were undertaken for some known, though criminal, purpose, such as expansion through colonization) and the "crime against humanity," whose intent and purpose were unprecedented, was clarified.

This page appears only in the second edition of the book.

The French translation of the passage is as follows:

> On avait assasiné des Juifs aux quatre coins de l'Europe . . . et leur extermination n'avait rien à voir avec l'expansion territoriale "à des fins de colonisation par les Allemands." Un tribunal préoccupé avant tout par un crime perpétré contre le peuple juif avait cet avantage: il pouvait faire la distinction . . . entre les "crimes de guerre" (fusiller des partisans, tuer des otages) et les "actes inhumains" ("expulser et annihiler" des populations entières de façon à rendre possible la colonisation par l'envahisseur, de certains territoires). Il savait aussi distinguer les "actes inhumains" (dont le mobile, la colonisation par exemple, était connu tout en étant criminel) et le "crime contre l'humanité" (dont le mobile comme le but étaient sans précédent).

The first occurence of *mobile* in French translates the English "purpose," while its second occurence translates probably the English "intent." Notwithstanding these slight discrepancies, the argument is clear: while in other cases the motive of the crime was known (colonization is the only example given by Arendt, but we could mention as well the will to homogenize a population, to unify a territory), it was "unprecedented" in the case of the Jewish Holocaust. With this somewhat loose distinction (although the word "unprecedented" has a very precise meaning in the author's philosophical view of History), Arendt summarizes the most important advance of the Jerusalem trial, and she produces as well the logical matrix through which all the "similar events of the century" were to be thought of afterward, with the key issue of the presence/absence of a recognizable motive or incentive for the crime.

13. This statement by Lacoue-Labarthe stems from his book, *La Fiction du politique* (Paris: Christian Bourgeois, 1987), 59. The quotation is on page 35 of the book's English translation by Chris Turner, under the title *Heidegger, Art and Politics* (Cambridge, Mass.: Basil Blackwell, 1990). Further, on the same page: "The extermination of the Jews . . . is a phenomenon which follows essentially no logic (political, economic, social, military, etc.) other than a spiritual one, degrated as it may be, and therefore a historial one." The absence of any rational motive is emphasized again on page 49: "without motives of a religious nature or indeed of any other nature." The argument relies on the matrix put forward by Arendt. But on the basis of this argument, Lacoue-Labarthe's main contention is that the only logic that governed the extermination was a "historial" one. The word "historial" is the not-so-common English rendition of *geschechtlich,* by which Heidegger meant—in an early stage of his philosophical inquiry—history understood as "appropriation of meaning," and in a later, more developed stage, the history of the West itself as the "history of being." Lacoue-Labarthe states: "In the Auschwitz apocalypse, it was nothing less than the West, in essence, that revealed itself" (35). The "historial" view of history appears again later in this essay in my account of Jean-Luc Nancy's statements on the uniqueness of the Holocaust.
14. Jay Winter, in the same article in *Le Monde,* says: "it is important to keep in mind that this chapter of the history of the World War, however vile it may be, is very different from those of Auschwitz and Treblinka."
15. On the twisted use of singularity as absolute and argument, see my essay, "L'Empire du sacrifice," *L'Intranquille* (Paris), no. 1 (1992). For a profound reflection on the theme of Singularity, see the interview with Jean-Luc Nancy, in *Le Monde,* March 29, 1994. I will come back to this interview in relation to the theme of "ethnic cleansing."
16. See United Nations Sub-Commission on the Prevention of Discrimination and the Protection of Minorities, *Revised and Updated Report on the Question of the Prevention and Punishment of the Crime of Genocide,* prepared by Benjamin Whitaker, U.N. Document E/CN.4/Sub.2/1985/6, July 2, 1985; Permanent People's Tribunal, *A Crime of Silence: The Armenian Genocide* (London: Zed Books, 1985); "Resolution on a Political Solution of the Armenian Question," European Parliament Resolution, Doc. A2–33/87, no. 10, 31 (1987).
17. See J. F. Lyotard, *Le Différend* (Paris: Editions de Minuit, 1983), 23–24: idem,

"Discussions, ou phraser après Auschwitz," in *Les Fins de l'homme, à partir du travail de Jacques Derrida,* ed. J. L. Nancy and P. Lacoue-Labarthe (Paris: Christian Bourgeois, 1981), 283–310. There is an English translation of this article: "Discussions or Phrasing 'after Auschwitz'," in *The Lyotard Reader,* ed. Andrew Benjamin (Cambridge, Mass.: Basil Blackwell, 1989). See also idem, *Peregrinations: Law, Form, Event* (New York: Columbia University Press, 1988).

18. A study by Hélène Piralian, *Génocide et transmission* (Paris: Éditions l'Harmattan, 1995), deals with this issue from the perspective of impossible mourning by using an approach that claims to be psychoanalytical. The "denial" at the heart of the genocidal act causes the impossibility of mourning, and consequently of transmission, for the victim. Hannah Arendt already spoke of this at the end of her book on totalitarian domination in the chapter on the concentration camps. The task of the SS was not so much one of annihilating the living as one of annihilating death. We find another thesis in Hélène Piralian's book: the descendants of the executioners are as much concerned with grasping the scene of murder as the descendents of the survivors. The psychic liberation from it will be common and reciprocal or will not occur at all.
19. The term "archive" is used to designate the historical concept; "archives" is reserved for the concrete records, whatever form they take.
20. Hagop Oshagan (1883–1948) is one of the most important Armenian writers of the twentieth century and probably the one who has taken the experience of the Catastrophe to its furthest possible point in his works. He encountered there the definitive and irrevocable character of our entry into the era of the archive. The above mentioned quotation is from Oshagan's monumental *Hamapatker Arevmtahay Grakanutian* (Panorama of Western-Armenian literature) (Antelias, Lebanon: Catholicosate of Cilicia Press, 1980), 9:287. Hagop Oshagan is also, to my knowledge, the only Armenian language writer who has spoken in a well-informed manner about the Holocaust of the Jewish people, in *Mitk ev Sirt* (Spirit and heart), in the periodical of the Armenian Patriarchate of Jerusalem, *Sion* (1948), the last of his writings published during his lifetime. See M. Nichanian, "Hagop Ochagan tel qu'en lui même," *Dissonanze* 1 (1983), and "L'Ecrit et le mutisme: Introduction à la littérature arménienne moderne," *Temps Modernes* 504–6 (September 1988).
21. This is a quotation from Aram Andonian. This author (born in 1875 in Constantinople, died in 1952 in Paris) is probably with Zabel Esayan the first Armenian writer who collected testimonies of the survivors. His book *Mets Vojire* (The great crime), Armenian original published in Boston in 1921, was based on these testimonies; it intended to exhibit the collected evidence of a well-planned genocidal action. It must be remembered that the French and English translations of this work were published before the Armenian original: *Documents relatifs aux massacres arméniens* (Paris: Imp. H. Turabian, 1920), and *The Memoirs of Naïm Bey* (London: Hodder and Stoughton, 1920). See also Andonian's *Ain Sev Orerun* (In those dark days) (Boston: Hairenik, 1919),

in which he tried to give a living account of the Catastrophe, such as he had experienced it, through the means of literary representation.

22. The proper name of the event in Armenian is *Aghed.* Like *Shoah* in Hebrew, it simply designates the Catastrophe, the unique one, and this forever. Of course, the common word *aghed* means "catastrophe" as well. The word has been used for the first time in its full extent by Hagop Oshagan in his *In the Shade of the Cedars,* published as an interview in the monthly *Hairenik* (Boston) in 1932 and in book form in 1983 (Antelias: Catholicosate of Cilicia Press). This essay, along with Oshagan's monograph on Andonian (*Hamapatker,* vol. 9) , contains the most powerful reflection to this day in the Armenian language upon the Catastrophe and its "reception" among the survivors. It shows that it is probably impossible to attain the essence of the Catastrophe without taking into consideration the forms of its "reception." See the first attempt of a commentary in M. Nichanian, "The Style of Violence," *Armenian Review* 38, no. 1 (Spring 1985): 1–26.
23. I explain this historical point in my lecture, "La dénégation au coeur du génocide," in *Rwanda: Un génocide du XX*e *siècle.* See also Yves Ternon, *Enquête sur la négation d'un génocide* (Marseilles: Parenthèses, 1989). For the first time, an author was able to analyze in an explicit way the working of denial in the very act of the executioner. In spite of this, a complete history of the annihilation, exhibiting all the wheels of its machinery (in particular the twofold structure of the Special Organization) and making use of the now available transcripts of the 1919 trials in Constantinople (see note 25) is still wanting.
24. For Aram Andonian, see note 21 above.
25. The supplements to the *Takvimi Vekayi,* the official Turkish journal which covered the period of the trials, were rediscovered and studied in the 1960s by an Armenian researcher who signed his works (written in Armenian) as Krieger (Krikor Gergerian). There exists as yet no complete translation of the trials of 1919 in European languages. We do not even possess a full edition of these trials in their original language. Only recently has Vahakn Dadrian finally devoted a complete study, written from a judicial point of view, to these trials. See Vahakn Dadrian, "Genocide as a Problem of National and International Law: The World War I Armenian Case and its Contemporary Legal Ramifications," *Yale Journal of International Law* 14, no. 2 (1989), translated into French by Mikaël Nichanian and myself as *Autopsie du génocide arménien* (Brussels: Ed. Complexe, 1995). See also Dadrian's "Documentation of the World War I Armenian Massacres in the Proceedings of the Turkish Military Tribunal," and "A Textual Analysis of the Key Indictment of the Turkish Military Tribunal Investigating the Armenian Genocide," *Journal of Political and Military Sociology* (*The Armenian Genocide in Official Turkish Records*) 22, no. 1 (Summer 1994). A partial translation of the trials has been published in German by Taner Akcam, *Armenien und der Völkermord: Die Istanbuler Prozesse und die türkische Nationalbewegung,* trans. Hayrettin Ayden (Hamburg: Hamburger Edition, 1996). See my review of this book in the literary supplement of the Paris Armenian newspaper *Haratch* in May 1997.

26. For this and subsequent quotations by Maggiori, see his "Lewis, tête de Turc," *Libération,* April 28, 1994.
27. In France, Faurisson is the archetype of the "negationist" discourse. He has cast doubt upon the very existence of the gas chambers and has been condemned more than once for doing so.
28. "Faussaires du passé" (Forgers of the past), *Le Monde des Débats,* February 1994. Eric Hobsbawm is a renowned Marxist historian, considered one of the specialists on the phenomenon of nationalisme in Europe. See in particular his *Nations et nationalism depuis 1780* (Paris: Gallimard, 1992), which includes a whole set of theses on nationalism as a "construction" or a dangerous "fiction."
29. T. Ferenczi, "Un entretien avec Jean-Luc Nancy," *Le Monde,* March 29, 1994.
30. For a brief explanation of the word "historial" in this context, see note 13.
31. J. P. Langellier and J. P. Péroncel-Hugoz, "Un entretien avec Anahide Ter-Minassian et Claude Mutafian," *Le Monde,* April 26, 1994.
32. "Raul Hilberg: Le film de Spielberg, c'est un histoire ce n'est pas l'Histoire," interview with P. Girard, *Globe Hebdo,* Paris, March 2–8, 1994.
33. See note 11.
34. The original French (Hilberg, "Le film de Spielberg") reads as follows:

> Je dois dire qu'aux États Unis est paru un livre, passé totalement inaperçu, d'un politologue nommé Melson, qui établissait une comparaison entre l'extermination des juifs et le massacre des Arméniens par les Turcs durant la première Guerre mondiale. Lorsque les Turcs ont commencé à déporter les Arméniens en 1915, ils l'ont fait au nom de la "purification ethnique," ils ne les ont pas tués systématiquement. Ils voulaient créer une Turquie ethniquement pure. C'est ce qui se passe aujourd'hui en Bosnie et ce n'est pas un hasard si ce sont les Serbes qui pratiquent la "purification ethnique." Ils ont été vaincus trois fois et occupés par les Ottomans. Ils ont donc été à bonne école pour apprendre comment purifier un territoire donné et c'est ce qu'ils mettent en pratique. Mais il ne s'agit pas d'une répétition de l'holocauste. Ceux qui le disent n'ont rien compris à l'histoire.

I offer a translation of the original French passage:

> I must say that a book by a political scientist, Robert Melson, appeared in the United States, though remaining totally unnoticed. It tended to establish a comparison between the extermination of the Jews and the massacre of Armenians by the Turks during World War I. When the Turks began to deport the Armenians in 1915, they did it in the name of "ethnic cleansing," they did not kill them in a systematic way. They wanted to create an ethnically pure Turkey. This is what is going on today in Bosnia, and it is not by accident that the Serbs are today those who carry out the "ethnic cleansing." They had been three times defeated and subjugated by the Turks. Consequently, they have learned from the best masters how to purify a territory and they are now implementing this knowledge. But this is far from being a repetition of the Holocaust. Those who think the contrary have never understood anything about History.

12

Professional Ethics and the Denial of the Armenian Genocide

ROGER W. SMITH, ERIC MARKUSEN, AND ROBERT JAY LIFTON

> The will to truth is cowed by pressure of numerous kinds, reasons of state on the one hand, economic necessities on the other, and, not least, the pure careerism of intellectuals who put their expertise in the service of power as a matter of course. When governments and professional elites find reward in the sophistries of might makes right, truth is bound to suffer.
>
> TERRENCE DES PRES[1]

It has been said that gentlemen do not read other gentlemen's mail. But suppose that one receives a letter from the Turkish ambassador to the United States rebuking one's scholarship because one has written about what the ambassador refers to as "the so-called 'Armenian genocide,' allegedly perpetrated by the Ottoman Turks during the First World War." Suppose that, inadvertently, the envelope also contains an internal memorandum written by the executive director of what claims to be a non-political, scholarly institute and that memorandum reveals much about the mentality of those who engage in denial of the Armenian Genocide. What then? The attempt to confuse and intimidate academics by such letters is an ongoing process. The letter that we shall present is from the current ambassador, but two of us have received such letters from his predecessor. The difference is that only in the letter to Robert Jay Lifton is there created an opportunity to see what takes place behind the scenes, what assumptions guide the work of scholars who engage in denial, and what the implications are in terms of professional ethics.

Our concern is not with the person who wrote the memorandum and drafted the letter, but with the role such scholars perform in the subversion of scholarship and with their assumptions which substitute a narrative of power for the search for truth. In such narratives, as Terrence Des Pres has noted, "knowledge" is what serves the interest of the powerful (particularly the state), the goal of knowledge is seen as control rather than freedom, and "truth" is whatever officials (and their adjuncts) say it is.[2]

The Armenian Genocide and Turkey's Attempts to Deny It

From 1915 to 1917, the Young Turk regime in the Ottoman Empire carried out a systematic, premeditated, centrally planned genocide against the Armenian people. One of the documents authenticated by Turkish authorities in 1919 is a telegram sent in June 1915 by Dr. Shakir, one of the leaders of the secret organization that carried out the planning and implementation of the genocide. He asks the provincial party official who is responsible for carrying out the deportations and massacres of Armenians within his district: "Are the Armenians, who are being dispatched from there, being liquidated? Are those harmful persons whom you inform us you are exiling and banishing, being exterminated, or are they being merely dispatched and exiled? Answer explicitly."[3]

The evidence of intent is backed also by the outcome of the actions against the Armenians: it is inconceivable that over a million persons could have died due to even a badly flawed effort at resettlement. Moreover, the pattern of destruction was repeated over and over in different parts of Turkey, many of them far from any war zone. Such repetition could only have come from a central design. Furthermore, the reward structure was geared toward destruction of the Christian minority. Provincial governors and officials who refused to carry out orders to annihilate the Armenians were summarily replaced.[4]

Armenian men were drafted into the army, set to work as pack animals, and subsequently killed. Leaders were arrested and executed. Then, the deportations of women, children, and the elderly to the deserts of Syria and Iraq began. The American ambassador to the Ottoman Empire, Henry Morgenthau, immediately recognized that the forced marches into the desert, and the atrocities that accompanied them, were a new form of massacre. "When the Turkish authorities gave the orders for these deportations, they were simply giving the death warrant to a whole race; they understood this well, and in their conversations with me, they made no particular attempt to conceal the fact."[5]

The ambassadors of Germany and Austria, representatives of governments allied with Turkey, also quickly realized what was taking place. As early as July 1915, the German ambassador reported to Berlin: "Turks began deportations from areas now not threatened by invasion. This fact and the manner in which the relocation is being carried out demonstrate that the government is really pursuing the aim of destroying the Armenian race in Turkey." By January 1917 his successor reported: "The policy of extermination has been largely achieved; the current leaders of Turkey fully subscribe to this policy."[6]

More than one million Armenians perished as the result of execution, starvation, disease, the harsh environment, and physical abuse. A people who lived in eastern Turkey for nearly 3,000 years lost its homeland and was profoundly decimated in the first large scale genocide of the twentieth century. At the beginning of 1915 there were some two million Armenians within Turkey; today there are fewer than 60,000.

Despite the vast amount of evidence that points to the historical reality of the Armenian Genocide—eyewitness accounts, official archives, photographic evidence, the reports of diplomats, and the testimony of survivors[7]—denial of the Armenian Genocide by successive regimes in Turkey has gone on from 1915 to the present.[8]

The basic argument of denial has remained the same—it never happened, Turkey is not responsible, the term "genocide" does not apply. The tactics of denial, however, have shifted over the years.[9] In the period immediately after World War I the tactic was to find scapegoats to blame for what was said to be only a security measure that had gone awry due to unscrupulous officials, Kurds, and common criminals. This was followed by an attempt to avoid the whole issue, with silence, diplomatic efforts, and political pressure used where possible. In the 1930s, for example, Turkey pressured the U.S. Department of State into preventing MGM Studios from producing a film based on Franz Werfel's *The Forty Days of Musa Dagh*, a book that depicted aspects of the genocide in a district located on the Mediterranean Sea, far from the Russian front.[10]

In the 1960s, prompted by the worldwide commemoration of the fiftieth anniversary of the genocide, efforts were made to influence journalists, teachers, and public officials to tell "the other side of the story." Foreign scholars were encouraged to revise the record of genocide, presenting an account largely blaming the Armenians or, in another version, wartime conditions that claimed the lives of more Turks than Armenians.[11] Thereafter, Turkey tried to prohibit any mention of the genocide in a United Nations report and was successful in its pressure on the Reagan and Bush administrations in defeating congressional resolutions that would have designated April 24 as a national day of remembrance of the Armenian Genocide.[12] The Turkish government has also attempted to exclude any mention of the genocide from American textbooks. Stronger efforts still have been made to prevent any discussion of the 1915 genocide being formally included in the social studies curriculum as part of Holocaust and genocide studies.[13]

There have also been attempts by the Turkish government to disrupt academic conferences and public discussions of the genocide. A notable example was the attempt by Turkish officials to force cancellation of a conference in Tel Aviv in 1982 if the Armenian Genocide were to be discussed, demands backed up with threats to the safety of Jews in Turkey.[14] The U.S. Holocaust Memorial Council reported similar threats over plans to include references to the Armenian Genocide within the interpretive framework of the Holocaust Memorial Museum in Washington.[15] At the same time, Turkey has sought to make an absolute distinction between the Holocaust and the Armenian Genocide, defining the latter as "alleged" or "so-called." The documents we have, however, show that, in private, such labeling drops off (a point we shall come back to and discuss in detail).

Finally, in the 1980s the Turkish government supported the establishment of "institutes," whose apparent purpose was to further research on Turkish history and culture. At least one also was used to further denial of Turkish genocide and otherwise improve Turkey's image in the West. To our knowledge, the memorandum and letters that we reproduce in full provide the first direct evidence of the close relationship between the Turkish government and one such institute. Before turning to that evidence, we shall provide background information on the origin, funding, stated purposes, and tax status of the institute from which that evidence comes.

The Institute of Turkish Studies

The Institute of Turkish Studies, Inc., located in Washington, D.C., was established in 1982 with a grant of three million dollars from the Republic of Turkey.[16] Information about its current finances is not readily available, but in 1989 it had expenditures of $264,593, of which $121,062 were for grants. That year it received gifts of nearly $240,000. The sources of the gifts are unknown to us, but in the past much of its financial support has come from American corporations that sell military equipment to the Turkish government. In 1992, the institute began a fund-raising campaign to double its endowment to six million dollars, with funds to be raised from businesses in America and Turkey. The organization itself has a staff of two: an executive director and a secretary. There is also a board of directors, which includes several academics among its members. In various directories of associations, its purposes and activities are listed as: "To provide funding for research centers and scholars interested in Turkish studies; to encourage development of Turkish studies in university curricula. Bestows awards. Maintains 5000 volume library on the Ottoman Empire, Turkey, and Turkish history." It also provides grants for the academic community of U.S. specialists in the field of Turkish studies; support includes awards to individual scholars and to institutions. The institute's fields of interest are said to be "Turkey, higher education." In terms of activities, it is said to provide grants to individuals and institutions for "research, publications, scholarship funds, fellowships, seed money, conferences and seminars, including matching funds, grants to individuals." Under United States tax law, the Institute falls within section 501(c)3 of the Internal Revenue Filing Status, meaning that it is non-profit and donations to it are tax deductible.

Its own brochure published within the first years of the founding of the institute, however, throws a somewhat different light on its stated purpose. The Institute states that it has received grants from major defense contractors, such as General Dynamics and Westinghouse, and with this support the Institute "shall continue to play a key role in furthering knowledge and understanding of a key NATO ally of the United States, the Republic of Turkey, among citizens of our country."[17] Unfortunately, the phrase "furthering knowledge and understanding" includes measures that have been construed as denial of the Armenian Genocide.

The executive director of the Institute from its inception to 1994 was Dr. Heath W. Lowry, who received his doctorate in history from UCLA. His mentor at UCLA was Stanford Shaw, whose history of Turkey strenuously denies the reality of the Armenian Genocide, while, at the same time, blaming the victims, who are depicted as disloyal, rebellious, and terroristic.[18] Lowry wrote the memorandum and drafted the letter for the ambassador that are made public for the first time.

In 1994, Dr. Lowry became the first incumbent of the Ataturk Chair in Turkish Studies at Princeton University. The chair was established through a $1.5 million grant from the Republic of Turkey. In its *Report of the Institute of Turkish Studies, Inc, 1982–1992*, the Institute cites its "key role . . . in encouraging the Government of Turkey to embark upon a plan of endowing a series of Chairs in Turkish Studies at major American Universities. In an advisory capacity the Institute has been involved in every stage of this process." The report notes that the chair at Princeton is "fully established and funded" and that the institute supports "the further creation of endowed chairs at three other U.S. Universities."[19]

Memorandum from Dr. Heath Lowry, Executive Director of the Institute of Turkish Studies, Inc., to Nuzhet Kandemir, Turkish Ambassador to the United States, September 6, 1990

MEMORANDUM

TO: H.E. AMBASSADOR NUZHET KANDEMIR;

FROM: DR. HEATH W. LOWRY;

REG.: COMMENTS ON THE "ARMENIAN GENOCIDE" INCLUDED IN THE ROBERT JAY LIFTON STUDY ENTITLED: THE NAZI DOCTORS, MEDICAL KILLING AND THE PSYCHOLOGY OF GENOCIDE;

DATE: SEPTEMBER 26, 1990.

PER YOUR REQUEST CONVEYED TO ME BY MS. HILAL BAŞKAL OF YOUR STAFF, I HAVE LOCATED AND READ LIFTON'S THE NAZI DOCTORS, WITH AN EYE TO DRAFTING A LETTER FOR YOUR SIGNATURE TO THE AUTHOR. LIFTON'S WORK, A MASSIVE TOME OF XIII + 561 PAGES, IS AUTHORED BY A PROFESSOR OF PSYCHIATRY AND PSYCHOLOGY AT JOHN JAY COLLEGE AND THE GRADUATE CENTER OF THE CITY UNIVERSITY OF NEW YORK [NOTE:THE LATTER IS THE SAME INSTITUTION WHERE PROFESSOR RUSTOW OF THE ITS BOARD TEACHES]. HE IS A WELL KNOWN AUTHORITY ON THE TRAUMA OF WAR AND HIS MAJOR BOOKS INCLUDE:

DEATH IN LIFE (1968)
HOME FROM THE WAR (1973)
THE LIFE OF THE SELF (1976)
THE BROKEN CONNECTION (1979)
INDEFENSIBLE WEAPONS (1982)

IN SHORT, LIFTON IS A RECOGNIZED AUTHORITY IN HIS OWN FIELD WHO CLEARLY KNOWS ABSOLUTELY NOTHING ABOUT THE SO-CALLED "ARMENIAN GENOCIDE." INDEED, A CAREFUL PERUSAL OF HIS BOOK, REVEALS THAT IN ITS 561 PAGES HE MAKES THE FOLLOWING FEW REFERENCES TO THE SUBJECT:

P. XII.: "BUT I FOUND THAT NAZI DOCTORS DIFFERED SIGNIFICANTLY FROM THESE OTHER GROUPS, NOT SO MUCH IN THEIR HUMAN EXPERIMENTATION BUT IN THEIR CENTRAL ROLE IN GENOCIDAL PROJECTS... (PERHAPS TURKISH DOCTORS, IN THEIR PARTICIPATION IN GENOCIDE AGAINST THE ARMENIANS, COME CLOSEST, AS I SHALL LATER SUGGEST).."

NOTE: LIFTON DOES NOT PROVIDE ANY SOURCE FOR THIS STATEMENT FOLLOWING THIS PASSAGE;

PP.466-7: "I SHALL REFER TO OTHER GENOCIDES--NOTABLY THE TURKS' ANNIHILATION OF ABOUT ONE MILLION ARMENIANS IN 1915- NOT WITH ANY CLAIM TO COMPREHENSIVENESS BUT ONLY TO SUGGEST WIDER APPLICATION."

NOTE: AGAIN NO FOOTNOTED SOURCE. MORE IMPORTANTLY IS LIFTON'S ADMISSION THAT HE DOESN'T CLAIM ANY EXPERTISE ON THE SUBJECT HE IS GOING TO ADDRESS;

P. 470: "THERE SEEM TO HAVE BEEN DEFINITE PARALLELS IN TURKISH HISTORICAL EXPERIENCE PRIOR TO THEIR MASS MURDER OF ARMENIANS IN 1915. WITHIN THE OTTOMAN EMPIRE, THROUGHOUT THE LATTER PART OF THE NINETEENTH CENTURY, THERE WAS AN ATMOSPHERE OF PROGRESSIVE 'DECAY AND DISINTEGRATION,' ALONG WITH A CONTINUOUS IF LOSING STRUGGLE FOR

SPIRITUAL AND POLITICAL UNIFICATION. THE TURKS ALSO EXPERIENCED HUMILIATING FORMS OF FAILED REGENERATION IN THEIR DISASTROUS MILITARY ENTERPRISES DURING THE 1912 BALKAN WAR (IGNOMINIOUS DEFEAT AT THE HANDS OF THEIR FORMER SLAVES AND WARDS, THE GREEKS AND THE BULGARIANS) AND THEIR ABORTIVE RUSSIAN CAMPAIGN IN 1915 AS A GERMAN ALLY. VAHAKN N. DADRIAN OBSERVES THAT THE TURKS MOVED CLOSER TO GENOCIDE AS THEIR PERCEPTION OF THEIR SITUATION PROCEEDED 'FROM THE CONDITION OF MERE STRAIN, TO THAT OF CRISIS, TO A PRECIPITATE CRISIS, AND EVENTUALLY TO THE CATACLYSM OF WAR.' 19

FOOTNOTE 19: VAHAKN N. DADRIAN, "THE ROLE OF TURKISH PHYSICIANS IN THE WORLD WAR I GENOCIDE OF OTTOMAN ARMENIANS," HOLOCAUST AND GENOCIDE STUDIES I (1986, FORTHCOMING); DADRIAN, "THE COMMON FEATURES OF THE ARMENIAN AND JEWISH CASES OF GENOCIDE: A COMPARATIVE VICTIMOLOGICAL PERSPECTIVE," IN ISRAEL DRAPKIN AND EMILIO VIANO, VICTIMOLOGY: A NEW FOCUS, VOL. IV (LEXINGTON, MASS: D.C. HEATH, 1974), PP. 99-120. SEE ALSO, HELEN FEIN, ACCOUNTING FOR GENOCIDE: VICTIM-AND SURVIVORS-OF THE HOLOCAUST (NEW YORK: FREE PRESS, 1979), PO. 10-18.

NOTE: THE SOLE SOURCE FOR LIFTON'S COMMENTS IS THE ARMENIAN AUTHOR: VAHAKN N. DADRIAN.

P. 473: "AGAIN, THERE ARE SUGGESTIONS OF SIMILAR CURRENTS IN THE TURKISH SITUATION. THE 'YOUNG TURKS' WHO SOUGHT TO REFORM THE OTTOMAN EMPIRE SPEARHEADED 'A MAJOR CAMPAIGN TO CHANGE THE SOCIAL STRUCTURE OF OTTOMAN SOCIETY AS AN ANTIDOTE TO INTERNAL DISCORD AND CONFLICT, AND ALSO AS A MEANS OF RECAPTURING IMPERIAL, PANTURKIC GLORY.' THEIR CURE INCLUDED 'AN ADMIXTURE OF RELIGIOUS AND POLITICAL IDEOLOGIES,' AND 'GENOCIDE BECAME A MEANS FOR [BRINGING ABOUT] A RADICAL .....CHANGE IN THE SYSTEM.'" 34

FOOTNOTE 34: SEE DADRIAN, "TURKISH PHYSICIANS" AND "COMMON FEATURES" [19].

NOTE: AGAIN, LIFTON'S SOLE SOURCE FOR HIS VIEWS ON THE TURCO-ARMENIAN QUESTION ARE THE TWO ARTICLES OF DADRIAN CITED IN FOOTNOTE 19.

P. 476: "IN THE CASE OF THE TURKS, WHATEVER THEIR ATTITUDE TOWARD SCIENCE, THEY DID PUT FORWARD A MYSTICAL VISION OF PAN-TURANIANISM (OR 'TURKIFICATION') 'WHICH ALLEGED A PREHISTORIC MYTHIC UNITY AMONG TURANIAN PEOPLES BASED ON RACIAL ORIGIN.' 43 AND ONE CANNOT DOUBT THE EXPERIENCE OF TRANSCENDENCE OF TURKISH NATIONALISTS IN THEIR REVERSION TO FUNDAMENTALIST MOHAMMEDANISM AS A CALL TO AN ANTI-ARMENIAN-CHRISTIAN CRUSADE-ALL ON BEHALF OF A NEW VISION OF OTTOMAN GLORY."

FOOTNOTE 43: DADRIAN, "TURKISH PHYSICIANS" [19].

NOTE: ONCE AGAIN, LIFTON'S SOLE SOURSE IS DADRIAN!

KANDEMIR 3:

p. 488: "ARMENIANS WERE DESCRIBED AS 'A CANKER, A MALIGNANCE WHICH LOOKS LIKE A SMALL PIMPLE FROM THE OUTSIDE, WHICH, IF NOT REMOVED BY A SKILLFUL SURGEON'S SCALPEL, WILL KILL THE PATIENT.'"108

FOOTNOTE 108: A YOUNG TURK ACTIVIST, QUOTED IN KUPER, GENOCIDE P. 40 [LEO KUPER, GENOCIDE: ITS POLITCAL USE IN THE TWENTIETH CENTURY (NEW HAVEN: YALE UNIVERSITY PRESS, 1981), PP.19-23, 210-214.

NOTE: AGAIN, LIFTON IS SIMPLY CITING AN ALREADY PUBLISHED (AND VERY WELL KNOWN) BOOK BY A JEWISH EXPERT ON THE HOLOCAUST.

p. 493: "ONE CANNOT SAY THAT ANY PARTICULAR LEVEL OF TECHNOLOGY IS REQUIRED FOR GENOCIDE: THE TURKS KILLED ABOUT ONE MILLION ARMENIANS BY MEANS OF SHOOTING, CLUBBING, BEATING, SLAVE LABOR, STARVATION, AND OTHER FORMS OF TORTURE."

NOTE: THERE IS NO FOOTNOTE APPENDED TO THIS STATEMENT, BUT IT CLEARLY IS TAKEN FROM THE DADRIAN ARTICLES AS WELL.

****

IN SUMMATION, WHAT WE ARE FACED WITH HERE ARE SEVEN REFERENCES (COMPRISING ABOUT ONE FULL PAGE OF TEXT) IN A BOOK OF 561 PAGES. THEY ARE BASED ALMOST EXCLUSIVELY ON THE ARTICLES BY DADRIAN (EACH OF WHICH HAVE BEEN THE SUBJECT OF DETAILED MEMOS BY THIS WRITER IN PAST YEARS), TOGETHER WITH REFERENCES TO THE WORK OF HELEN FEIN (WHOSE BOOK INCLUDES A FULL CHAPTER ON THE ARMENIAN GENOCIDE) AND LEO KUPER (WHOSE BOOK CONTAINS A VERY LONG CHAPTER ON THE GENOCIDE). STATED DIFFERENTLY, LIFTON, IN HIS BOOK PUBLISHED FOUR YEARS AGO IN 1986, IS SIMPLY USING THE EXISTING LITERATURE ON THE HOLOCAUST AND GENOCIDE. CONSEQUENTLY, OUR BASIC PROBLEM IS WITH AUTHORS SUCH AS DADRIAN, FEIN AND KUPER, EACH OF WHOM ARE NOW SERVING AS SOURCES FOR AUTHORS SUCH AS LIFTON. THESE FACTS MAKE IT RATHER DIFFICULT TO REGISTER OUR UNHAPPINESS WITH LIFTON PER SE, AS HE WILL QUITE JUSTIFIABLY RESPOND BY GIVING US REFERENCES TO HIS SOURCES, I.E., DADRIAN, FEIN AND KUPER.

OUR PROBLEM IS LESS WITH LIFTON THAN IT IS WITH THE WORKS UPON WHICH HE RELIES. LIFTON IS SIMPLY THE END OF THE CHAIN, THAT IS, FROM NOW ON WE WILL SEE ALL WORKS ON THE GENOCIDE OF THE JEWS, INCLUDING REFERENCES SUCH AS THOSE MADE BY LIFTON ON THE BASIS OF THE WORKS OF DADRIAN, FEIN, KUPER, HOVANNISIAN, ET.AL. THOUGH THIS POINT HAS BEEN REPEATEDLY STRESSED BOTH IN WRITING AND VERBALLY TO IADA-ANKARA, WE HAVE NOT YET SEEN AS MUCH AS A SINGLE ARTICLE BY ANY SCHOLAR RESPONDING TO D A D R I A N (OR ANY OF THE OTHERS AS WELL).

I STRONGLY RECOMMEND THAT IT BE POINTED OUT TO ANKARA THAT LIFTON'S BOOK IS SIMPLY THE END RESULT OF THE TURKISH FAILURE TO RESPOND IN A PROMPT FASHION TO THE DADRIAN ARTICLES AND THE FEIN AND KUPER BOOKS.

ON THE CHANCE THAT YOU STILL WISH TO RESPOND IN WRITING TO LIFTON, I HAVE DRAFTED THE FOLLOWING LETTER, WHICH, DUE TO THE ABSENCE OF AN ADDRESS FOR LIFTON WILL HAVE TO BE SENT TO HIM CARE OF HIS PUBLISHER:

Draft of Letter to Dr. Robert Jay Lifton, Prepared by Dr. Heath Lowry, to be signed by Ambassador Nuzhet Kandemir

KANDEMIR 4:

DRAFT LETTER

MR. ROBERT JAY LIFTON
% BASIC BOOKS, INC.
10 E 53RD. STREET
NEW YORK, NEW YORK 10022

DEAR MR. LIFTON:

YOUR 1986 PUBLICATION ENTITLED: THE NAZI DOCTORS, MEDICAL KILLING AND THE PSYCHOLOGY OF GENOCIDE WAS RECENTLY BROUGHT TO MY ATTENTION. NEEDLESS TO SAY, I WAS SHOCKED BY REFERENCES IN YOUR WORK (PP. XII., 466-7, 470, 473, 476, 488, & 493) TO THE SO-CALLED "ARMENIAN GENOCIDE," ALLEGEDLY PERPETRATED BY THE OTTOMAN TURKS DURING THE FIRST WORLD WAR. I WAS EVEN MORE DISTURBED WHEN YOUR CITATIONS REVEALED THAT YOUR SOURCES CONSISTED OF ARTICLES AND BOOKS BY THREE INDIVIDUALS (VAHAKN N. DADRIAN, HELEN FEIN AND LEO KUPER), NONE OF WHOM ARE HISTORIANS OF THE PERIOD IN QUESTION AND NONE OF WHOM RELY ON PRIMARY RESEARCH IN THEIR OWN WORKS.

IN SHORT, YOU HAVE SIMPLY PASSED ALONG QUESTIONABLE SECONDARY SOURCES AS EVIDENCE FOR A NUMBER OF CONTENTIONS WHICH ARE, TO SAY THE LEAST, HOTLY DEBATED AMONG CONTEMPORARY SCHOLARS WRITING ON THE PERIOD AND EVENTS IN QUESTION.

IT IS PARTICULARLY DISTURBING TO SEE A MAJOR SCHOLAR ON THE HOLOCAUST, A TRAGEDY WHOSE ENORMITY AND BARBARITY MUST NEVER BE FORGOTTEN, SO CARELESS IN HIS REFERENCES TO A FIELD OUTSIDE HIS OWN AREA OF EXPERTISE. FOR TURKS, WHO ARE JUSTIFIABLY PROUD OF OUR LONG AND CONTINUING ROLE AS A HAVEN FOR MINORITIES (INCLUDING THE JEWS EVICTED FROM SPAIN BY THE INQUISITION), IT IS PARTICULARLY DISQUIETING TO FIND OUR OWN HISTORY DISTORTED IN WORKS DEVOTED TO THE HOLOCAUST OF WORLD WAR II.

TO COMPARE A TRAGIC CIVIL WAR (PERPETRATED BY MISGUIDED ARMENIAN NATIONALISTS) AND THE HUMAN SUFFERING IT WROUGHT ON BOTH THE MUSLIM AND CHRISTIAN POPULATIONS, WITH THE HORRORS OF A PREMEDITATED ATTEMPT TO SYSTEMATICALLY ERADICATE A PEOPLE, IS, TO ANYONE FAMILIAR WITH THE HISTORY IN QUESTION, SIMPLY LUDICROUS.

I AM ENCLOSING COPIES OF WORKS BY TWO AMERICAN EXPERTS ON THE HISTORY OF TURCO-ARMENIAN RELATIONS, PROFESSORS JUSTIN MCCARTHY AND HEATH LOWRY, AND WOULD HOPE THAT IN THE INTERESTS OF OBJECTIVITY AND FAIRNESS YOU WILL NOT ONLY READ THEM, BUT REFLECT HAVING DONE SO IN ANY FUTURE WORKS YOU MAY PUBLISH.

SINCERELY YOURS,

NUZHET KANDEMIR
AMBASSADOR, REPUBLIC OF TURKEY
WASHINGTON, D.C.

Letter from Ambassador Nuzhet Kandemir to Robert Jay Lifton, 2 October 1990

TURKISH EMBASSY
WASHINGTON, D.C.

October 2, 1990

Mr. Robert Jay Lifton
c/o Basic Books, Inc.
10 E 53rd Street
New York, NY 10022

Dear Mr. Lifton:

Your 1986 publication, The Nazi Doctors: Medical Killing and the Psychology of Genocide, was recently brought to my attention. Needless to say, I was shocked by references in your work (pp. xii, 466-7, 470, 473, 476, 488, and 493) to the so-called "Armenian genocide," allegedly perpetrated by the Ottoman Turks during the First World War. I was even more disturbed when your citations revealed that your sources consisted of articles and books by three individuals: Vakahn N. Dadrian, Helen Fein and Leo Kuper, none of whom are historians of the period in question and none of whom rely on primary research in their own works.

In short, you have simply passed along questionable secondary sources as evidence for a number of contentions which are, to say the least, hotly debated among contemporary scholars writing on the period and events at issue.

It is particularly disturbing to see a major scholar on the Holocaust, a tragedy whose enormity and barbarity must never be forgotten, so careless in his references to a field outside his area of expertise. For Turks, who are justifiably proud of our long and continuing role as a haven for minorities (including the Jews evicted from Spain by the Inquisition), it is particularly disquieting to find our own history distorted in works devoted to the Holocaust of World War II.

To compare a tragic civil war (initiated by Armenian nationalists) and the human suffering it wrought on both the Muslim and Christian populations with the horrors of a premeditated attempt to systematically eradicate a peaceable people, is, to anyone familiar with the history in question, simply ludicrous.

I am enclosing copies of works by two American experts on the history of Turco-Armenian relations, Professors Justin McCarthy and Heath Lowry, and would hope that in the interests of objectivity and fairness you will not only read them but also reflect having done so in any future works you may publish.

Yours Sincerely,

Nuzhet Kandemir
Ambassador

Analysis of the Lowry Memorandum

Lowry's memorandum indicates that he has been engaged in an ongoing relationship with the Turkish government, and that he has regularly offered advice on denial both to the Turkish ambassador to the United States and to other persons in Turkey (IADA-Ankara). The memorandum also provides evidence of the desire to check scholars from referring to an Armenian genocide. The process may even be bureaucratic. Someone at the embassy identifies books and articles that mention the genocide. (Perhaps denial is part of his or her official duties.) The list is turned over to Lowry at the request of the ambassador, and Lowry examines the works in question, provides a report in the form of a memorandum, and then prepares a letter for the ambassador's signature. Lowry reads Lifton's book, not out of interest or to be informed: he does it as a service to the Turkish government, "with an eye to drafting a letter for your [the ambassador's] signature to the author."

Why a scholar would conceive of his or her craft in this fashion is not a question that admits of easy answers. But, as we shall suggest in another section of the article, it is not uncommon. What is clear from the memorandum, though, is that Lowry identifies with the power of the Turkish government. He twice refers to "our problem," that is, the availability of works that discuss the Armenian Genocide, suggesting that he sees himself as part of a power constellation engaged in furthering the perceived interests of Turkey.

Lowry is critical of the ineptitude of the deniers who fail to serve what he assumes are Turkey's interests. Verbally and in writing, he repeatedly told those in power that they must attack and discredit articles or books by Dadrian, Fein, Kuper, and others, yet not a single attack has been written. He underlines the date of Lifton's book—1986—and suggests implicitly that four years is simply too long: material must be subjected to damage control at the earliest possible moment. One wonders why it took so long in this case, since Markusen and Smith received letters similar to the one addressed to Lifton within months of the appearance of their essays in *Genocide and the Modern Age.*[20]

Lowry's own work contains many questionable assertions and conclusions. He denies that Hitler ever uttered the widely quoted remark: "Who, after all, speaks today of the annihilation of the Armenians?"[21] In his booklet, *The Story behind Ambassador Morgenthau's Story,* he asserts that Morgenthau's account of the genocide is nothing but "crude half-truths and outright falsehoods . . . from cover to cover."[22] His conclusions do not follow from his analysis or the evidence he can marshal. Quite astonishing, however, is his claim that what Talaat, a principal architect of the Armenian Genocide, had in mind for the Armenians was not destruction, but "segregation," that the fate of the Armenians was to be that of African-Americans in the South in 1915.[23]

Lowry apparently seeks to discredit the work of any author who treats the Armenian Genocide as historical reality. Nevertheless, those in Ankara, whom he has communicated with again and again on how to discredit works on the Armenian Genocide, have not heeded his words. "I strongly recommend that it be pointed out to Ankara." Had people listened to me, he suggests, "we" wouldn't be faced with "our" present "problem."

Analysis of the Letter to Lifton

Various perspectives on denial can be brought to bear on the content of the letter. Smith notes that typically the denial of genocide involves denial that the events took place, that the perpetrator bears any responsibility for the destruction, and that the term "genocide" is applicable to what occurred. Deborah Lipstadt, in her work on the Holocaust, speaks of the "Yes, but" mode of denial: applied to the present case, Yes, Armenians died, but so did Turks. Yes, Armenians were killed, but they brought it on themselves. Yes, the conflict took place, but it was a civil war within a global war. Likewise, Israel Charny has pointed to a "template of denial," the rules of which include: Do not acknowledge that the genocide took place; transform it into other kinds of events; portray the victims as the perpetrators; insist more victims were from the perpetrator's group; and relativize the genocide in whatever way possible.[24] The letter is too limited in purpose to display all of the elements depicted in these overlapping perspectives, but they are found in the larger literature of denial of the 1915 genocide.

In terms of the letter itself, however, we want to call attention to two aspects of denial that are part and parcel of Turkey's denial tactics. The goal of each is to prevent recognition of the fact that what the Ottoman government did to the Armenians in 1915 constitutes genocide. First, there is an attempt to remove the label "genocide" from the Armenian experience. This is done in part by not differentiating between the victims of the massacre and of warfare, of blaming the victims as the initiators of violence (thus suggesting that they got what they deserved, even though it never happened), and describing the genocide as a civil war within a global war. In the end, the genocide of over a million Armenians is made to appear like an "amorphous human disaster."[25]

A second theme, unique to the Turkish case, is the determination to deny the Armenian Genocide by acknowledging the Holocaust.[26] This involves in part special efforts by Turkey to recognize the tragedy of the Holocaust and show compassion for its victims. At the same time, Turkey has gone to extraordinary lengths, including threats and disruption of academic conferences, to prevent Jews from learning about the Armenian Genocide. One notes, too, Lowry's memorandum stresses that Lifton relied on the work of other scholars, but this, he argues, is precisely why it is necessary to discredit at the outset authors such as Dadrian, Fein, and Kuper. The danger Lowry sees is that "from now on we will see *all* works on the genocide of the Jews" containing references to the Armenian Genocide. Such references would allow for comparison and the conclusion that, for different reasons, both Jews and Armenians have been victims of genocide. There is another aspect to this, however, that can best be addressed in terms of the letter—the attempt of the Turkish government and its intellectuals to draw a sharp and decisive distinction between the Holocaust and the experience of the Armenians in 1915.

The letter states that to make any comparison of the Holocaust and the Armenian Genocide is ludicrous. But it is not ludicrous: the similarities have been pointed out by many scholars, most recently by Robert Melson in his major work on *Revolution and Genocide: On the Origins of the Armenian Genocide and the Holocaust.*[27] Other leading Jewish scholars of the Holocaust, in fact, describe the Armenian massacres and deportations into the desert as genocide, and one that approximates the Holocaust in important respects. Yehuda Bauer, for example, not only points out the similarities between the Armenian Genocide and the Holocaust, but states that on a "continuum of murderous behavior, the Armenian massacres would figure nearest to the Holocaust."[28] Similarly, the late Lucy Dawidowicz stated that the Armenian Genocide in its "extent and horror most closely approximated the murder of the European Jews." She continued: "The once unthinkable 'Armenian solution' became, in our time, the achievable 'Final Solution,' the Nazi code name for the annihilation of the European Jews."[29]

Concluding Reflections on the Memorandum and Letter

To confront denial is to face a recurrent question: do those who engage in denial of a well-documented genocide actually believe their own words, or do they know better, but disregard the facts for personal or political reasons? The issue is complicated in that denial is, at times, a matter of lying—a deliberate distortion of the facts to serve some presumed advantage. Denial may also be a "defense mechanism" that functions to reduce stress and inner conflict. As a defense mechanism, the events and feelings that one wants to deny are not completely removed from consciousness, but are rather placed in a more favorable light through a kind of selective emphasis and reappraisal. Although this distorts the truth, the person who uses such a strategy may not be aware that he or she is doing so to make the situation less threatening. Nevertheless, denial as lie and as self-serving rationalization are often intertwined and reinforce each other.

In the case of Lowry and the ambassador, there is a sense in which their whole enterprise involves a retelling of the Armenian Genocide to place Turks in a favorable light and Armenians in a bad light. In such accounts the victim is invariably blamed for the genocide; indeed, is cast in the role of perpetrator. But for all the reinterpretation and selective uses of history, there is a clue that the ambassador and Lowry know that the Armenian Genocide took place, which would make their public statements to the contrary appear to be calculated distortions of the truth.

To go back to the documents at hand. The letter Lifton received and the draft of it by Lowry are explicit in denying the genocide, and speak of the "so-called 'Armenian genocide,' allegedly perpetrated by the Ottoman Turks during the First World War." When we examine the memorandum, however, a different story appears, with a decided gap between the public discourse of the letter and the private discourse of the memorandum. On the first page of the memorandum, the executive director of the Institute of Turkish Studies approaches the subject, and the ambassador, delicately, referring to the "so-called 'Armenian genocide'." Yet a few pages later, when he gives his "summation," Lowry speaks openly without using such terms as "alleged" or "so-called." He writes, without quotation marks, about "the Armenian genocide" and "the genocide." It is hard to believe that he would present such language to the ambassador unless he knew that the ambassador would not be offended.

The Harm of Genocide Denial

We should not be surprised by instances of what many would consider to be inappropriate use of academic credentials and skills, since, after all, academics and professionals have contributed in direct ways to genocidal killing projects, including the Armenian Genocide and the Holocaust. They have done so by lending their talents and prestige to racist, victimizing ideologies that are central features of many genocides, by helping to create and administer the policies and technologies of mass killing, and by actually engaging in the killing.[30] If highly educated academics and professionals have been able to repudiate their ethical codes and serve as accomplices and perpetrators of actual genocides, it is likely that they would be even more able to engage in an activity in which no one is killed.

It would be a mistake, however, to underestimate the serious harm caused by denial of genocide, particularly denial wrapped in the guise of legitimate scholarship. In this section, we examine the harm done by pseudo-scholarly denial of known genocides and consider the assertion, put forth by some scholars, that deliberate denial is a form of aggression that ought to be regarded as a contribution to genocidal violence in its own right. Then we briefly address the question of what might motivate academics to make a career out of denial of genocide.

Some of the ways in which denial of genocide causes "violence to others" have been identified by Israel W. Charny in his essay on "The Psychology of Denial of Known Genocides."[31] Charny emphasizes that denial conceals the horror of the crimes and exonerates those responsible for it. This point is echoed by historian Deborah Lipstadt, who, in her recent book on denial of the Holocaust, writes that "Denial aims to reshape history in order to rehabilitate the perpetrators and demonize the victims."[32] Denial also, according to Charny, "attacks the historical spirit and morale" of the survivors and the descendants of those killed and places "further burdens on their recovery."[33] In short, denial prevents healing of the wounds inflicted by genocide.[34] Furthermore, it constitutes an "attack on the collective identity and national cultural continuity of the victim people."[35]

A number of scholars have argued that the deliberate denial of a known genocide is a harmful act that deserves to be included in the same moral domain with indirect and direct contributions to the actual genocides. Thus, Charny states that "*Denials of genocide make no sense unless one sees in them renewed opportunities for the same passions, meanings, and pleasures that were at work in the genocide itself,* now revived in symbolic processes of murdering the dignity of the survivors, rationality, dignity, and even history itself" (emphasis in original).[36] Indeed, denial may be thought of as the last stage of genocide, one that continues into the present. A kind of double killing takes place: first the physical deed, followed by the destruction of remembrance of the deed.

Historian and Holocaust survivor Erich Kulka regards the denial of genocide as an offense in its own right, asserting that "Attempts to rewrite Holocaust history on the pretext of 'revisionism,' aided by scholars with academic backgrounds, must be viewed as intellectual aggression," a repetition in thought of what was enacted earlier as physical deed.[37] In his recent book on denial of the Holocaust, historian Pierre Vidal-Naquet characterizes Robert Faurisson, whose "scholarly" denials of the Holocaust have been widely disseminated, as a "paper Eichmann."[38]

We concur with Charny, Kulka, and Vidal-Naquet in regarding denial of genocide as an egregious offense that warrants being regarded as a form of contribution to genocidal violence. Denial contributes to genocide in at least two ways. First of all, genocide does not end with its last human victim; denial continues the process, but if denial points to the past and the present, it also has implications for the future. By absolving the perpetrators of past genocides from responsibility for their actions and by obscuring the reality of genocide as a widely practiced form of state policy in the modern world, denial may increase the risk of future outbreaks of genocidal killing.

Why Might Intellectuals Engage in Denial of Known Genocides?

There are several possible motivations for denial of genocide, and these can be complex. The motivations that we would call attention to include: self-serving ideology, bigotry, intellectual confusion, careerism, identification with power, and a particular conception of knowledge. It seems unlikely, however, that denial rests only on one of these motivations; moreover, the particular combinations of motivations may vary with individuals. Also, what prompts denial may vary with different examples of genocide: anti-Zionism, for example, may help explain denial of the Holocaust, but in terms of its content tells us nothing about why the Armenian Genocide has been denied. On the other hand, if we focus not on the content of the motivation, but on its form (ideology) and goals (political and psychological purposes), then the motivations for denial in these two cases may have more in common than appear at first glance.

Scholars who have analyzed deniers of the Holocaust have concluded that they are primarily motivated by ideology. Thus, Vidal-Naquet, in his examination of Faurisson and other French "revisionists," asserts that "all revisionists are resolute anti-Zionists."[39] Similarly, on the basis of her even more comprehensive survey of Holocaust deniers, Lipstadt concludes that "it is clear that deniers have no interest in scholarship or reason. Most are antisemites or bigots."[40]

These answers are no doubt correct, but they are incomplete. It may be that all revisionists are anti-Zionists, but there are surely anti-Zionists (some of them Jewish) who do not deny the reality of the Holocaust. Similarly, there are people who are highly anti-Semitic, but acknowledge that the Holocaust took place.

Clues to the thinking of academics who question the reality of the Armenian Genocide have been provided by Israel Charny and his colleague Daphna Fromer, who sent questionnaires to sixty-nine scholars who signed an advertisement which, in the words of Charny and Fromer, "questioned insidiously the evidence of the Armenian genocide" and appeared in several newspapers, including the *New York Times* and the *Washington Post*.[41] In analyzing the comments of the seventeen scholars who provided "active responses" to their mailing, Charny and Fromer discerned a number of "thinking defense-mechanisms" that enabled the scholars to engage in "the denial of genocide." These mechanisms included what the authors term "scientificism in the service of denial," i.e., the claim that not enough empirical evidence is available to justify an unequivocal position on the reality of the genocide; and "definitionalism," i.e., acknowledging deaths, but denying that they were the result of "genocide," thus shifting responsibility for the genocide away from the Turkish government and trivializing the killing of over a million Armenians as the inadvertent result of famine, war, and disease. Whether anyone is led into denial by such reasoning is an open question, but such thinking does serve to make denial easier thereafter, while, at the same time, it preserves the appearance of objectivity.

"Careerism" is a complicated phenomenon, but for our purposes we would identify two (non-exclusive) forms that it may take: one that is oriented more toward material goals, and one that involves more the satisfactions that go with power. Both share the "thoughtlessness" that Hannah Arendt saw as the essence of the "banality of evil": an imaginative blindness that prevents one from reflecting upon the consequences of one's actions.[42] Elsewhere, however, Arendt also speaks of a "willed evil," and the second type of careerism is not far removed from this: not simply the obliviousness to hurt, but the calculated infliction of hurt.[43]

Intellectuals who engage in the denial of genocide may be motivated in part by either type of careerism, or by them in combination. The more insidious form, however, is the second type of careerism. Here material rewards are important, but more so, the opportunity for certain psychological and social satisfactions: a sense of importance, of status, of being in control, all of which can come through identification with power, something we believe we have shown in the memorandum we have analyzed. The price for intellect in the service of denial, however, is a particular conception of knowledge, one in which knowledge not only serves the ends of those in power, but is defined by power. To define truth in terms of power, however, is to reveal the bankruptcy, irrationality, and above all, danger of the whole enterprise of denial of genocide. Inherent in such a view of knowledge is both a deep-seated nihilism and an urge to tyranny.

Scholars and Truth

Scholarship is, or should be, a quest for truth. What scholars write and say in that quest matters a great deal. Directly or indirectly, our words contribute to shared consciousness—to the constellation of beliefs that a society forms in connection with issues of any kind. Scholars' contributions to that shared consciousness become especially important in relation to a society's struggles with large, disturbing, and threatening historical events.

Nowhere is scholarly research and commentary more significant than in connection with genocide where the scope of mass murder and the depth of its moral violation defy understanding and arouse every kind of confusion, whether in the form of diffuse passions or resistance to painful evidence. Careful scholarly evaluation can hardly eliminate these confusions, but it can diminish them in favor of reasoned interpretation and the channeling of passion into constructive policy. Generally speaking, the extremity of human harm brought about by genocide raises the stakes of scholarly commentary.

Where scholars deny genocide, in the face of decisive evidence that it has occurred, they contribute to a false consciousness that can have the most dire reverberations. Their message, in effect, is: murderers did not really murder; victims were not really killed; mass murder requires no confrontation, no reflection, but should be ignored, glossed over. In this way scholars lend their considerable authority to the acceptance of this ultimate human crime. More than that, they encourage—indeed invite—a repetition of that crime from virtually any source in the immediate or distant future. By closing their minds to truth such scholars contribute to the deadly psychohistorical dynamic in which unopposed genocide begets new genocides.

Those of us who wish to be true to our scholarly calling have a clear obligation. We must first expose this form of denial. At the same time we must ourselves bear witness to historical truths—to the full narrative of mass murder and human suffering. To be witnessing professionals in this way requires that we take in grim details so that we can tell the story with accuracy and insight. It is a task to which we must bring both heart and mind, an approach that combines advocacy and detachment. We require sufficient detachment to maintain rigorous intellectual standards in evaluating evidence and drawing conclusions. At the same time our moral advocacy should require us to open ourselves to suffering as a way of taking a stand against cruelty and killing, whatever its source.

Notes

This essay was first published in *Holocaust and Genocide Studies* 9, no. 1 (Spring 1995).

1. Terrence Des Pres, "Introduction: Remembering Armenia," in *The Armenian Genocide in Perspective,* ed. Richard G. Hovannisian (New Brunswick, N.J.: Transaction Books, 1986), 10.
2. On scholarship as commitment to power, see Terrence Des Pres, "On Governing Narratives: The Turkish-Armenian Case," *Yale Review* 75, no. 4 (October 1986): 517–31.
3. Vahakn N. Dadrian, "A Textual Analysis of the Key Indictment of the Turkish Military Tribunal Investigating the Armenian Genocide," *Armenian Review* 44, no. 1 (Spring 1991): 26–27.
4. Vahakn N. Dadrian, "The Documentation of the World War I Armenian Massacres in the Proceedings of the Turkish Military Tribunal," *International Journal of Middle East Studies* 23, no. 4 (November 1991): 560.
5. Henry Morgenthau, *Ambassador Morgenthau's Story* (Garden City, N.Y.: Doubleday, Page, 1918; reprint, Plandome, N.Y.: New Age Publishers, 1975), 309.
6. Dadrian, "Documentation of the World War I Armenian Massacres," 568.
7. Here we can cite only a few of the many works that document the Armenian Genocide. Among the contemporary accounts, see Leslie Davis, *The Slaughterhouse Province: An American Diplomat's Report on the Armenian Genocide, 1915–1917* (New Rochelle, N.Y.: Aristide D. Caratzas, 1989); Morgenthau, *Ambassador Morgenthau's Story*; Arnold J. Toynbee, ed., *The Treatment of Armenians in the Ottoman Empire, 1915–16: Documents Presented to Viscount Grey of Fallodon, Secretary of State for Foreign Affairs* (London: Sir Joseph Causton and Sons, 1916). *The Armenian Genocide in the U.S. Archives, 1915–1918* (Alexandria, Va.: Chadwyck-Healey Inc., 1990) provides 37,000 pages of documentation on microfiche. For recent studies, see three articles by Vahakn N. Dadrian, "The Secret Young-Turk Ittihadist Conference and the Decision for the World War I Genocide of the Armenians," *Holocaust and Genocide Studies* 7, no. 2 (Fall 1993): 173–201; idem, "The Documentation of the World War I Armenian Massacres in the Proceedings of the Turkish Military Tribunal," *International Journal of Middle East Studies* 23, no. 4 (November 1991): 549–76; idem, "Documentation of the Armenian Genocide in Turkish Sources," in *Genocide: A Critical Bibliographic Review,* ed. Israel W. Charny (New York: Facts on File, 1991), 2: ch. 4; Tessa Hofmann and Gerayer Koutcharian, " 'Images that Horrify and Indict': Pictorial Documents on the Persecution and Extermination of the Armenians from 1877 to 1922," *Armenian Review* 45, no. 1–2 (Spring/Summer 1992): 53–184; Robert Melson, *Revolution and Genocide: On the Origins of the Armenian Genocide and the Holocaust* (Chicago: University of Chicago Press, 1992); Donald E.

Miller and Lorna Touryan Miller, *Survivors: An Oral History of the Armenian Genocide* (Berkeley: University of California Press, 1993). For an extensive bibliography on the Armenian Genocide, see Richard G. Hovannisian, *The Armenian Holocaust: A Bibliography Relating to the Deportations, Massacres, and Dispersion of the Armenian People, 1915–1923,* 2d ed. (Cambridge, Mass.: Armenian Heritage Press, 1980). On the availability of survivor testimony in the form of oral history, see Miller and Miller, *Survivors,* 212–13. Most of the oral histories are in Armenian and have not been translated; on the other hand, many survivor memoirs exist in English. Among the more detailed are Abraham H. Hartunian, *Neither to Laugh nor to Weep: A Memoir of the Armenian Genocide* (Boston: Beacon Press, 1968; reprint, Cambridge, Mass.: Armenian Heritage Press, 1986), and Ephraim K. Jernazian, *Judgment unto Truth: Witnessing the Armenian Genocide* (New Brunswick, N.J.: Transaction Books, 1990).

8. There is a substantial literature on denial of the Armenian Genocide. See Rouben Adalian, "The Armenian Genocide: Revisionism and Denial," in *Genocide in Our Time: An Annotated Bibliography with Analytical Introductions,* ed. Michael N. Dobkowski and Isidor Wallimann (Ann Arbor: Pierian Press, 1992), ch. 5; Marjorie Housepian Dobkin, "What Genocide? What Holocaust? News from Turkey, 1915–1923: A Case Study," in *The Armenian Genocide in Perspective,* ed. Hovannisian, ch. 5; Richard G. Hovannisian, "The Armenian Genocide and Patterns of Denial," in ibid., ch. 6; Clive Foss, "The Turkish View of Armenian History: A Vanishing Nation," in *The Armenian Genocide: History, Politics, Ethics,* ed. Richard G. Hovannisian (New York: St. Martin's Press, 1992), ch. 11; Vahakn N. Dadrian, "Ottoman Archives and Denial of the Armenian Genocide," in *The Armenian Genocide,* ed. Hovannisian, ch. 12; Vigen Guroian, "The Politics and Morality of Genocide," in *The Armenian Genocide,* ed. Hovannisian, ch. 13; Roger W. Smith, "Genocide and Denial: The Armenian Case and Its Implications," *Armenian Review* 42, no. 1 (Spring 1989): 1–38; idem, "Denial of the Armenian Genocide," in Charny, *Genocide,* vol. 2, ch. 3; and "The Armenian Genocide: Memory, Politics, and the Future," in *The Armenian Genocide,* ed. Hovannisian, ch. 1. See also the wide-ranging discussion by Israel W. Charny, "The Psychology of Denial of Known Genocides," in Charny, *Genocide,* ch. 1.
9. See, for example, Hovannisian, "The Armenian Genocide and Patterns of Denial," 115–31; Smith, "Genocide and Denial," 15–20.
10. Edward Minasian, "Musa Dagh: The Film That Was Denied," *Journal of Armenian Studies,* 1, no. 2 (Fall/Winter 1985–86): 63–73; Hovannisian, "The Armenian Genocide and Patterns of Denial," 120–21.
11. Ibid., 113–14, 124–27, 129–30.
12. Leo Kuper, *Genocide: Its Political Use in the Twentieth Century* (New Haven: Yale University Press, 1981), 219–20; Smith, "Genocide and Denial," 22–23.
13. Leo Kuper, "Problems in Education on Genocide," *Internet on the Holocaust and Genocide,* 14 (February 1988): special supplement, p. 1.
14. Israel W. Charny and Shamai Davidson, eds., *The Book of the International Conference on the Holocaust and Genocide*: Book 1: *The Conference Program and*

Crisis (Tel Aviv: Institute of the International Conference on the Holocaust and Genocide, 1983), 269–315; Israel W. Charny, ed., *Toward the Understanding and Prevention of Genocide* (Boulder, Colo.: Westview Press, 1984), 364–72.

15. *New York Times,* June 22, 1982, A4.
16. Our description of the Institute of Turkish Studies, Inc., is drawn from the following sources: *The Institute of Turkish Studies, Inc.,* a brochure published in Washington, D.C. by the institute, not dated, but includes the Director's Report for 1983–84; *Report of the Institute of Turkish Studies, Inc.,* 1982–1992 (Washington, D.C.: Institute of Turkish Studies, Inc., 1992); *Encyclopedia of Associations,* 26th ed., 1992 (Detroit: Gale Research Inc., 1991), 1:1133; Stan Olson, ed., *The Foundation Directory* (New York: The Foundation Center, 1992), 228; William Wade, ed., *National Directory of Nonprofit Organizations, 1991,* vol. I: *Organizations with Revenues of $100,000 or More,* pt. 1: A–O (Rockville, Md.: The Taft Group, 1991), ix, 1078; and Speros Vryonis, Jr., *The Turkish State and History: Clio Meets the Grey Wolf,* 2d ed. (Thessaloniki and New Rochelle, N.Y.: Institute for Balkan Studies and Aristide D. Caratzas, 1993), pt. III. We are grateful to Dr. Rouben Adalian for making available to us a copy of the brochure published by the Institute of Turkish Studies.
17. *The Institute of Turkish Studies, Inc.,* 11.
18. Smith, "Denial of the Armenian Genocide," 83. Stanford Shaw, *Turkey and the Holocaust: Turkey's Role in Rescuing Turkish and European Jewry from Nazi Persecution, 1933–1945* (New York: New York University Press, 1993), 22, 27. This book accuses some Armenians residing in Turkey during World War II of being pro-Nazi and anti-Semitic. See the devastating review of Shaw's book by Bernard Wasserstein in *The Times Literary Supplement,* January 7, 1994, 4–6.
19. *Report of the Institute of Turkish Studies, Inc., 1982–1992,* xi–xii. The next chair in Turkish studies will be in the School of Foreign Service at Georgetown University in Washington, D.C. The Turkish government has contributed $1.5 million toward establishing the professorship. See *Georgetown Magazine* (Spring/Summer 1994): 12.
20. Isidor Wallimann and Michael N. Dobkowski, eds., *Genocide and the Modern Age* (Westport, Conn.: Greenwood Press, 1987).
21. Heath W. Lowry, "The U.S. Congress and Adolf Hitler on the Armenians," *Political Communication and Persuasion* 3, no. 2 (1985): 111–40. For a thorough discussion of the Hitler remark and its authenticity, see Kevork B. Bardakjian, *Hitler and the Armenians* (Cambridge, Mass.: Zoryan Institute, 1985).

    The statement attributed to Hitler is contained in a summary of Hitler's speech to his generals on August 22, 1939 about his plans to wage a ruthless war against Poland. Within days Louis P. Lochner of the Associated Press in Berlin received from an "informant" a copy of the document, which is based on notes taken by Admiral Wilhelm Canaris, head of Hitler's military intelligence. Lochner immediately brought the account to the attention of the American and British embassies. He subsequently published the document in translation in his book *What About Germany?* (New York: Dodd, Mead and Co., 1942), 1–4.

    The important issue is less the authenticity of the remark than what lessons Hitler drew from the Armenian case, and how these affected his actions in conducting the war and subsequently the decisions to annihilate the Jews and Gypsies. Bardakjian provides evidence (25–35) that Hitler was very familiar with the Armenian Genocide, believed that the Armenians, like the Jews, were a "degenerate race," and was aware that Turkey had been able to exterminate a people with impunity. The lessons he drew were even more pointed in his 1931 interview with Richard Breiting of the *Leipziger Neueste Nachrichten.* Here he invoked the destruction of the Armenians within a context of deportation, resettlement, and massacre as means to secure "living space" for Germany and the Aryan race. "Think of the biblical deportations and the massacres of the Middle Ages . . . and remember the extermination of the Armenians." Hitler added: "One eventually reaches the conclusion that masses of men are mere biological plasticine." Quoted in Bardakjian, *Hitler and the Armenians,* 28, quoting from Edouard Calic, *Unmasked,* trans. Richard Barry (London: Chatto and Windus, 1971), 81.

22. Heath W. Lowry, *The Story Behind Ambassador Morgenthau's Story* (Istanbul: The Isis Press, 1990), 60.
23. Ibid., 49–50. Lowry has also written "op-ed" articles in an attempt to defeat Congressional resolutions that would officially recognize the Armenian genocide. A good example of this appears in the *Wall Street Journal,* November 15, 1989, A26.
24. Smith, "Genocide and Denial," 6–9; Deborah E. Lipstadt, "Deniers, Relativists, and Pseudo-Scholarship," *Dimensions* 6, no. 1 (1991): 7; Israel W. Charny, "The Psychology of Denial of Known Genocides," in Charny, *Genocide,* 2:13–15.
25. Dadrian, "Ottoman Archives and Denial of the Armenian Genocide," in *The Armenian Genocide,* ed. Hovannisian, 283–86. An excellent example of denial through the means of which Dadrian speaks is contained in Stanford J. Shaw and Ezel Kural Shaw, "The Authors Respond," *International Journal of Middle East Studies* 9, no. 3 (1978): 399–400.
26. Hovannisian, "The Armenian Genocide and Patterns of Denial," 128–29; Smith, "Genocide and Denial," 16–18.
27. Richard G. Hovannisian lists many of the common features in his study, "The Historical Dimensions of the Armenian Question, 1878–1923," in *The Armenian Genocide in Perspective,* ed. Hovannisian, 30. Melson's book, published by the University of Chicago Press in 1992, provides a sustained analysis of the similarities between the two genocides, which he describes as "total genocides," born of revolution and war. But, like others, he suggests there are also some differences. See, in particular, chapter 8 of his book.
28. Yehuda Bauer, "Essay: On the Place of the Holocaust in History," *Holocaust and Genocide Studies* 2, no. 2 (1987): 217.
29. Lucy Dawidowicz, *The Holocaust and the Historians* (Cambridge, Mass.: Harvard University Press, 1981), 20.
30. For a survey of the roles of several professions in the Holocaust and other cases of genocidal killing, see Eric Markusen, "Professions, Professionals, and Genocide," in Charny, *Genocide,* 2:264–98. With few exceptions, studies of

the role of specific professions in genocide focus on the Holocaust, but see the path-breaking article by Vahakn N. Dadrian, "The Role of Turkish Physicians in the World War I Genocide of the Ottoman Armenians," *Holocaust and Genocide Studies* 1, no. 2 (1986): 169–92. On the involvement of various professions in the Holocaust, see, among others, Omer Bartov, *The Eastern Front, 1941–45: German Troops and the Barbarisation of Warfare* (New York: St. Martin's Press, 1986); idem, *Hitler's Army: Soldiers, Nazis, and War in the Third Reich* (New York: Oxford University Press, 1991); Alan D. Beyerchen, *Scientists under Hitler: Politics and the Physics Community in the Third Reich* (New Haven: Yale University Press, 1977); Christopher R. Browning, *The Final Solution and the German Foreign Office: A Study of Referat D III of Abteilung Deutschland* (New York: Holms and Meier, 1977); idem, "Genocide and Public Health: German Doctors and Polish Jews, 1939–41," *Holocaust and Genocide Studies* 3, no. 1 (1988): 21–36; Michael H. Kater, *Doctors under Hitler* (Chapel Hill: University of North Carolina Press, 1989); Peter Hayes, *Industry and Ideology: I. G. Farben in the Nazi Era* (New York: Cambridge University Press, 1987); Herbert Hirsch, "Nazi Education: A Case of Political Socialization," *Educational Forum* 53, no. 1 (1988): 63–76; Robert J. Lifton, *The Nazi Doctors: Medical Killing and the Psychology of Genocide* (New York: Basic Books, 1986); Ingo Muller, *Hitler's Justice: The Courts of the Third Reich,* trans. Deborah Lucas Schneider (Cambridge, Mass.: Harvard University Press, 1991); Benno Muller-Hill, *Murderous Science: Elimination by Scientific Selection of Jews, Gypsies, and Others, Germany 1933–1945* (New York: Oxford University Press, 1988); Robert Proctor, *Racial Hygiene: Medicine under the Nazis* (Cambridge, Mass.: Harvard University Press, 1988); Gunter W. Remmling, "Discrimination, Persecution, Theft, and Murder under Color of Law: The Totalitarian Corruption of the German Legal System, 1933–1945," in *Genocide and the Modern Age: Etiology and Case Studies of Mass Death,* ed. Isidor Wallimann and Michael N. Dobkowski (Westport, Conn.: Greenwood Press, 1987), ch. 10; Telford Taylor, "The Legal Profession," in *The Holocaust: Ideology, Bureaucracy, and Genocide,* ed. Henry Friedlander and Sybil Milton (Millwood, N.Y.: Kraus International Publications, 1980), 133–40; Max Weinreich, *Hitler's Professors: The Part of Scholarship in Germany's Crimes against the Jewish People* (New York: YIVO Institute for Jewish Research, 1946).

31. Charny, "The Psychology of Denial of Known Genocides," 23.
32. Deborah E. Lipstadt, *Denying the Holocaust: The Growing Assault on Truth and Memory* (New York: The Free Press, 1993, and Toronto: Maxwell MacMillan, 1993.), 217.
33. Charny, "The Psychology of Denial of Known Genocides," 22.
34. See, for example, Levon Boyajian and Haigaz Grigorian, "Psychological Sequelae of the Armenian Genocide," in *The Armenian Genocide in Perspective,* ed. Hovannisian, ch. 10; and Miller and Miller, *Survivors: An Oral History of the Armenian Genocide,* ch. 8.
35. Charny, "The Psychology of Denial of Known Genocides," 23.
36. Ibid., 18.

37. Erich Kulka, "Denial of the Holocaust," in Charny, *Genocide,* 2:57.
38. Pierre Vidal-Naquet, *Assassins of Memory: Essays on the Denial of the Holocaust* (New York: Columbia University Press, 1992), 57.
39. Ibid., 87.
40. Lipstadt, *Denying the Holocaust,* 206.
41. Israel W. Charny and Daphna Fromer, "A Follow-Up of the Sixty-Nine Scholars Who Signed an Advertisement Questioning the Armenian Genocide," *Internet on the Holocaust and Genocide* no. 25/26 (April 1990): 6–7.
42. Hannah Arendt, *Eichmann in Jerusalem: A Report on the Banality of Evil* (New York: The Viking Press, 1964), 49, 278–88.
43. Hannah Arendt, *The Human Condition* (Chicago: University of Chicago Press, 1958), 239–40.

Works Cited

Adalian, Rouben. "The Armenian Genocide: Revisionism and Denial." In *Genocide in Our Time: An Annotated Bibliography with Analytical Introductions,* ed. Michael N. Dobkowski and Isidor Wallimann. Ann Arbor, Mich.: Pierian Press, 1992.

———., ed. *The Armenian Genocide in the U.S. Archives, 1915–1918.* Alexandria, Va.: Chadwick-Healey, 1991. (Microfiche compilation.)

Agayef, Ahmed. "Turk Alemi" (The Turkish world). Part 4, *Türk Yurdu* 1, no. 5 (July 17, 1328 [1912]).

Ahmad, Feroz. "War and Society under the Young Turks, 1908–18." *Review: Fernand Braudel Center* 11, no. 2 (Spring 1988).

Akarlı, Engin Deniz, trans. and ed. *Belgelerle Tanzimat: Osmanlı Sadrıazamlarından Ali ve Fuad Paşaların Siyasî Vasiyyetnâmeleri* (The Tanzimat with documents: The political testaments of the Ottoman grand viziers Ali and Fuad Pashas). İstanbul: Boğaziçi Üniversitesi Matbaası, 1978.

Akçam, Taner. *Armenien und der Völkermord: Die Istanbuler Prozesse und die türkische Nationalbewegung.* Trans. Hayrettin Aydin. Hamburg: Hamburger Edition, 1996.

A. Y. [Yusuf Akçura]. "1329 Senesinde Türk Dünyası" (The Turkish world in the year 1913). *Türk Yurdu* 6, no. 3 (June 3, 1330 [1914]).

———. "İktisad" (Economy). *Türk Yurdu* 12, no. 12 (August 2, 1333 [1917]).

Alexander, Edward. *The Resonance of Dust: Essays on Holocaust Literature and Jewish Fate.* Columbus: Ohio State University Press, 1979.

Alp, Tekin (Moiz Cohen). *Turan.* İstanbul: "Kader" Matbaası, 1330 [1914–15].

———. *Türkismus und Pantürkismus.* Weimar: Gustav Kiepenheuer, 1915.

———. *Türkleşdirme* (Turkification). İstanbul: "Resimli Ay" Matbaası, 1928.

———. *Yeni Hayat* (New life). İstanbul: Evkaf-i İslamiyye, 1918.

American Committee for Armenian and Syrian Relief. "Latest News Concerning the Armenian and Syrian Sufferers (January 2, 1916)." New York, 1916.

Andonian, Aram. *Ain Sev Orerun* (In those dark days). Boston: Hairenik, 1919.

———. *Documents officiels concernant les massacres arméniens.* Paris: Imp. H. Turabian, 1920.

———. *Documents relatifs aux massacres arméniens.* Paris: Imp. H. Turabian, 1920.

———. *The Memoirs of Naïm Bey.* London: Hodder and Stoughton, 1920.

———. *Mets Vojire* (The great crime). Boston: Pahak, 1921.

Apélian, Albert S. *The Antiochians.* New York: Vantage Press, 1960.

App, Austin J. *History's Most Terrifying Peace.* San Antonio: Austin J. App, 1974.

———. *The Six Million Swindle: Blackmailing the German People for Hard Marks with Fabricated Corpses.* Tacoma Park, Md.: N.p., 1973.

Arai, Masami. *Turkish Nationalism in the Young Turk Era.* Leiden: E. J. Brill, 1992.

Arendt, Hannah. *Eichmann à Jérusalem.* Paris: Seuil, 1966.

———. *Eichmann in Jerusalem: A Report on the Banality of Evil.* New York: Viking, 1964. Reprint, New York: Penguin, 1966.

———. *The Human Condition.* Chicago: University of Chicago Press, 1958.

Armenian National Committee. *The Armenian Genocide: As Reported in the Australian Press.* Sydney: Armenian National Committee, 1983.

Armenian Youth Federation of Canada. *The Armenian Genocide in the Canadian Press,* vol. 1: *1915–1916.* Montreal: Armenian National Committee of Canada, 1985.

Assembly of Turkish American Associations. *Setting the Record Straight on Armenian Propaganda against Turkey.* Washington, D.C.: Assembly of Turkish American Associations, 1982.

Astourian, Stephan H. "Genocidal Process: Reflections on the Armeno-Turkish Polarization." In *The Armenian Genocide: History, Politics, Ethics,* ed. Richard G. Hovannisian. New York: St. Martin's Press, 1992.

Baghdjian, Kevork K. *La confiscation, par le gouvernement turc, des biens arméniens . . . dits "abandonnés."* Montreal: N.p., 1987.

Balakian, Krikoris (Grigoris Palakian). *Hai Goghgotan* (Armenian calvary). Vol. 2. Paris: N.p., 1959.

Baldwin, Peter, ed. *Reworking the Past: Hitler, the Holocaust and the Historians' Debate.* Boston: Beacon Press, 1990.

Banker, Marie Sarrafian. *Armenian Romance.* Grand Rapids, Mich.: Wm. B. Eerdmans Publishing Co., 1941.

Bardakjian, Kevork B. *Hitler and the Armenians.* Cambridge, Mass.: Zoryan Institute, 1985.

Bardèche, Maurice. *Nuremberg: Ou, la terre promise.* Paris: Les Sept Couleurs, [1948].

———. *Nuremberg II: Ou, les faux monnayeurs.* Paris: Les Sept Couleurs, [1950].

Barnes, Harry Elmer. *Revisionism and Brainwashing: A Survey of the War Guilt Question of Germany after Two World Wars.* N.p., 1962.

Barsoumian, Hagop Levon. "The Armenian Amira Class of Istanbul." Ph.D. diss., Columbia University, 1980.

Bartholomew, Alan Alfred. "Tarsus American School, 1888–1988: The Evolution of a Missionary Institution in Turkey." Ph.D. diss., Bryn Mawr College, 1989.

Bartov, Omer. *The Eastern Front, 1941–45: German Troops and the Barbarisation of Warfare.* New York: St. Martin's Press, 1986.

———. *Hitler's Army: Soldiers, Nazis, and War in the Third Reich.* New York: Oxford University Press, 1991.

Baskakov, Nikolai A., et al. *Turetsko-Russkii Slovar'*. Moscow: Russkii Iazyk, 1977.

Bauer, Yehuda. "Essay: On the Place of the Holocaust in History." *Holocaust and Genocide Studies* 2, no. 2 (1987).

Bayur, Yusuf Hikmet. *Türk İnkılabi Tarihi* (History of the Turkish revolution). Vol. 3, part 3. İstanbul: Maarif Matbaası, 1957.

Beaty, John. *The Iron Curtain over America.* Dallas: Wilkinson Pub. Co., 1951.

Becker, Helmut. *Äskulap zwischen Reichsadler und Halbmond: Seuchenbekämpfung und Sanitätswesen im türkischen Reich während des Ersten Weltkriegs.* Herzogenrath: Verlag Murken-Altrogge, 1990.

Bedoukian, Kerop. *The Urchin: An Armenian's Escape.* London: John Murray, 1978.

Beilinson, Moshe. "A Monument to the Glory of Israeli Alienation," *Davar,* January 22, 1936.

Beledian, Krikor. *Vayrer* (Loci). Paris: N.p., 1983.

Berberian, Houri. "The Delegation of Integral Armenia: From Greater Armenia to Lesser Armenia." *Armenian Review* 44, no. 3 (Autumn 1991).

Berkes, Niyazi. *The Development of Secularism in Turkey.* Montreal: McGill University Press, 1964.

Beyerchen, Alan D. *Scientists under Hitler: Politics and the Physics Community in the Third Reich.* New Haven: Yale University Press, 1977.

Beylerian, Arthur, ed. *Les Grandes puissances, l'Empire Ottoman et les Arméniens dans les archives françaises (1914–1918): Recueil de documents.* Paris: Publications de la Sorbonne, 1983.

Binark, İsmet. *Ermeni Olayları Tarihi* (History of the Armenian incidents [Hüseyin Nazim Pasha's papers]). Ankara: Turkish Prime Ministry General Directorate of State Archives, 1994.

Bonifas, Aimé. "The French Revisionists and the Myth of Holocaust." *Remembering for the Future.* Vol. 2. Oxford: Pergamon Press, 1988.

Braham, Randolph L. "Historical Revisionism and the New Right." *Remembering for the Future.* Vol. 2. Oxford: Pergamon Press, 1988.

Bishop, Harry Coghill Watson. *A Kut Prisoner.* London: John Lane and Co., 1920.

Blumer, Herbert. "Race Prejudice as a Sense of Group Position." *Pacific Sociological Review* 1, no. 1 (Spring 1958).

Boyajian, Levon, and Haigaz Grigorian. "Psychological Sequelae of the Armenian Genocide." In *The Armenian Genocide in Perspective,* ed. Richard G. Hovannisian. New Brunswick, N.J.: Transaction Books, 1986.

Brenner, Uri. *Facing the Threat of German Invasion of Eretz Israel in the Years 1940–1942.* Yad Tabenkin, Research Booklets, 3 (1981).

Bridoux, André. *Le Souvenir.* Paris: Presses Universitaires de France, 1956.

Brown, Rupert. *Group Processes: Dynamics within and between Groups.* New York: Basil Blackwell, 1988.

Browning, Christopher R. *The Final Solution and the German Foreign Office: A Study of Referat D III of Abteilung Deutschland.* New York: Holms and Meier, 1977.

———. "Genocide and Public Health: German Doctors and Polish Jews, 1939–41." *Holocaust and Genocide Studies* 3, no. 1 (1988).

Bryce, James. *Transcaucasia and Ararat, Being Notes of a Vacation Tour in the Autumn of 1876.* London: Macmillan and Co., Ltd., 1877.

Burnett, Philip Mason. *Reparations at the Paris Peace Conference: From the Standpoint of the American Delegation.* New York: Columbia University Press, 1940. 2 vols.

Butz, Arthur R. *The Hoax of the Twentieth Century.* Torrance, Calif.: Institute for Historical Review, 1976.

Buzanski, Peter M. "Admiral Mark L. Bristol and U.S.–Turkish Relations, 1919–1922." Ph.D. diss., University of California, Berkeley, 1960.

Calic, Edouard. *Unmasked.* Trans. Richard Barry. London: Chatto and Windus, 1971.

Çambel, Hasan Cemil. *Makaleler, Hâtıralar* (Articles, memoirs). 1964. Reprint, Ankara: Türk Tarih Kurumu, 1987.

Caraman, Elizabeth. *Daughter of the Euphrates.* New York: Harper and Brothers, 1939. Reprint, Paramus, N.J.: Armenian Missionary Association of America, Inc., 1979.

Çark, Y. G. *Türk Devleti Hizmetinde Ermeniler, 1453–1953* (Armenians in the service of the Turkish state, 1453–1953). İstanbul: Yeni Matbaa, 1953.

Cevdet Paşa. *Tezâkir* (Memoranda), I, ed. Cavid Baysun. 1953. Reprint, Ankara: Türk Tarih Kurumu, 1953.

Chalk, Frank, and Kurt Jonassohn. *The History and Sociology of Genocide: Analyses and Case Studies.* New Haven: Yale University Press, 1990.

Charny, Israel W. "The Conference Crisis: The Turks, Armenians and Jews." In Israel W. Charny and Shamai Davidson, eds. *The Book of the International Conference on the Holocaust and Genocide.* Vol. 2: *The Conference Program and Crisis.* Tel Aviv: Institute of the International Conference on the Holocaust and Genocide, 1983.

———. *How Can We Commit the Unthinkable? Genocide, the Human Cancer.* Boulder, Colo.: Westview Press, 1982.

———. "The Psychology of Denial of Known Genocides." In *Genocide: A Critical Bibliographic Review.* Vol. 2. Ed. Israel W. Charny. New York: Facts on File, 1991.

———., ed. *Genocide: A Critical Bibliographic Review.* New York: Facts on File, 1988–1991. 2 vols.

———., ed. *Toward the Understanding and Prevention of Genocide.* Boulder, Colo.: Westview Press, 1984.

Charny, Israel W., and Shamai Davidson, eds. *The Book of the International Conference on the Holocaust and Genocide*: Book 1: *The Conference Program and Crisis.* Tel Aviv: Institute of the International Conference on the Holocaust and Genocide, 1983.

Charny, Israel W., and Daphna Fromer. "A Follow-Up of the Sixty-Nine Scholars

Who Signed an Advertisement Questioning the Armenian Genocide." *Internet on the Holocaust and Genocide* no. 25/26 (April 1990).

Cohen, Richard. "Killing Truth," *Washington Post,* May 31, 1983.

Cohen-Adler, Ra'ya. "Franz Werfel's The Forty Days of Mussa Dag, as Investigative Literature." *State, Government and International Relations* 32 (Spring 1990).

Comité de l'oeuvre de secours 1915 aux Arméniens. *Quelques documents sur le sort des Arméniens en 1915–1916.* Geneva: Société Générale d'Imprimerie, 1916.

Committee on Armenian Atrocities. "October 4, 1915 Press Release." New York, 1915.

Cretan, Lawrence. "The Armenian Remnants in Turkey: 1918–1922." Seminar paper, University of California, Los Angeles, 1976.

Dadrian, Vahakn N. "Documentation of the Armenian Genocide in German and Austrian Sources." In *Genocide: A Critical Bibliographic Review,* vol. 2, ed. Israel W. Charny. New York: Facts on File, 1988–1991.

———. "Documentation of the Armenian Genocide in Turkish Sources." In Israel W. Charny and Shamai Davidson, eds. *The Book of the International Conference on the Holocaust and Genocide.* Vol. 2: *The Conference Program and Crisis.* Tel Aviv: Institute of the International Conference on the Holocaust and Genocide, 1983.

———. "The Documentation of the World War I Armenian Massacres in the Proceedings of the Turkish Military Tribunal." *International Journal of Middle East Studies* 23, no. 4 (November 1991).

———. "The Documentation of the World War I Armenian Massacres in the Proceedings of the Turkish Military Tribunal." *Journal of Political and Military Sociology* (*The Armenian Genocide in Official Turkish Records*) 22, no. 1 (Summer 1994).

———. "Genocide as a Problem of National and International Law: The World War I Armenian Case and Its Contemporary Legal Ramifications." *Yale Journal of Internationl Law* 14, no. 2 (Summer 1989). French trans. Marc and Mikaël Nichanian. *Autopsie du génocide arménien.* Brussels: Ed. Complexe, 1995.

———. *German Responsibility in the Armenian Genocide: A Review of the Historical Evidence of German Complicity.* Watertown, Mass.: Blue Crane Books, 1996.

———. *The History of the Armenian Genocide: Ethnic Conflict from the Balkans to Anatolia to the Caucasus.* Providence, R.I.: Berghahn Books, 1995.

———. "The Naim-Andonian Documents on the World War I Destruction of Ottoman Armenians: The Anatomy of a Genocide." *International Journal of Middle East Studies* 18 (1986).

———. "Ottoman Archives and Denial of the Armenian Genocide." In *The Armenian Genocide: History, Politics, Ethics,* ed. Richard G. Hovannisian. New York: St. Martin's Press, 1992.

———. "The Role of Turkish Physicians in the World War I Genocide of the Ottoman Armenians." *Holocaust and Genocide Studies* 1, no. 2 (1986).

———. "The Secret Young-Turk Ittihadist Conference and the Decision for the World War I Genocide of the Armenians." *Holocaust and Genocide Studies* 7, no. 2 (Fall 1993).

———. "A Textual Analysis of the Key Indictment of the Turkish Military Tribunal Investigating the Armenian Genocide." *Armenian Review* 44, no. 1 (Spring 1991), and *Journal of Political and Military Sociology* (*The Armenian Genocide in Official Turkish Records*) 22, no. 1 (Summer 1994).

Davidson, Khoren K. *Odyssey of an Armenian of Zeitoun.* New York: Vantage Press, 1985.

Davis, Leslie. *The Slaughterhouse Province: An American Diplomat's Report on the Armenian Genocide, 1915–1917.* New Rochelle, N.Y.: Aristide D. Caratzas, 1989.

Davison, Roderic H. "The Question of Fuad Paşa's 'Political Testament'." *Belleten* 23 (January 1959).

Dawidowicz, Lucy. *The Holocaust and the Historians.* Cambridge, Mass.: Harvard University Press, 1981.

De Nogales, Rafael. *Four Years Beneath the Crescent.* Trans. Muna Lee. New York: Scribner's Sons, 1926.

Deny, Jean. *Grammaire de la langue turque* (*dialecte osmanli*). 1921. Reprint, Wiesbaden: Dr. Martin Sandig, 1971.

Der-Vartanian, Hovsep. *Intilli-Airani Spande, 1916: Mut Mnatsats Ech Me Mets Eghernen* (The slaughter of Entilli-Airan 1916: A dark page remaining from the Great Catastrophe). Jerusalem: St. James Press, 1928.

Des Pres, Terrence. "On Governing Narratives: The Turkish-Armenian Case." *Yale Review* 75, no. 4 (October 1986).

———. "Introduction: Remembering Armenia." In *The Armenian Genocide in Perspective,* ed. Richard G. Hovannisian. New Brunswick, N.J.: Transaction Books, 1986.

Devereux, Georges. "L'identité ethnique: Ses bases logiques et ses dysfonctions." *Ethnopsychanalyse complémentariste.* Paris: Flammarion, 1985.

Dinkel, Christoph. "German Officers and the Armenian Genocide." *Armenian Review* 44, no. 1 (Spring 1991).

Dobkin, Marjorie Housepian. "What Genocide? What Holocaust? News from Turkey, 1915–1923: A Case Study." In *The Armenian Genocide in Perspective,* ed. Richard G. Hovannisian. New Brunswick, N.J.: Transaction Books, 1986.

Dror, Zvika. "Life with Kushmar." *Davar,* June 8, 1990.

Edib, Halidé. *The Turkish Ordeal.* New York: The Century Co., 1928.

Elmajian, Eflatoon E. *In the Shadow of the Almighty: My Life Story.* Pasadena, Calif.: N.p., 1982.

Emin, Ahmed. *Turkey in the World War.* New Haven: Yale University Press, 1930.

Erol, Mine. *Türkiye'de Amerikan Mandası Meselesi: 1919–1920* (The American mandate question in Turkey, 1919–1920). Giresun: İleri Basımevi, 1972.

Ezrahi, Sidra DeKoven. *By Words Alone: The Holocaust in Literature*. Chicago: University of Chicago Press, 1982.

Eyüboğlu, E. Kemal. *On Üçüncü Yüzyıldan Günümüze Kadar Şiirde ve Halk Dilinde Atasözleri ve Deyimler* (Proverbs and idioms in poetry and popular language from the thirteenth century until now). İstanbul: N.p., 1973–1975. 2 vols.

Fairclough, Norman. *Language and Power.* 1989. Reprint, New York: Longman, 1991.

Farley, J. Lewis. *Egypt, Cyprus and Asiatic Turkey.* London: Trubner and Co., 1878.

Faurisson, Robert. *Mémoire en défense: Contre ceux qui m'accusent de falsifier l'histoire: La question des chambres à gaz.* Paris: La Vieille Taupe, [1980].

———. *The "Problem of the Gas Chambers."* Rochelle Park, N.J.: The Revisionist Press, 1979.

Feldman, Gerald D. "Die Deutsche Bank vom Ersten Weltkrieg bis zur Weltwirtschaftskrise." In *Die Deutsche Bank 1870–1995,* ed. Lothar Gall et al. Munich: C. H. Beck Verlag, 1995.

Ferenczi, Thomas. "Un entretien avec Jean-Luc Nancy." *Le Monde,* March 29, 1994.

Findley, Carter V. *Bureaucratic Reform in the Ottoman Empire: The Sublime Porte, 1789–1922.* Princeton: Princeton University Press, 1980.

Fischer, Fritz. *Krieg der Illusionen: Die deutsche Politik von 1911–1914.* 2d ed. Düsseldorf: Droste Verlag, 1978.

Foley, Barbara. "Fact, Fiction, Fascism: Testimony and Mimesis in Holocaust Narrative." *Comparative Literature* 34, no. 4 (1982).

Foss, Clive. "The Turkish View of Armenian History: A Vanishing Nation." In *The Armenian Genocide: History, Politics, Ethics,* ed. Richard G. Hovannisian. New York: St. Martin's Press, 1992.

Fraschery, Samy-Bey. *Dictionnaire français-turc.* 2d rev. ed. Constantinople: Mihran, 1898.

Fraser, Angus. *The Gypsies.* 1992. Reprint, Oxford: Blackwell, 1993.

Gelber, Yoav. *Massada: The Defense of Eretz Israel in World War II.* Bar-Ilan: Bar-Ilan University, 1990.

Gelzer, Heinrich. *Geistliches und Weltliches aus dem türkisch-griechischen Orient.* Leipzig: B. G. Teubner, 1900.

Genç Kalemler 2, no. 8 (July 26, 1327 [1911]).

Georgeon, François. *Aux origines du nationalisme turc: Yusuf Akçura (1876–1935).* Paris: Editions ADPF, 1980.

Germany, Turkey and Armenia: A Selection of Documentary Evidence Relating to the Armenian Atrocities from German and Other Sources. London: J. J. Keliher and Co., 1917.

Gidney, James B. *A Mandate for Armenia.* Kent, Ohio: Kent State University Press, 1967.

Giesl, Baron Wladimir. *Zwei Jahrzehnte im Nahen Orient.* Berlin: Verlag für Kulturpolitik, 1927.

Gleich, Gerold von. *Vom Balkan nach Bagdad: Militärisch-politische Erinnerungen an den Orient.* Berlin: Scherl, 1921.

Gök Alp, Ziya. "İktisadî Vatanperverlik" (Economic patriotism). *Yeni Mecmua* 2, no. 43 (May 9, 1918).

———. *Kızıl Elma* (The red apple). İstanbul, 1330 [1914–15].

———. *Makaleler* (Articles). Vol. 2. Ed. Süleyman Hayri Bolay. Ankara: Başbakanlık Basımevı, 1982.

———. "Rusya'daki Türkler Ne Yapmalı?" (What ought the Turks of Russia to do?). *Yeni Mecmua* 2, no. 38 (June 4, 1918).

———. " 'Turan' Nedir?" (What is "Turan"?). *Yeni Mecmua* 2, no. 31 (February 8, 1918).

———. "Türkçülük Nedir?" (What is Turkism?). *Yeni Mecmua* 1, no. 25 (December 27, 1917).

———. "Türkleşmek, İslamlaşmak, Muasırlaşmak" (Turkification, Islamization, modernization). *Türk Yurdu* 1, no. 2 (7 Mart 1329 [1913]).

Gözler, H. Fathi. *Örnekleriyle Türkçemizin Açıklamalı Büyük Deyimler Sözlüğü* [A–Z] (Great dictionary of our Turkish idioms explained with examples). İstanbul: İnkılâp ve Aka Kitabevleri, 1975.

Great Britain. *Parliamentary Debates.* 5th series. London: His Majesty's Stationery Office, 1920–1923.

Grew, Joseph Clark. *Turbulent Era: A Diplomatic Record of Forty Years, 1904–1945.* Boston: Houghton Mifflin Co., 1921. 2 vols.

Grossman, Haike. *The People of the Underground.* Tel-Aviv: Sifriyat Poalim, 1965.

Guroian, Vigen. "The Politics and Morality of Genocide." In *The Armenian Genocide: History, Politics, Ethics,* ed. Richard G. Hovannisian. New York: St. Martin's Press, 1992.

Gürün, Kamuran. *The Armenian File: The Myth of Innocence Exposed.* Nicosia, Istanbul: K. Rustem and Brother, 1985.

Gutman, Yisrael. "The Denial of the Holocaust and Its Consequences." *Remembering for the Future.* Vol. 2. Oxford: Pergamon Press, 1988.

Haig, H. H. *The First Genocide.* New York: Vantage Press, 1967.

Haig, Kerest. *Dictionary of Turkish-English Proverbial Idioms.* Amsterdam: Philo Press, 1969.

Hairapetian, Armen. " 'Race Problems' and the Armenian Genocide: The State Department Files." *Armenian Review* 37, no. 1 (Spring 1984).

Hartunian, Abraham H. *Neither to Laugh nor to Weep: A Memoir of the Armenian Genocide.* Boston: Beacon Press, 1968. Reprint, Cambridge, Mass.: Armenian Heritage Press, 1986.

Hashian, Jack. *Mamigon.* New York: Coward, McCann and Geoghan, 1982.

Hayes, Peter. *Industry and Ideology: I. G. Farben in the Nazi Era.* New York: Cambridge University Press, 1987.

Heyd, Uriel. *Foundations of Turkish Nationalism: The Life and Teachings of Ziya Gökalp.* London: Luzac and Company and The Harvill Press, 1950.

Highgas, Dirouhi Kouymjian. *Refugee Girl.* Watertown, Mass.: Baikar Publications, 1985.

Hirsch, Herbert. "Nazi Education: A Case of Political Socialization." *Educational Forum* 53, no. 1 (1988).

Hobsbawm, Eric. "Faussaires du passé" (Forgers of the past). *Le Monde des Débats,* February 1994.

Hodge, Robert, and Gunther Kress. *Language as Ideology.* 2d ed. New York: Routledge, 1993.

Hofmann, Tessa, and Gerayer Koutcharian. "The History of Armenian-Kurdish Relations in the Ottoman Empire." *Armenian Review* 33, no. 4 (Winter 1986).

———. " 'Images That Horrify and Indict': Pictorial Documents on the Persecution and Extermination of the Armenians from 1877 to 1922." *Armenian Review* 45, nos. 1–2 (Spring/Summer 1992).

Hony, H. C. *A Turkish-English Dictionary.* 2d ed. Oxford: Clarendon Press, 1980.

Housepian, Marjorie. *Smyrna 1922: The Destruction of a City.* London: Faber and Faber, 1972.

Hovannisian, Richard G. "The Armenian Diaspora and the Narrative of Power." In *Diasporas in World Politics,* ed. Dimitri C. Constas and Athanassios G. Platias. London: MacMillan, 1993.

———. "The Armenian Genocide and Patterns of Denial." In *The Armenian Genocide in Perspective,* ed. Richard G. Hovannisian. New Brunswick, N.J.: Transaction Books, 1986.

———. *The Armenian Holocaust: A Bibliography Relating to the Deportations, Massacres, and the Dispersion of the Armenian People, 1915–1923.* 2d ed. Cambridge, Mass.: Armenian Heritage Press, 1980.

———. "The Historical Dimensions of the Armenian Question, 1878–1923." In *The Armenian Genocide in Perspective,* ed. Richard G. Hovannisian. New Brunswick, N.J.: Transaction Books, 1986.

———. *The Republic of Armenia.* Berkeley: University of California Press, 1971–1996. 4 vols.

İnönü, İsmet. *Hatıralar* (Memoirs) Vol. 2. Ankara: Bilgi Yayınevi, 1987.

Institut für Armenische Fragen. *The Armenian Genocide: Documentation.* Vol. 2. Munich: Institut für Armenische Fragen, 1988.

Institute of Turkish Studies. *Report of the Institute of Turkish Studies, Inc.,1982–1992.* Washington, D.C.: Institute of Turkish Studies Inc., 1992.

Irving, David. *Hitler's War.* New York: The Viking Press, 1977.

Jäckh, Ernst. *Der aufsteigende Halbmond: Beiträge zur türkischen Renaissance.* Berlin: Buchverlag der "Hilfe," 1911.

Jernazian, Ephraim K. *Judgment unto Truth: Witnessing the Armenian Genocide.* New Brunswick, N. J.: Transaction Books, 1990.

Jungk, Peter Stephan. *Franz Werfel: Une vie de Prague à Hollywood.* Paris: Albin Michel, 1990.

Kadri, Hüseyin Kâzim. *Türk Lûgati* (Turkish dictionary). Vol. 4. İstanbul: Cumhuriyet Matbaası, 1945.

Karal, Enver Zia. *Armenian Question (1878–1923).* Ankara: Imprimerie Gündüz, 1975.

Kater, Michael H. *Doctors under Hitler.* Chapel Hill: University of North Carolina Press, 1989.

Katz, Steven T. *The Holocaust in Historical Context.* Vol. I: *The Holocaust and Mass Death before the Modern Age.* New York: Oxford University Press, 1994.

Katznelson, Yitzhak. *Last Writings, 1940–1944.* New ed. Beit Lohamei Hagettoat: Hakkibutz Hameu'had, 1956.

Keeling, Edward Herbert. *Adventures in Turkey and Russia.* London: John Murray, 1924.

Kenaan, Haviv. *200 Days of Fear.* Tel-Aviv: Mol-Art Publisher, n.d.

Kerr, Stanley. *The Lions of Marash: Personal Experiences with American Near East Relief, 1919–1922.* Albany: State University of New York Press, 1973.

Kévorkian, Raymond H. "Recueil de témoignages sur l'extermination des amele tabouri ou bataillons de soldats-ouvriers arméniens de l'armée ottomane." *Revue d'histoire arménienne contemporaine* 1 (1995).

Kiesling, Hans von. *Orientfahrten: Zwischen Ägeis und Zagros: Erlebtes und Erschautes aus schwerer Zeit.* Leipzig: Dieterich'sche Verlagsbuchhandlung, 1921.

Kiliç, Altemur. *Turkey and the World.* Washington, D.C.: Public Affairs Press, 1959.

Kimhi, Dov. *Massot Ketanot.* Jerusalem: Reuven Mass., 1938.

Kloian, Richard, comp. *The Armenian Genocide: News Accounts from the American Press.* Berkeley: Anto Press, 1985.

Körte, Alfred. *Anatolische Skizzen.* Berlin: Julius Springer, 1896.

Kressenstein, Friedrich Freiherr Kress von. *Mit den Türken zum Suezkanal.* Berlin: Vorhut Verlag Otto Schlegel, 1938.

Kulka, Erich. "Denial of the Holocaust." In *Genocide: A Critical Bibliographic Review.* Vol. 2. Ed. Israel W. Charny. New York: Facts on File, 1991.

Künzler, Jacob. *Im Lande des Blutes und der Tränen: Erlebnisse in Mesopotamien während des Weltkrieges.* Potsdam: Tempelverlag, 1921.

Kuper, Leo. *Genocide: Its Political Use in the Twentieth Century.* New Haven: Yale University Press, 1981.

———. *The Pity of It All: Polarisation of Racial and Ethnic Relations.* Minneapolis: University of Minnesota Press, 1977.

———. "Problems in Education on Genocide." *Internet on the Holocaust and Genocide* 14 (February 1988).

Kushner, David. *The Rise of Turkish Nationalism, 1876–1908.* London: Frank Cass, 1977.

Lacoue-Labarthe, Philippe. *La fiction du politique.* Paris: Christian Bourgeois, 1987.

———. *Heidegger, Art and Politics.* Trans. Chris Turner. Cambridge, Mass.: Basil Blackwell, 1990.

Landau, Jacob M. "Munis Tekinalp's Economic Views Regarding the Ottoman Empire and Turkey." In *Osmanistische Studien zur Wirtschafts- und Sozialgeschichte: In Memoriam Vančo Boškov,* ed. Hans Georg Majer. Wiesbaden: Otto Harrassowitz, 1986.

———. *Pan-Turkism in Turkey: A Study of Irredentism.* Hamden, Conn.: Archon Books, 1981.

———. *Tekinalp, Turkish Patriot, 1883–1961.* Istanbul: Nederlands Historisch-Archeologisch Instituut, 1984.

Langer, Lawrence. *The Holocaust and the Literary Imagination.* New Haven: Yale University Press, 1975.

———., ed. *Art from the Ashes: A Holocaust Anthology.* New York: Oxford University Press, 1995.

Laughlin, H. P. *The Ego and Its Defenses.* 2d ed. New York: Jason Aronson, 1979.

Lepsius, Johannes. *Le Rapport secret sur les massacres d'Arménie.* 1916. Reprint, Beirut: Hamaskaine, 1968.

———., ed. *Deutschland und Armenien 1914–1918: Sammlung diplomatischer Aktenstücke.* Potsdam: Tempelverlag, 1919. Reprint, Bremen: Donat and Temmen Verlag, 1986.

Leverkuehn, Paul. *Posten auf ewiger Wache: Aus dem abenteuerlichen Leben des Max von Scheubner-Richter.* Essen: Essener Verlagsanstalt, 1938.

Lewis, Bernard. *The Emergence of Modern Turkey.* Oxford: Oxford University Press, 1961.

———. *Islam et Laïcité: La naissance de la Turquie moderne.* Paris: Fayard, 1988.

Lifton, Robert J. *Boundaries.* Toronto: CBC Publications, 1969.

———. *The Nazi Doctors: Medical Killing and the Psychology of Genocide.* New York: Basic Books, 1986.

Lipstadt, Deborah E. "Deniers, Relativists, and Pseudo-Scholarship." *Dimensions* 6, no. 1 (1991).

———. *Denying the Holocaust: The Growing Assault on Truth and Memory.* New York: The Free Press, and Toronto: Maxwell MacMillan, 1993.

———. "The Evolution of American Holocaust Revisionism." In *Remembering for the Future: The Impact of the Holocaust and Genocide on Jews and Christians.* Supplementary Volume. Oxford: Pergamon Press, 1988.

Lochner, Louis P. *What about Germany?* New York: Dodd, Mead and Co., 1942.

Loraux, Patrice. "Consentir." *Le Genre humain* (1990).

Lowry, Heath W. *The Story Behind Ambassador Morgenthau's Story.* Istanbul: The Isis Press, 1990.

———. "The U.S. Congress and Adolf Hitler on the Armenians." *Political Communication and Persuasion* 3, no. 2 (1985).

Lyotard, Jean-François. *Le Différend.* Paris: Editions de Minuit, 1983.

———. "Discussions or Phrasing 'after Auschwitz'." In *The Lyotard Reader,* ed. Andrew Benjamin. Cambridge, Mass.: Basil Blackwell, 1989.

———. "Discussions, ou phraser après Auschwitz." In J. L. Nancy and P. Lacoue-Labarthe, eds. *Les Fins de l'homme, à partir du travail de Jacques Derrida.* Paris: Galilée, 1981.

———. *Peregrinations: Law, Form, Event.* New York: Columbia University Press, 1988.

McCarthy, Justin, and Carolyn McCarthy. *Turks and Armenians: A Manual on the Armenian Question.* Washington, D.C.: Assembly of Turkish American Associations, 1989.

MacColl, Malcolm. "The Constantinople Massacre and Its Lesson." *Contemporary Review* (November 1895).

Malade, Theo. *Von Amiens bis Aleppo: Ein Beitrag zur Seelenkunde des grossen Krieges: Aus dem Tagebuch eines Feldarztes.* Munich: Lehmann, 1930.

Mandelstam, André N. *Confiscation des biens des réfugiés arméniens par le gouvernement turc.* Paris: Imp. Massis, 1929.

Marashlian, Levon. "Economic and Moral Influences on U.S. Policies toward Turkey and the Armenians, 1919–1923." *11. Türk Tarih Kongresi: Kongreye Sunulan Bildiriler.* Vol. 5. Ankara: Türk Tarih Kurumu Basımevi, 1994.

———. "The London and San Remo Conferences and the Armenian Settlement: The Belated Decisions, February–April, 1920." *Armenian Review* 30, no. 3 (Autumn 1977); no. 4 (Winter 1977–78).

———. "The Status of Armenian Oral History." *Society for Armenian Studies Bulletin* 5 (Spring 1980).

Margosian, Bedros. *Of Desert Bondage.* Boston: The Van Press, 1940.

Markusen, Eric. "Professions, Professionals, and Genocide." In *Genocide: A Critical Bibliographic Review,* ed. Israel W. Charny, 264–98. New York: Facts on File, 1988–1992.

Marrus, Michael R. *The Holocaust in History.* Hanover, N.H.: University Press of New England, 1987.

Martin, Ramela. *Out of Darkness.* Cambridge, Mass.: The Zoryan Institute, 1989.

Masis, Antranik. *The Question of the American Mandate over Armenia.* Nicosia: Proodos Ltd., 1980.

Melson, Robert. *Revolution and Genocide: On the Origins of the Armenian Genocide and the Holocaust.* Chicago: University of Chicago Press, 1992.

Messerlian, Zaven. "Turkio Nerkin Gavarneru Hayots Partadir Artagaghte, 1929–1930" (The forced exodus of the Armenians of the interior provinces of Turkey). *Haykazian Hayagitakan Handes* 3 (1972).

Miles, Robert. *Racism.* Key Ideas series. London: Routledge, 1989.

Miller, Donald E., and Lorna Touryan Miller. *Survivors: An Oral History of the Armenian Genocide.* Berkeley: University of California Press, 1993.

Minasian, Edward. "Musa Dagh: The Film That Was Denied." *Journal of Armenian Studies* 1, no. 2 (Fall/Winter 1985–86).

Molinié, Georges. *Dictionnaire de rhétorique.* Paris: Le livre de poche, 1992.

Moran, A. Vahid. *Türkçe-İngilizce Sözlük* (Turkish-English dictionary). 1945. Reprint, İstanbul: Millî Eğitim Basımevi, 1971.

Morgenthau, Henry. *Ambassador Morgenthau's Story.* Garden City, N.Y.: Doubleday, Page, 1918. Reprint, Plandome, N.Y.: New Age Publishers, 1975.

Moranian, Suzanne Elizabeth. "The American Missionaries and the Armenian Question: 1915–1927." Ph.D. diss., University of Wisconsin, Madison, 1994.

Mühlens, Peter. "Vier Jahre Kriegshygiene in der Türkei und auf dem Balkan." *Vor 20 Jahren* 2. Folge (1935).

Mühlmann, Carl. *Das deutsch-türkische Waffenbündnis im Weltkrieg.* Leipzig: Köhler and Amelang, 1940.

Muller, Ingo. *Hitler's Justice: The Courts of the Third Reich.* Trans. Deborah Lucas Schneider. Cambridge, Mass.: Harvard University Press, 1991.

Muller-Hill, Benno. *Murderous Science: Elimination by Scientific Selection of Jews, Gypsies, and Others, Germany 1933–1945.* London: Croom Helm, 1988.

The Myth of the Six Million. Los Angeles: Noontide Press, 1969.

Nassibian, Akaby. *Britain and the Armenian Question, 1915–1923.* New York: St. Martin's Press, 1984.

Near East Relief. *Reports to the Congress of the United States, 1920–1925.* New York, 1921–26.

Nichanian, Marc. "L'Ecrit et le mutisme: Introduction à la littérature arménienne moderne." *Temps Modernes* 504–6 (September 1988).

———. "L'Empire du sacrifice." *L'Intranquille* no. 1 (1992).

———. "Hagop Ochagan tel qu'en lui-même." *Dissonanze* 1 (1983).

———. "The Style of Violence." *Armenian Review* 38, no. 1 (Spring 1985).

Niepage, Martin. *Ein Wort an die berufenen Vertreter des deutschen Volkes: Eindrücke eines deutschen Oberlehrers aus der Türkei.* Berlin: Als Manuskript gedruckt, n.d. [1916].

Noradoungian, Gabriel. "Antip Husher: Gabriel Efendi Noradoungiani, Nakhkin Osmanian Artakin Gordsots Nakharar" (Unpublished memoirs: Gabriel Effendi Noradoungian, former Ottoman minister of foreign affairs). *Baikar* (June 17, 1952).

Nur, Riza. *Hayat ve Hatıratım* (Life and my memoirs). Vol. 3. İstanbul: Altındağ Yayınevi, 1968.

Ohandjanian, Artem. *Armenien: Der verschwiegene Völkermord.* Vienna: Böhlau Verlag, 1989.

Öke, Mim Kemal. *The Armenian Question, 1914–1923.* Nicosia: K. Rustem and Brother, 1988.

Orel, Şinasi, and Süreyya Yuca. *The Talât Pasha Telegrams: Historical Fact or Armenian Fiction?* Nicosia: K. Rustem and Brother, 1986.

Oshagan, Hagop. *Hamapatker Arevmtahay Grakanutian* (Panorama of Western-Armenian literature). 10 vols. Jerusalem: St. James Press, and Antelias: Catholicosate of Cilicia Press, 1945–1982.

———. *Spiurke ev Irav Banasteghtsutiune* (Diaspora and the true poetry). Jerusalem: St. James Press, 1945.

———. *Mitk ev Sirt* (Spirit and heart). *Sion* (1948).

———. *Vkayutiun Me* (A testimony). Aleppo: Nayiri Press, 1946.

Özdemir, Mehmet. "Birinci Dünya Savaşı'nda Demiryollarının Kullanımı ve Bunun Savaşın Sonucuna Etkisi" (The use of railroads in World War I and its effect on the outcome of the war). *Dördüncü Askeri Tarih Semineri.* Ankara: Genelkurmay Basımevi, 1989.

Özön, Mustafa Nihat. *Ata Sözleri* (Proverbs). İstanbul: İnkilâp Kitabevi, 1956.

Paksoy, H. B. *Central Asian Reader: The Rediscovery of History.* Armonk, N.Y.: M. E. Sharpe, 1994.

Parla, Taha. *The Social and Political Thought of Ziya Gökalp 1876–1924.* Leiden: E. J. Brill, 1985.

Permanent People's Tribunal. *A Crime of Silence: The Armenian Genocide.* London: Zed Books, 1985.

Peroomian, Rubina. *Literary Responses to Catastrophe: A Comparison of the Armenian and the Jewish Experience.* Atlanta: Scholars Press, 1993.

Piralian, Hélène. *Génocide et transmission.* Paris: Éditions l'Harmattan, 1995.

Pomiankowski, Joseph. *Der Zusammenbruch des Ottomanischen Reiches: Erinnerungen an die Türkei aus der Zeit des Weltkrieges.* Vienna: Amalthea Verlag, 1928. Reprint, Graz: Akademische Druck- u. Verlagsanstalt, 1969.

Porter, Carlos Whitlock, ed. *Made in Russia: The Holocaust.* N.p.: Historical Review Press, 1988.

Proctor, Robert. *Racial Hygiene: Medicine under the Nazis.* Cambridge, Mass.: Harvard University Press, 1988.

Raith, Oberstltn. a.D. "Deutschtum in Persien." *Mitteilungen des Bundes der Asienkämpfer* 11 (1929).

Rassinier, Paul. *Debunking the Genocide Myth: A Study of the Nazi Concentration Camps and the Alleged Extermination of European Jewry.* Torrance, Calif.: Institute for Historical Review, 1978.

———. *The Real Eichmann Trial: Or the Incorrigible Victors.* Chapel Ascote, U.K.: Historical Review Press, 1979.

Redhouse, James W. *A Turkish and English Lexicon.* 1890. Reprint, Beirut: Librairie du Liban, 1974.

Redhouse Çağdaş Türkçe-İngilizce Sözlüğü (Redhouse contemporary Turkish-English dictionary). İstanbul: Redhouse Yayınevi, 1983.

Redhouse Yeni Türkçe-Ingilizce Sözlük (New Redhouse Turkish-English dictionary). 2d ed. İstanbul: Redhouse Yayınevi, 1974.

Refik, Ahmet (Altınay). *İki Komite, İki Kıtâl* (Two committees, two massacres). Ed. Hamide Koyukan. Ankara: Kebikeç Yayınları, 1994.

Remmling, Gunter W. "Discrimination, Persecution, Theft, and Murder under Color of Law: The Totalitarian Corruption of the German Legal System, 1933–1945." In *Genocide and the Modern Age: Etiology and Case Studies of Mass*

Death, ed. Isidor Wallimann and Michael N. Dobkowski. Westport, Conn.: Greenwood Press, 1987.

Rex, John. *Race Relations in Sociological Theory.* 2d ed. London: Routledge and Kegan Paul, 1987.

Rex, John, and David Mason, eds. *Theories of Race and Ethnic Relations.* 2d ed. Cambridge: Cambridge University Press, 1990.

Robert, Marthe. "Les Génocides ou la dernière trouvaille d'un révisionnisme plus subtil." *Passages* (April–May 1995).

Rodenwaldt, Ernst. *Seuchenkämpfe: Bericht des beratenden Hygienikers der V. kaiserlich-osmanischen Armee.* Heidelberg: Carl Winter Verlag, 1921.

Rosenfeld, Alvin. *A Double Dying: Reflections on Holocaust Literature.* 2d ed. Bloomington: Indiana University Press, 1988.

Rutland, Peter. "Democracy and Nationalism in Armenia." *Europe-Asia Studies* 46, no. 5 (September 1994).

Sahakian, Ruben G. *Turk-Fransiakan Haraberutiunnere ev Kilikian 1919–1921* (Turkish-French relations and Cilicia, 1919–1921). Erevan: Gitutiunneri Akademia, 1970.

Sami, Şemseddin. *Kâmûs-i Türkî* (The Turkish dictionary). 1899. Reprint, Beirut: Librairie du Liban, 1989.

Şapolyo, Enver Behnan. *Ziya Gökalp: İttihat ve Terakki ve Meşrutiyet Tarihi* (Ziya Gökalp: Union and Progress and the history of the constitutional period). İstanbul: Güven Basımevi, 1943.

Sarafian, Ara. "The Paper Trail: The American State Department and the Report of Committee on Armenian Atrocities." *Revue du Monde Arménien* 1 (1994).

———., comp. *United States Official Documents on the Armenian Genocide.* Vols. 1–3. Watertown, Mass: Armenian Review, 1993–1996.

Sarid, Levy Aryeh. "The Fighting Jewish Underground in Byalistok." *Moreshet* no. 55 (October 1993).

Saupp, Norbert. "Das Deutsche Reich und die Armenische Frage 1878–1914." Ph.D. diss., Cologne, 1990.

Schilling, Viktor. *Kriegshygienische Erfahrungen in der Türkei (Cilicien, Nordsyrien).* Leipzig: J. A. Barth, 1921.

———. "Über die schwere cilicische Malaria." *Archiv für Schiffs- und Tropen-Hygiene* 23 (1919).

Schröder, Christoph. "Die armenischen Greuel." *Berliner Stadt Anzeiger,* September 25, 1919.

Schutz, Alfred. *The Phenomenology of the Social World.* Evanston, Ill.: Northwestern University Press, 1967.

Seydi, Ali, Ali Reşad, Mehmed İzzet, and L. Feuillet, eds. *Musavver Dâiret ül-Maârif* (Illustrated encyclopedia). Vol. 1. Dersaadet [İstanbul]: Kanaat, 1332/1913.

Shahmuratian, Samuel, ed. *The Sumgait Tragedy: Pogroms against Armenians in Soviet Azerbaijan,* Vol. 1: *Eyewitness Accounts.* New Rochelle, N.Y.: Aristide D. Caratzas and Zoryan Institute, 1990.

Shahnur, Shahan. *Nahanje Arants Ergi* (Retreat without song). 4th ed. Beirut: Sevan Press, 1981.

Shavit, David. *Hunger for the Printed Word.* Jefferson: McFarland, 1997.

Shaw, Stanford. *Turkey and the Holocaust: Turkey's Role in Rescuing Turkish and European Jewry from Nazi Persecution, 1933–1945.* New York: New York University Press, 1993.

Shaw, Stanford J., and Ezel Kural Shaw, *History of the Ottoman Empire and Modern Turkey.* Vol. 2. *Reform, Revolution, and Republic: The Rise of Modern Turkey, 1808–1975.* New York: Cambridge University Press, 1977.

Şinasi, İbrahim. *Durûb-ı Emsâl-i Osmaniyye* (Ottoman proverbs). 3d ed. Dersaadet [İstanbul]: Matbaa-i Ebüzziya, 1302/1886–87.

Smith, Roger W. "The Armenian Genocide: Memory, Politics, and the Future." In *The Armenian Genocide: History, Politics, Ethics,* ed. Richard G. Hovannisian. New York: St. Martin's Press, 1992.

———. "Denial of the Armenian Genocide." In *Genocide: A Critical Bibliographic Review.* Vol. 2. Ed. Israel W. Charny. New York: Facts on File, 1991.

———. "Genocide and Denial: The Armenian Case and Its Implications." *Armenian Review* 42, no. 1 (Spring 1989).

Sommer, Ernst. *Die Wahrheit über die Leiden des armenischen Volkes in der Türkei während des Weltkriegs.* Frankfurt a.M.: Verlag Orient, 1919.

Sonyel, Salahi R. *Minorities and the Destruction of the Ottoman Empire.* Turkish Historical Society, vol. 7, no. 129. Ankara: Turkish Historical Society Printing House, 1993.

———. "Turco-Armenian Relations and British Propaganda during the First World War." *Belleten* 58 (August 1994).

———. *Turkish Diplomacy from Mudros to Lausanne, 1918–1923: Mustafa Kemal and the Turkish National Movement.* London: Sage Publications, 1975.

Still, John A. *A Prisoner in Turkey.* London: John Lane and Co., 1920.

Tableau approximatif des réparations et indemnités pour les dommages subis par la nation arménienne en Arménie de Turquie et dans la République Arménienne du Caucase. Paris: Imp. P. Dupont, 1919.

Taft, Elise Hagopian. *Rebirth.* Plandome, N.Y.: New Age Publishers, 1981.

[Talaat]. "Posthumous Memoirs of Talaat Pasha." *Current History* 15 (November 1921).

Tannenbaum-Tamaroff, Mordechai. *Pages from Fire.* Rev. ed. Jerusalem: Yad Vashem and Beit Lohamei Hagettaot, 1984.

Tashian, B. *Mairineru Shukin Tak: Grakan Zruits H. Oshakani Het* (In the shade of the cedars: A literary discussion with H. Oshagan). Beirut: Altapress, 1983.

Taylor, Telford. "The Legal Profession." In *The Holocaust: Ideology, Bureaucracy, and Genocide,* ed. Henry Friedlander and Sybil Milton. Millwood, N.Y.: Kraus International Publications, 1980.

Teodik. *Amenun Taretsuitse* (Everyone's almanac). Constantinople: K. Keshishian, 1920.

Ternon, Yves. *Enquête sur la négation d'un génocide.* Marseilles: Parenthèses, 1989.

———. *L'État criminel: Les génocides au XXe siècle.* Paris: Ed. du Seuil, 1995.

Thomas, Lewis V., and Richard N. Frye. *The United States and Turkey and Iran.* Cambridge, Mass.: Harvard University Press, 1951.

Toprak, Zafer. "İslam ve İktisat: 1913–1914 Müslüman Boykotajı" (Islam and the economy: The Muslim boycott of 1913–1914). *Toplum ve Bilim* no. 29/30 (Spring–Summer 1985).

———. "II. Meşrutiyet'te Solidarist Düşünce: Halkçılık" (Solidarist thought in the second constitutional period: Populism). *Toplum ve Bilim* 1 (Spring 1977).

———. *Millî İktisat—Milli Burjuvazi* (National economy—national bourgeoisie). İstanbul: Tarih Vakfı Yurt Yayınları, 1995.

———. "Türkiye'de Korporatizmin Doğuşu" (The birth of corporatism in Turkey). *Toplum ve Bilim* 12 (Winter 1980).

———. *Türkiye'de "Millî İktisat," 1908–1918* ("National economy" in Turkey, 1908–1918). Ankara: Yurt Yayınları A. Ş., 1982.

Toynbee, Arnold J. *Armenian Atrocities: The Murder of a Nation, With a Speech Delivered by Lord Bryce in the House of Lords.* London: Hodder and Stoughton, 1915.

———., ed. *Key to Names of Persons and Places Withheld from Publication in the Original Edition of "The Treatment of Armenians in the Ottoman Empire, 1915–16: Documents Presented to Viscount Grey of Fallodon by Viscount Bryce."* Miscellaneous no. 31, 1916. London, 1916.

———., ed. *The Treatment of Armenians in the Ottoman Empire, 1915–16: Documents Presented to Viscount Grey of Fallodon, Secretary of State for Foreign Affairs.* London: Sir Joseph Causton and Sons, 1916. Reprint, Astoria, N.Y.: J. C. and L. Fawcett, 1990.

"Treaty of Peace between the British Empire and Allied Powers . . . and Turkey, Sèvres, August 10, 1920." In *British and Foreign State Papers.* Vol. 113: *1920.* Ed. Edward Parkes et al. London: His Majesty's Stationery Office, 1923.

Trumpener, Ulrich. *Germany and the Ottoman Empire, 1914–1918.* Princeton: Princeton University Press, 1968. Reprint: Delmar, N.Y.: Caravan Press, 1989.

Tülbentçi, Feridun Fazıl. *Türk Atasözleri ve Deyimleri* (Turkish proverbs and sayings). İstanbul: İnkilâp ve Aka Kitabevleri, 1963.

Tunaya, Tarık Zafer. *Türkiye'de Siyasal Partiler,* vol. 3: *İttihat ve Terakki: Bir Çağın, Bir Kuşağın, Bir Partinin Tarihi* (Political parties in Turkey, vol. 3: Union and Progress: The history of a period, a generation, a party). İstanbul: Hürriyet Vakfı Yayınları, 1989.

Türk Dil Kurumu, comp. *Bölge Ağızlarında Atasözleri ve Deyimler* (Proverbs and idioms in regional dialects), with introduction by Ömer Asım Aksoy. Ankara: Ankara Üniversitesi Basımevi, 1969.

Turkey, Foreign Policy Institute. *The Armenian Issue in Nine Questions and Answers.* Ankara: Foreign Policy Institute, 1982.

Turkey, Prime Ministry. Directorate General of Press and Information. *Documents,* Vol. 1 Ankara: Başarı Matbaacılık Sanayii, 1983.

Turkey, Prime Ministry. *Armenian Atrocities in the Caucasus and Anatolia According to Archival Documents.* Ankara: Prime Ministry State Archives, 1995.

Türkiye Cumhuriyeti, Başbakanlık Devlet Arşivleri Genel Müdürlüğü. *Osmanlı Belgelerinde Ermeniler (1915–1920)* (The Armenians in Ottoman documents, [1915–1920]). Ankara: Başbakanlık Basımevi, 1994.

United Nations. *Convention on the Prevention and Punishment of the Crime of Genocide,* December 9, 1948.

United Nations. Sub-Commission on the Prevention of Discrimination and the Protection of Minorities. *Revised and Updated Report on the Question of the Prevention and Punishment of the Crime of Genocide.* Prepared by Benjamin Whitaker. U.N. Document E/CN.4/Sub.2/1985/6, July 2, 1985.

United States, Congress. *Congressional Record,* 128, 97th Congress, 2d sess. Washington, D.C.: GPO, 1982.

United States, Department of State. *Papers Relating to the Foreign Relations of the United States, 1915, Supplement, The World War.* Washington, D.C.: GPO, 1928.

Vefik Paşa, Ahmed. *Müntahabât-ı Durûb-ı Emsal* (Anthology of proverbs). [İstanbul]: N.p., [1871].

Verdier, Raymond, Emmanuel Decaux, and Jean-Pierre Chrétien, eds. *Rwanda: Un génocide du XXe siècle.* Paris: Ed. l'Harmattan, 1996.

Vidal-Naquet, Pierre. *Assassins of Memory: Essays on the Denial of the Holocaust.* New York: Columbia University Press, 1992.

———. *Les Assassins de la mémoire.* Paris: La Découverte, 1987.

Vryonis, Speros, Jr. *The Turkish State and History: Clio Meets the Grey Wolf.* 2d ed. Thessaloniki and New Rochelle, N.Y.: Institute for Balkan Studies and Aristide D. Caratzas, 1993.

Wajsbort, Inka. *Together and Yet Alone in the Face of the Terror.* Tel-Aviv: Moreshet, with Beit Lohamei Hagettaot, 1992.

Walker, Christopher J. *Armenia: The Survival of a Nation.* New York: St. Martin's Press, 1980.

Wallimann, Isidor, and Michael N. Dobkowski, eds. *Genocide and the Modern Age.* Westport, Conn.: Greenwood Press, 1987.

Weber, Frank G. *Eagles on the Crescent: Germany, Austria, and the Diplomacy of the Turkish Alliance, 1914–1918.* Ithaca, N.Y.: Cornell University Press, 1970.

Wegner, Armin T. *Der Weg ohne Heimkehr: Ein Martyrium in Briefen.* Berlin: Fleischel and Co., 1919.

Wehr, Hans. *A Dictionary of Modern Written Arabic.* Ed. J. M. Cowan. 3d rev. ed. Ithaca, N.Y.: Spoken Language Services, 1976.

Weinreich, Max. *Hitler's Professors: The Part of Scholarship in Germany's Crimes against the Jewish People.* New York: YIVO Institute for Jewish Research, 1946.

Weisgal, Meyer. *Ad Kan* (So far). Jerusalem: Weidenfeld and Nicholson, Ma'ariv Library Publishing Press, 1971.

Werfel, Franz. *The Forty Days of Musa Dagh.* New York: The Modern Library, 1934.

White, Hayden. *Tropics of Discourse: Essays in Cultural Criticism.* Baltimore: Johns Hopkins University Press, 1978.

Wiesel, Elie. "Understanding Eyes." *Hadassah Magazine,* March 1987.

Wilson, William J. *Power, Racism, and Privilege: Race Relations in Theoretical and Sociohistorical Perspectives.* New York: The Free Press, 1973.

Winter, Jay. "Les Massacres des Arménies." *Le Monde,* August 3, 1994.

Woodward, W. L., and Rohan Butler, eds. *Documents on British Foreign Policy 1919–1939,* first series, 17. London: Her Majesty's Stationery Office, 1970.

Young, James E. *Writing and Rewriting the Holocaust: Narrative and the Consequences of Interpretation.* Bloomington: Indiana University Press, 1988.

Yurtbaşı, Metin. *A Dictionary of Turkish Proverbs.* Ankara: Turkish Daily News, 1993.

Zarevand (Zaven and Nartouhie Nalbandian). *United and Independent Turania: Aims and Designs of the Turks.* Trans. Vahakn N. Dadrian. Leiden: E. J. Brill, 1971.

Zaven, Archbishop [Eghiayan]. *Patriarkakan Hushers, Vaveragirner u Vkayutiunner* (Patriarchal memoirs, documents, and testimonies). Cairo: Nor Astgh, 1947.

Ziya Paşa. *Zafernâme Şerhi* (Commentary on the epic of victory). İstanbul: 1289/1872–73.

Zürcher, Erik J. *Turkey: A Modern History.* New York: I. B. Tauris, 1994.

Index

Abandoned Properties Law, 115–16, 118, 119
Abdülhamid II, Sultan, 27–28
Adana, 55, 76, 78, 81, 89, 90, 123, 124, 125
Adil, Hadji, 125
aggregation, 40
Aghayef, Ahmed, 45n. 41
Aghopian, Senator, 117
Aharonian, Avetis, 116
Ahmed Jevdet Pasha, 26
Ahmed Riza, 116
Ahmed Vefik Pasha, 44n. 31, 48n. 71
Aintab, 111n. 102, 123, 137
Akchura, Yusuf, 31–32, 37
Aleppo, 41, 65n. 39, 68, 76, 78, 92, 136, 137, 257
Alexander, Edward, 178
Alexandropol, 130
Ali Pasha, Grand Vizier, 26, 28
Amanus Mountains, 72, 78, 87, 90, 91, 92, 93, 94, 100n. 29
American Board of Commissioners for Foreign Missions (ABCFM), 53, 54
American Committee for Armenian and Syrian Relief (ACASR), 54, 58
American Embassy, pro-Turkish atmosphere at, 131
American Near East Relief (NER), 120, 122, 135
American observers, evidence from, 129
amir, 28, 42n. 13
amira class, 26
Andonian, Aram, 100n. 29, 108n. 78, 175, 177, 178, 257, 268n. 21
Angora, 80, 119, 120, 130, 134, 138; government of, 122, 125, 126, 128, 131
  Turkish Nationalists in, 113
Anne Frank's diary, 178
annihilation, completed by denial or banishment of memory, 202, 230, 286, 289
antisemitism, 201, 227, 287. *See also* Holocaust
  history of, 263
Apélian, Albert S., 168
apologists. *See* deniers
Apostolic Armenians, 116
App, Austin, 212
Arabs, 38, 91, 101n. 34, 128
Arendt, Hannah, 252, 266n. 12, 268n. 18, 288
Armenian captives, recovery of, 120–22
"Armenian destiny," 151–53
Armenian Genocide
  avoiding discussion of, 16. *See also* censorship; Turkish government
  compared with other massacres, 20, 197–99. *See also* Holocaust
  description of, 272–73
  finishing, on road to Lausanne, 135–38
  revival of interest in, 16
  sources of evidence regarding, 51–65, 165–73, 246
Armenian Mixed Council, 117
Armenian National Assembly, 116
Armenian National Delegation, 116, 117
Armenian National Home, 137

Armenian Revolutionary Federation (ARF), 56
Armenian workers. *See* Baghdad Railway
Armenians. *See also* Christians; non-Muslims
collective image of
economic superiority, 39
greed, 31
as liberal, 36
symbol of Western modernity and exploitation, 31, 39
vicious and cunning, 39
hated because of their craftiness and commercial talent, 30
as overstepping boundaries of their position, 27, 30
reformist and decentalizing aspirations of, 36
assimilation, goal of, 14
Astourian, Stephan, 19
Auschwitz, 178, 181, 213, 252, 267n. 13
Avni Bey, Col., 89

Baghche, 79, 111n. 102
Baghdad Railway, 19, 69, 76–78, 92–96
construction works in Amanus Mountains, 86–88, 92
decision on deportation and company's reaction, 82–86
deportation and concentration camps and, 72–76, 92–93
deportation of Armenian workers on, 88–91
during first months of war, 70–72
between humanitarian aid and resistance, 78–79
map of, 73–74
massacre of deportees, 91–92
Ottoman government's demands regarding, 79
struggle for Armenian employees and workers on, 79–82
Bagradian, Gabriel, 153, 160–61
Baiburt, 52
Baku massacres, 192–96
Balkan Wars, 37
Banker, Marie Sarrafian, 168
Bardèche, Maurice, 205, 207, 217
Bardizag, 55
Barnes, Harry Elmer, 205, 211, 212, 227
Baroutdjibashian, Victoria Khatchadour, 52
Bartevian, Suren, 175, 180–82
Barton, Rev. James L., 54–55, 57, 63n. 19, 63n. 20
Batz, Meir, 155
Bauer, Yehuda, 229, 284
Beaty, John, 212
Beckett, Samuel, 180
Bedoukian, Kerop, 170
Beilinson, Moshe, 151–53
Beledian, Krikor, 182, 183
Berkes, Niyazi, 42n. 13
Binark, Ismet, 52
Bitlis, 125, 128, 210
Blumer, Herbert, 24–25
Board of Foreign Missions of the Presbyterian Church (BFMPC), 55, 58
Böttrich, Lt. Col., 71, 72, 82–86, 89–90, 92–93, 95, 97n. 13
bourgeoisie, 35, 36, 48n. 69
boycotting of non-Muslim groups, 37, 40
as nationalistic, 37
non-Muslim, ridding economy of, 29
Bristol, Rear Admiral Mark Lambert, 122–24, 129
British reactions to renewed persecutions, 132–35
Bronsart von Schellendorf, General Fritz, 81, 82–84, 93
brotherhood, feeling of, 37
Bryce, Lord James, 51, 52, 54–58, 61n. 1, 63n. 12, 65n. 39, 133
Büge, Eugen, 76–78, 79
Butz, Arthur, 207, 210, 211, 217

Cambodian genocide, 227, 230, 239
Cannon, Bishop James, Jr., 134–35
Caraman, Elizabeth, 167–68, 171
"careerism," 288
"caste system." *See* hierarchies
Caucasus, 34, 38, 165, 215, 228; campaign of, 209
Cecil, Lord Robert, 133–34
Celan, Paul, 181, 182
censorship of mention of genocide, 273–74, 282–85
Central Powers, 52, 67
Chaliand, Gerard, 241–42
Chambers, William N., 55
Charny, Israel, 229, 230, 283, 286, 287, 288
Chomsky, Noam, 227
Christians, 118–20, 122, 124, 128, 130, 136–38. *See also* Armenians; non-Muslims
Cilicia, 30, 31, 122, 124, 136, 141n. 40, 210; massacres in (1909), 180
"civil war," genocide called, 204
class struggle, 37
  vs. cooperation, 35
coexistence, viewed only in terms of domination or hostility, 28
Cohen, Moiz. *See* Tekin Alp
Cohen, Richard, 204–5
Cold, Edith, 65n. 39
Cold War, 221–25
Committee for the Defense of the American Cause (CDCA), 245
Committee of Union and Progress (CUP), 14, 15, 19, 32, 34, 41, 72, 77, 78, 79, 80, 81, 87, 91, 93, 94, 95, 126, 213, 214, 220, 239, 240, 257, 272
"common conscience," 35
compensation, 48n. 76
confiscation, policy of, 136. *See also* properties
Constantinople, 67, 68, 70, 71, 72, 82, 88, 114, 116, 118, 120, 122, 129, 131, 136, 204, 220, 240
cosmopolitanism, 38
  opposition to, 36
Curzon, Foreign Secretary George Nathaniel, 124, 125

Dachau, 212
Dadrian, Vahakn, 69, 94, 95, 277, 280, 282, 284
Damascus, 65n. 39
Dardanelles, 71
Dawidowicz, Lucy, 284
deaths. *See* killing(s)
defense mechanisms, 284–85, 288. *See also* denial; rationalization; relativization; trivialization
"definitionalism," 288
Deir-el-Zor, 76, 92, 112n. 108, 145n. 79, 216
denial, 19–21, 229–31, 237–38, 261, 283–84. *See also* censorship; defense mechanisms; Holocaust denial: "Lewis Affair"
  attacks the historical spirit and morale, 286
  attacks the victim, 207–11, 217–18, 273, 285, 286, 289
  belief in one's own, 284
  as defense mechanism, 284–85
  denouncement of, 230
  discourse of, 261
  as essence of genocide, 259
  as final stage of genocide, 202, 230
  harm done by, 230, 285–87, 289
  institutionalization of, 202–3
  literature on, 291n. 8
  professional ethics and, 271–72
  psychology of denial, 286
  reasons intellectuals engage in, 287–89
  "scientificism" in service of, 288
  Turkey's efforts in, 272–74
  wartime propaganda and, 205–7
  "Yes, but" mode of, 283
deniers, 20, 201, 205, 220, 237–38, 248, 259

arguments and strategies of, 20, 219–26, 231
attempt to discredit survivor testimony, 206
fear of eyewitness accounts, 207
points emphasized by, 203–4
self-portrayal as warriors for truth, 204, 225–27
deportation, 38. *See also* Baghdad Railway
resumption of, 122–24
Des Pres, Terrence, 21, 221. 271–72
devaluation of subordinate group, 24
Diarbekir, 125
Dinkel, Christoph, 69, 95
distinctiveness, feeling of, 24
Djemal Pasha, 77, 106n. 65, 111n. 102, 220
Dodd, William, 65n. 39
Dresden, 212
Dror, Zvika, 160
Dulles, Allen, 129

economic nationalism, 29, 36
economic patriotism, 36
economic problems, 26. *See also* poverty
economy
national. *See* Millî İktisat
economy, control of
"laissez-faire" liberalism as hindrance to, 36
Edib, Halidé, 121–22
Egan, Eleanor Franklin, 56
Elekdağ, Şükrü, 208
elite, reaction to emancipation of non-Muslims, 28
emancipation of non-Muslims, 28. *See also* Hatt-i Hümayun
Engert, C. H. Van, 122–23
England. *See* British reactions to renewed persecutions
Entilli, 79, 87
entitlement to exclusive rights, feeling of, 24, 27
Enver Pasha, 34, 41, 78, 79, 80, 81, 83, 85, 89, 93, 96n. 5, 106n. 65, 209, 220, 246
envy, 39
Eregli, 75
Erzerum, 52, 56, 124, 210
Erzinjan, 52
Esayan, Zabel, 175, 177, 180, 268n. 21
Eskishehir, 80
"ethnic cleansing/purification," 262–64, 270n. 34
ethnic identity, 38
Even-Shushan, Shlomo, 159
"exclusive" ideologies
and ejection of Armenians, 31
racism and, 40
Turkish identity and, 31
expulsion, policy of, 136

facts and opinions, 258–60
Falkenhayn, General Erich von, 84–86, 89, 93, 106n. 69
Faurisson, Robert, 205, 207, 227, 259, 287
Favre, Leopold, 64n. 27
Fein, Helen, 230, 280, 282, 284
Ferid Pasha, Grand Vizier Damad, 117–18, 137, 220
Fethi Bey, 126
Forster, Lev, 245
Forty Days of Musa Dagh, The (Werfel), 147–49, 160–62, 273
characters' self-perception as victims who struggle, 161–62
and Eretz Israel during World War II, 154–56
impact in Europe during World War II, 156–60
initial Jewish responses to, 149–54
Jewish symbolism in, 148, 160–61
magnetism of, 161
moral questions arising from, 162
suppression of film, 222
tragic, existential setting of, 161

free will, *Millî İktisat*'s opposition to, 35
Freud, Sigmund, 251
Fromer, Daphna, 288
Fuad Pasha, 28, 42n. 14
Fundajak, 91
future, promise of glorious and powerful, 40.
future civilization, based on "genuine values," 40

Gallipoli peninsula, 80, 94
Gayssot law, 20, 245, 258
gendarmes, 87
Genghis Khan, 32
genocide
  ambiguities and differing interpretations of, 239. *See also* defense mechanisms
  central characteristic, 203
  definition, 14, 211
  future generations impacted by, 17
  nature of evidence concerning, 246
  withholding of the label of, 202
genocide literature, 20. *See also* "Lewis Affair"; *Treatment of Armenians in the Ottoman Empire, The*
  of atrocities, 181–82
  and denial literature, 16
  emotional breakdown in, 179–80
  and first-generation survivor-writers, 175
  Holocaust compared with Armenian Genocide literature, 20
  problematic aspects of reading, 175, 179–83
  questions regarding, 176–78
  reading and writing about, 183–85
Georgeon, François, 45n. 41
German diplomats, 68
German Foreign Office, 69, 76, 84
  denial of German involvement, 68
  strategy, 68
German involvement in Armenian Genocide, 67, 95–96. *See also* Baghdad Railway
  absence of uniform policy, 95
  complicity, 68
  denial and evidence, 76–78
  limited impact, 68–69
  participation, 67–68
German officers and consuls, 68, 96
ghiaours, 28
  collective image of, 28–30
    disloyalty, 28
    trickery, 30
    ungratefulness, 28–29
Gibbons, Herbert, 129, 131–32, 135
Gillespie, Julian, 134, 135
Gök Alp (Gökalp), Ziya, 31–36, 40, 46n. 48, 47n. 58
  theoretical treatises, 33–35
Goltz Pasha, Colmar von der, 69, 93
Gorrini, Giacomo, 51, 65n. 39
Graffam, Mary, 65n. 39
Grant, Charles P., 130
Greek/Greeks, 27, 30, 36, 37, 125, 128, 129, 130, 133, 134, 135, 136, 139n. 11; expulsion from Asia Minor, 14; property, 119; traders and artisans, 35; uprising, 126
Greek Ottoman shops, boycott of, 37
Grew, Joseph Clark, 129
Gröner, Wilhelm, 86
Grossman, Haike, 157
guilt. *See* survivor shame
Günther, Franz J., 70, 72, 75, 77, 79–86, 88, 94
Gürün, Kamuran, 205, 206, 208, 210, 213–14, 218
Gutman, Yisrael, 230
Gwinner, Arthur von, 77, 81, 86
Gypsies, 27, 42n. 11, 293n. 21

Hadjin, 65n. 39, 79, 124
Haig, H. H., 168
Hamid Bey, 137
Harley, Isabel, 127
Harmsworth, Cecil, 125, 134

Hartunian, Abraham H., 95, 111n. 102
Hasanbeyli, 79
Hashian, Jack, 168
Hatt-i Hümayun (Imperial Rescript), 25–26
  Muslim resentment against, 26
Hatti-i Sherif-i Gülhane (Noble Rescript of Rose Chamber), 25
hegemony, delusory vision of world, 31
Heizer, Oscar, 51, 65n. 39, 114
Herbert, Aubrey, 133, 134
Herzl, Theodore, 148, 153
hierarchies, 27–28, 30, 42nn. 11, 13
Highgas, Dirouhi Kouymjian, 171
Hilberg, Raul, 230, 264, 270n. 34
Himmler, Heinrich, 212
Hiroshima, 208, 212
historians, responsibility of, 237–40, 246–48
  "Lewis Affair" and, 240–43
historians' debate, 227, 259
historical facts, interpretation of, 258–61. *See also* defense mechanisms; revisionism
Hitler, Adolf, 212, 292n. 21
Hobsbawm, Eric, 260–61
Hohenlohe-Langenburg, Acting Ambassador Ernst zu, 77, 80, 81, 102n. 37
Holocaust, 179, 267n. 13
  rationalization of, 207
Holocaust denial
  compared with Armenian Genocide denial, 201, 203–5, 229–31
  academic freedom and, 225–27
  blaming alleged victims, 207–11, 217, 273, 285, 286, 289
  Cold War, national security, and, 221–25
  differences between, 202–4, 206, 227
  manipulation of statistics in, 217–19
  and question of intent, 211–17
  trial of war criminals and, 219–21
  trivialization in, 227–29
  wartime propaganda and, 205–7
homogeneity, goal of, 14
Hovadjian, K., 51
Hovannisian, Richard, 20, 140n. 25
Huguenin, Eduard, 86

ideology, guiding, 31
industrialists, 26
inferiority feelings, 39
"infidels," 28, 29
Institute of Turkish Studies, 274–78
intent, question of
  as fundamental, 203, 211, 213
  rationalization and relativization, 211–17
ırk, 31, 45n. 45
Irving, David, 205, 212
Islahia, 89
Ismail Hakkı Pasha, 72
Ismet Pasha, 137
Ittihad ve Terakki party, 115, 118. *See also* Committee of Union and Progress

Jäckh, Ernst, 31
Jackson, Jesse B., 65n. 39, 123, 124
Jagow, Gottlieb von, 83–85
Jaquith, Captain Harold C., 130, 132, 135
Jews, 27, 37, 42n. 11, 208. See also *Forty Days of Musa Dagh, The* (Werfel)
  antisemitism, 263, 287
  extermination of, 267n. 13. *See also* Holocaust
  perception of, 30
Johannsen, Alma, 65n. 39
Jonassohn, Kurt, 203

Kaiser, Hilmar, 19
Kaiseri (Kayseri), 124, 132
Kandemir, Ambassador Nuzhet, 276, 279–81

Kaplan, Khaem, 180
Karakilisse, 130
Karal, Enver Zia, 52
Kars, 130
Katma, 75
Katz, Steven, 228, 229
Katznelson, Yitzhak, 158–59
Kemal Pasha (Atatürk), Mustafa, 15, 19, 33, 119, 126, 132, 165, 220, 222
  Turkish Nationalist movement, success of, 220
Kenaan, Haviv, 155, 163n. 14
Kenworthy, Joseph M., 132–34
Kharpert (Kharput, Harput), 52, 65n. 39, 122, 125, 127, 128, 130, 131
killing(s)
  denial of, 217–19
  mass. *See also* massacres
    before Armenian Genocide, 14
  methods of, 76
  number of, 15, 273
Killis, 78, 123
Kimhi, Dov, 149–50
Klibansky, Bronka, 157
Konia, 65n. 39, 75, 99n. 27, 123, 124
Köppel, Engineer, 87
Kübel, Major, 71, 97n. 17
küfran, 28–29, 43n. 20
Kulka, Erich, 286
Kundera, Milan, 17
Kuper, Leo, 278, 280, 282, 284
Kurds, 15, 17, 23, 38, 117, 120, 128, 213, 215, 273
Kut-el-Amara, 89

Lacoue-Labarthe, Philippe, 252, 267n. 13
Langer, Lawrence, 177, 181
Laughlin, H. P., 48nn. 71, 76
Lausanne peace conference (1923), 15, 113, 120, 136, 137, 138, 220
Lefort, Claude, 243
Lepsius, Johannes, 52, 68, 96n. 5, 159
Leslie, Davis, 65n. 39
Leslie, Francis, 65n. 39
Lewin, Abraham, 180
Lewis, Bernard, 20, 209, 226, 238, 254, 258, 264. *See also* "Lewis Affair"
"Lewis Affair," 20–21, 240–43, 246–47, 249–52
  Paris phase, 243–46
liberalism, *Millî İktisat*'s opposition to, 35
Lifton, Robert Jay, 21, 230, 276, 279. See also *Nazi Doctors*
  Turkish ambassador's letter to, 271, 280–81, 283–85
Liman von Sanders, General Otto, 67
Lipstadt, Deborah, 228, 230, 283, 286, 287
Lloyd George, David, 132
Lossow, General Otto von, 81, 82, 84, 89
Lowry, Heath, 224, 275, 281, 284, 285
  work of, questionable assertions and conclusions in, 282–83
Lowry memorandum, 276–79, 282–85
Lyotard, J. F., 254, 255

Maggiori, Robert, 258–59
Malatia, 131
Malta, 124, 125, 126, 220
Marash, 91, 92, 94, 111n. 102, 123, 137
Marashlian, Levon, 19
Marcher, Hansina, 52
Mardin, 92, 136, 137
Margosian, Bedros, 168
Markusen, Eric, 21, 282
Marian, Michel, 243
Marrus, Michael, 202, 228
Martin, Ramela, 170
massacre
  of deportees via Baghdad Railway, 91–92
massacres. *See also* killing(s)
  Armenian Genocide compared with other, 20, 197–99
  Baku, 192–96
  resumption of, 122–24
  Sumgait, 188–92, 198

McCarthy, Justin, 206, 210–11, 213, 215–16, 218, 225, 226, 281
McNaughton, James, 55
media, propaganda in, 127–32
Melson, Robert, 230, 264, 265n. 11, 284
memory
  historical, role in interpreting events, 187–88
  subversion of, 221
  targeted as the last victim, 202, 230, 286, 289
Mersina, 65n. 39, 123
Midhat Pasha, 28
Miles, Robert, 41n. 7
Miller, Donald, 20, 166
Miller, Lorna Touryan, 166
Millî İktisat (national economy)
  results of, 40
  theories and policies, 35, 39
    eliminating Armenians and Ottoman Greeks, 35
  Turkism, Pan-Turkism, and, 36–40
Mohring, Schwester, 65n. 39
Morgenthau, Henry, 52, 272, 282
Moush, 65n. 39
Mudros Armistice, 117, 132
Musa Dagh. See *Forty Days of Musa Dagh, The*
Muslim Ottomans
  self-identification of Turkish speaking, as Turks, 38
  superior status threatened by Tanzimat, 26
Muslim unity, 27
Muslims
  inequality between non-Muslims and, 27
Muslims, non-Turkish
  suppression of, 14

Nagasaki, 208, 212
Nagorno-Karabagh, 20, 188, 191, 198
nakibs, 28, 42n. 13
Nancy, Jean-Luc, 262–63
Narekatsi, Grigor, 177
Nathan, Edward, 65n. 39
national bourgeois class, 48n. 69
national economy. See *Millî İktisat*
national greatness, sense of, 31
"national idealization, 40
national security, 221–25
"national solidarism," 35
nationalism, 23, 31, 37–39, 220, 264
  economic, 29, 36
naturalization
  used in struggle to legitimize power, 24
Nazi Doctors (Lifton), 279, 280, 282
negation. *See* defense mechanisms; denial
Nezihe Hanum, 121
Nichanian, Marc, 21, 183
Niepage, Martin, 88
Nietzsche, Friedrich, 33
Nolte, Ernst, 227
non-Muslims. *See also* Armenians; Christians; ghiaours
  economic power ostracized, 29
  emancipation of. *See also* Hatt-i Hümayun
    elite reaction to, 28
  exclusion of, 23, 29. *See also* "exclusive" ideologies
    roots of, 23
Noradoungian, Gabriel, 117–18
Nubar, Boghos, 116
Nuremberg trials, 220, 245

O'Conner, T. P., 126, 133, 134
Öke, Mim Kemal, 52
Orel, Şinasi, 53
orphanages, 121, 122, 127
Osborne, D. G., 125, 134
Oshagan, Hagop, 175, 177–79, 181, 182, 185n. 11, 256, 268n. 20, 269n. 22
Oshagan, Vahé, 177, 185n. 5
Osmanieh, 75, 78, 93, 98n. 23
Ottoman constitution, 27, 38
  anticonstitutionalism and, 27

suspension of, 28
Ottoman Empire
defeat of, 15
at turn of century, 23
Ottoman government, 14, 26, 79
Ottomanism, 26
opposition to, 26–31
outgroup. *See also* ghiaours
raising self-esteem by degrading the, 38
suspicion of subordinate, 25

Palmon, Yehoshua (Josh), 163n. 14
Pan-Turanian dreams, 36
Pan-Turkic activities, 32
Pan-Turkism, 39, 40
as monomania, 34
Turkism and, 31
paranoia. *See* suspicion
parasitism, mutual, 35
Paris Peace Conference, 113, 116, 117
Parla, Taha, 33, 48n. 69
Parmalee, Ruth, 127
Partridge, Ernest, 65n. 39
patriotism, economic, 36. *See also* nationalism
peasants, 38
Permanent Peoples' Tribunal, 242, 253
Peroomian, Rubina, 20
perpetrators
postgenocide attitudes, 15–16
release of, 15
persecutions. *See also* massacres
in Anatolia, 127–32
British reactions to, 132–35
resumption of, 124, 127
Piralian, Hélène, 268n. 18
plural society, repudiation of, 14
pogroms. *See* massacres
Post, Wilfred, 65n. 39
postmodernism, 260
poverty, 30
power
narrative of, 221–23, 271–72
naturalization used to legitimize, 24
prejudice. *See also* racist nationalism
causes
economic, 31
predisposing conditions, 24–25
feelings that characterize, 24
rationalization of, 201
prisoners from Malta, union with nationalists in Angora, 124–27
propaganda
in media, 127–32
Turkish, 205–6
wartime, 205–7
properties, expropriation of, 113–20, 136
proprietary claims, 24–25

racial greatness, sense of, 31
racism
biological, 31, 38, 39, 41
toward ghiaours, 38
uses of, 38–41
racist nationalism, transition from prejudice to, 23
racist theories, 39–40
rank structure, 27–28
Ras-ul-Ain, 75, 76, 92, 101n. 33
Rassinier, Paul, 205, 207, 213, 217, 221, 227
rationalization, 16, 201, 202, 208–11, 216–17, 222, 223
rationalizer-relativizers, 218, 248
attacks on victims, 207, 218
points emphasized by, 203–4
self-portrayal as warriors for truth, 204, 225–27
use of established power structures, 221
Refik Bey, Lt. Col., 90–91
refugees, plight of, 196. *See also* survivors
relativist arguments, 204–5. *See also* rationalizer-relativizers
relativization, 16, 201, 213–19

Rendel, W. G., 125, 134, 135, 143n. 60
"Reordering." *See* Tanzimat
revisionism, 238, 262, 286
  neorevisionism, 250, 262
    law, facts, and, 253–54
    meaning, reality, and, 260–62
    state of belligerency in, 250–52, 265n. 11
    "truth of the facts" and essence of genocide, 258–60
    validation of facts and, 255–57
revisionists. *See* deniers; rationalizer-relativizers
Rex, John, 25
Riggs, Ernest, 65n. 39
Riza Nur Pasha, 137
Rockwell, Rev. William, 56
Rosenfeld, Alvin, 176, 178–80
Rosenthal, Herschel, 156
Rössler, Walter, 68
Rue, Larry, 130, 143n. 60
Rumbold, Sir Horace, 119, 124, 129

Shakir, Dr., 272
Salonika, 126
salvation, fantasy of, 31
Sami Bey, 129
Samsun, 126
Şapolyo, Enver Behnan, 35
Sarafian, Ara, 19
Sarafian, Nikoghayos, 183
Schäfer, Paula, 91
Schnebel, Ernst, 178
scholars, truth and, 289–90
Schutz, Alfred, 187
şerif, 28, 42n. 13
Sèvres, Treaty of, 15, 128, 138, 220
seyyid, 28, 42n. 13
Shabin-Karahisar, 210
Shahnur, Shahan, 177, 182–83
shaikhs, 42n. 13
Shahmuratian, Samvel, 191
Shaw, Stanford, 209–10, 214–15, 218–19, 223n. 40, 226, 275
Shemseddin Sami, 28
Shinasi, 30
Shirinian, Lorne, 19
Siamanto, 175, 178, 180
Singer, Isaac Bashevis, 178
Sivas (Sebastia), 65n. 39, 125, 210
Smith, Roger, 21, 282
Smyrna, 134
social equality. *See* Hatt-i Hümayun; Ottomanism
social identities, 24
Sonyel, Salahi, 54
spiritual knowledge, 30
Stapleton, Rev. Robert, 56
Staub, Erwin, 17
Stepanakert, 188
stereotyping, 23–24
  legitimizes domination, 31
  prepares for collective slaughter, 31
  raises self-esteem by degrading outgroup, 38
  rationalization of, 201
sultan, 27
Sumgait massacres, 188–92, 198
superiority, feeling of, 24, 27, 33
survival, struggle for, 13–4
survivor shame, 255
survivor testimony, attempts to discredit, 206
survivor-writers
  first-generation, 175
  memoirs, 19, 166–171
  as cultural history, 171–72
survivors
  blaming the, 207–11, 217, 218, 273, 285, 286, 289
  inability to deal with their trauma, 16
  postgenocide experiences of, 15–16, 19, 165–67, 196
  psychological effects on, 16
  repatriation, rehabilitation, and compensation
    Turkish Nationalists' refusal of, 15

revictimization, 16
suspicion, of subordinate outgroup, 25
symbolic interactionist perspective, 24

Taft, Elise Hagopian, 169–71
Talaat Bey, 76–78, 80, 81, 87, 94. *See also* Talaat (Tâlat) Pasha
Talaat (Tâlat) Pasha, 41, 100n. 29, 102n. 37, 106n. 65, 108n. 78, 112n. 106, 111n. 102, 126–27, 208, 213, 220, 246, 283
Tanzimat, 25–26, 27, 28, 30
Tashian, Beniamin, 178
Taurus Mountains, 72, 76, 89, 92, 100n. 29
Tehlirian, Soghomon, 127
Tekeyan, Vahan, 175
Tekin Alp, 31–37
Tell Abiad, 76, 101n. 34
Ternon, Yves, 21
territorial integrity, threat to, 27
territorial nationalism, ethnic purification in the name of, 264
Thomas, David, 45n. 41
Thomas, Lewis V., 223
Townsend, Charles, 132–34
Toynbee, Arnold, 19, 51–58, 61n. 1, 63n. 12, 64n. 35, 65n. 39
trade unions, "honorable silence" of
    misinterpreted as acceptance of guilt, 217
Treatment of Armenians in the Ottoman Empire, The, 19, 51–52
    and deviant historiography, 52–54
    Key to Names of Persons and Places Withheld from Publication in Original Edition of, 53, 54, 57
    and role of U.S. and Rev. James L. Barton, 1915–16, 54–57
Trebizond, 51, 52, 65n. 39, 114, 129, 135
Treutler, Carl Georg von, 84
trivialization, 201, 202, 227–29
Trumpener, Ulrich, 68–69
truth, 258–60, 289–90
    as last victim of genocide, 205
Turan, 32–34
    realization of, 32
Turco-Tatar Committee, 32
turkification, goal of, 14
Turkish ambassador. *See* Lifton, Robert Jay
Turkish government. *See also specific topics*
    attempts to deny genocide, 272–74
    attempts to prevent discussion of genocide, 273–74, 282–85
Turkish identity, 38
Turkish nation. *See also specific topics*
    formation of homogeneous, 40
Turkish Nationalists, 15, 220. *See also* Kemal Pasha (Atatürk), Mustafa,
Turkish racism, as cause of Armenian Genocide, 40
Turkism, 31–32. *See also* Pan-Turkism
Turks, as victims of Greeks and Armenians, 36

ulema (learned men of Islam), 27, 28
Ulukishla,76
umma, 42n. 13
United Nations Genocide Convention, 14, 211, 214, 218, 239, 250
United States
    discovery of Armenian Genocide, 122–23
    efforts to save Armenians, 122
    State Department Records, 60
Urfa, 65n. 39, 91, 92, 210
Urmia, 55

validation, narration and, 255
Van, 55, 210
Varuzhan, Daniel, 175
Vaughan, Olive, 55
Venizelos, Eleutherios, 133
Veranshehir, 91
Vidal-Naquet, Pierre, 221, 286–87

Vorbuni, Zareh, 183

Wajsbort, Inka, 158
Wangenheim, Hans von, 71
war criminals, trials of, 219–21
Ward, Mark, 127, 128, 131, 134, 135
Wedgewood, Col., 141n. 40
Wegner, Armin T., 101n. 33, 112n. 108
Weisgal, Meyer, 154
Werfel, Franz, 19, 147, 222, 273. See also *Forty Days of Musa Dagh, The*
  Jewishness of, 163n. 13
Weizmann, Chaim, 207, 227
West, opposition to, 27, 31, 39
Wiesel, Elie, 165, 225
Williams, Aneurin, 125
Winkler, Engineer, 78–79, 81, 82, 88–91
Winter, Jay, 250–51, 267n. 14
Wolff-Metternich, Paul von, 85, 91, 115
Woods, Edith, 131
World War I, 29, 33, 34, 37, 38, 39, 57, 67, 68, 70, 113, 133, 134, 201, 209, 211, 247, 271, 285
  Ottoman Empire's entry into, 32
World War II, 16, 201, 207, 208, 211
  blaming the Allied Powers for, 212
Wyschogrod, Michael, 181

Yarlesberg, Flora A. Wedel, 52
Yarrow, Ernest, 55
Yerevan, 188
Young, Greg, 65n. 39
Young, James E., 184
Young Turk party. *See* Committee of Union and Progress
Young Turk regime, 67, 272–74
youth movements, 157, 160
Yowell, Major Forrest D., 127, 130, 134, 135

Zaven, Patriarch, 117, 120, 137
Zavrieff, Ivan (Hovhannes Zavrian), 52
Zeitun, 72, 75, 79, 98n. 23
Zeligman, R., 151
Zimmermann, Arthur, 83
Ziya Pasha, 26
Zuckerman, Yitzhak, 159–60